鳥 山 明

I am fairly confident about my health. I hardly ever get stiff shoulders, but recently, my right hand has been sore and it's getting to the point where it's painful. When I think about it, it's been almost eleven years of straight manga-drawing since I started **Dr. Slump** on through to **Dragon Ball**, and I haven't had much time off. Hey, maybe a doctor will force me to take three months off! (Though actually, my hand has been fine since yesterday...darn it!)

       —Akira Toriyama, 1990

Artist/writer Akira Toriyama burst onto the manga scene in 1980 with the wildly popular **Dr. Slump**, a science fiction comedy about the adventures of a mad scientist and his android "daughter." In 1984 he created his hit series **Dragon Ball**, which ran until 1995 in Shueisha's best-selling magazine **Weekly Shonen Jump**, and was translated into foreign languages around the world. Since **Dragon Ball**, he has worked on a variety of short series, including **Cowa!**, **Kajika**, **SandLand**, and **Neko Majin**, as well as a children's book, **Toccio the Angel**. He is also known for his design work on video games, particularly the **Dragon Warrior** RPG series. He lives with his family in Japan.

DRAGON BALL Z VOL. 7
The SHONEN JUMP Manga Edition

This graphic novel is number 23 in a series of 42.

STORY AND ART BY
AKIRA TORIYAMA

ENGLISH ADAPTATION BY
GERARD JONES

Translation/Lillian Olsen
Touch-Up Art & Lettering/Wayne Truman
Cover Design/Izumi Evers & Dan Ziegler
Graphics & Design/Sean Lee
Senior Editor/Jason Thompson

Editor in Chief, Books/Alvin Lu
Editor in Chief, Magazines/Marc Weidenbaum
VP of Publishing Licensing/Rika Inouye
VP of Sales/Gonzalo Ferreyra
Sr. VP of Marketing/Liza Coppola
Publisher/Hyoe Narita

The rights of the author(s) of the work(s) in this publication to be so
identified have been asserted in accordance with the Copyright,
Designs and Patents Act 1988. A CIP catalogue record for this book is
available from the British Library.

Printed in Canada

In the original Japanese edition, DRAGON BALL and DRAGON BALL
Z are known collectively as the 42-volume series DRAGON BALL. The
English DRAGON BALL Z was originally volumes 17-42 of the
Japanese DRAGON BALL.

Published by VIZ Media, LLC
P.O. Box 77010 • San Francisco, CA 94107

The SHONEN JUMP Manga Edition
10 9 8 7 6 5 4
First printing, March 2003
Fourth printing, March 2008

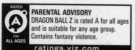

PARENTAL ADVISORY
DRAGON BALL Z is rated A for all ages
and is suitable for any age group.
Contains fantasy violence.
ratings.viz.com

THE WORLD'S
MOST POPULAR MANGA

www.viz.com
VIZ media
www.shonenjump.com

SHONEN JUMP MANGA

DRAGON BALL Z

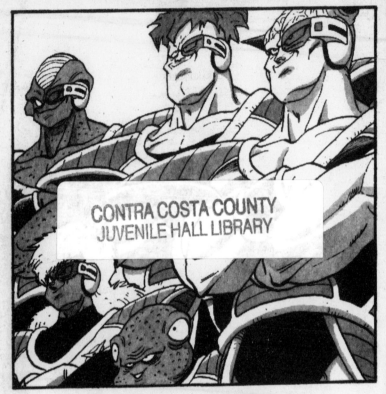

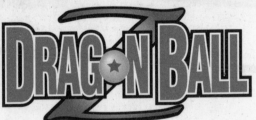

Vol. 7

DB: 23 of 42

STORY AND ART BY
AKIRA TORIYAMA

THE MAIN CHARACTERS

Bulma

Goku's oldest friend, Bulma is a scientific genius. She met Goku while on a quest for the seven magical Dragon Balls which, when gathered together, can grant any wish.

Son Goku

The greatest martial artist on Earth, he owes his strength to the training of Kame-Sen'nin and Kaiô-sama, and the fact that he's one of the alien Saiyans. To get even stronger, he is training under 30 times Earth's gravity.

The Great Elder

The sole survivor of a cataclysm that nearly destroyed all the Namekians. All the current Namekians (except Piccolo) are its children.

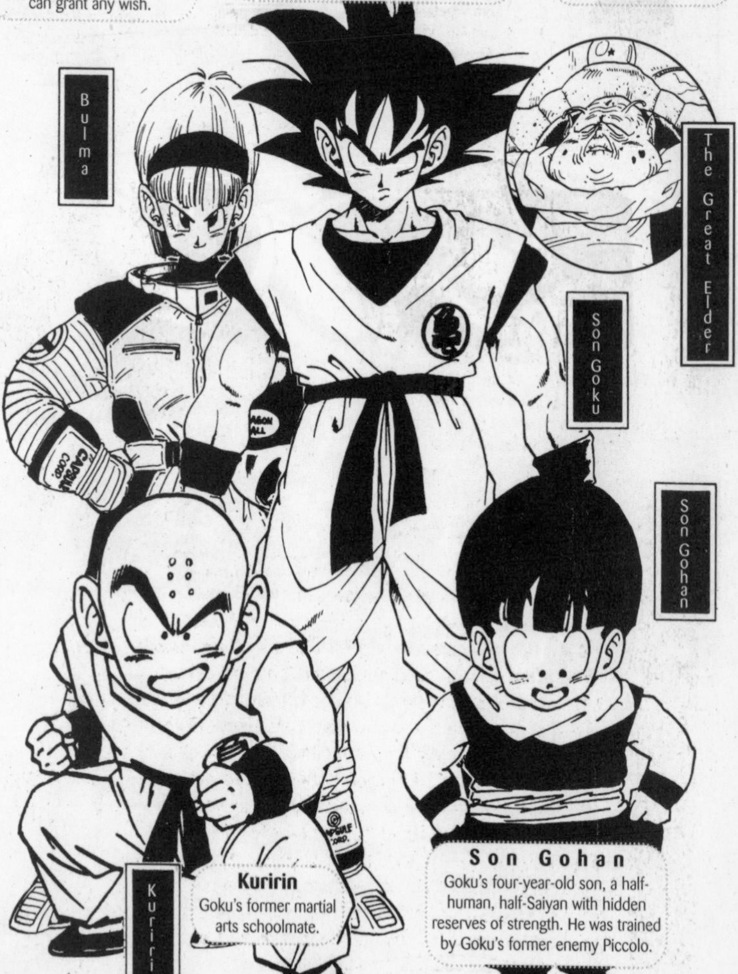
Bulma
The Great Elder
Son Goku
Son Gohan
Kuririn

Kuririn

Goku's former martial arts schoolmate.

Son Gohan

Goku's four-year-old son, a half-human, half-Saiyan with hidden reserves of strength. He was trained by Goku's former enemy Piccolo.

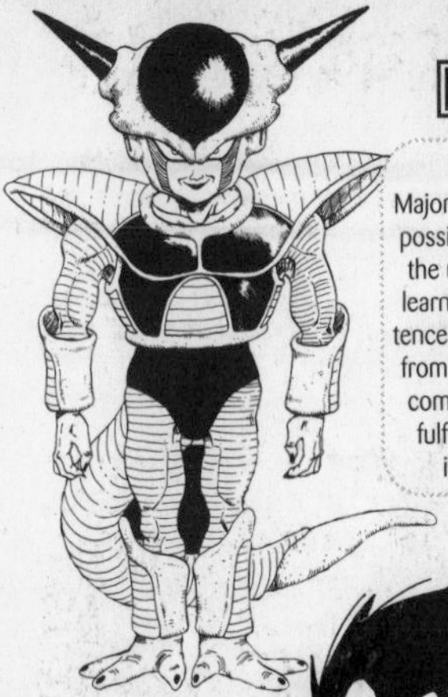

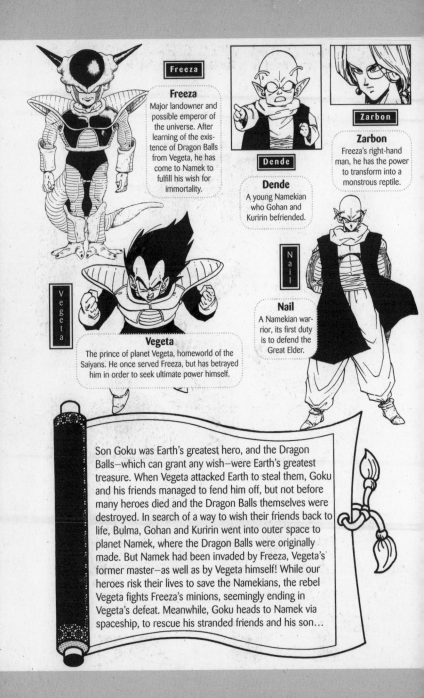

Freeza

Freeza

Major landowner and possible emperor of the universe. After learning of the existence of Dragon Balls from Vegeta, he has come to Namek to fulfill his wish for immortality.

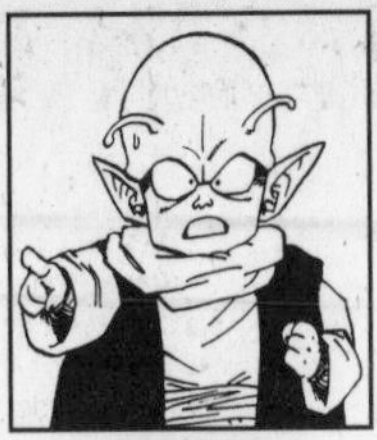

Dende

Dende

A young Namekian who Gohan and Kuririn befriended.

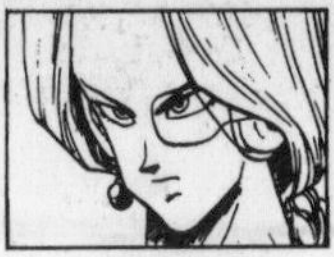

Zarbon

Zarbon

Freeza's right-hand man, he has the power to transform into a monstrous reptile.

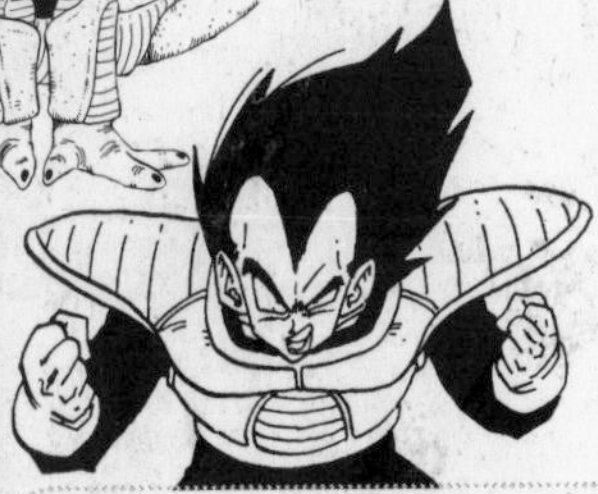

Vegeta

Vegeta

The prince of planet Vegeta, homeworld of the Saiyans. He once served Freeza, but has betrayed him in order to seek ultimate power himself.

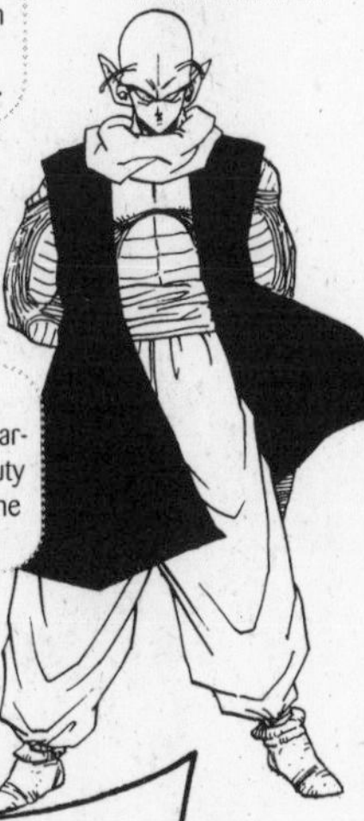

Nail

Nail

A Namekian warrior, its first duty is to defend the Great Elder.

Son Goku was Earth's greatest hero, and the Dragon Balls—which can grant any wish—were Earth's greatest treasure. When Vegeta attacked Earth to steal them, Goku and his friends managed to fend him off, but not before many heroes died and the Dragon Balls themselves were destroyed. In search of a way to wish their friends back to life, Bulma, Gohan and Kuririn went into outer space to planet Namek, where the Dragon Balls were originally made. But Namek had been invaded by Freeza, Vegeta's former master—as well as by Vegeta himself! While our heroes risk their lives to save the Namekians, the rebel Vegeta fights Freeza's minions, seemingly ending in Vegeta's defeat. Meanwhile, Goku heads to Namek via spaceship, to rescue his stranded friends and his son…

DRAGON BALL Z 7

CONTENTS

DRAGON BALL

ドラゴンボール

DBZ:71 • The Dragon Balls Change Hands

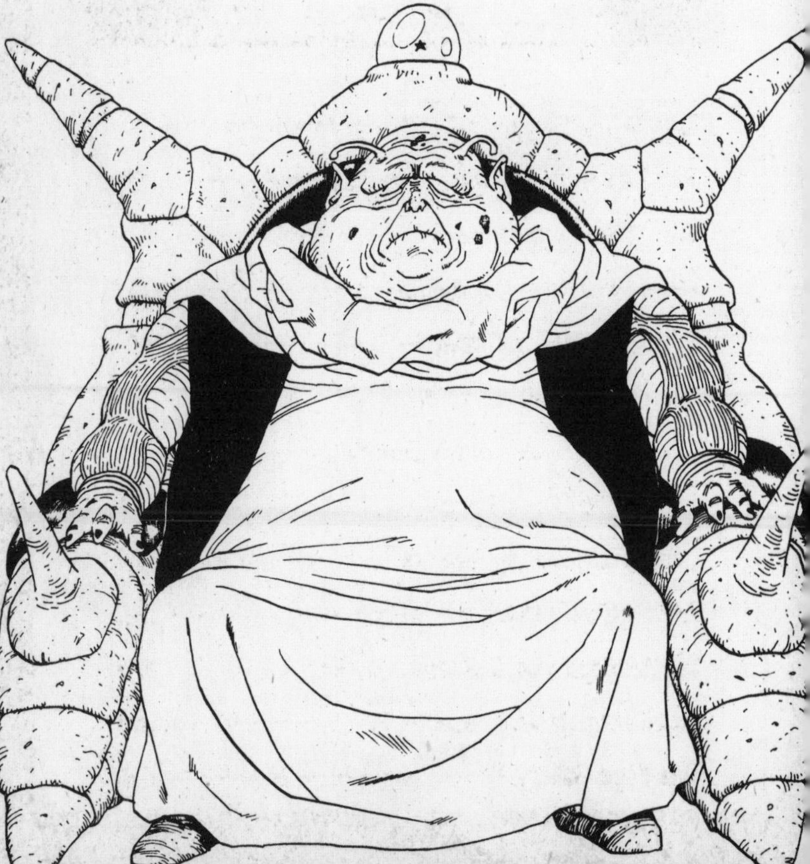

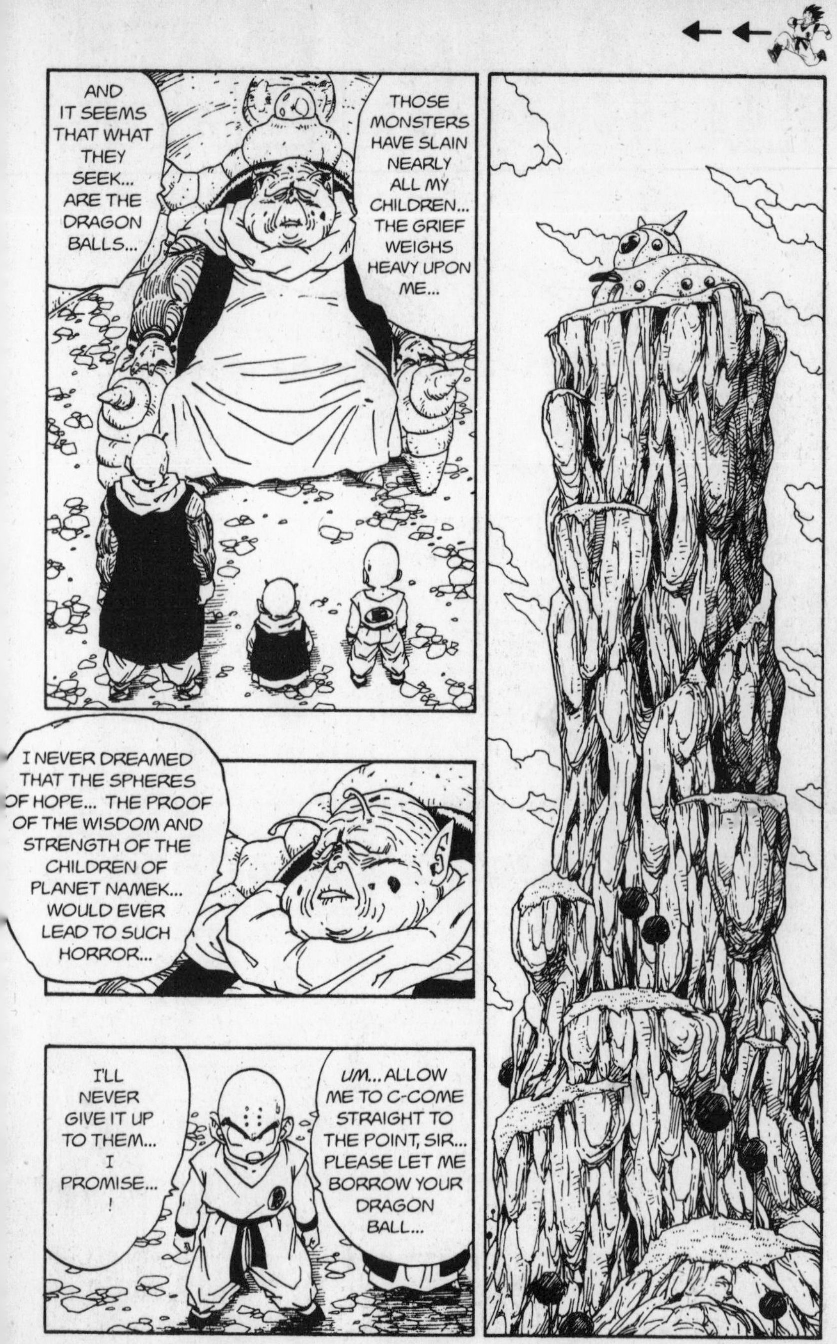
THOSE MONSTERS HAVE SLAIN NEARLY ALL MY CHILDREN... THE GRIEF WEIGHS HEAVY UPON ME...
AND IT SEEMS THAT WHAT THEY SEEK... ARE THE DRAGON BALLS...
I NEVER DREAMED THAT THE SPHERES OF HOPE... THE PROOF OF THE WISDOM AND STRENGTH OF THE CHILDREN OF PLANET NAMEK... WOULD EVER LEAD TO SUCH HORROR...
UM... ALLOW ME TO C-COME STRAIGHT TO THE POINT, SIR... PLEASE LET ME BORROW YOUR DRAGON BALL...
I'LL NEVER GIVE IT UP TO THEM... I PROMISE... !

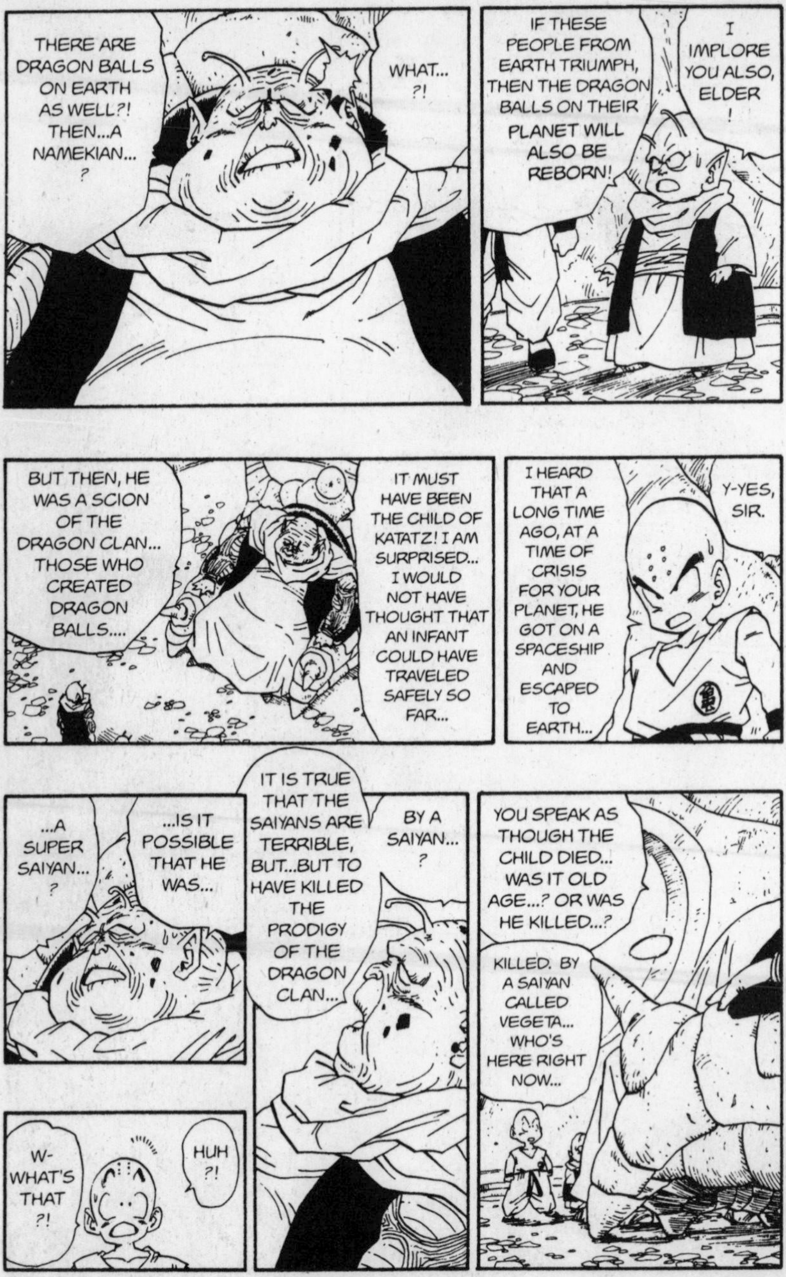
I IMPLORE YOU ALSO, ELDER!
IF THESE PEOPLE FROM EARTH TRIUMPH, THEN THE DRAGON BALLS ON THEIR PLANET WILL ALSO BE REBORN!
WHAT...?!
THERE ARE DRAGON BALLS ON EARTH AS WELL?! THEN...A NAMEKIAN...?
Y-YES, SIR.
I HEARD THAT A LONG TIME AGO, AT A TIME OF CRISIS FOR YOUR PLANET, HE GOT ON A SPACESHIP AND ESCAPED TO EARTH...
IT MUST HAVE BEEN THE CHILD OF KATATZ! I AM SURPRISED... I WOULD NOT HAVE THOUGHT THAT AN INFANT COULD HAVE TRAVELED SAFELY SO FAR...
BUT THEN, HE WAS A SCION OF THE DRAGON CLAN... THOSE WHO CREATED DRAGON BALLS....
YOU SPEAK AS THOUGH THE CHILD DIED... WAS IT OLD AGE...? OR WAS HE KILLED...?
KILLED. BY A SAIYAN CALLED VEGETA... WHO'S HERE RIGHT NOW...
BY A SAIYAN...?
IT IS TRUE THAT THE SAIYANS ARE TERRIBLE, BUT...BUT TO HAVE KILLED THE PRODIGY OF THE DRAGON CLAN...
...IS IT POSSIBLE THAT HE WAS...
...A SUPER SAIYAN...?
HUH?!
W-WHAT'S THAT?!

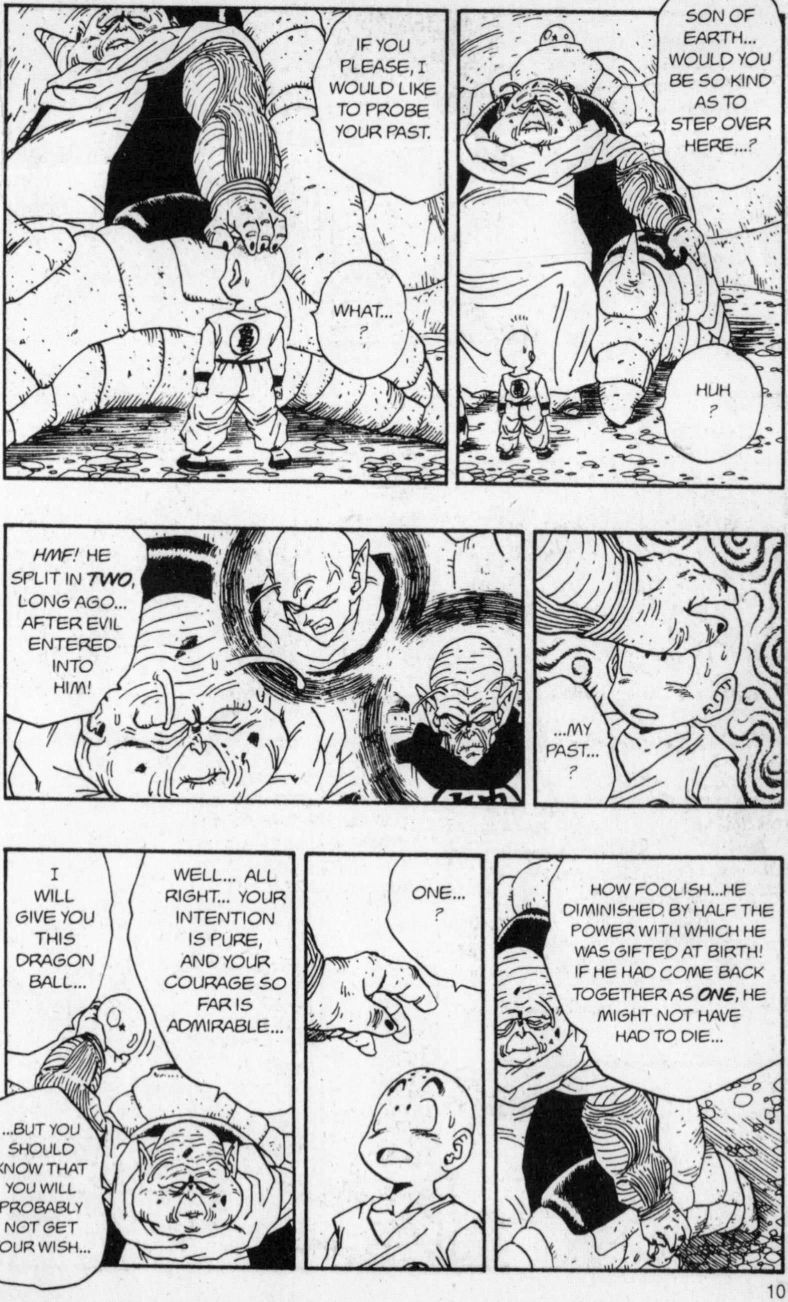
SON OF EARTH... WOULD YOU BE SO KIND AS TO STEP OVER HERE...?
HUH ?
IF YOU PLEASE, I WOULD LIKE TO PROBE YOUR PAST.
WHAT... ?
...MY PAST... ?
HMF! HE SPLIT IN ***TWO***, LONG AGO... AFTER EVIL ENTERED INTO HIM!
HOW FOOLISH...HE DIMINISHED BY HALF THE POWER WITH WHICH HE WAS GIFTED AT BIRTH! IF HE HAD COME BACK TOGETHER AS ***ONE***, HE MIGHT NOT HAVE HAD TO DIE...
ONE... ?
WELL... ALL RIGHT... YOUR INTENTION IS PURE, AND YOUR COURAGE SO FAR IS ADMIRABLE...
I WILL GIVE YOU THIS DRAGON BALL...
...BUT YOU SHOULD KNOW THAT YOU WILL PROBABLY NOT GET YOUR WISH...

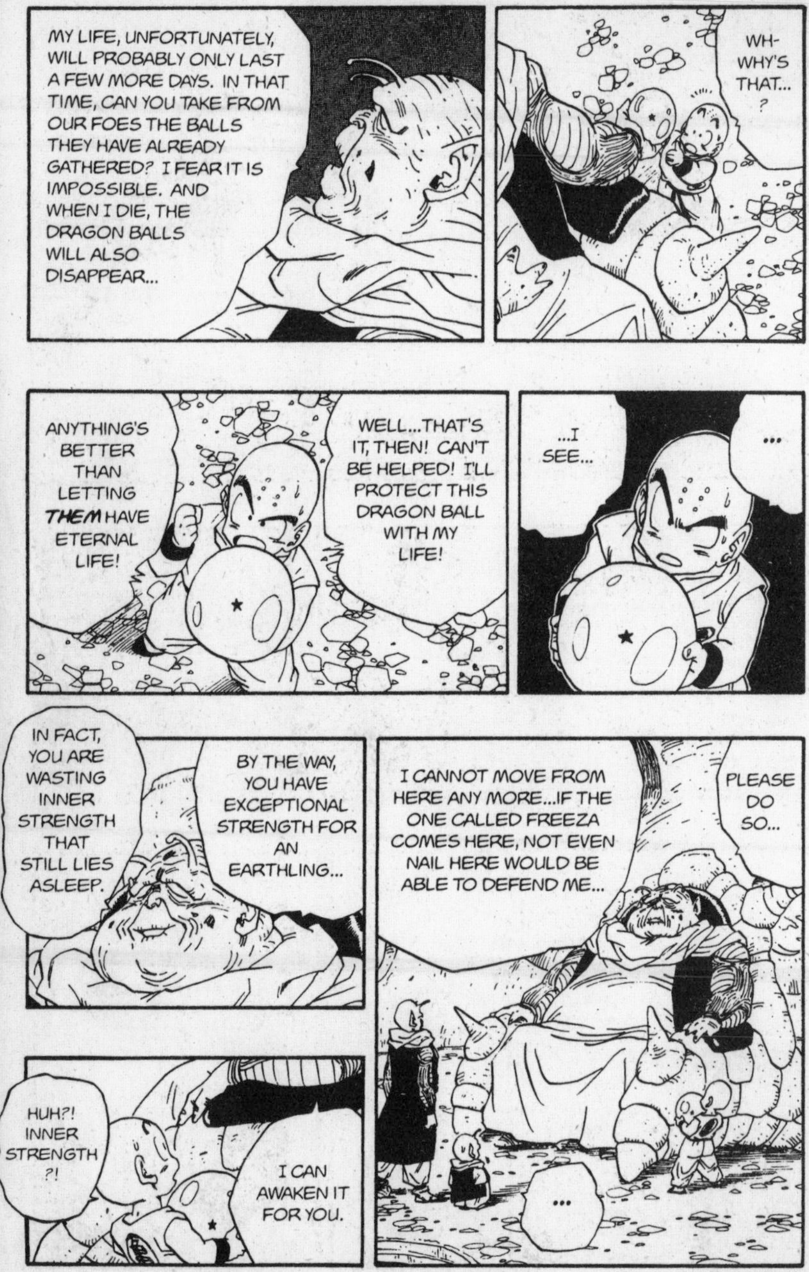
WH- WHY'S THAT... ?
MY LIFE, UNFORTUNATELY, WILL PROBABLY ONLY LAST A FEW MORE DAYS. IN THAT TIME, CAN YOU TAKE FROM OUR FOES THE BALLS THEY HAVE ALREADY GATHERED? I FEAR IT IS IMPOSSIBLE. AND WHEN I DIE, THE DRAGON BALLS WILL ALSO DISAPPEAR...
...
...I SEE...
WELL...THAT'S IT, THEN! CAN'T BE HELPED! I'LL PROTECT THIS DRAGON BALL WITH MY LIFE!
ANYTHING'S BETTER THAN LETTING *THEM* HAVE ETERNAL LIFE!
PLEASE DO SO...
I CANNOT MOVE FROM HERE ANY MORE...IF THE ONE CALLED FREEZA COMES HERE, NOT EVEN NAIL HERE WOULD BE ABLE TO DEFEND ME...
...
BY THE WAY, YOU HAVE EXCEPTIONAL STRENGTH FOR AN EARTHLING...
IN FACT, YOU ARE WASTING INNER STRENGTH THAT STILL LIES ASLEEP.
I CAN AWAKEN IT FOR YOU.
HUH?! INNER STRENGTH ?!

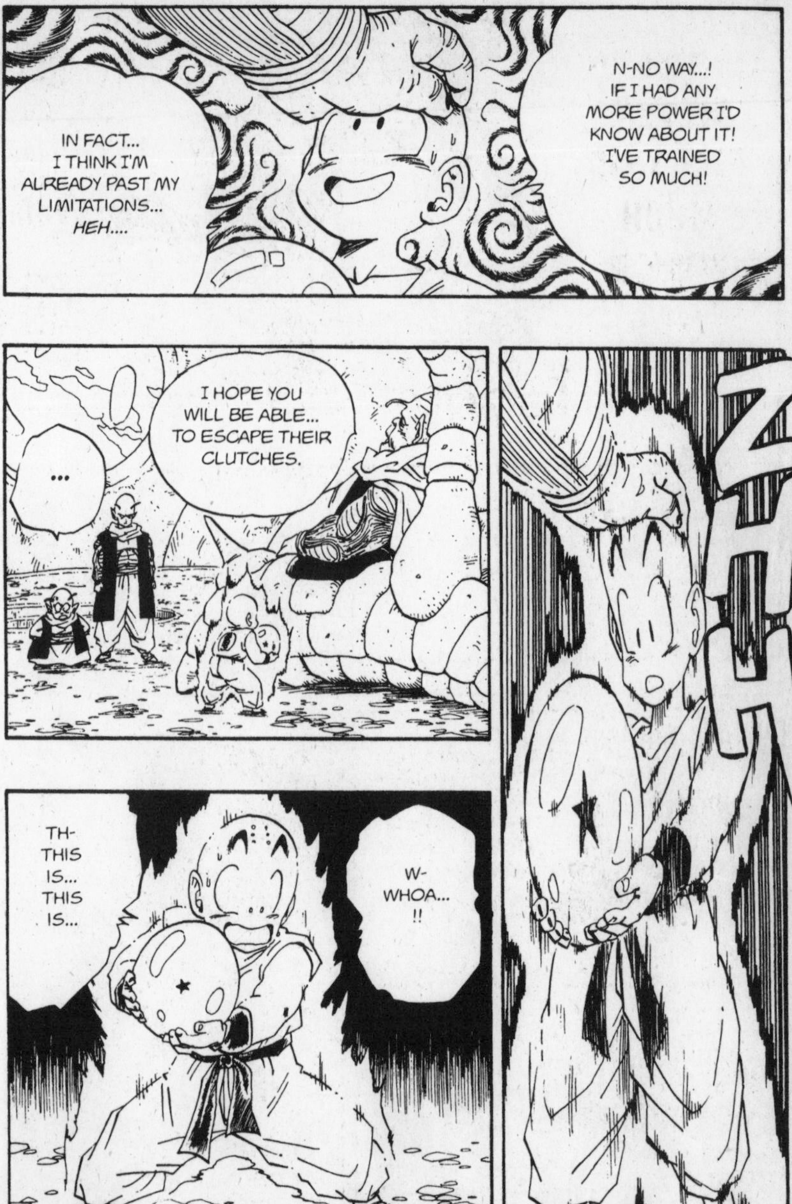
N-NO WAY...! IF I HAD ANY MORE POWER I'D KNOW ABOUT IT! I'VE TRAINED SO MUCH!
IN FACT... I THINK I'M ALREADY PAST MY LIMITATIONS... HEH....
ZHH
I HOPE YOU WILL BE ABLE... TO ESCAPE THEIR CLUTCHES.
...
W-WHOA... !!
TH-THIS IS... THIS IS...

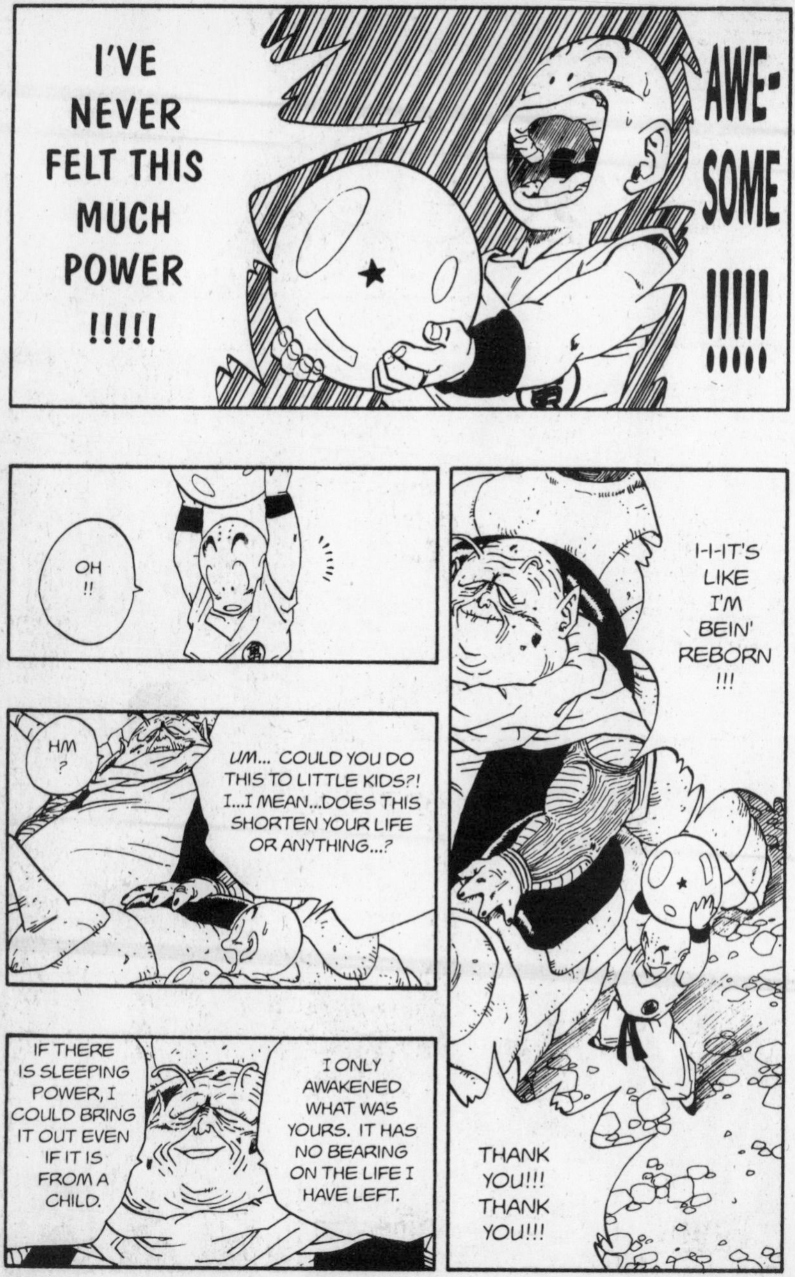
AWE-SOME!!!!!
I'VE NEVER FELT THIS MUCH POWER!!!!!
I-I-IT'S LIKE I'M BEIN' REBORN!!!
THANK YOU!!! THANK YOU!!!
OH!!
UM... COULD YOU DO THIS TO LITTLE KIDS?! I...I MEAN...DOES THIS SHORTEN YOUR LIFE OR ANYTHING...?
HM?
I ONLY AWAKENED WHAT WAS YOURS. IT HAS NO BEARING ON THE LIFE I HAVE LEFT.
IF THERE IS SLEEPING POWER, I COULD BRING IT OUT EVEN IF IT IS FROM A CHILD.

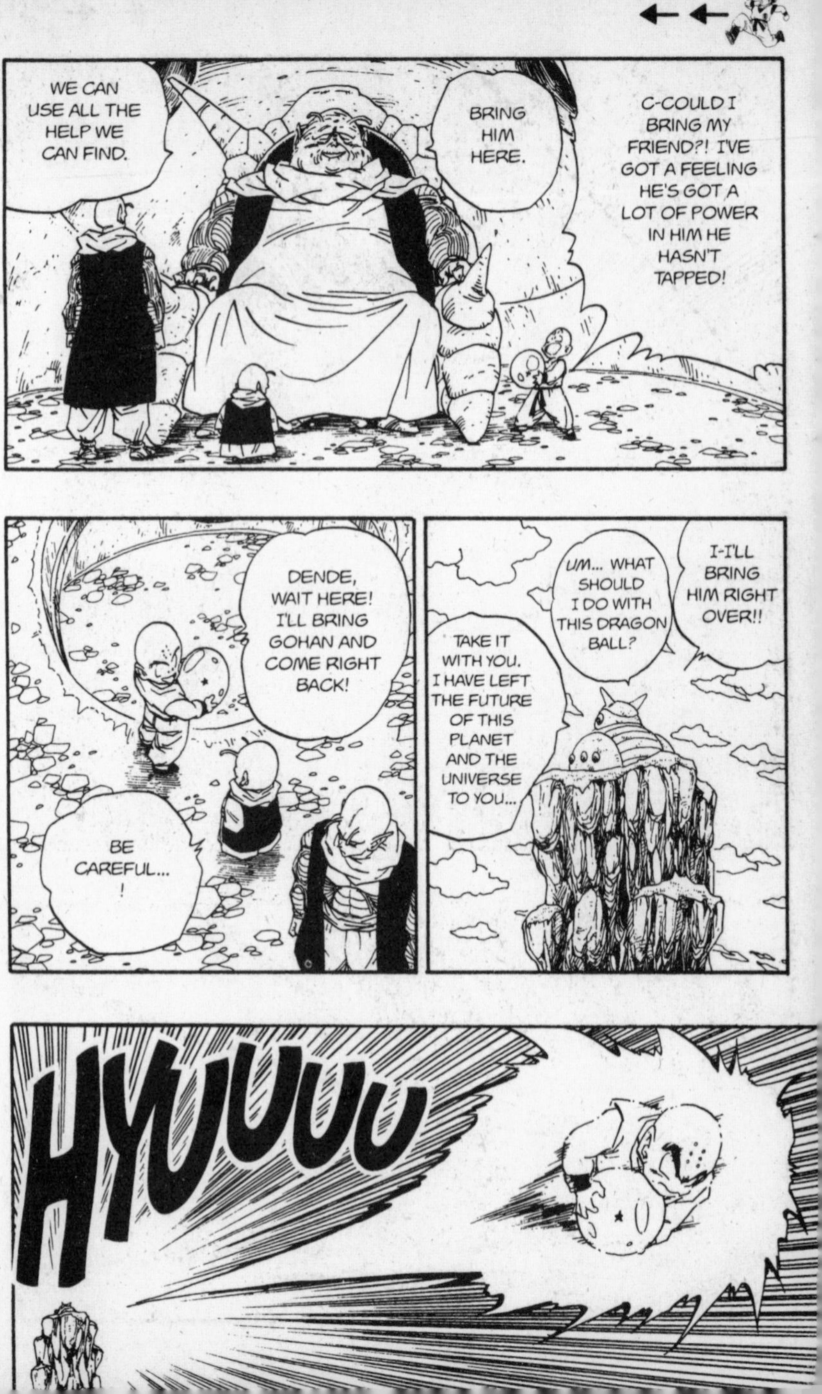
C-COULD I BRING MY FRIEND?! I'VE GOT A FEELING HE'S GOT A LOT OF POWER IN HIM HE HASN'T TAPPED!
BRING HIM HERE.
WE CAN USE ALL THE HELP WE CAN FIND.
I-I'LL BRING HIM RIGHT OVER!!
UM... WHAT SHOULD I DO WITH THIS DRAGON BALL?
TAKE IT WITH YOU. I HAVE LEFT THE FUTURE OF THIS PLANET AND THE UNIVERSE TO YOU...
DENDE, WAIT HERE! I'LL BRING GOHAN AND COME RIGHT BACK!
BE CAREFUL... !
HYUUUU

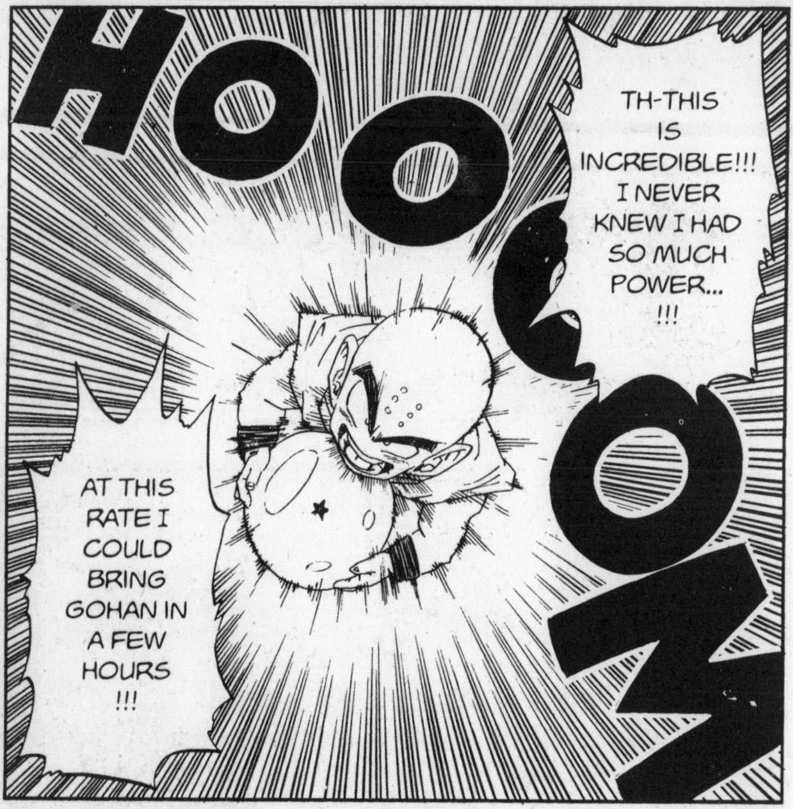
TH-THIS IS INCREDIBLE!!! I NEVER KNEW I HAD SO MUCH POWER... !!!
HOOOOM
AT THIS RATE I COULD BRING GOHAN IN A FEW HOURS !!!

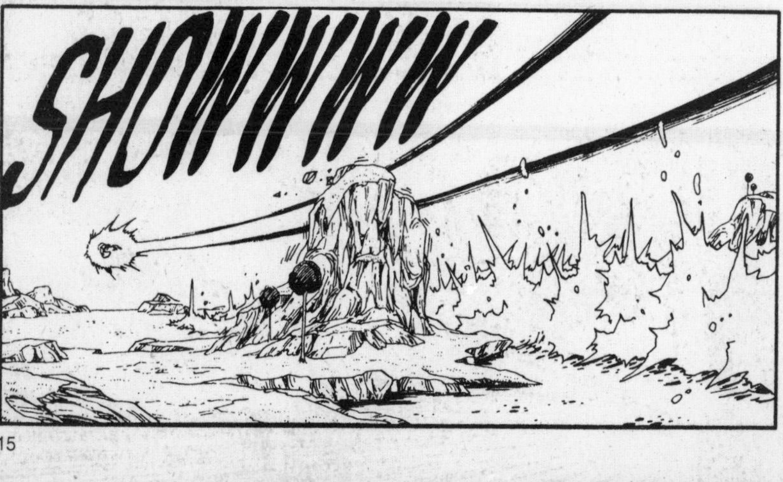
SHOWWWW

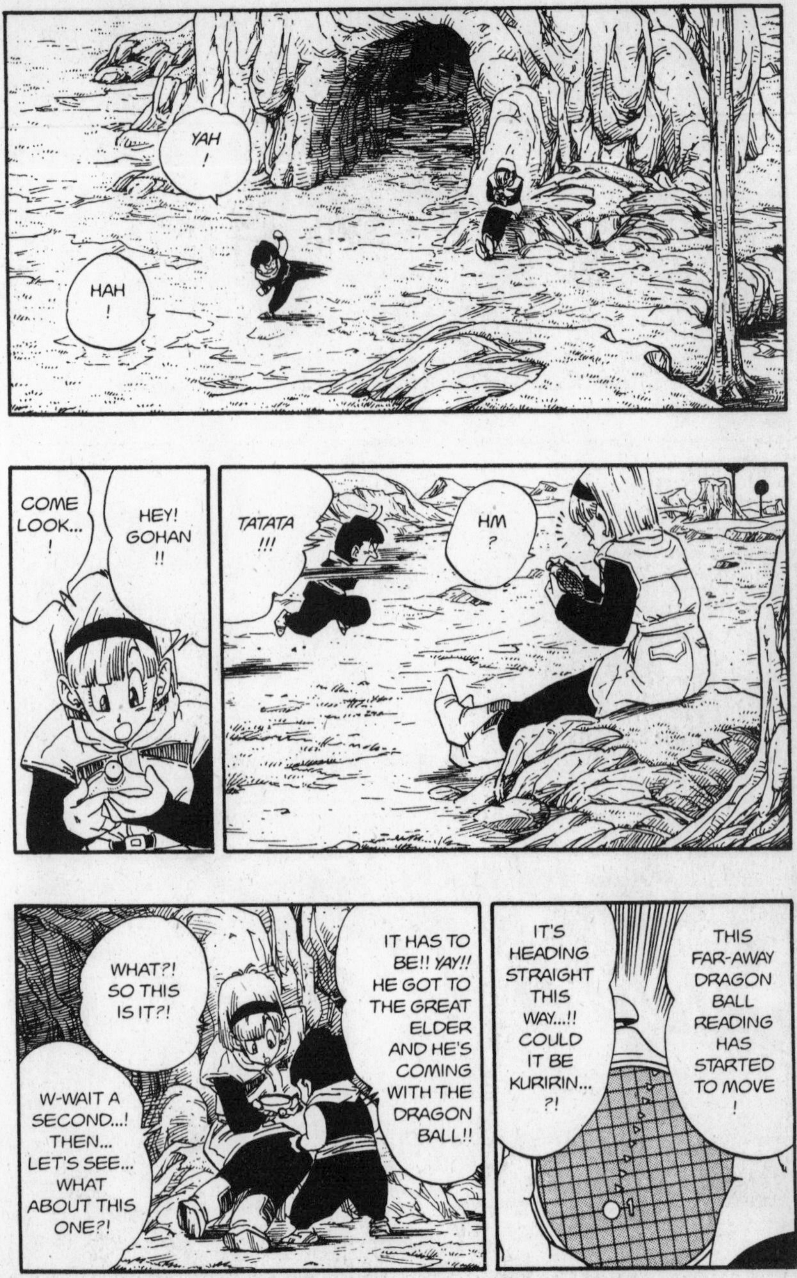
YAH!
HAH!
HM?
TATATA!!!
HEY! GOHAN!!
COME LOOK...!
THIS FAR-AWAY DRAGON BALL READING HAS STARTED TO MOVE!
IT'S HEADING STRAIGHT THIS WAY...!! COULD IT BE KURIRIN...?!
IT HAS TO BE!! YAY!! HE GOT TO THE GREAT ELDER AND HE'S COMING WITH THE DRAGON BALL!!
WHAT?! SO THIS IS IT?!
W-WAIT A SECOND...! THEN... LET'S SEE... WHAT ABOUT THIS ONE?!

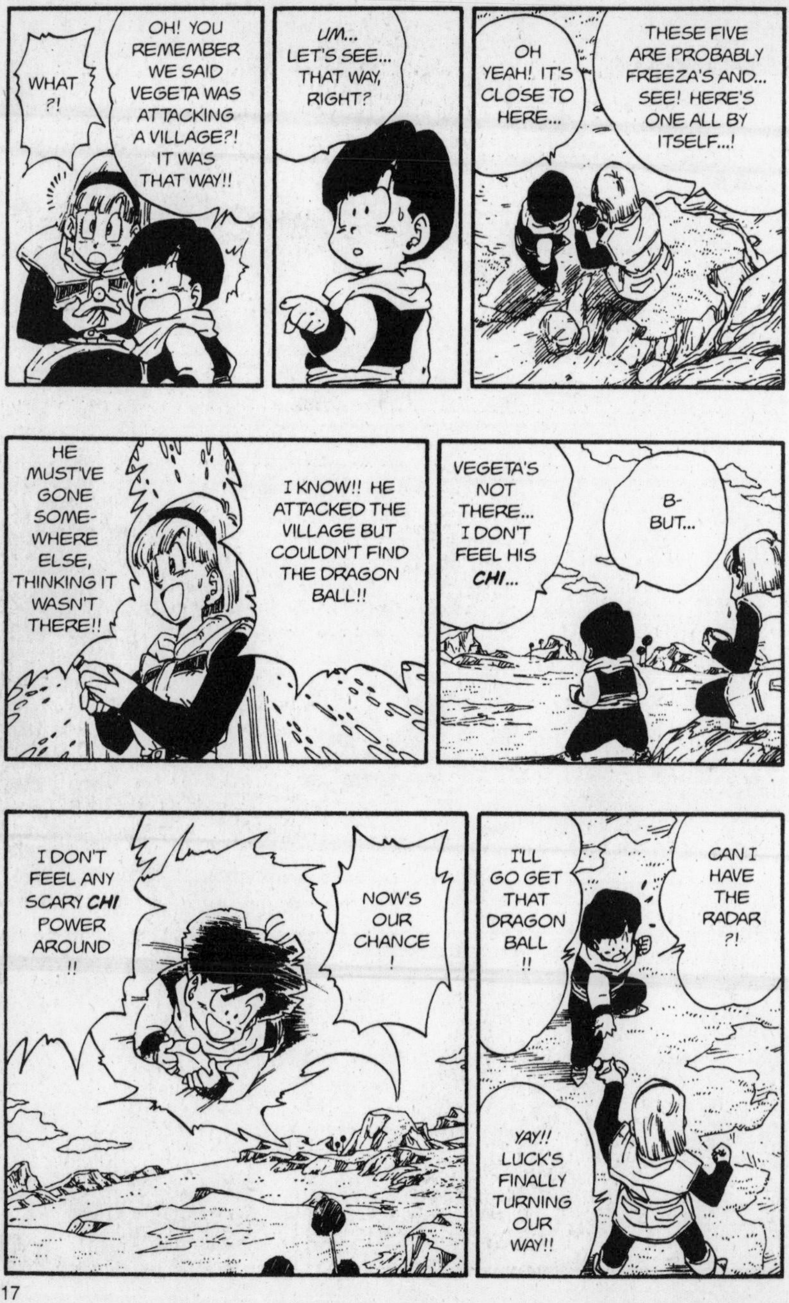
THESE FIVE ARE PROBABLY FREEZA'S AND... SEE! HERE'S ONE ALL BY ITSELF...!
OH YEAH! IT'S CLOSE TO HERE...
UM... LET'S SEE... THAT WAY, RIGHT?
OH! YOU REMEMBER WE SAID VEGETA WAS ATTACKING A VILLAGE?! IT WAS THAT WAY!!
WHAT ?!
B- BUT...
VEGETA'S NOT THERE... I DON'T FEEL HIS ***CHI***...
I KNOW!! HE ATTACKED THE VILLAGE BUT COULDN'T FIND THE DRAGON BALL!!
HE MUST'VE GONE SOME- WHERE ELSE, THINKING IT WASN'T THERE!!
CAN I HAVE THE RADAR ?!
I'LL GO GET THAT DRAGON BALL !!
YAY!! LUCK'S FINALLY TURNING OUR WAY!!
NOW'S OUR CHANCE !
I DON'T FEEL ANY SCARY ***CHI*** POWER AROUND !!

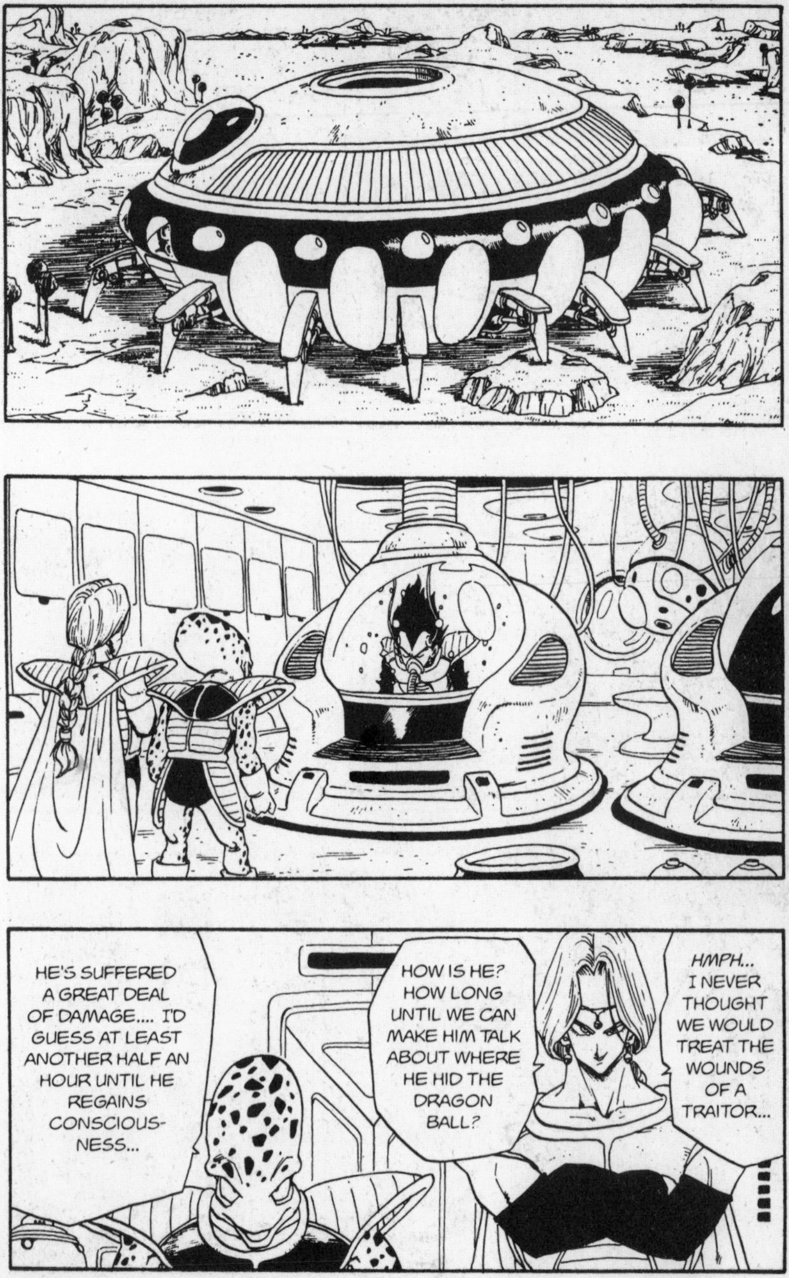
HMPH... I NEVER THOUGHT WE WOULD TREAT THE WOUNDS OF A TRAITOR...
HOW IS HE? HOW LONG UNTIL WE CAN MAKE HIM TALK ABOUT WHERE HE HID THE DRAGON BALL?
HE'S SUFFERED A GREAT DEAL OF DAMAGE.... I'D GUESS AT LEAST ANOTHER HALF AN HOUR UNTIL HE REGAINS CONSCIOUS-NESS...

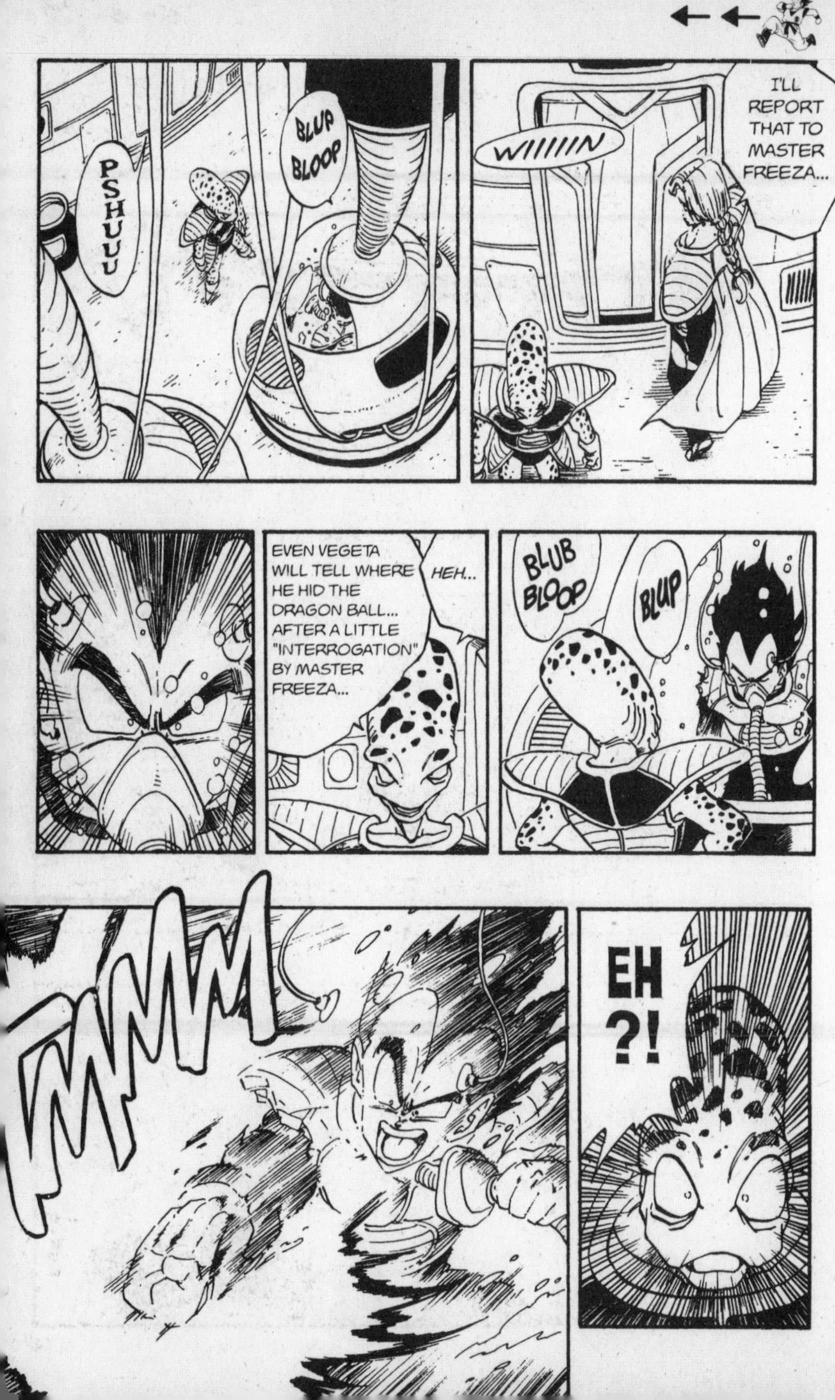
I'LL REPORT THAT TO MASTER FREEZA...
WIIIIIN
BLUP BLOOP
PSHUUU
BLUB BLOOP
BLUP
EVEN VEGETA WILL TELL WHERE HE HID THE DRAGON BALL... AFTER A LITTLE "INTERROGATION" BY MASTER FREEZA...
HEH...
EH?!
FWMM

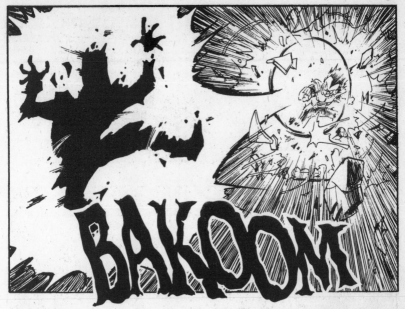

BAKOOM
THANKS SO MUCH...
PITY YOU UNDER-ESTIMATED MY RE-CUPERATIVE POWERS !!!
WH-WHAT WAS THAT SOUND ?!
IT COULDN'T BE... !!!
V-VEGETA... !!

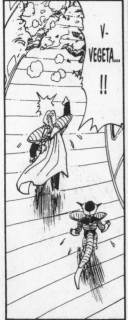

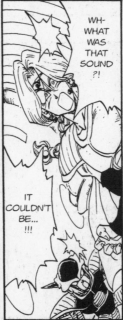

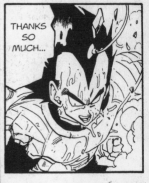

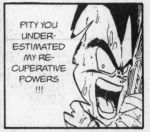

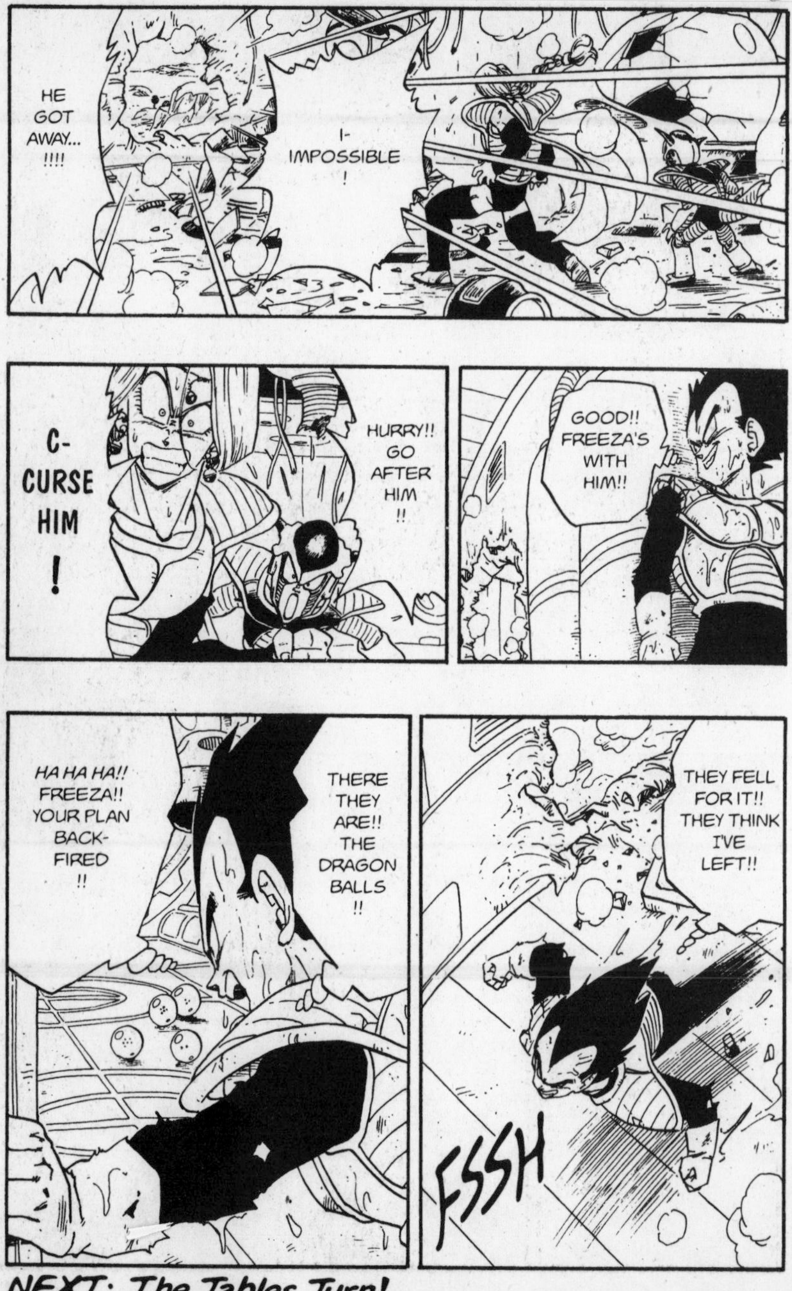
I-IMPOSSIBLE!
HE GOT AWAY...!!!!
GOOD!! FREEZA'S WITH HIM!!
HURRY!! GO AFTER HIM!!
C-CURSE HIM!
THEY FELL FOR IT!! THEY THINK I'VE LEFT!!
FSSH
THERE THEY ARE!! THE DRAGON BALLS!!
HA HA HA!! FREEZA!! YOUR PLAN BACK-FIRED!!

NEXT: The Tables Turn!

DBZ:72 • Vegeta's Laughter, Freeza's Rage

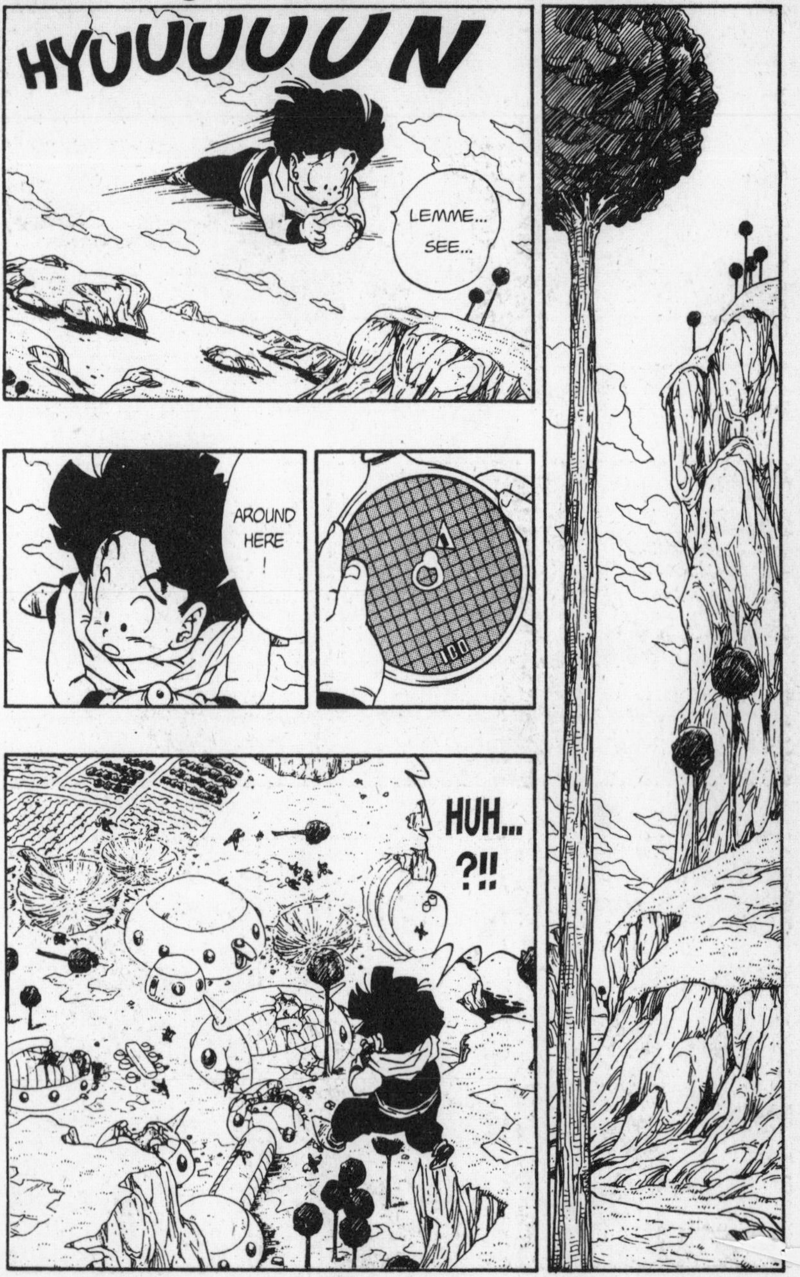
HYUUUUUN
LEMME... SEE...
AROUND HERE!
HUH... ?!!

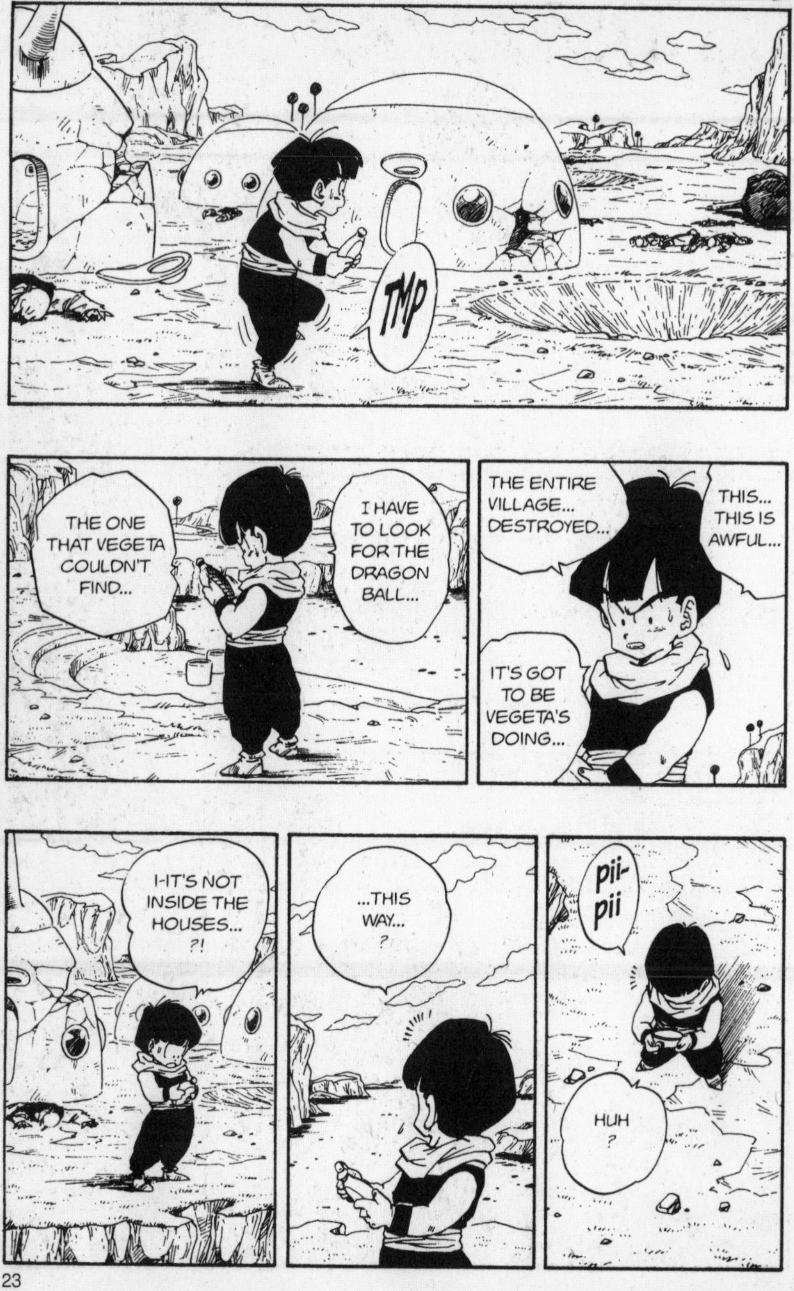
TMP
THIS... THIS IS AWFUL...
THE ENTIRE VILLAGE... DESTROYED...
IT'S GOT TO BE VEGETA'S DOING...
I HAVE TO LOOK FOR THE DRAGON BALL...
THE ONE THAT VEGETA COULDN'T FIND...
pii-pii
HUH ?
...THIS WAY... ?
I-IT'S NOT INSIDE THE HOUSES... ?!

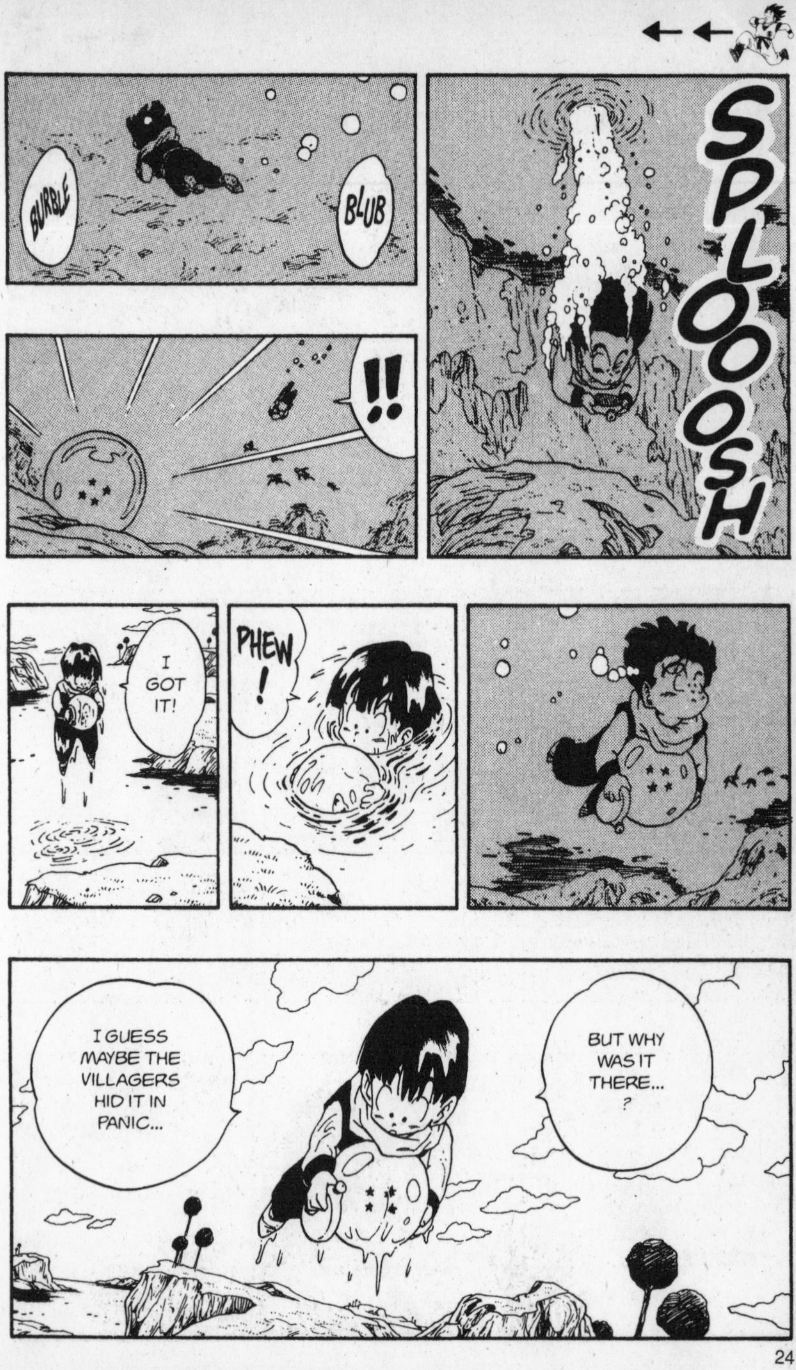
SPLOOOOSH
BLUB
BURBLE
!!
PHEW!
I GOT IT!
I GUESS MAYBE THE VILLAGERS HID IT IN PANIC...
BUT WHY WAS IT THERE... ?

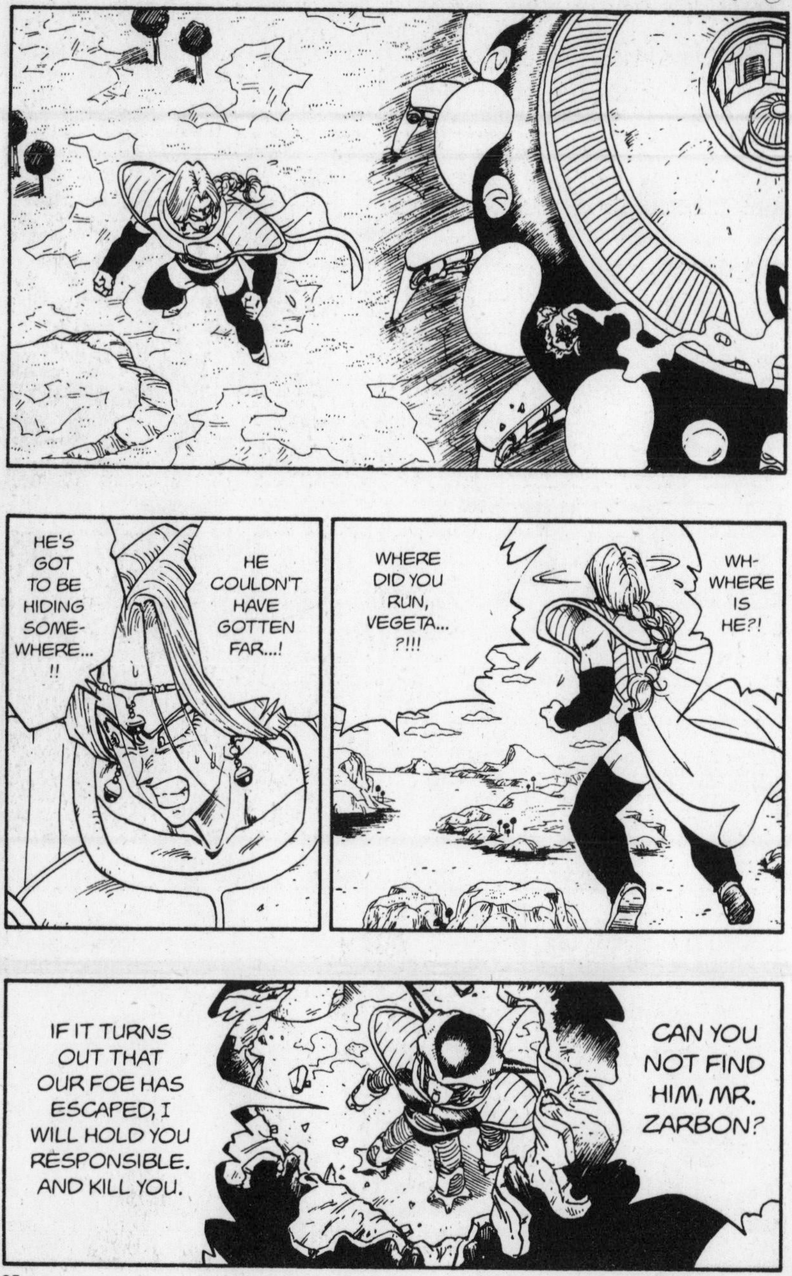
WH- WHERE IS HE?!
WHERE DID YOU RUN, VEGETA...?!!!
HE COULDN'T HAVE GOTTEN FAR...!
HE'S GOT TO BE HIDING SOMEWHERE...!!
CAN YOU NOT FIND HIM, MR. ZARBON?
IF IT TURNS OUT THAT OUR FOE HAS ESCAPED, I WILL HOLD YOU RESPONSIBLE. AND KILL YOU.

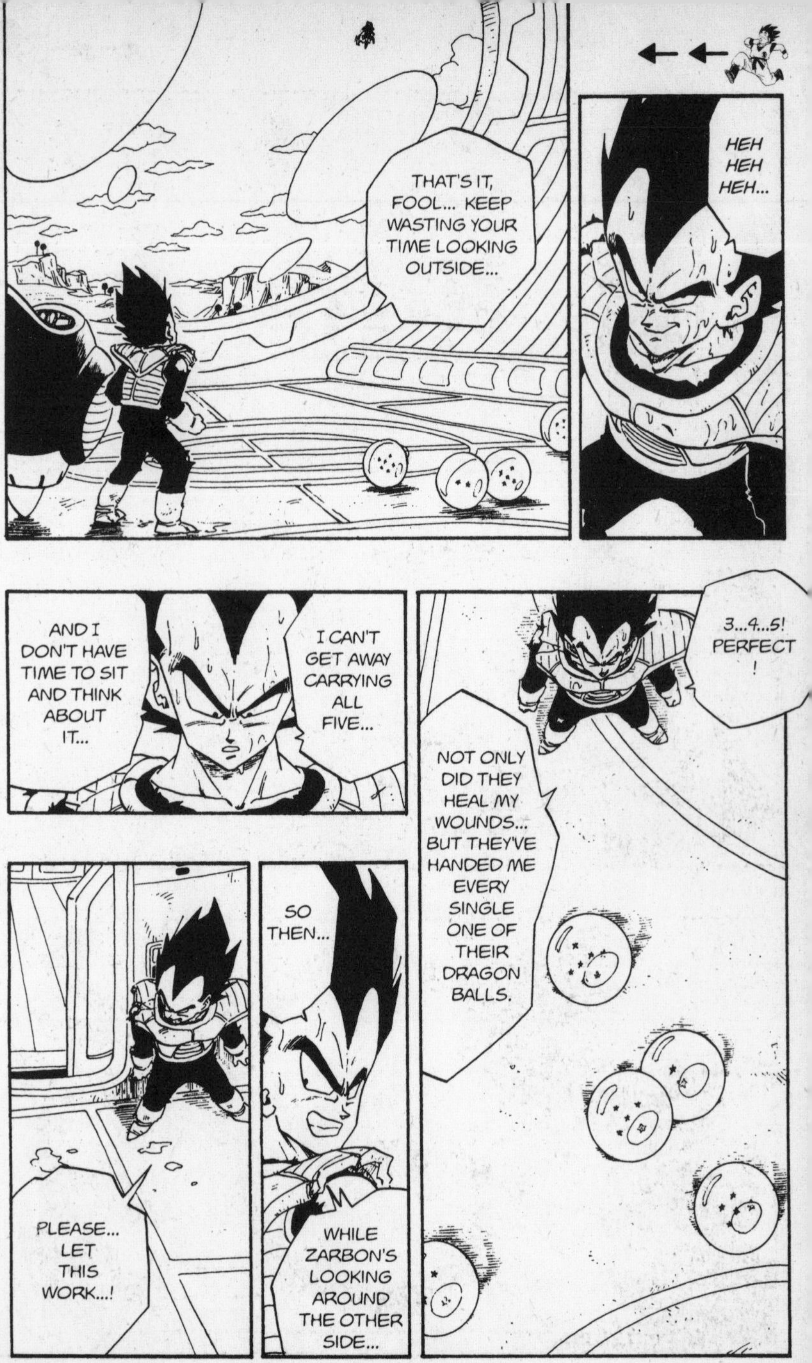
HEH HEH HEH...
THAT'S IT, FOOL... KEEP WASTING YOUR TIME LOOKING OUTSIDE...
3...4...5! PERFECT!
NOT ONLY DID THEY HEAL MY WOUNDS... BUT THEY'VE HANDED ME EVERY SINGLE ONE OF THEIR DRAGON BALLS.
I CAN'T GET AWAY CARRYING ALL FIVE...
AND I DON'T HAVE TIME TO SIT AND THINK ABOUT IT...
SO THEN...
WHILE ZARBON'S LOOKING AROUND THE OTHER SIDE...
PLEASE... LET THIS WORK...!

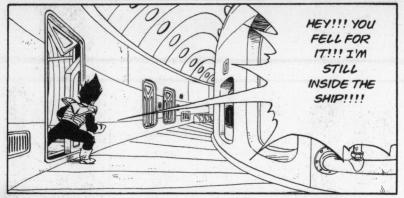

HEY!!! YOU FELL FOR IT!!! I'M STILL INSIDE THE SHIP!!!!

WHAT...?!!

WHAT...?!!

ZMMM

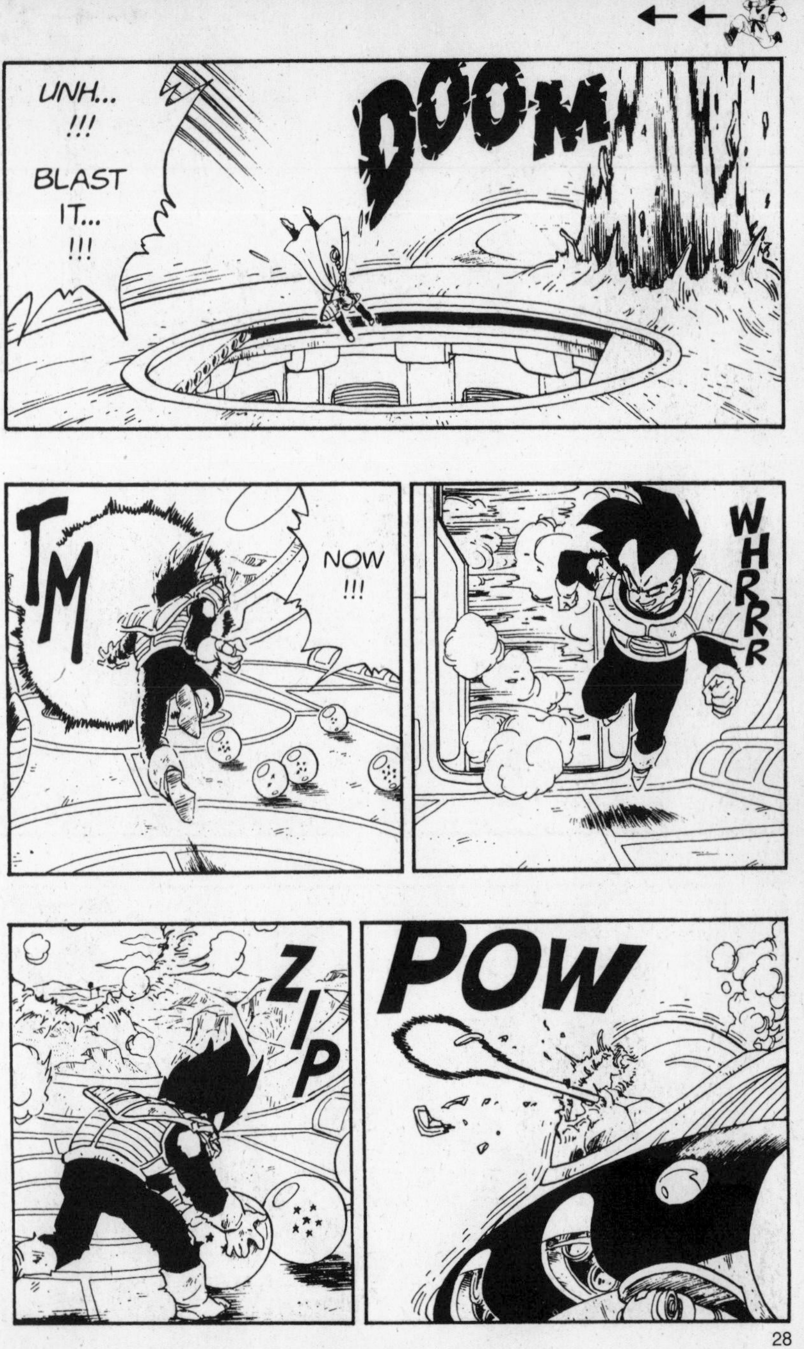

DOOM
UNH... !!!
BLAST IT... !!!
WHRRR
TM
NOW !!!
POW
ZIP

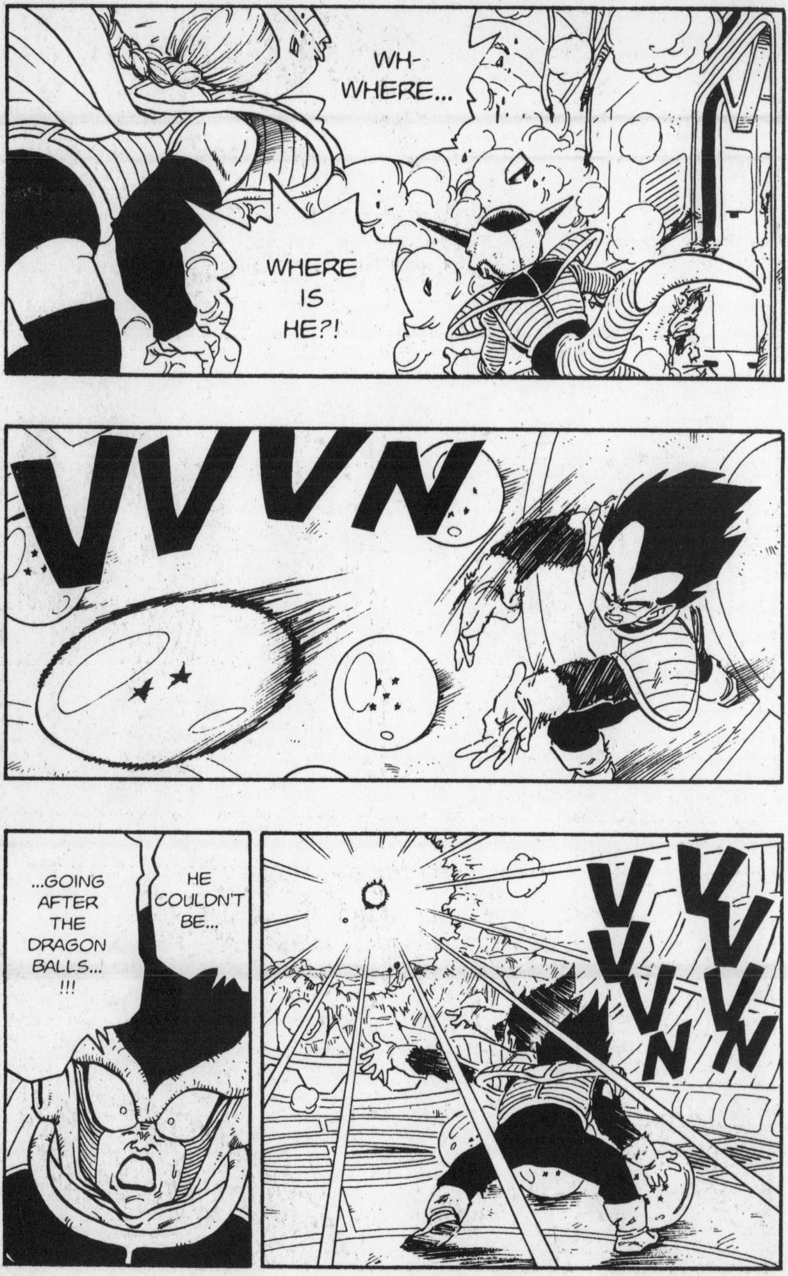
WH- WHERE...
WHERE IS HE?!
VVVN
VVVN
VVVN
HE COULDN'T BE...
...GOING AFTER THE DRAGON BALLS...!!!

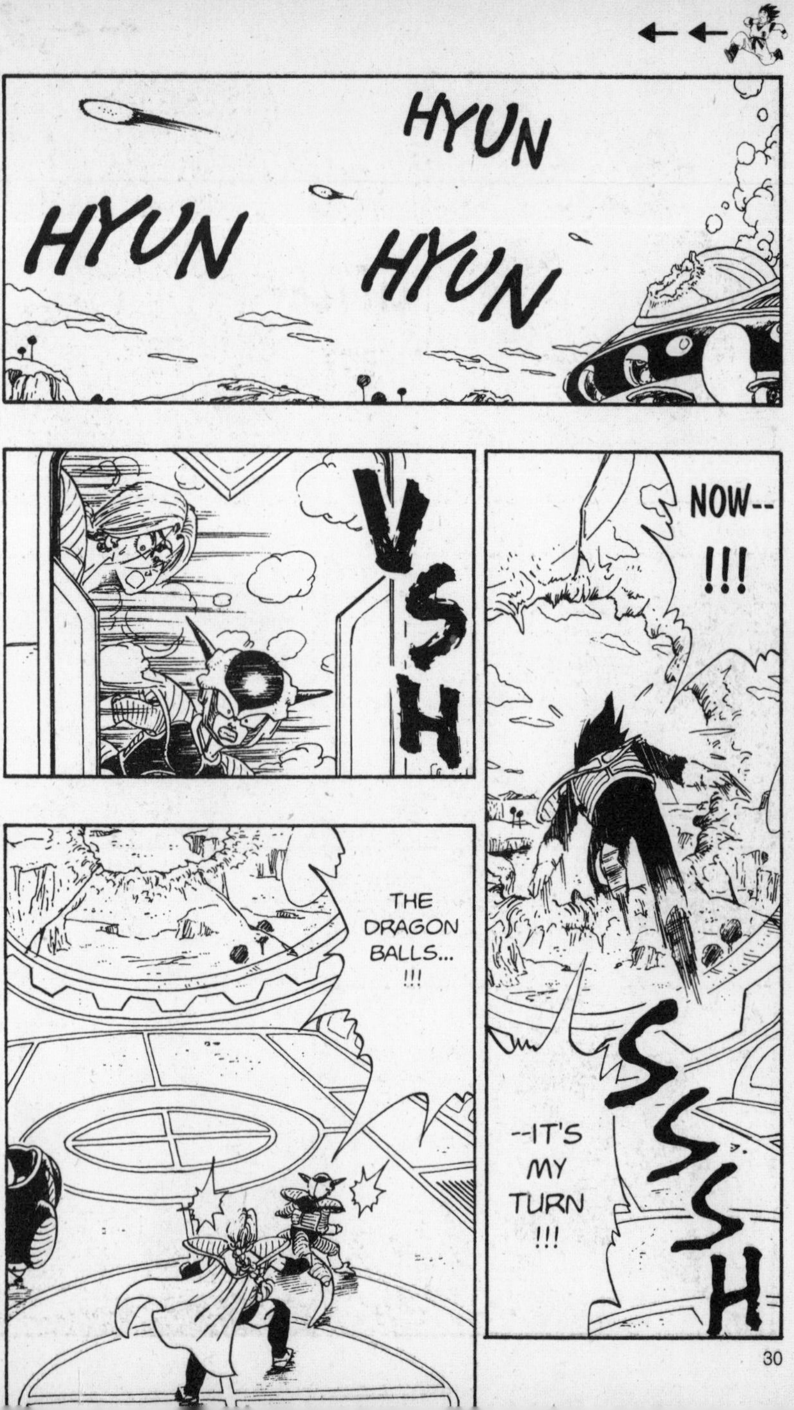
HYUN
HYUN
HYUN
NOW-- !!!
SSSH
--IT'S MY TURN !!!
VSH
THE DRAGON BALLS... !!!

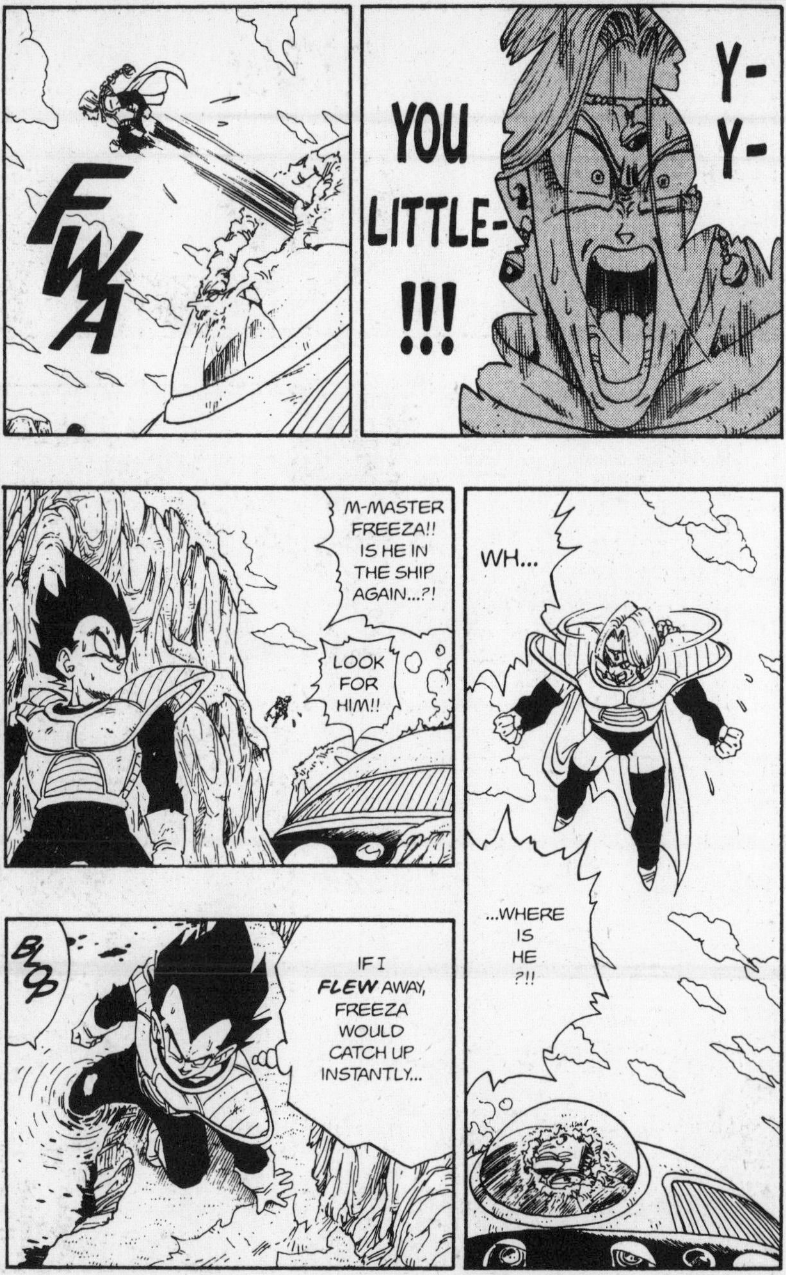
Y-Y-
YOU LITTLE-!!!
FWA
WH...
...WHERE IS HE?!!
M-MASTER FREEZA!! IS HE IN THE SHIP AGAIN...?!
LOOK FOR HIM!!
BLOP
IF I FLEW AWAY, FREEZA WOULD CATCH UP INSTANTLY...

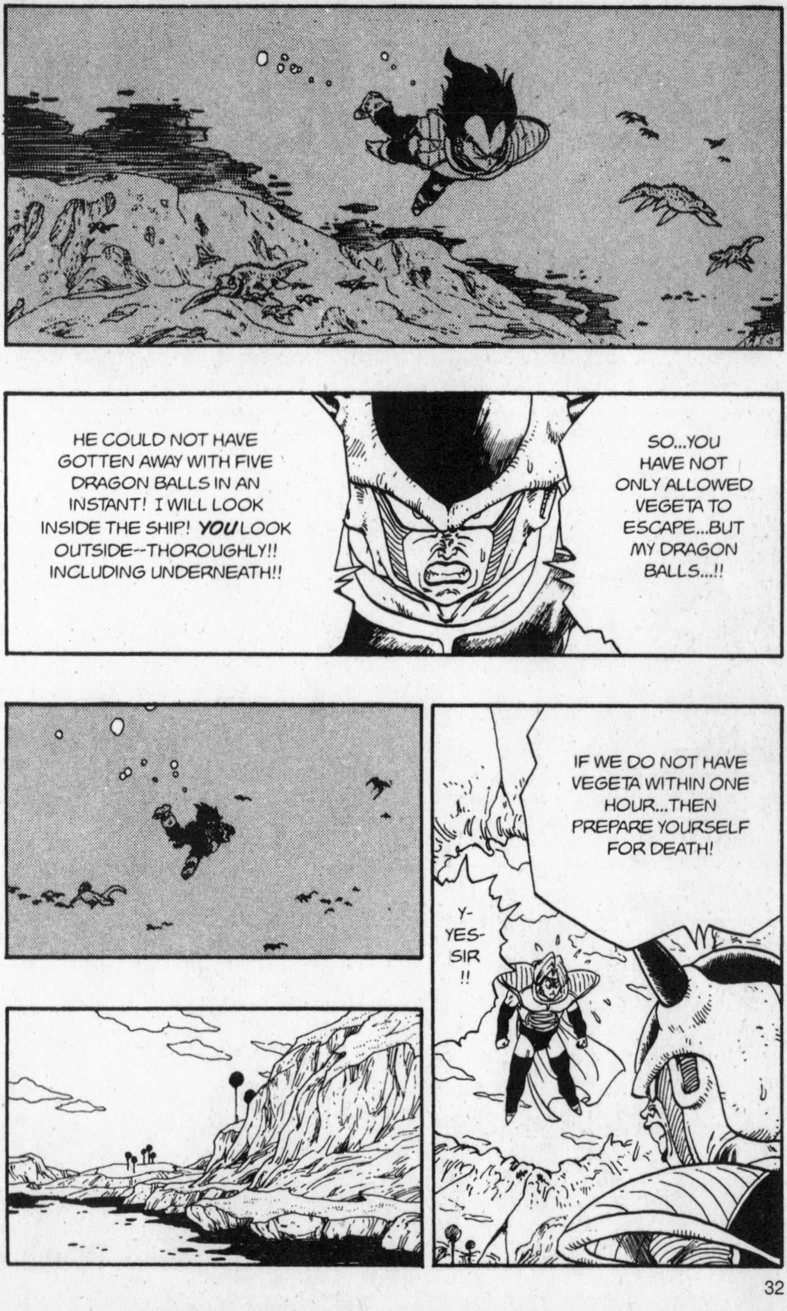
SO...YOU HAVE NOT ONLY ALLOWED VEGETA TO ESCAPE...BUT MY DRAGON BALLS...!!
HE COULD NOT HAVE GOTTEN AWAY WITH FIVE DRAGON BALLS IN AN INSTANT! I WILL LOOK INSIDE THE SHIP! **YOU** LOOK OUTSIDE--THOROUGHLY!! INCLUDING UNDERNEATH!!
IF WE DO NOT HAVE VEGETA WITHIN ONE HOUR...THEN PREPARE YOURSELF FOR DEATH!
Y-YES-SIR!!

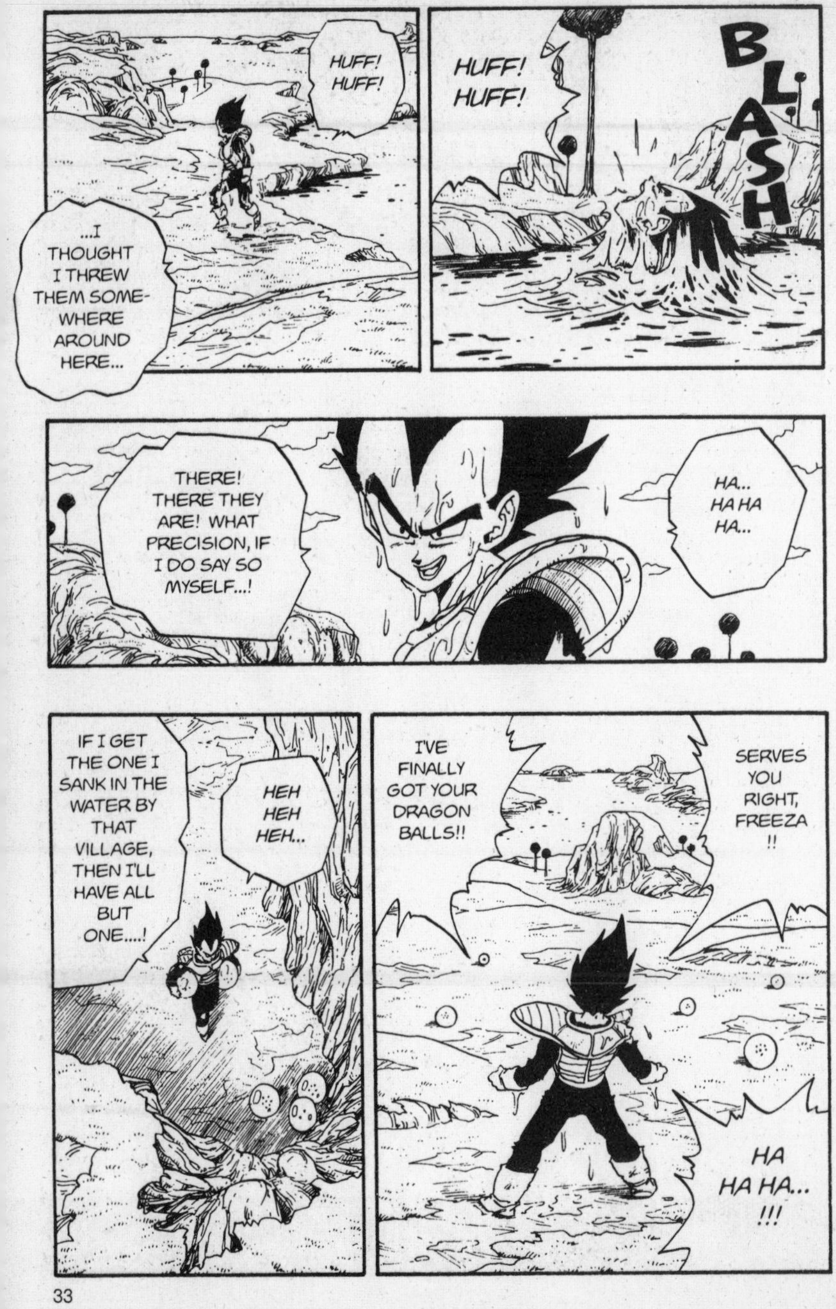

HUFF! HUFF!
BLASH
HUFF! HUFF!
...I THOUGHT I THREW THEM SOMEWHERE AROUND HERE...
HA... HA HA HA...
THERE! THERE THEY ARE! WHAT PRECISION, IF I DO SAY SO MYSELF...!
SERVES YOU RIGHT, FREEZA !!
I'VE FINALLY GOT YOUR DRAGON BALLS!!
HA HA HA... !!!
HEH HEH HEH...
IF I GET THE ONE I SANK IN THE WATER BY THAT VILLAGE, THEN I'LL HAVE ALL BUT ONE....!

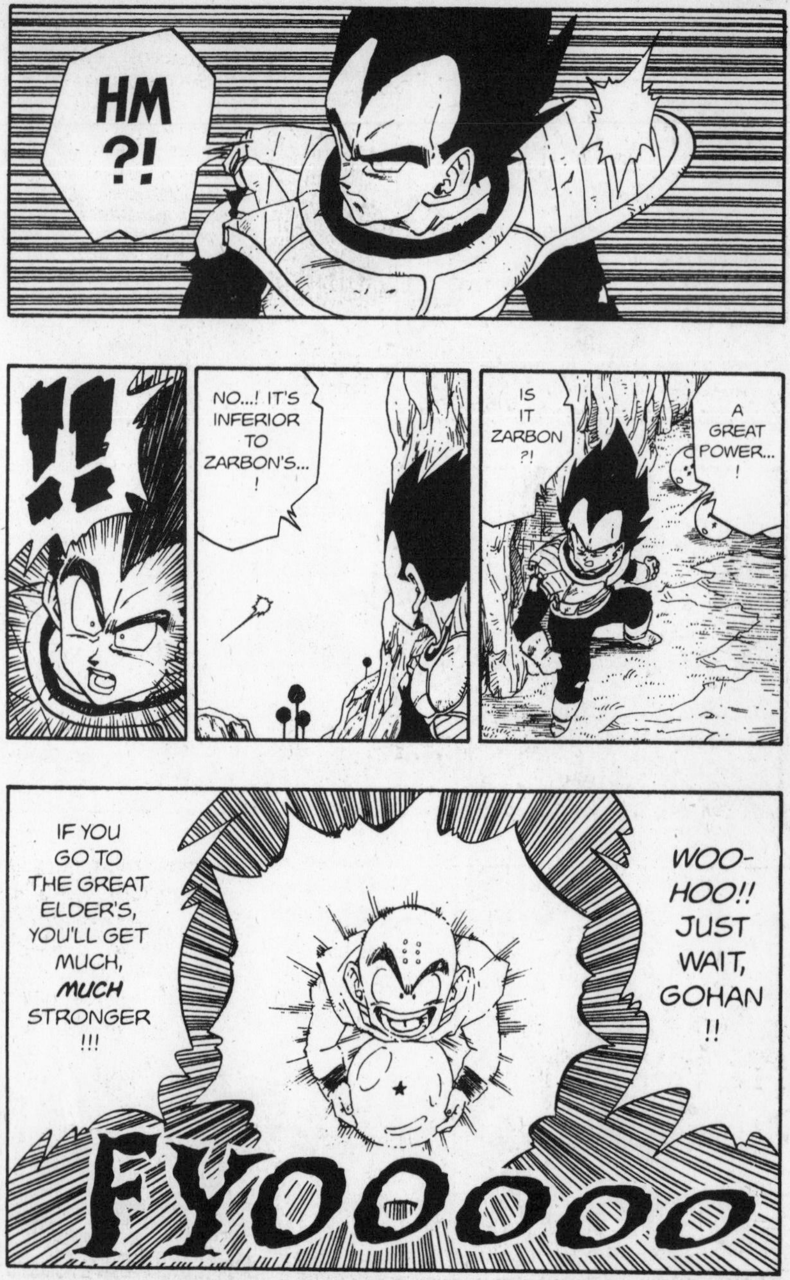
HM ?!
A GREAT POWER...!
IS IT ZARBON ?!
NO...! IT'S INFERIOR TO ZARBON'S...!
!!
WOO-HOO!! JUST WAIT, GOHAN !!
IF YOU GO TO THE GREAT ELDER'S, YOU'LL GET MUCH, MUCH STRONGER !!!
FYOOOOOO

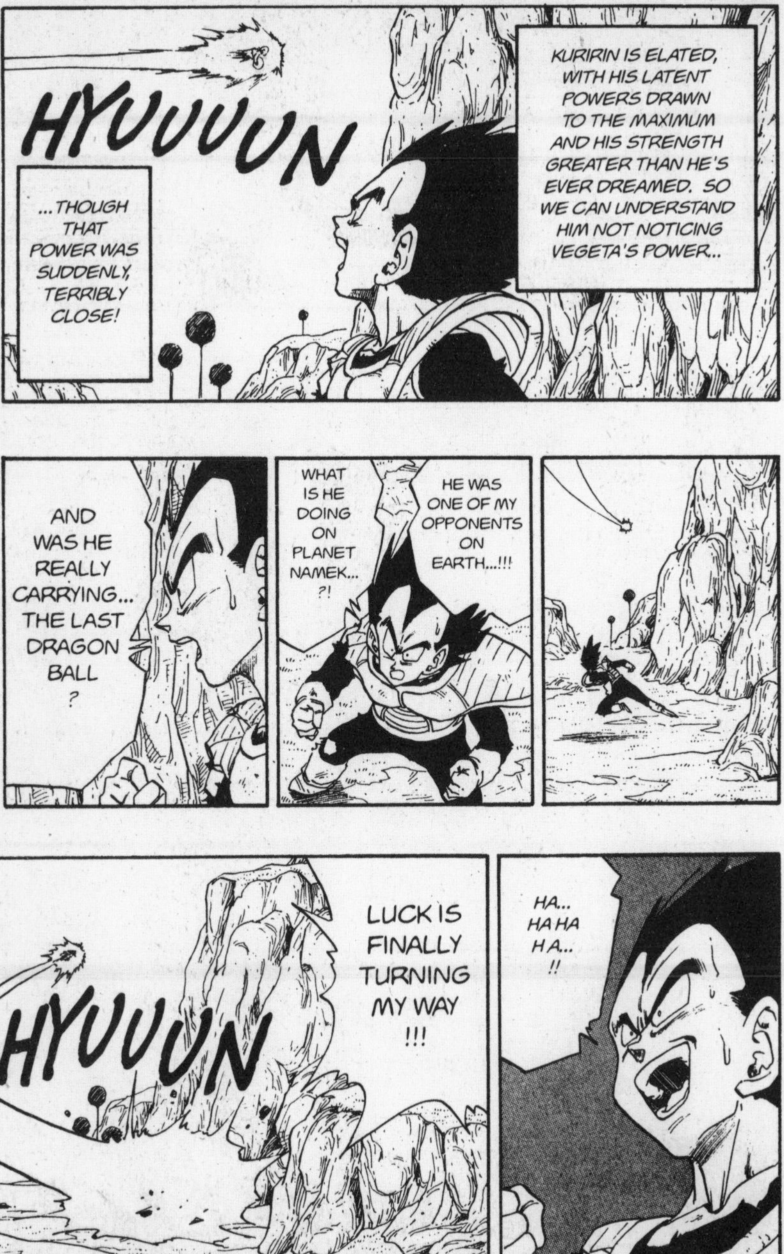

KURIRIN IS ELATED, WITH HIS LATENT POWERS DRAWN TO THE MAXIMUM AND HIS STRENGTH GREATER THAN HE'S EVER DREAMED. SO WE CAN UNDERSTAND HIM NOT NOTICING VEGETA'S POWER...
HYUUUUN
...THOUGH THAT POWER WAS SUDDENLY, TERRIBLY CLOSE!
HE WAS ONE OF MY OPPONENTS ON EARTH...!!!
WHAT IS HE DOING ON PLANET NAMEK...?!
AND WAS HE REALLY CARRYING... THE LAST DRAGON BALL?
HA... HA HA HA...!!
LUCK IS FINALLY TURNING MY WAY!!!
HYUUUN

NEXT: Reunion of Terror!

DBZ:73 • Reunion of Terror!

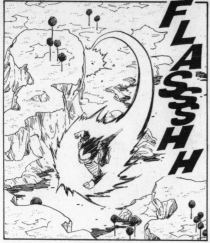

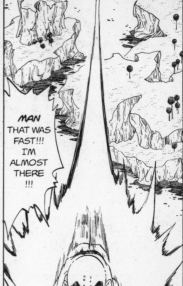

MAN THAT WAS FAST!!! I'M ALMOST THERE !!!
FLASSSHH
SO. THE EARTHLING SEEMS TO BE AFTER THE DRAGON BALLS TOO...
WELL, THEN--I'D BETTER TAKE YOURS !!

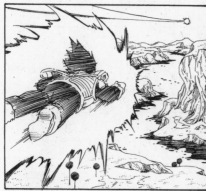

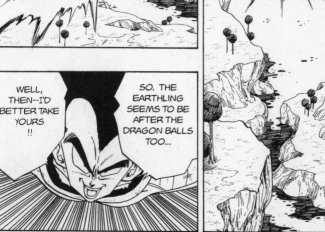

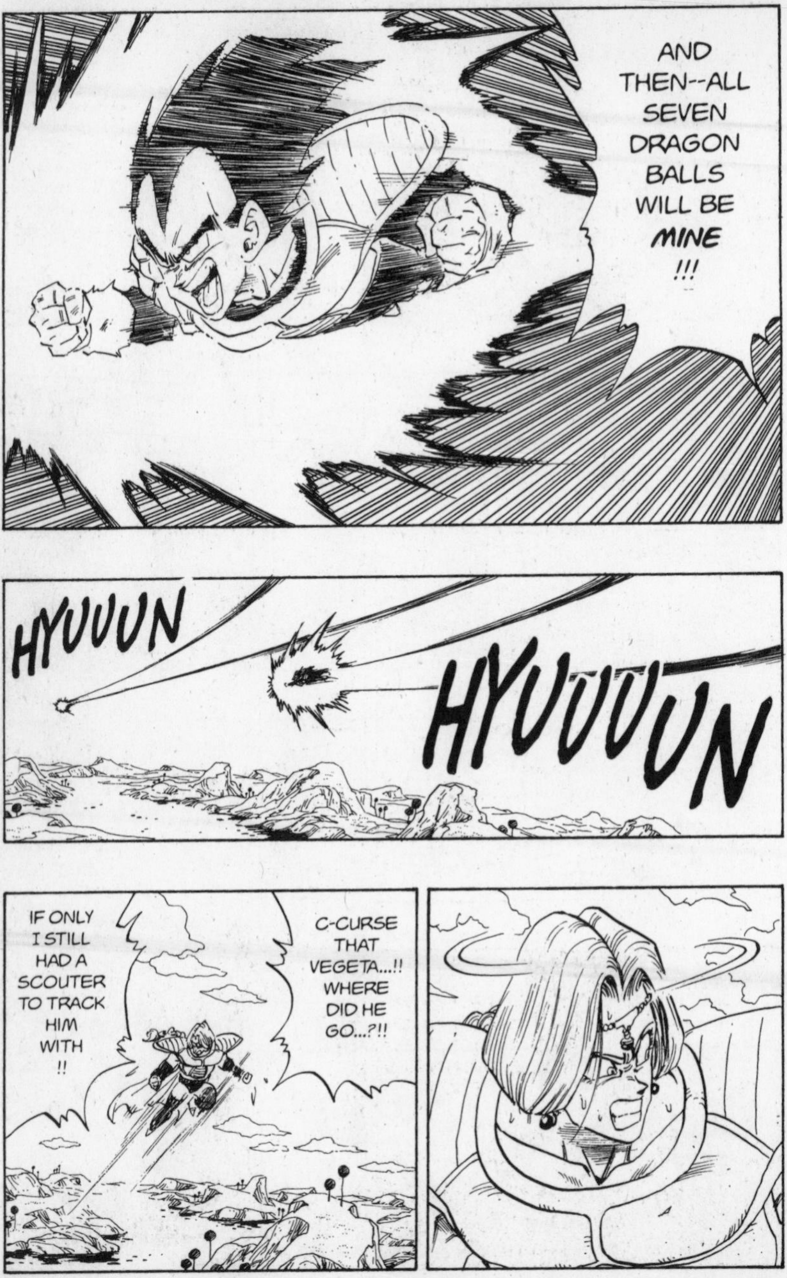
AND THEN--ALL SEVEN DRAGON BALLS WILL BE MINE !!!
HYUUUUN
HYUUUN
C-CURSE THAT VEGETA...!! WHERE DID HE GO...?!!
IF ONLY I STILL HAD A SCOUTER TO TRACK HIM WITH !!

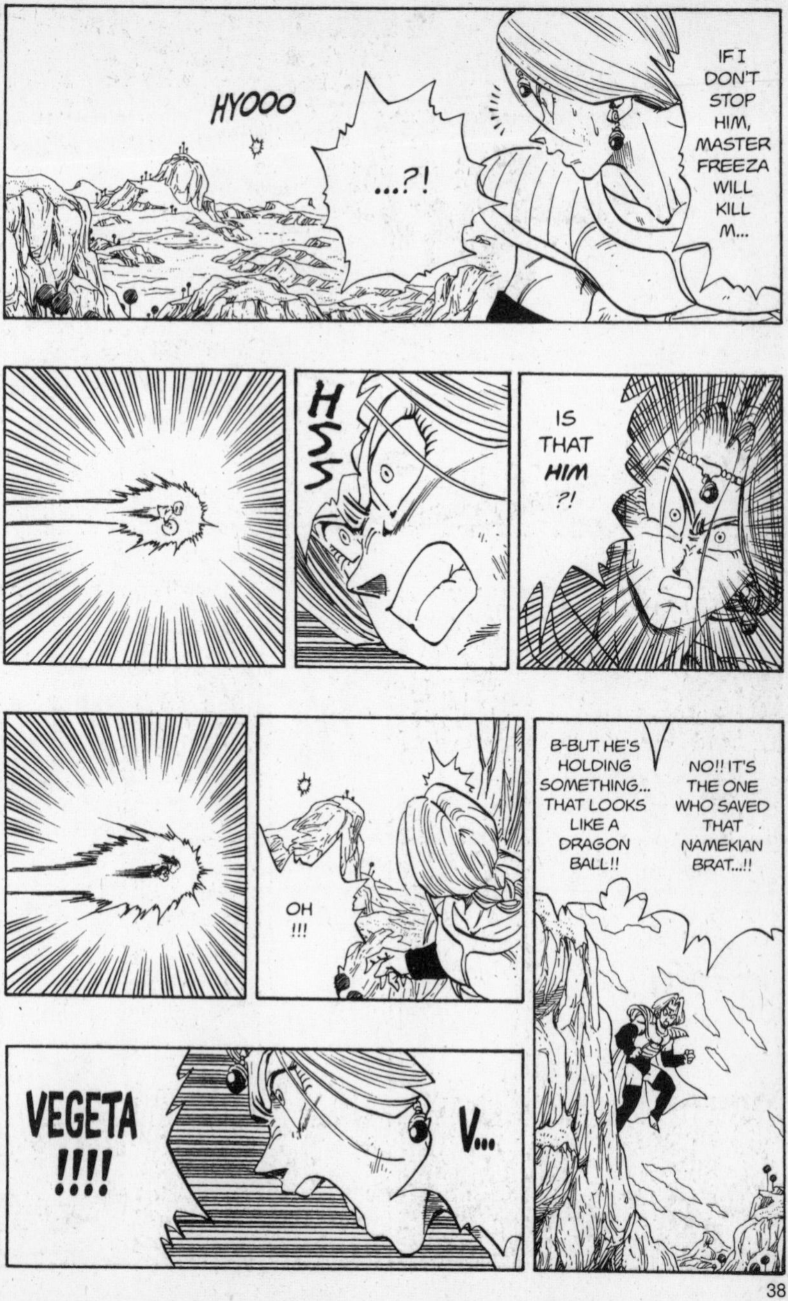
IF I DON'T STOP HIM, MASTER FREEZA WILL KILL M...
...?!
HYOOO
IS THAT HIM ?!
HSS
NO!! IT'S THE ONE WHO SAVED THAT NAMEKIAN BRAT...!!
B-BUT HE'S HOLDING SOMETHING... THAT LOOKS LIKE A DRAGON BALL!!
OH !!!
V...
VEGETA !!!!

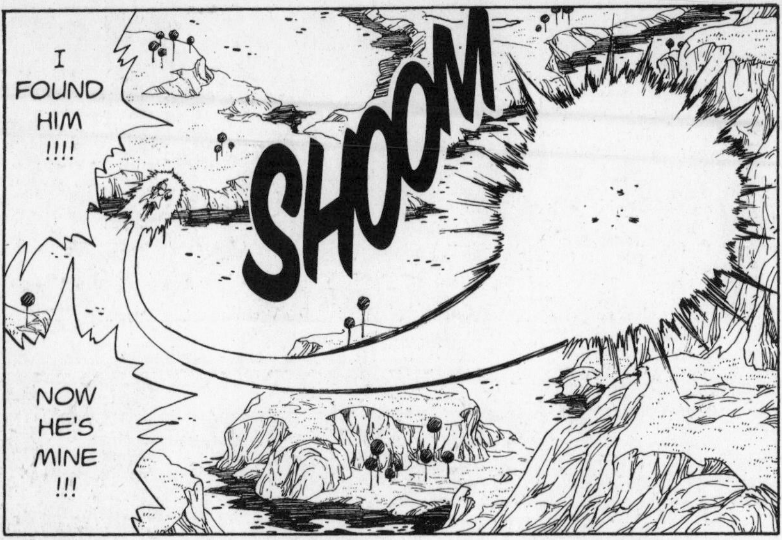
I FOUND HIM !!!!
NOW HE'S MINE !!!
SHOOM

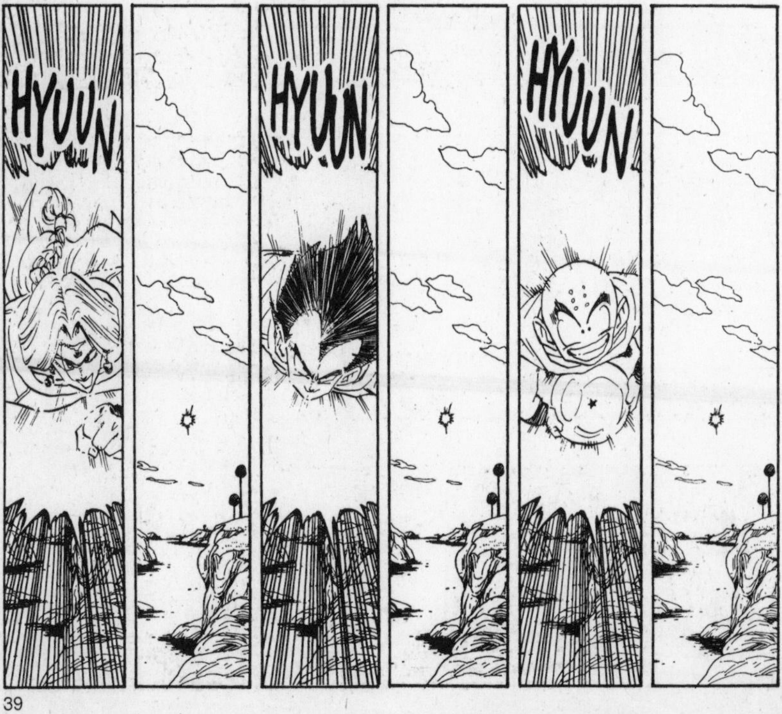
HYUUN
HYUUN
HYUUN

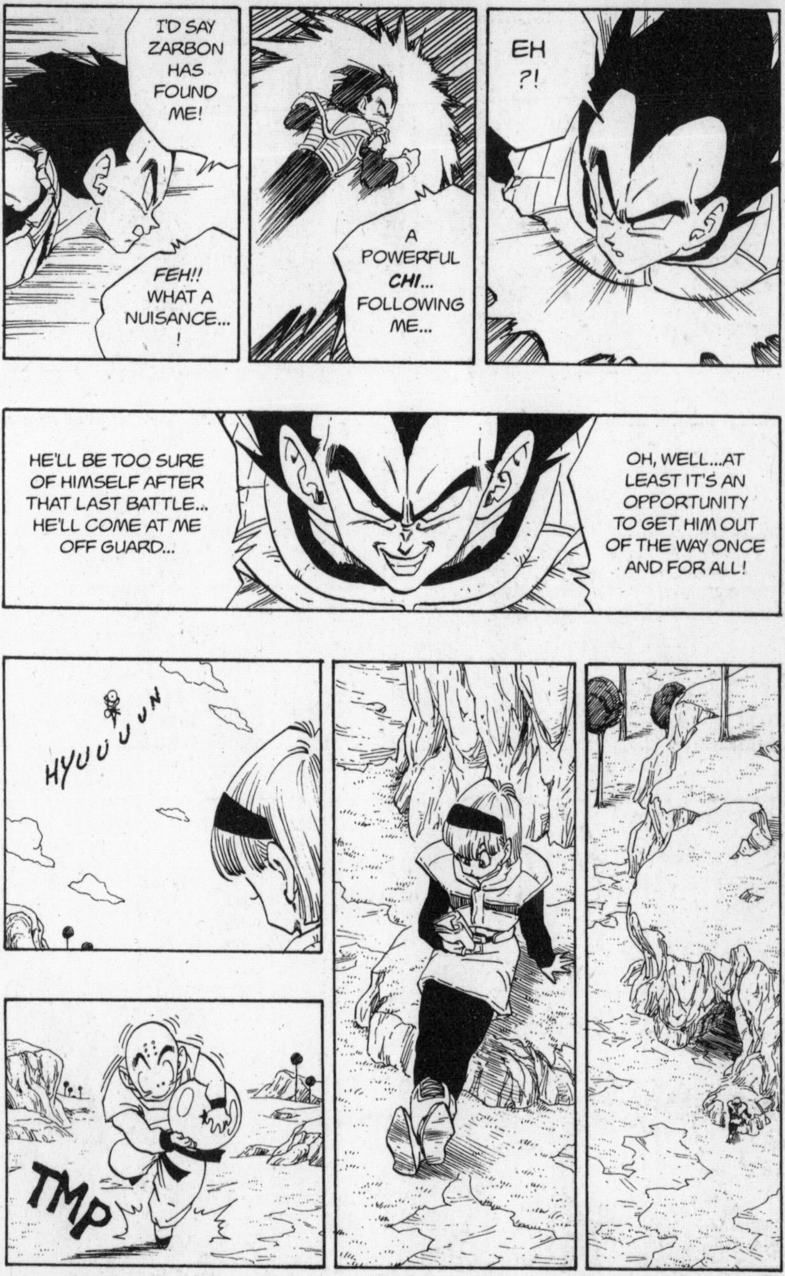
EH ?!
A POWERFUL CHI... FOLLOWING ME...
I'D SAY ZARBON HAS FOUND ME!
FEH!! WHAT A NUISANCE...!
OH, WELL...AT LEAST IT'S AN OPPORTUNITY TO GET HIM OUT OF THE WAY ONCE AND FOR ALL!
HE'LL BE TOO SURE OF HIMSELF AFTER THAT LAST BATTLE... HE'LL COME AT ME OFF GUARD...
HYUUUUUN
TMP

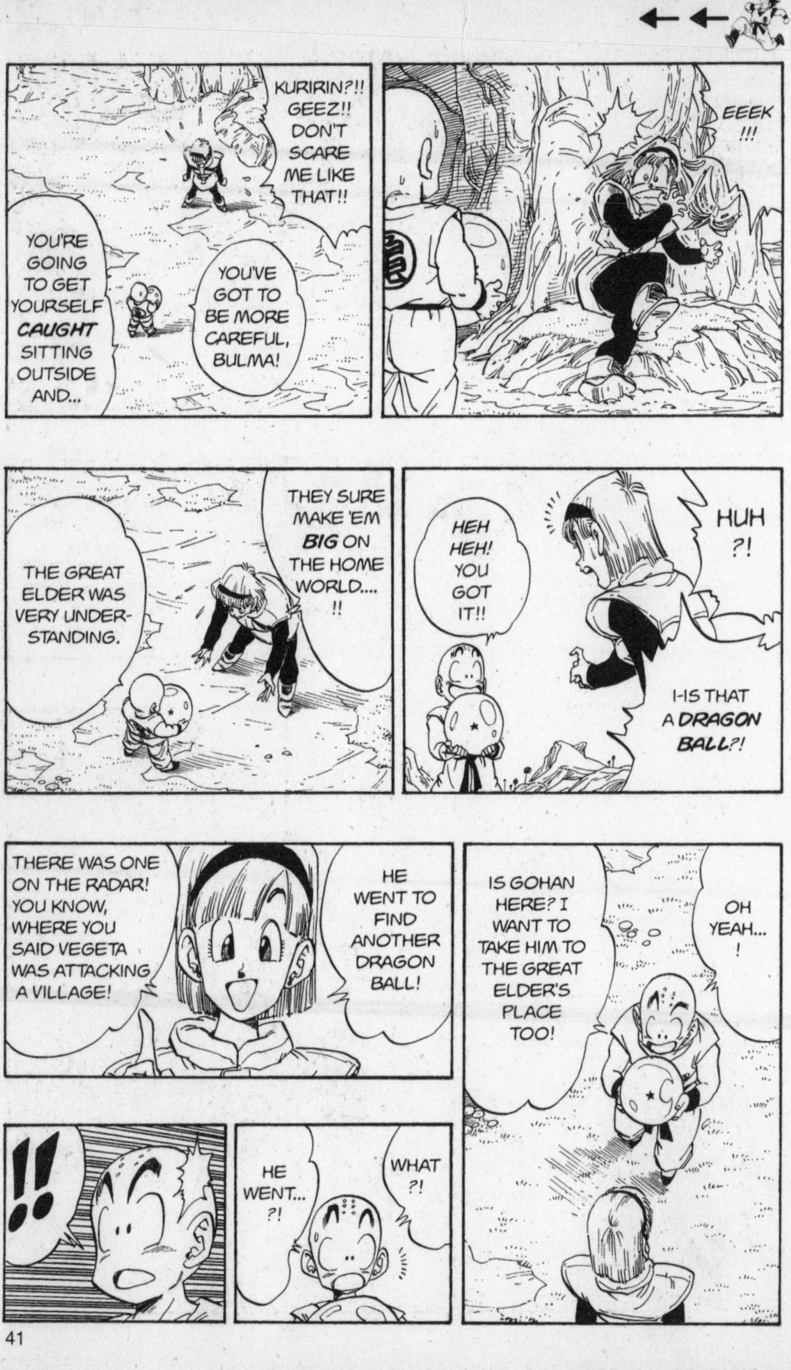
EEEK !!!
KURIRIN?!! GEEZ!! DON'T SCARE ME LIKE THAT!!
YOU'VE GOT TO BE MORE CAREFUL, BULMA!
YOU'RE GOING TO GET YOURSELF CAUGHT SITTING OUTSIDE AND...
HUH ?!
I-IS THAT A DRAGON BALL?!
HEH HEH! YOU GOT IT!!
THEY SURE MAKE 'EM BIG ON THE HOME WORLD.... !!
THE GREAT ELDER WAS VERY UNDER-STANDING.
OH YEAH... !
IS GOHAN HERE? I WANT TO TAKE HIM TO THE GREAT ELDER'S PLACE TOO!
HE WENT TO FIND ANOTHER DRAGON BALL!
THERE WAS ONE ON THE RADAR! YOU KNOW, WHERE YOU SAID VEGETA WAS ATTACKING A VILLAGE!
WHAT ?!
HE WENT... ?!
!!

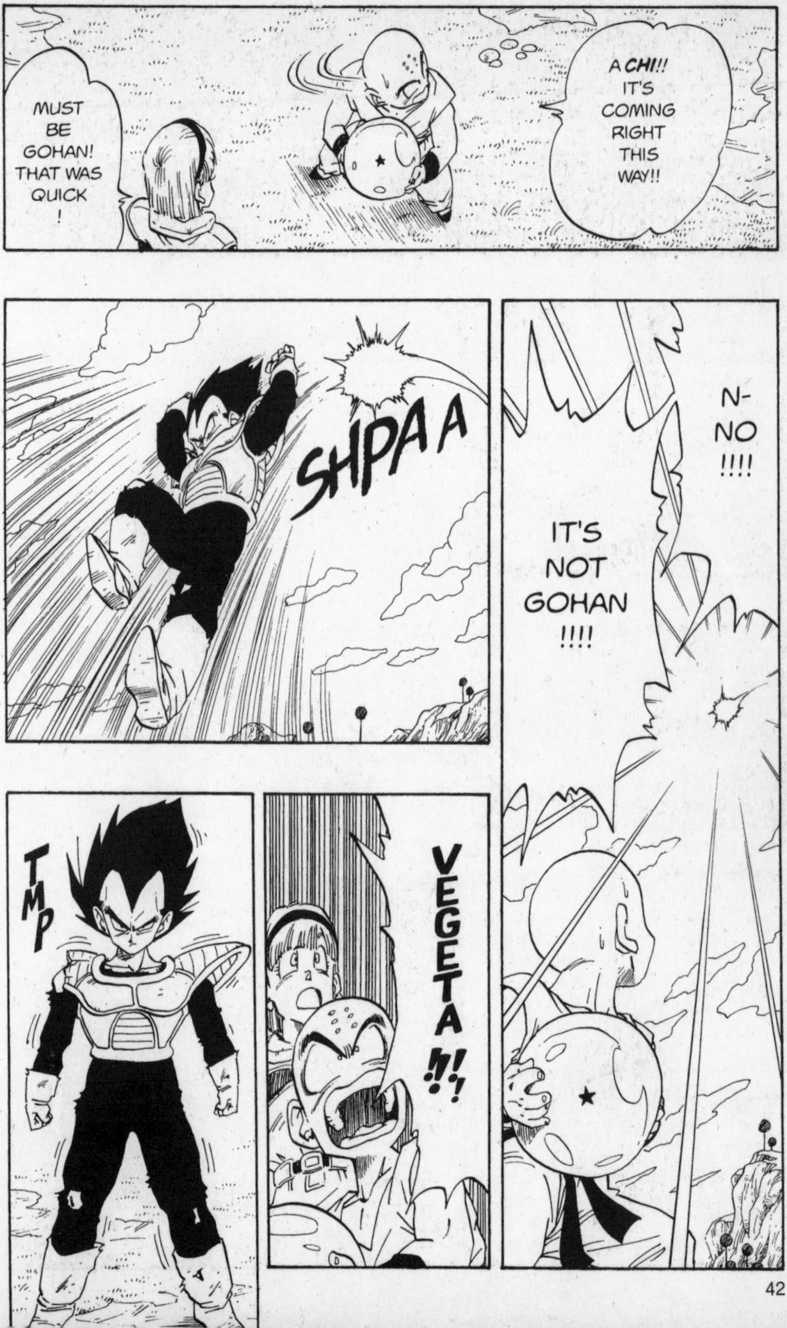
A CHI!! IT'S COMING RIGHT THIS WAY!!
MUST BE GOHAN! THAT WAS QUICK!
N-NO!!!!
IT'S NOT GOHAN!!!!
SHPAA
VEGETA!!!
TMP

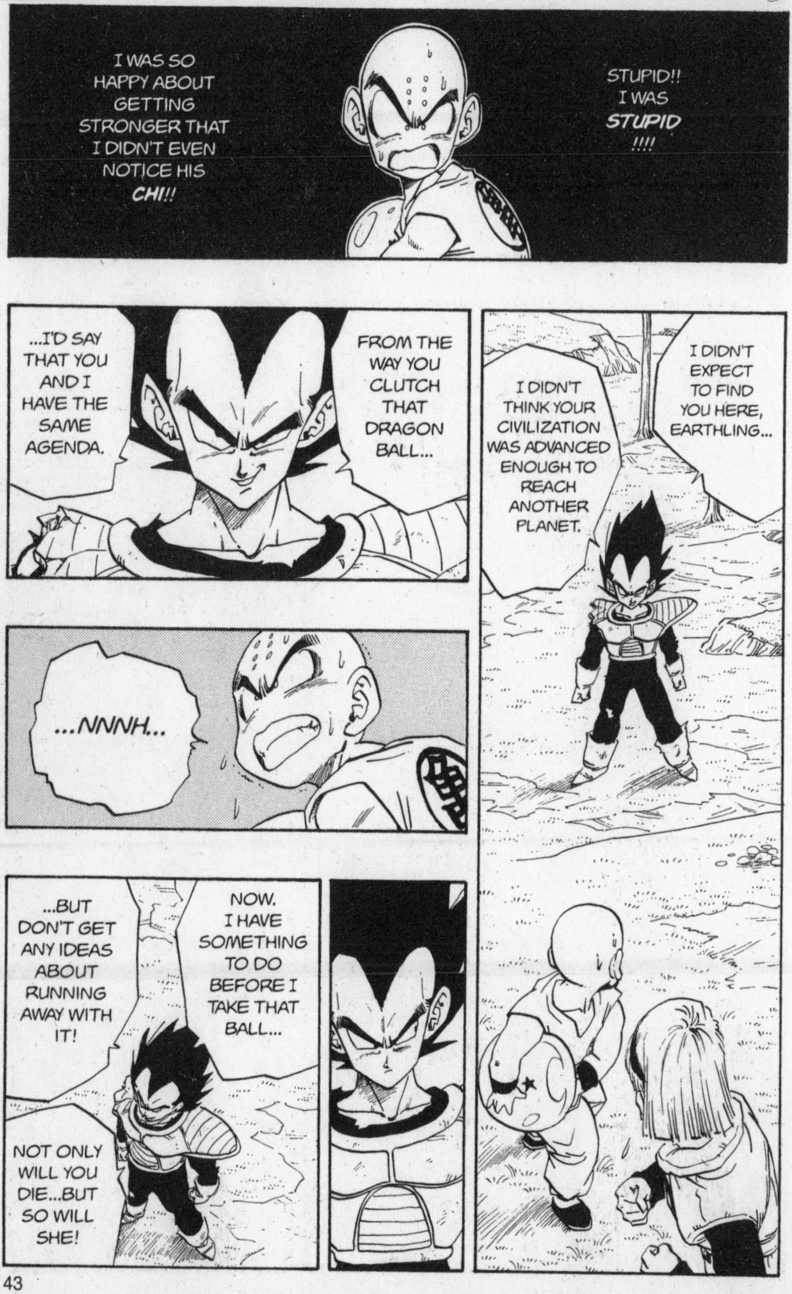
STUPID!! I WAS STUPID!!!!
I WAS SO HAPPY ABOUT GETTING STRONGER THAT I DIDN'T EVEN NOTICE HIS CHI!!
I DIDN'T EXPECT TO FIND YOU HERE, EARTHLING...
I DIDN'T THINK YOUR CIVILIZATION WAS ADVANCED ENOUGH TO REACH ANOTHER PLANET.
FROM THE WAY YOU CLUTCH THAT DRAGON BALL...
...I'D SAY THAT YOU AND I HAVE THE SAME AGENDA.
...NNNH...
NOW. I HAVE SOMETHING TO DO BEFORE I TAKE THAT BALL...
...BUT DON'T GET ANY IDEAS ABOUT RUNNING AWAY WITH IT!
NOT ONLY WILL YOU DIE...BUT SO WILL SHE!

OH
!!!

HE'S
HERE...

HUH
?!

TMP

VWOOSH!

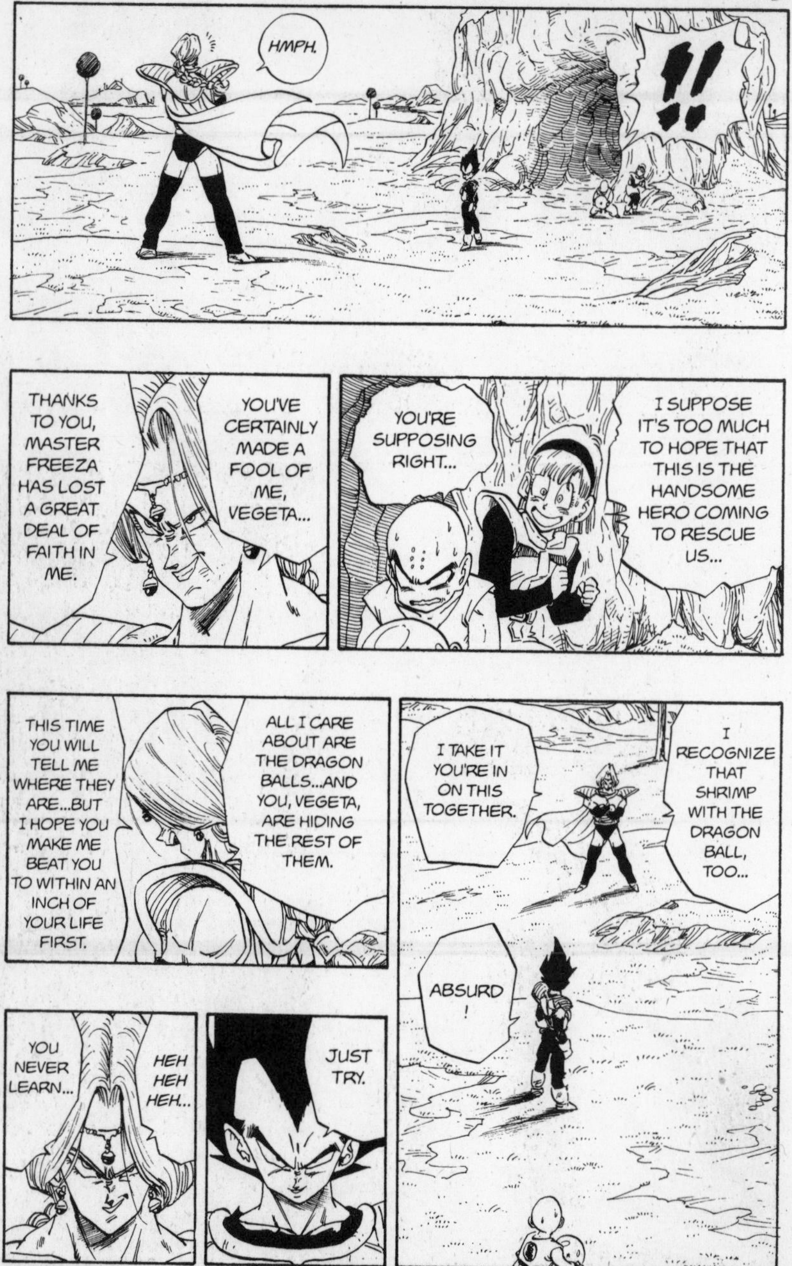
!!
HMPH.
I SUPPOSE IT'S TOO MUCH TO HOPE THAT THIS IS THE HANDSOME HERO COMING TO RESCUE US...
YOU'RE SUPPOSING RIGHT...
YOU'VE CERTAINLY MADE A FOOL OF ME, VEGETA...
THANKS TO YOU, MASTER FREEZA HAS LOST A GREAT DEAL OF FAITH IN ME.
I RECOGNIZE THAT SHRIMP WITH THE DRAGON BALL, TOO...
I TAKE IT YOU'RE IN ON THIS TOGETHER.
ABSURD!
ALL I CARE ABOUT ARE THE DRAGON BALLS...AND YOU, VEGETA, ARE HIDING THE REST OF THEM.
THIS TIME YOU WILL TELL ME WHERE THEY ARE...BUT I HOPE YOU MAKE ME BEAT YOU TO WITHIN AN INCH OF YOUR LIFE FIRST.
JUST TRY.
HEH HEH HEH...
YOU NEVER LEARN...

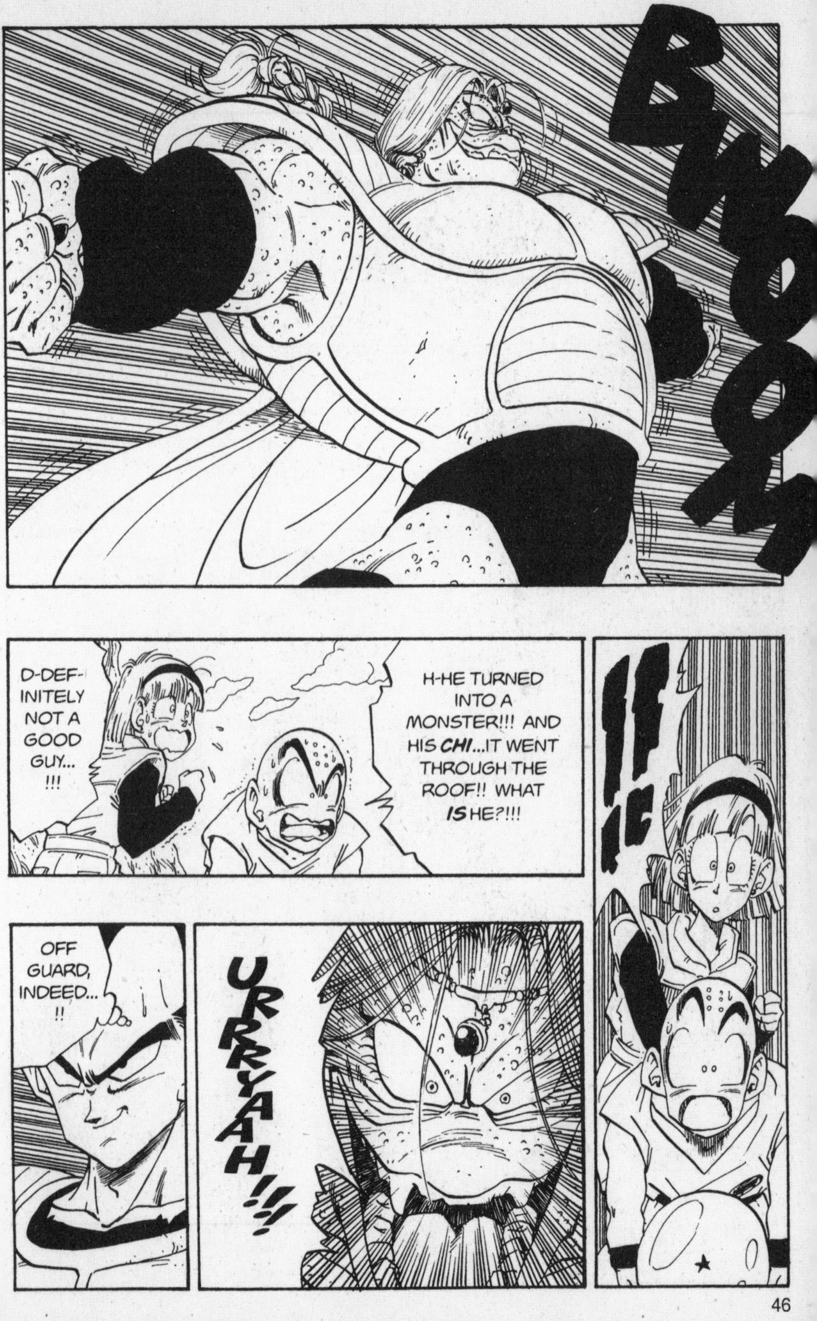
BWOOOM
!!
H-HE TURNED INTO A MONSTER!!! AND HIS *CHI*...IT WENT THROUGH THE ROOF!! WHAT *IS* HE?!!!
D-DEFINITELY NOT A GOOD GUY... !!!
URRYAAH!!!
OFF GUARD, INDEED... !!

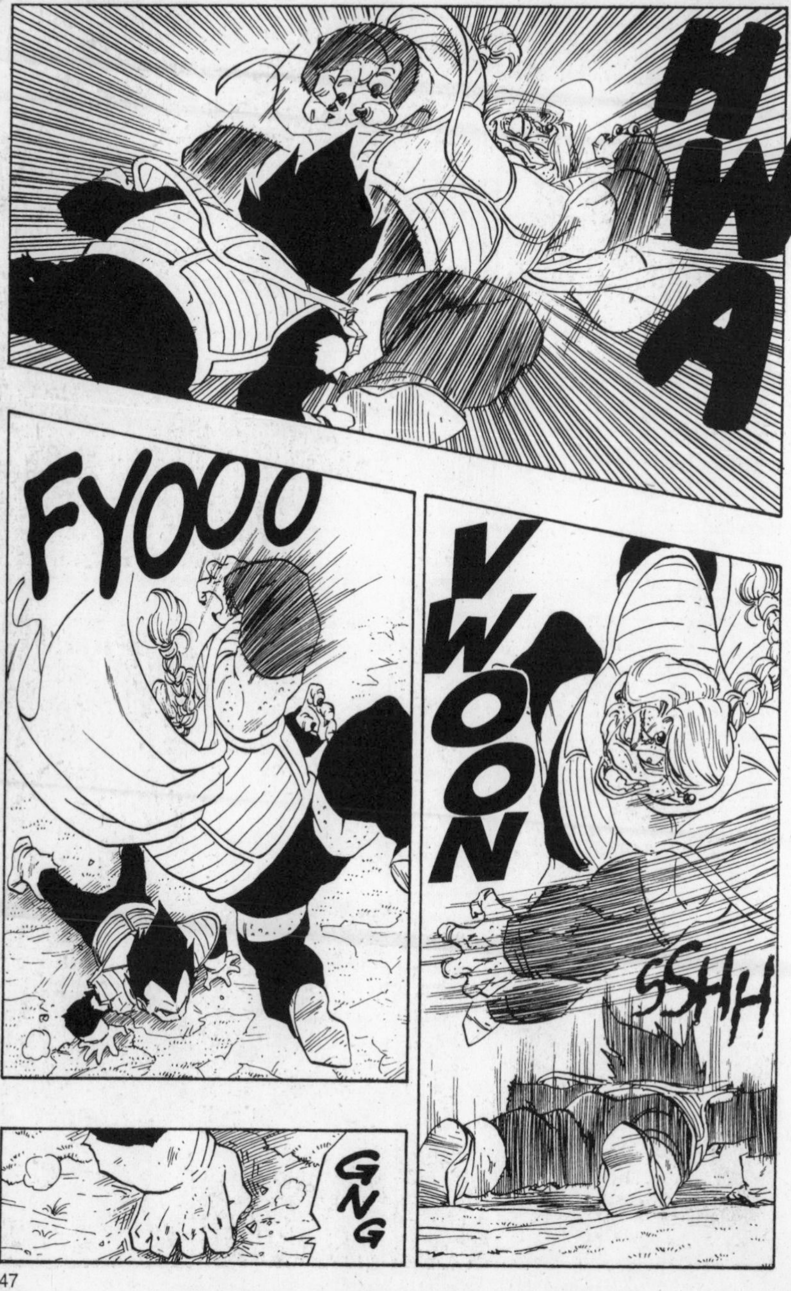
HWA
VWOON
SSHH!
FYOOO
GNG

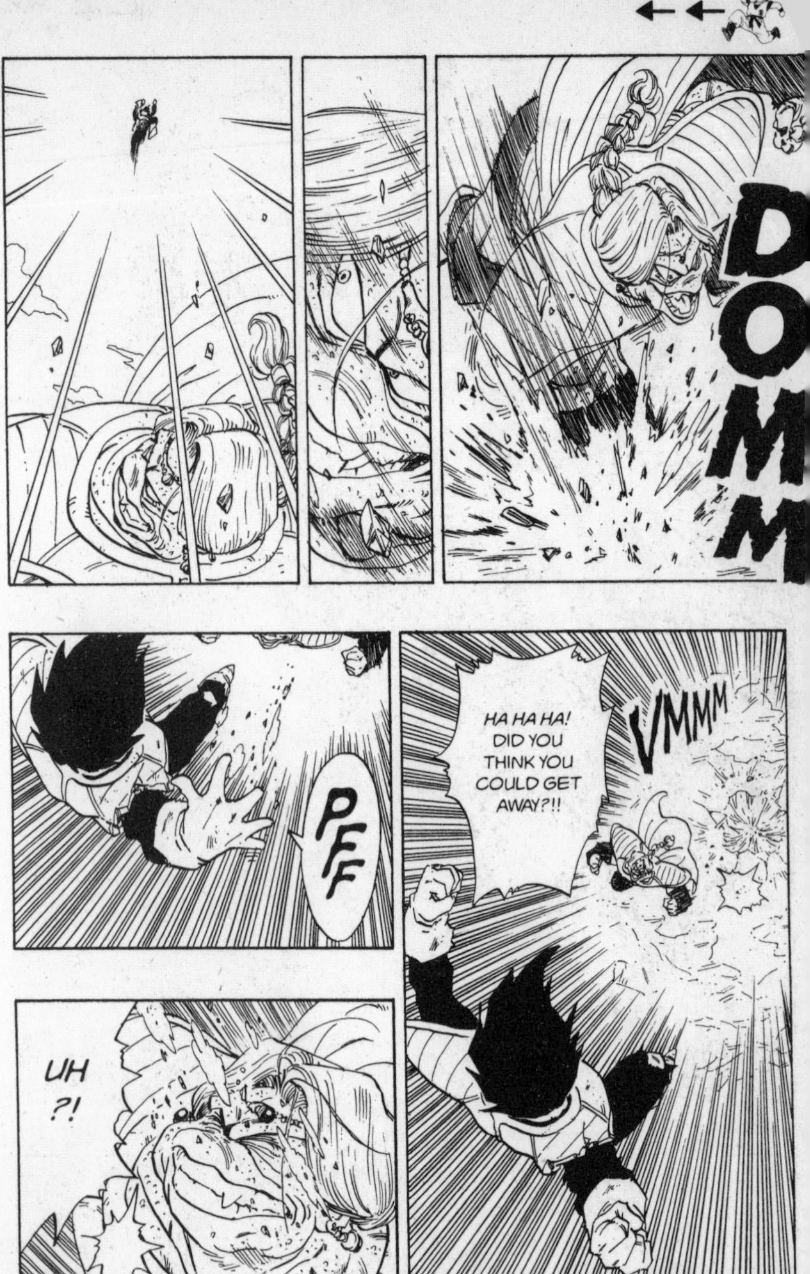
DOMM
HA HA HA! DID YOU THINK YOU COULD GET AWAY?!!
VMMM
PFF
UH ?!

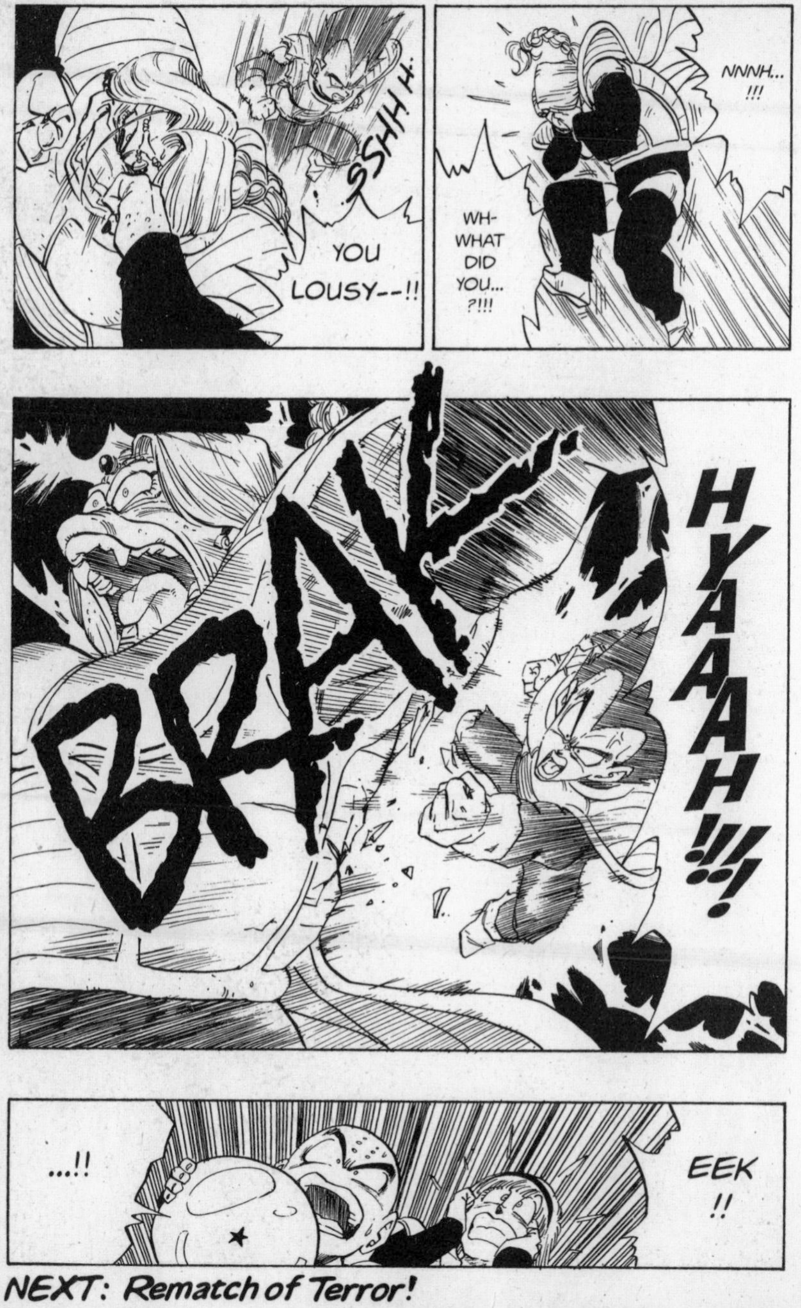
NNNH... !!!
WH- WHAT DID YOU... ?!!!
SSHH
YOU LOUSY--!!
HYAAAH!!!!
BRAK
EEK !!
...!!

NEXT: Rematch of Terror!

DBZ:74 • Vegeta in Overdrive!

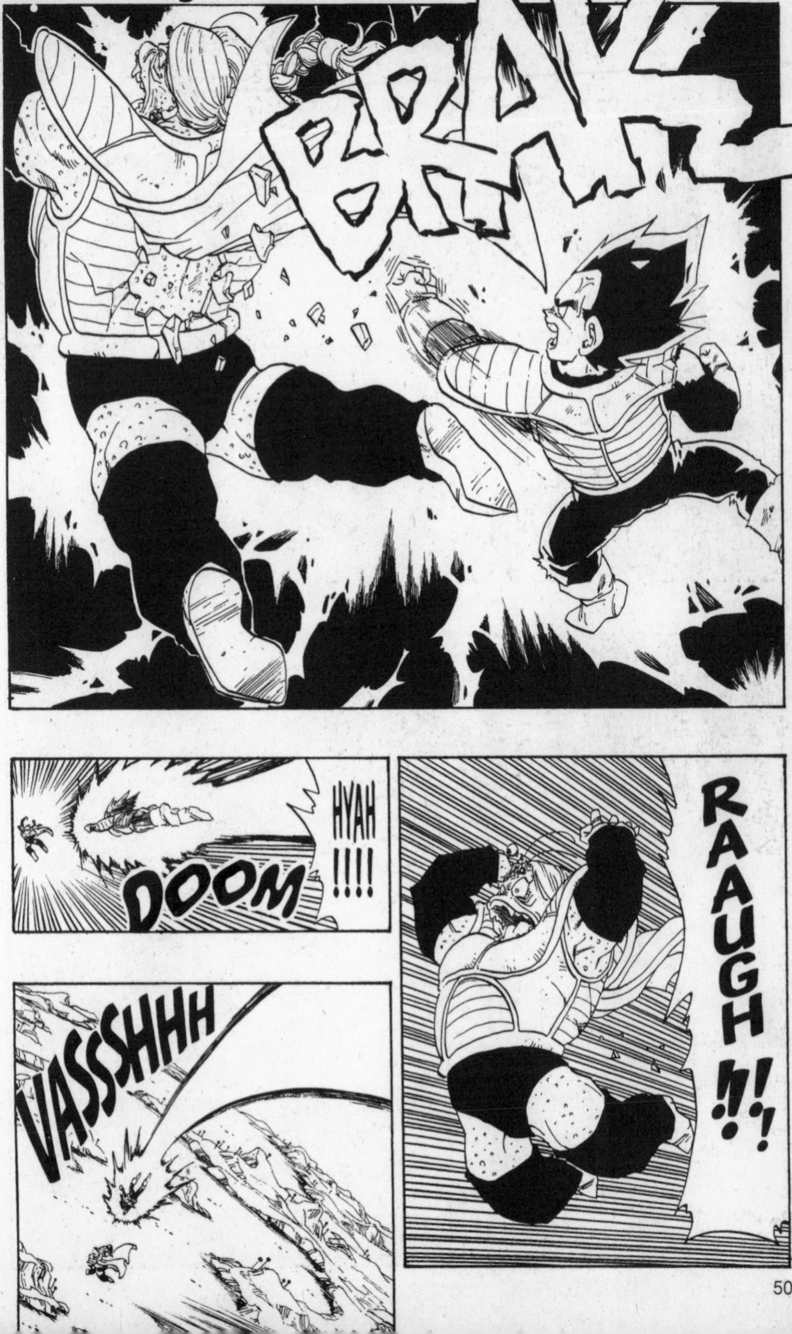
BRAK
RAAUGH!!!
HYAH!!!!
DOOM
VASSHHH

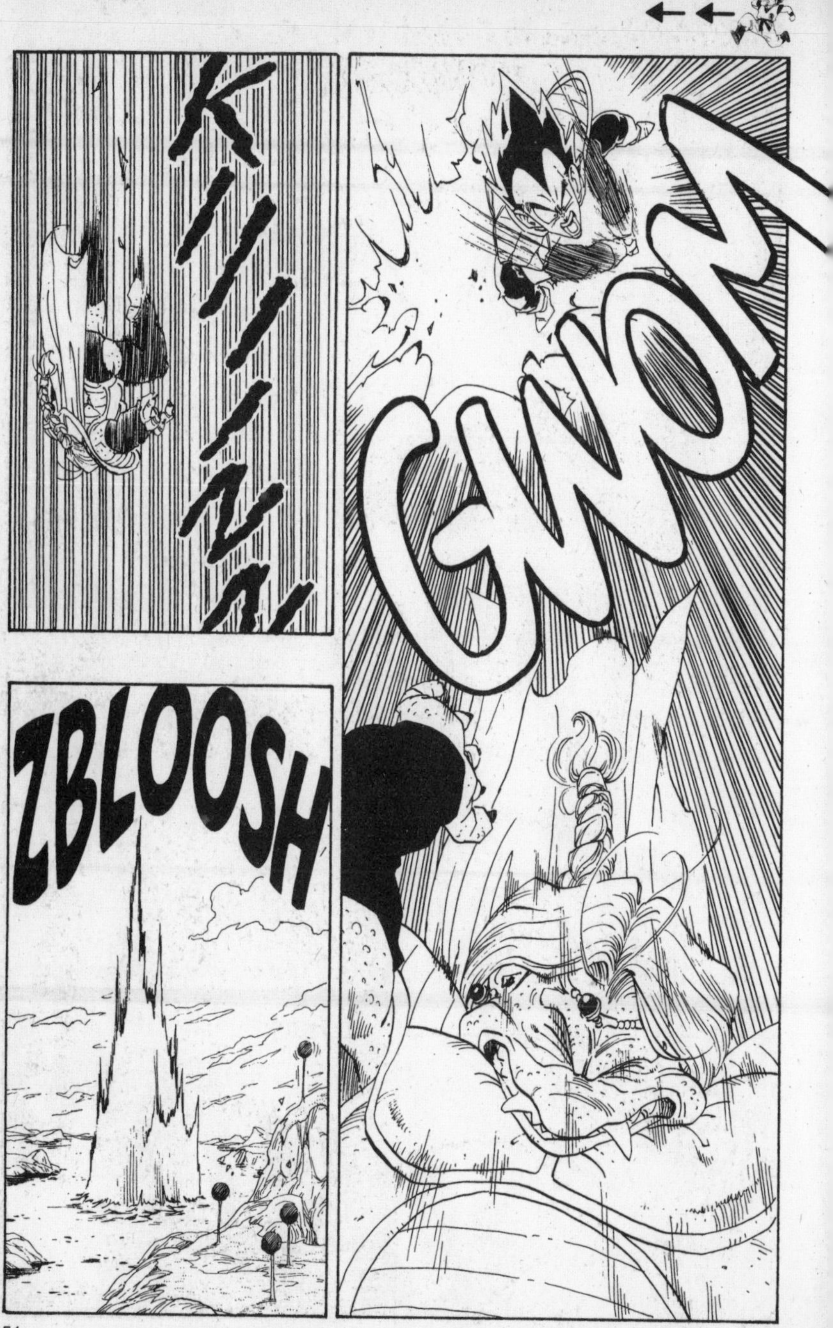
GWOM
KIIIIN
ZBLOOSH

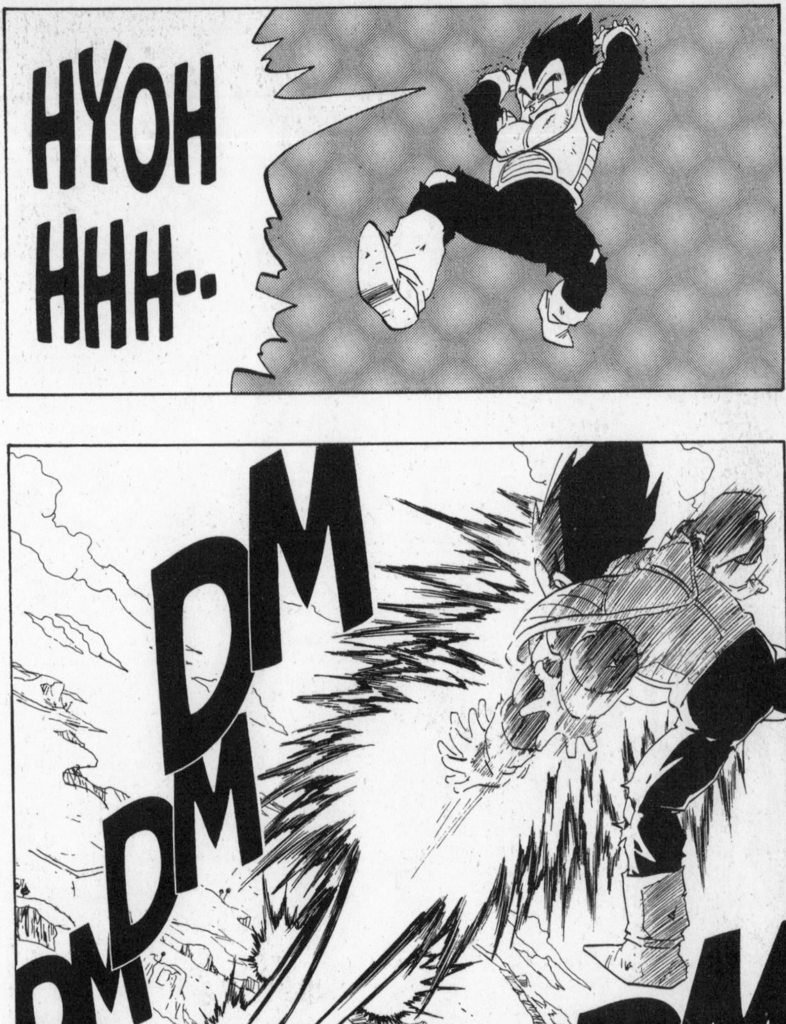
HYOH HHH-..
DM DM
DM DM
DM DM
DM DM

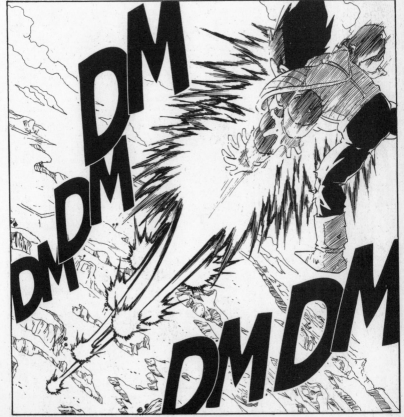

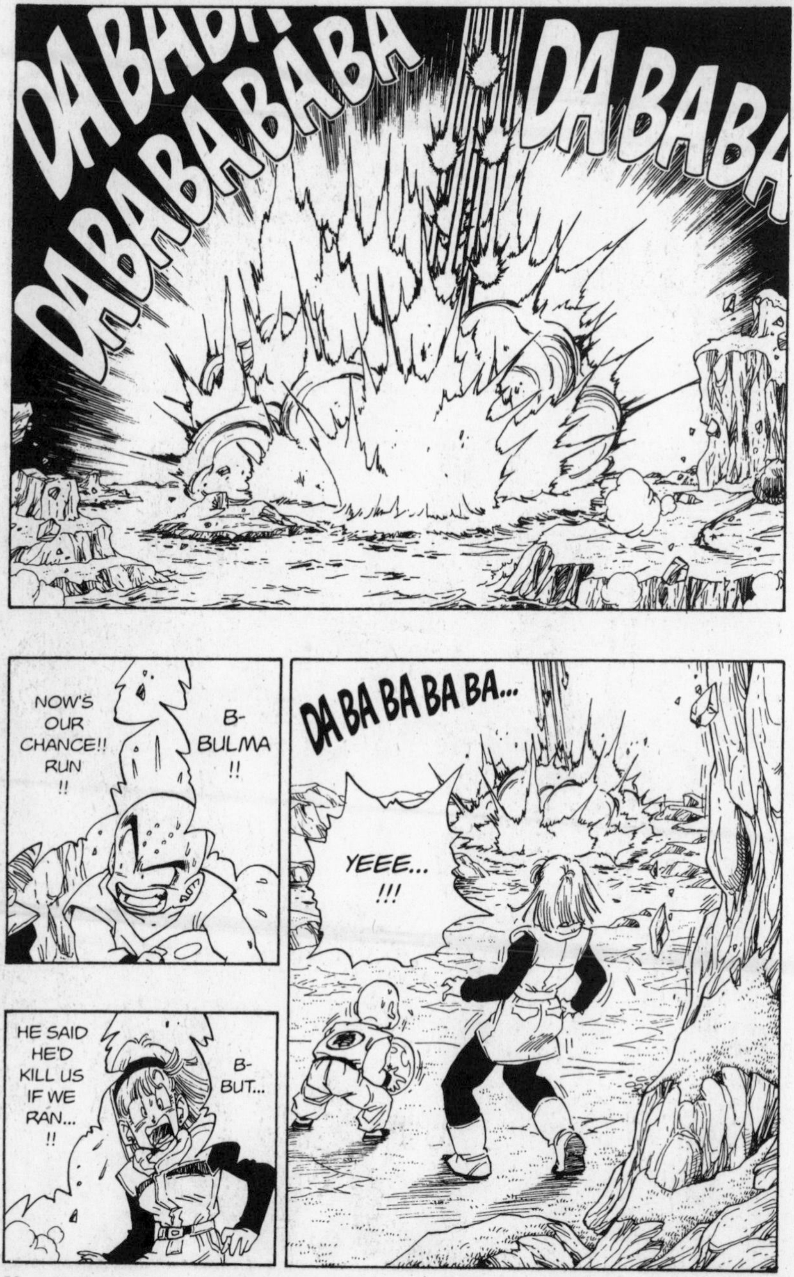
DA BABA
DABABA
DABABABABABA
DA BA BA BA BA...
YEEE... !!!
B- BULMA !!
NOW'S OUR CHANCE!! RUN !!
B- BUT...
HE SAID HE'D KILL US IF WE RAN... !!

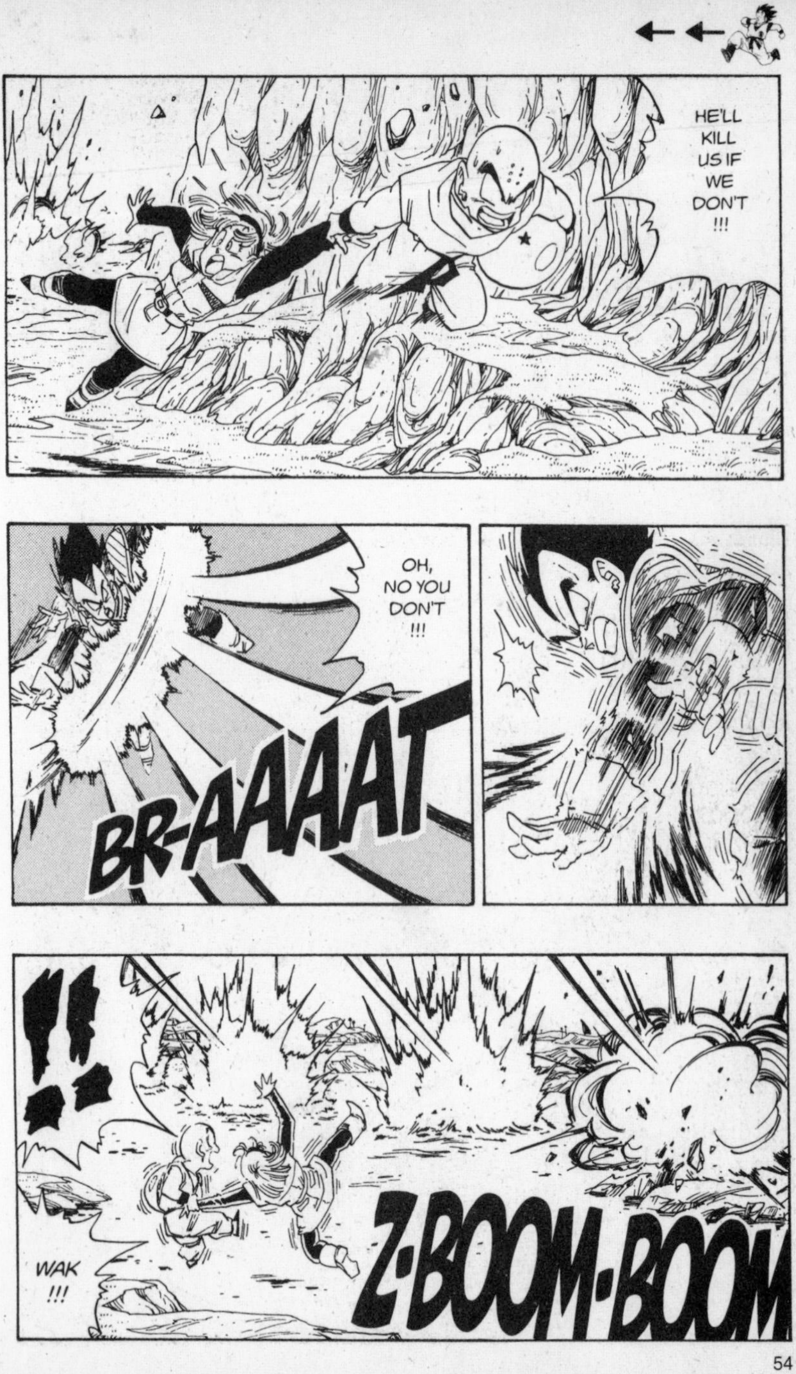
HE'LL KILL US IF WE DON'T !!!
OH, NO YOU DON'T !!!
BR-AAAAT
!!
Z-BOOM-BOOM
WAK !!!

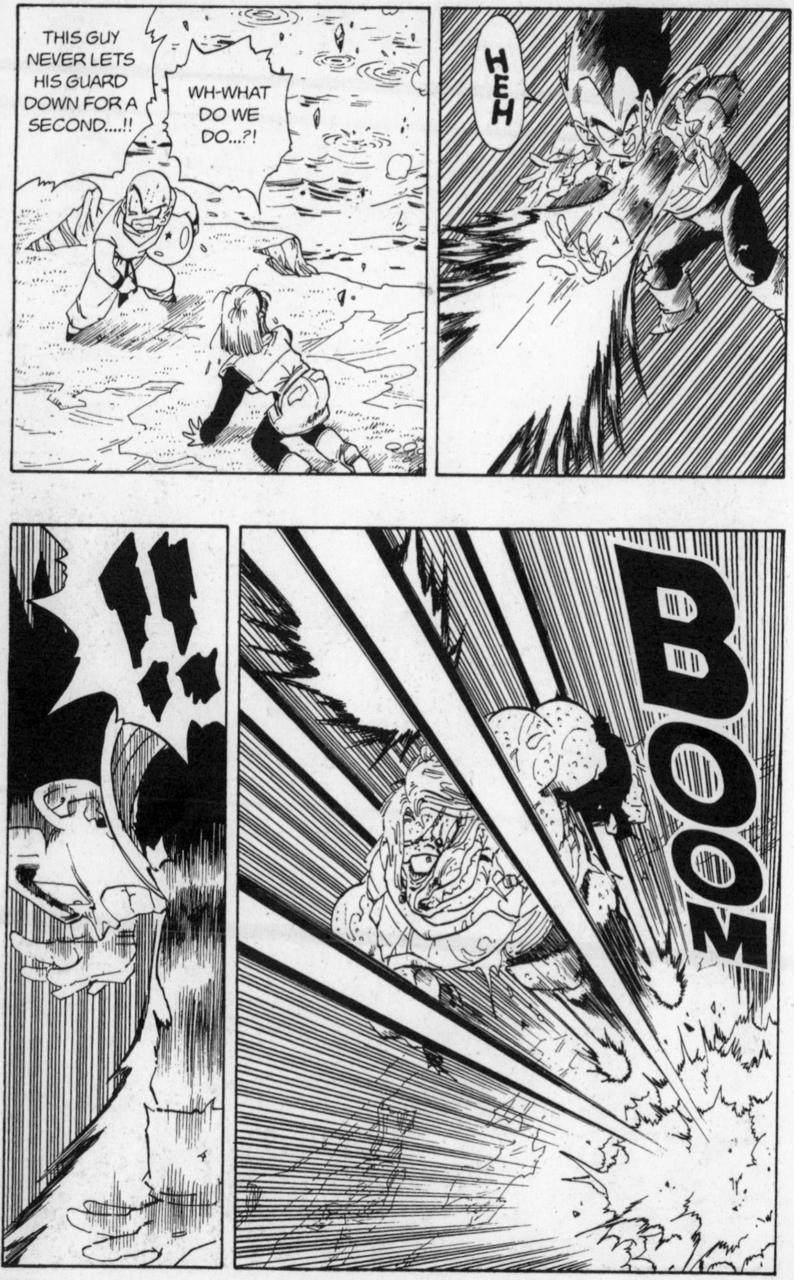
HEH
THIS GUY NEVER LETS HIS GUARD DOWN FOR A SECOND....!!
WH-WHAT DO WE DO...?!
BOOM
!!

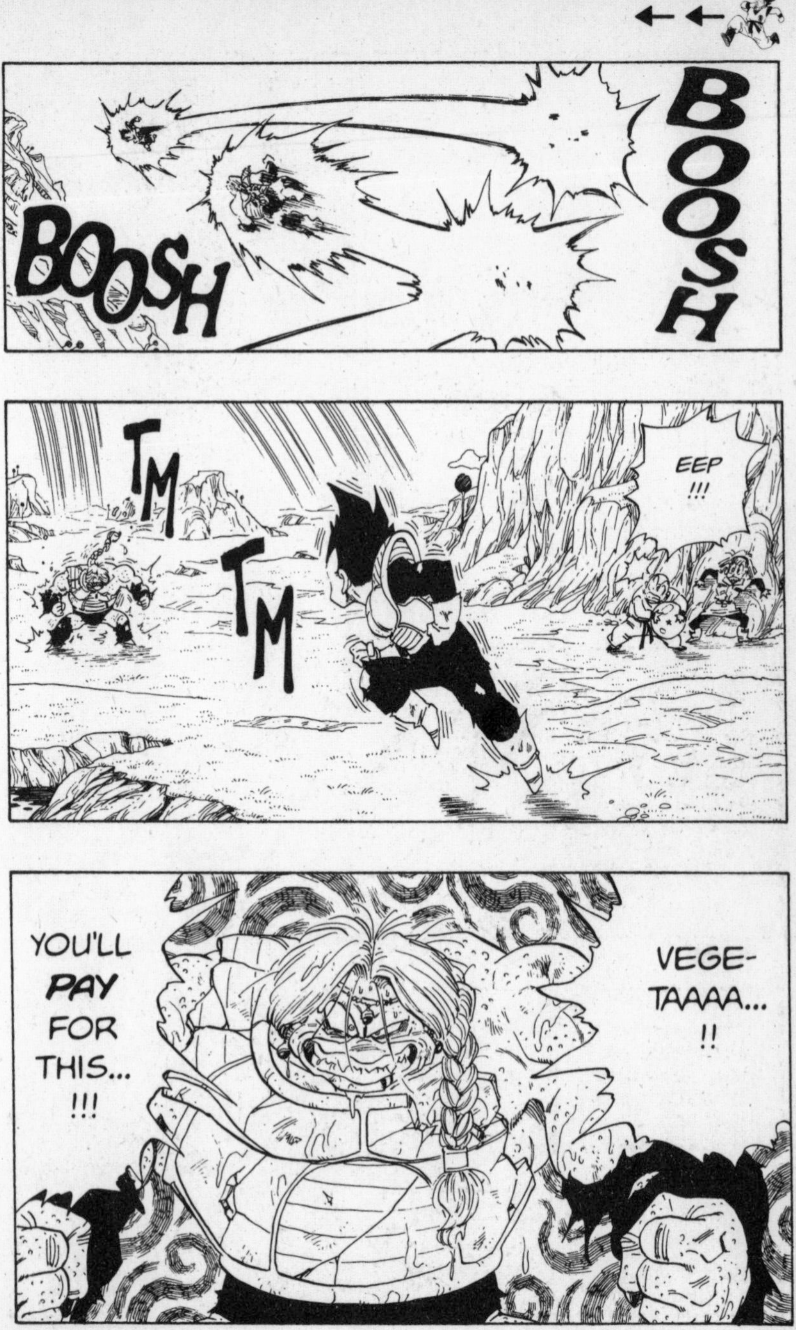
BOOSH
BOOSH
TM
TM
EEP !!!
VEGE-TAAAA... !!
YOU'LL PAY FOR THIS... !!!

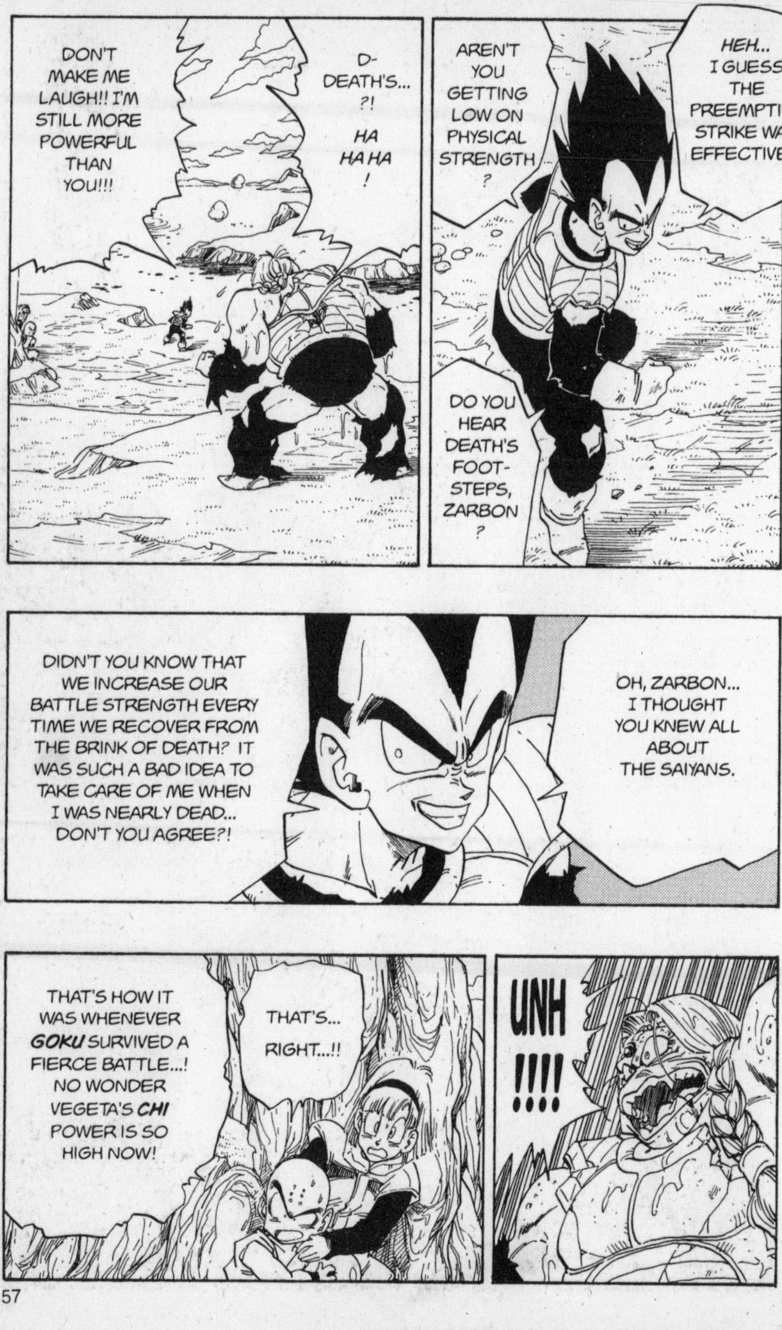
HEH... I GUESS THE PREEMPTIVE STRIKE WAS EFFECTIVE...
AREN'T YOU GETTING LOW ON PHYSICAL STRENGTH?
DO YOU HEAR DEATH'S FOOT-STEPS, ZARBON?
D-DEATH'S...?!
HA HA HA!
DON'T MAKE ME LAUGH!! I'M STILL MORE POWERFUL THAN YOU!!!
OH, ZARBON... I THOUGHT YOU KNEW ALL ABOUT THE SAIYANS.
DIDN'T YOU KNOW THAT WE INCREASE OUR BATTLE STRENGTH EVERY TIME WE RECOVER FROM THE BRINK OF DEATH? IT WAS SUCH A BAD IDEA TO TAKE CARE OF ME WHEN I WAS NEARLY DEAD... DON'T YOU AGREE?!
UNH !!!!
THAT'S... RIGHT...!!
THAT'S HOW IT WAS WHENEVER *GOKU* SURVIVED A FIERCE BATTLE...! NO WONDER VEGETA'S *CHI* POWER IS SO HIGH NOW!

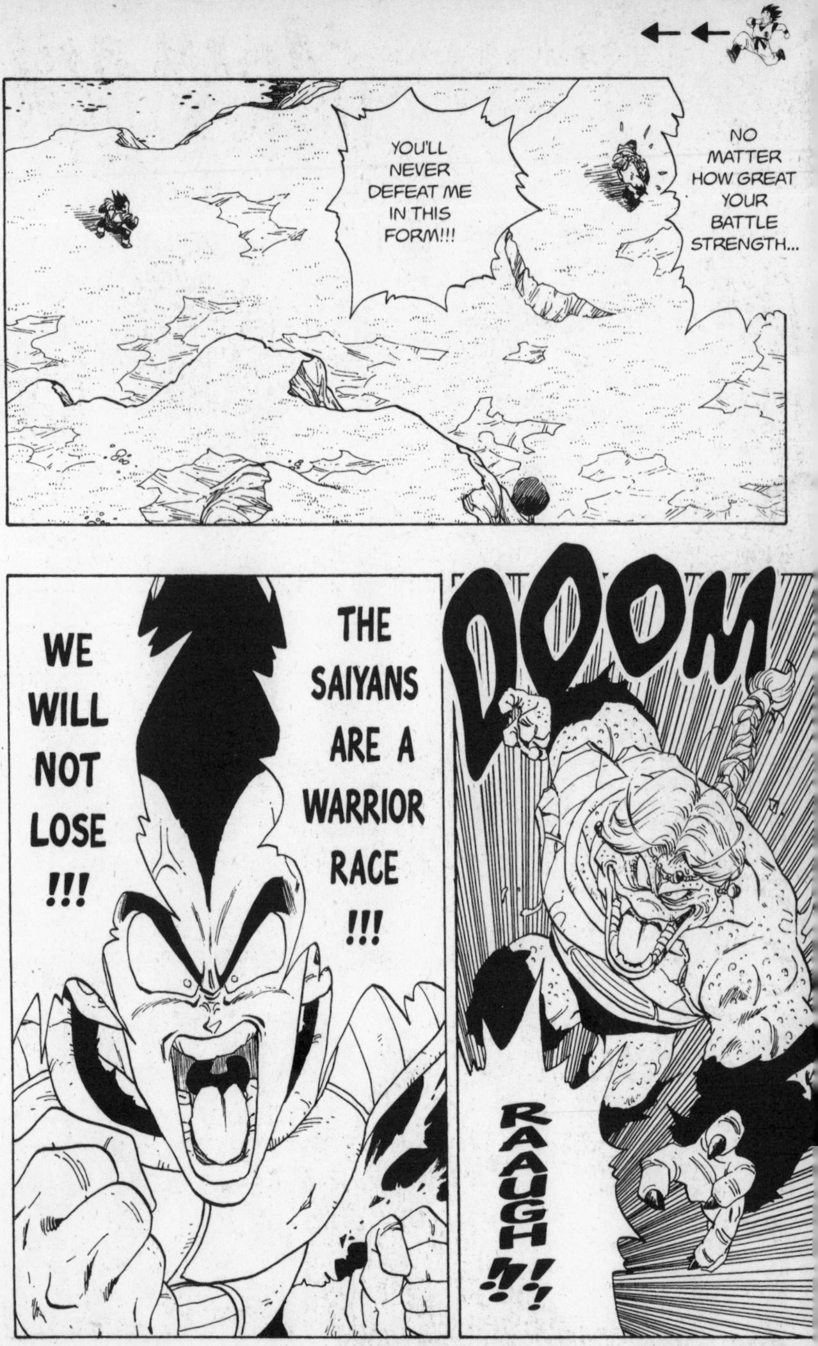
NO MATTER HOW GREAT YOUR BATTLE STRENGTH...
YOU'LL NEVER DEFEAT ME IN THIS FORM!!!
DOOM
RAAUGH!!!
THE SAIYANS ARE A WARRIOR RACE!!!
WE WILL NOT LOSE!!!

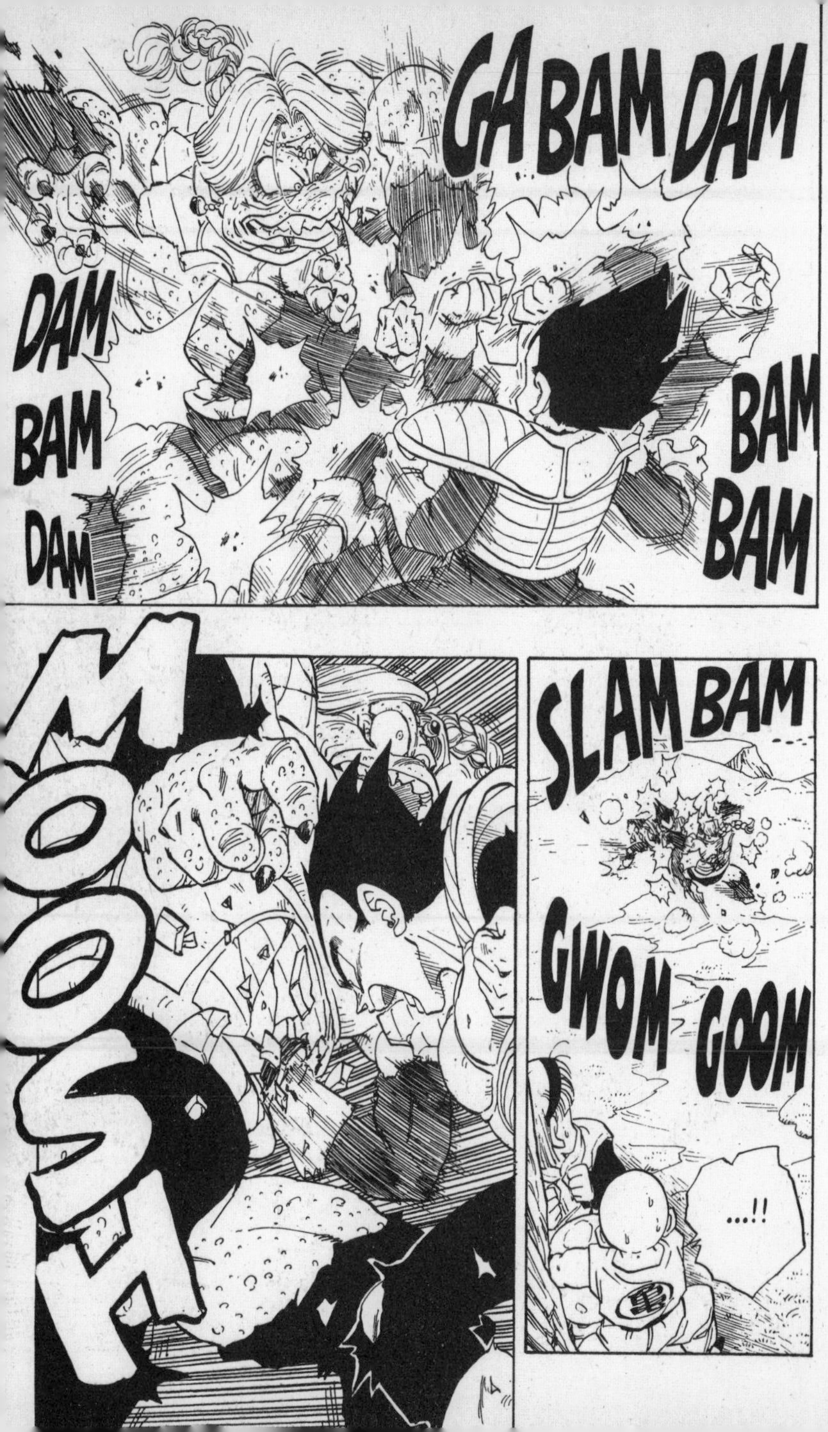
GA BAM DAM
BAM BAM
DAM BAM DAM
SLAM BAM
GWOM GOOM
...!!
WOOSH

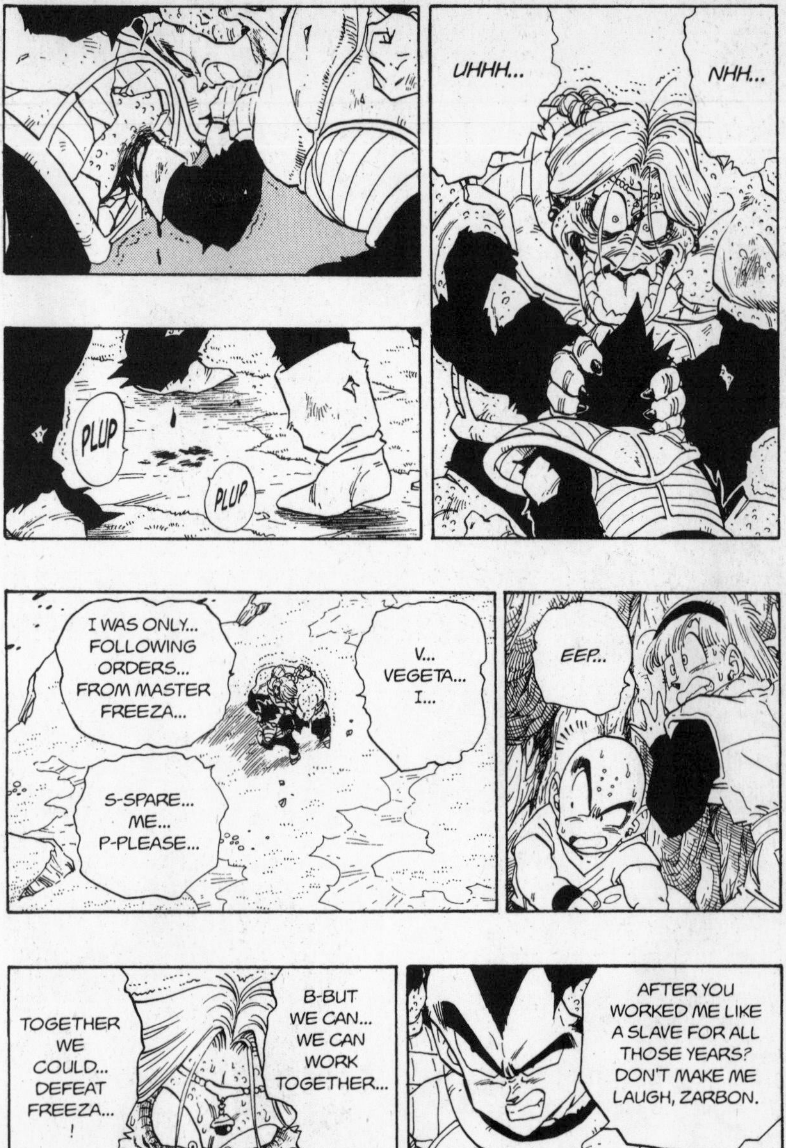
NHH...
UHHH...
PLUP
PLUP
EEP...
V... VEGETA... I...
I WAS ONLY... FOLLOWING ORDERS... FROM MASTER FREEZA...
S-SPARE... ME... P-PLEASE...
AFTER YOU WORKED ME LIKE A SLAVE FOR ALL THOSE YEARS? DON'T MAKE ME LAUGH, ZARBON.
B-BUT WE CAN... WE CAN WORK TOGETHER...
TOGETHER WE COULD... DEFEAT FREEZA... !

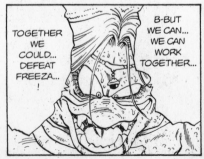

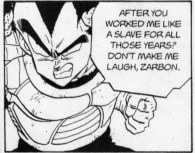

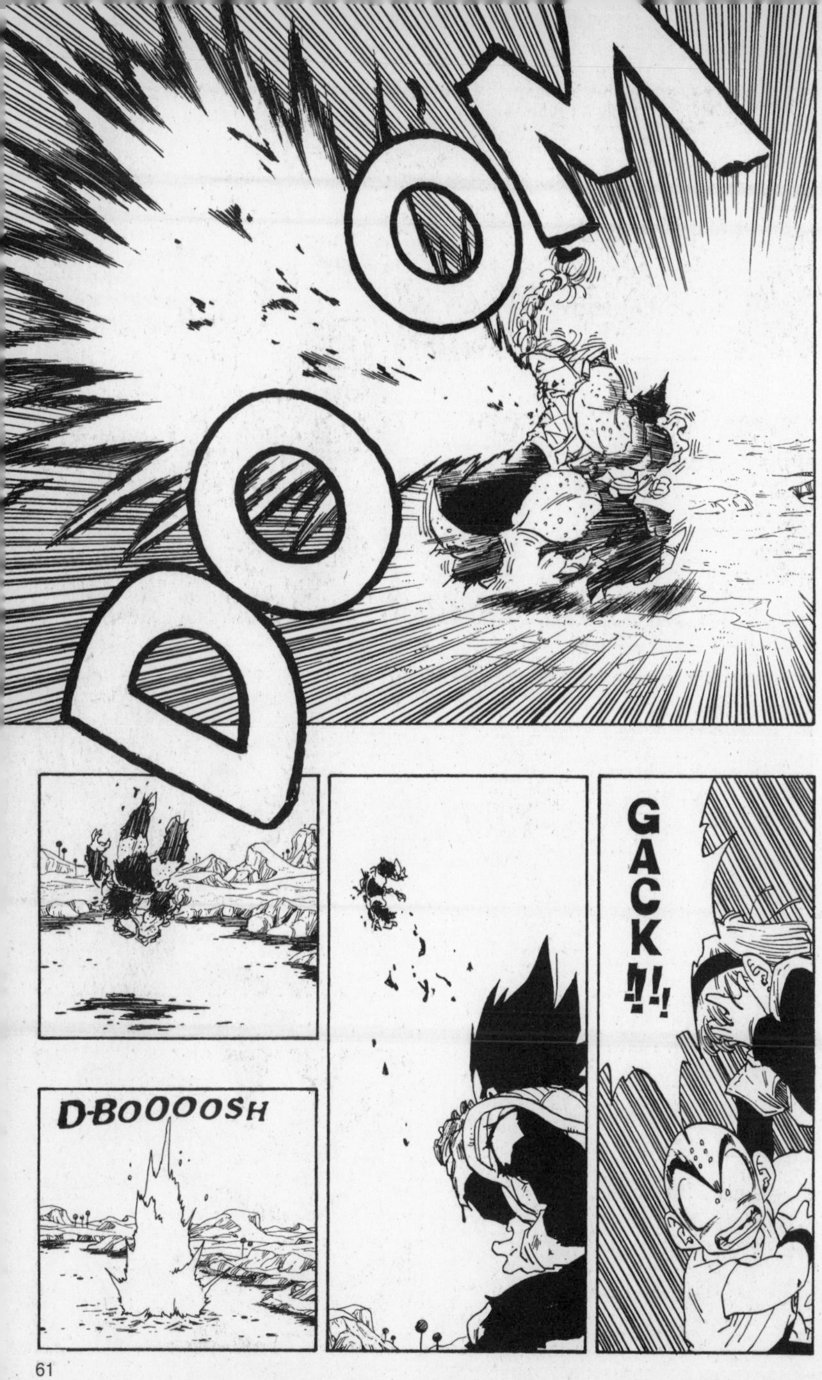
DOOM
GACK!!!
D-BOOOOSH

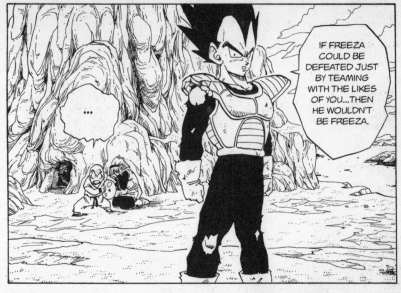

IF FREEZA COULD BE DEFEATED JUST BY TEAMING WITH THE LIKES OF YOU...THEN HE WOULDN'T BE FREEZA.
...
HSSS
NOW THEN...
HM ?
MY, MY. SOMEHOW YOU'VE IMPROVED QUITE A BIT SINCE WE MET ON EARTH...
ALTHOUGH OF COURSE, YOU'RE STILL FAR BELOW A LEVEL AT WHICH YOU COULD LAST LONG AGAINST ME...
NOW WHAT? ARE YOU WILLING TO HAND OVER THAT DRAGON BALL?
I KNOW IT'S P-P-POINTLESS TO ASK ...
...B-BUT WILL YOU JUST GO AWAY IF I GIVE THIS TO YOU?!

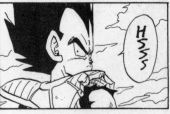

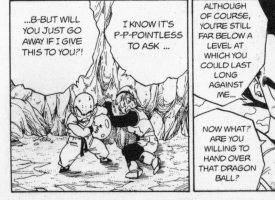

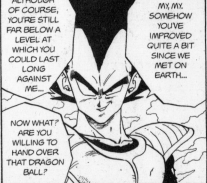

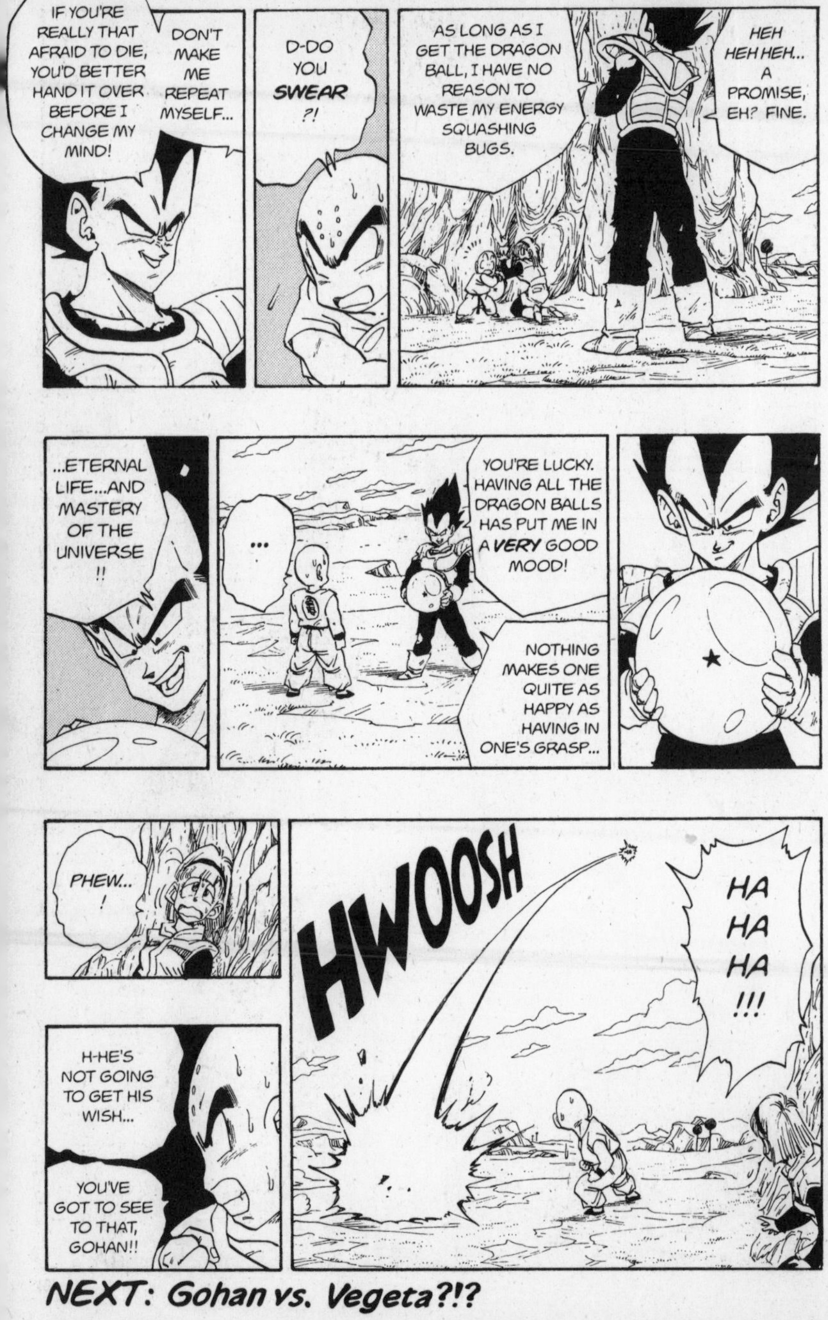
HEH HEH HEH... A PROMISE, EH? FINE.
AS LONG AS I GET THE DRAGON BALL, I HAVE NO REASON TO WASTE MY ENERGY SQUASHING BUGS.
D-DO YOU SWEAR ?!
DON'T MAKE ME REPEAT MYSELF...
IF YOU'RE REALLY THAT AFRAID TO DIE, YOU'D BETTER HAND IT OVER BEFORE I CHANGE MY MIND!
YOU'RE LUCKY. HAVING ALL THE DRAGON BALLS HAS PUT ME IN A VERY GOOD MOOD!
...
NOTHING MAKES ONE QUITE AS HAPPY AS HAVING IN ONE'S GRASP...
...ETERNAL LIFE...AND MASTERY OF THE UNIVERSE !!
HA HA HA !!!
HWOOSH
PHEW... !
H-HE'S NOT GOING TO GET HIS WISH...
YOU'VE GOT TO SEE TO THAT, GOHAN!!

NEXT: Gohan vs. Vegeta?!?

DBZ:75 • Brains and Brawn

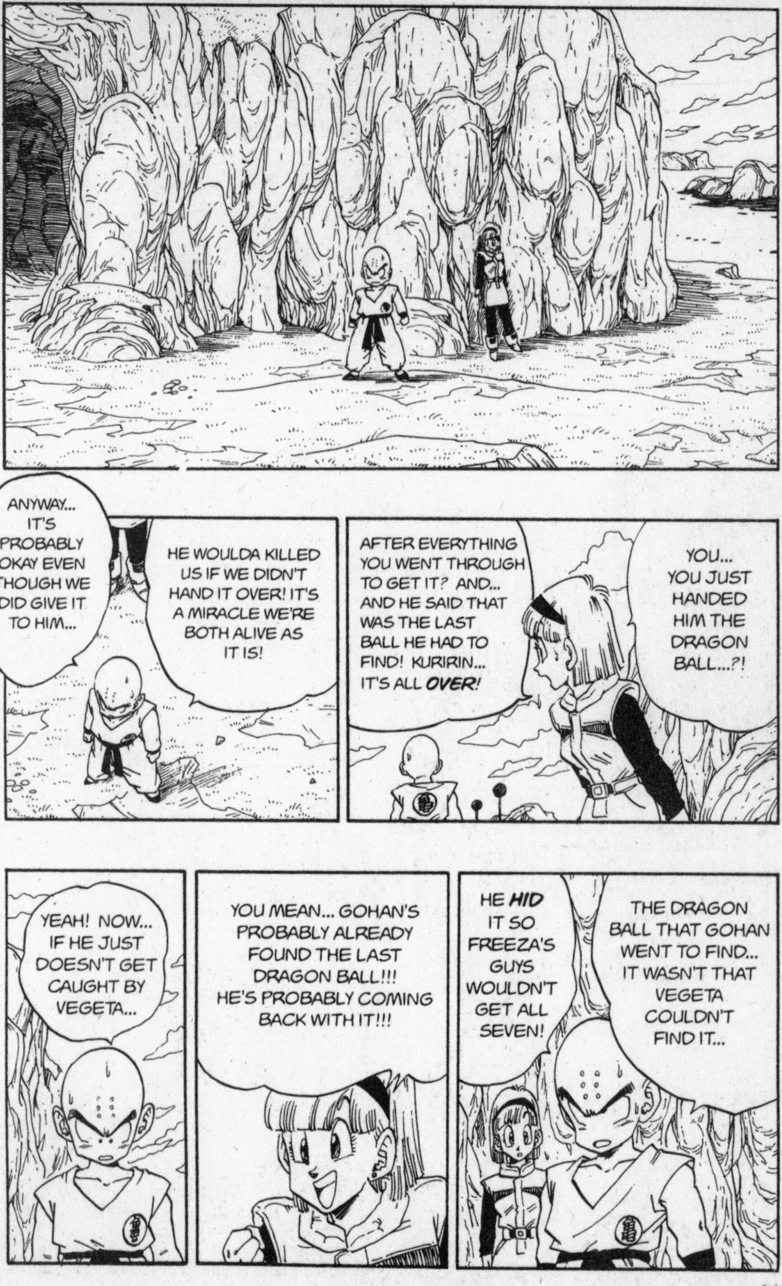

YOU... YOU JUST HANDED HIM THE DRAGON BALL...?!
AFTER EVERYTHING YOU WENT THROUGH TO GET IT? AND... AND HE SAID THAT WAS THE LAST BALL HE HAD TO FIND! KURIRIN... IT'S ALL ***OVER***!
HE WOULDA KILLED US IF WE DIDN'T HAND IT OVER! IT'S A MIRACLE WE'RE BOTH ALIVE AS IT IS!
ANYWAY... IT'S PROBABLY OKAY EVEN THOUGH WE DID GIVE IT TO HIM...
THE DRAGON BALL THAT GOHAN WENT TO FIND... IT WASN'T THAT VEGETA COULDN'T FIND IT...
HE ***HID*** IT SO FREEZA'S GUYS WOULDN'T GET ALL SEVEN!
YOU MEAN... GOHAN'S PROBABLY ALREADY FOUND THE LAST DRAGON BALL!!! HE'S PROBABLY COMING BACK WITH IT!!!
YEAH! NOW... IF HE JUST DOESN'T GET CAUGHT BY VEGETA...

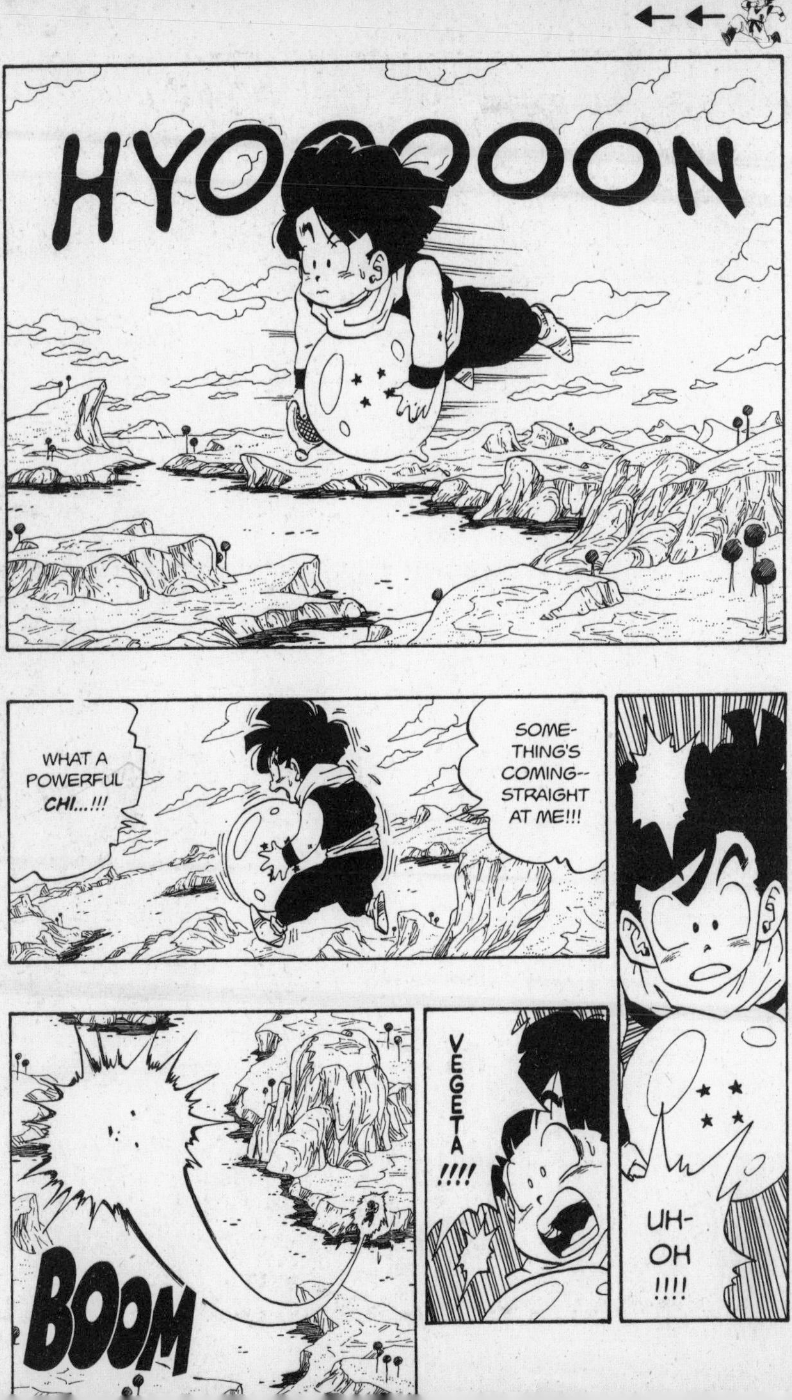
HYOOOOON
UH-OH !!!!
SOME-THING'S COMING--STRAIGHT AT ME!!!
WHAT A POWERFUL CHI...!!!
VEGETA !!!!
BOOM

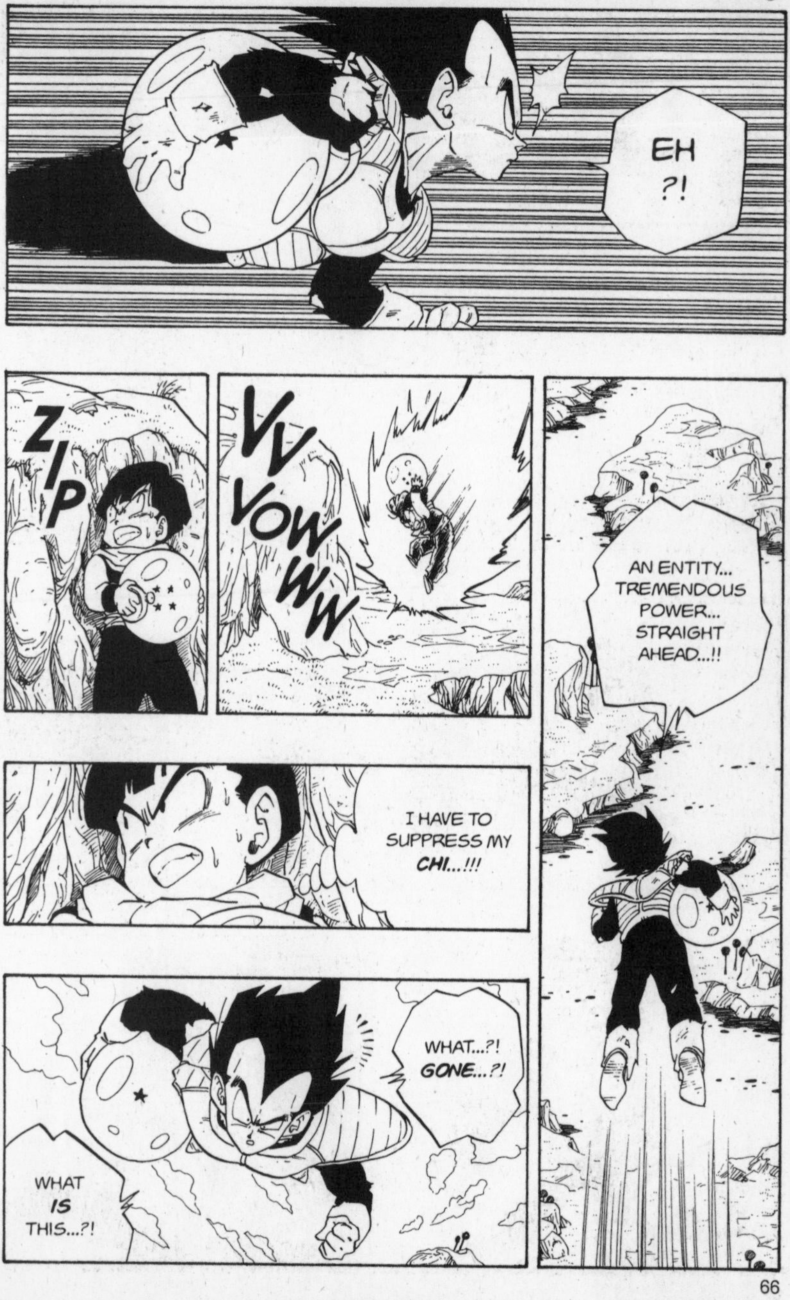
EH ?!
AN ENTITY... TREMENDOUS POWER... STRAIGHT AHEAD...!!
VVVOWWW
ZIP
I HAVE TO SUPPRESS MY CHI...!!!
WHAT...?! GONE...?!
WHAT IS THIS...?!

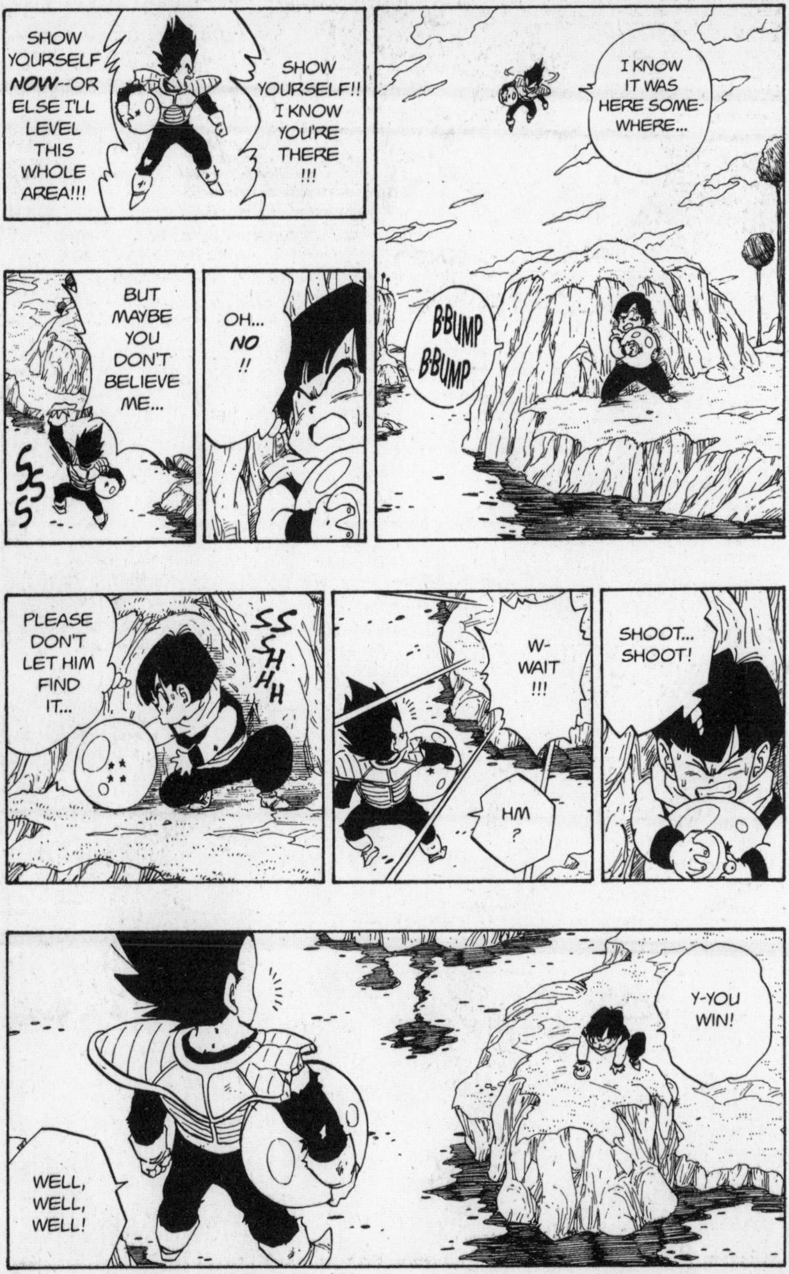
I KNOW IT WAS HERE SOME-WHERE...
B-BUMP B-BUMP
SHOW YOURSELF!! I KNOW YOU'RE THERE !!!
SHOW YOURSELF NOW--OR ELSE I'LL LEVEL THIS WHOLE AREA!!!
OH... NO !!
BUT MAYBE YOU DON'T BELIEVE ME...
SSS
SHOOT... SHOOT!
W-WAIT !!!
HM ?
SSSHHH
PLEASE DON'T LET HIM FIND IT...
Y-YOU WIN!
WELL, WELL, WELL!

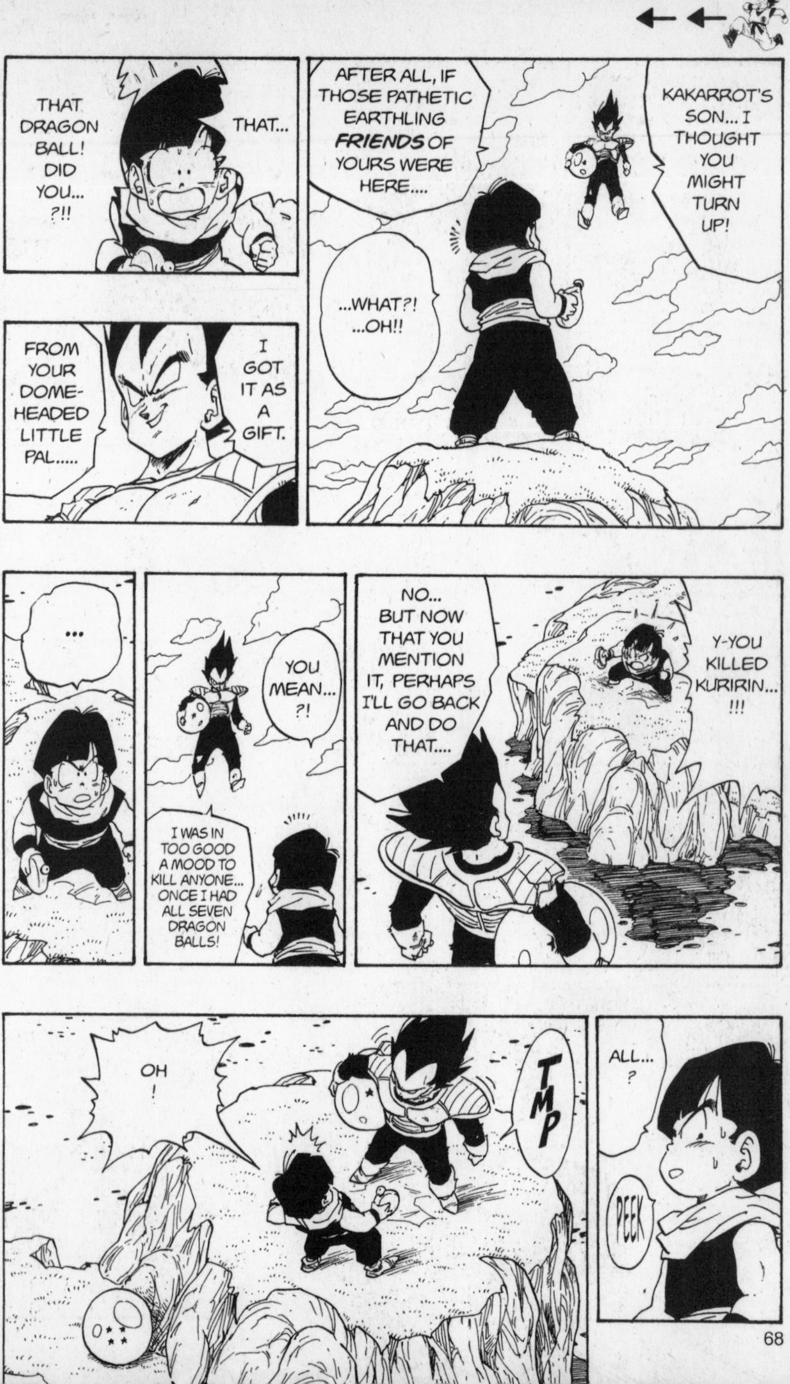
KAKARROT'S SON... I THOUGHT YOU MIGHT TURN UP!
AFTER ALL, IF THOSE PATHETIC EARTHLING **FRIENDS** OF YOURS WERE HERE....
...WHAT?! ...OH!!
THAT...
THAT DRAGON BALL! DID YOU... ?!!
I GOT IT AS A GIFT.
FROM YOUR DOME-HEADED LITTLE PAL.....
Y-YOU KILLED KURIRIN... !!!
NO... BUT NOW THAT YOU MENTION IT, PERHAPS I'LL GO BACK AND DO THAT....
YOU MEAN... ?!
I WAS IN TOO GOOD A MOOD TO KILL ANYONE... ONCE I HAD ALL SEVEN DRAGON BALLS!
...
ALL... ?
PEEK
TMP
OH !

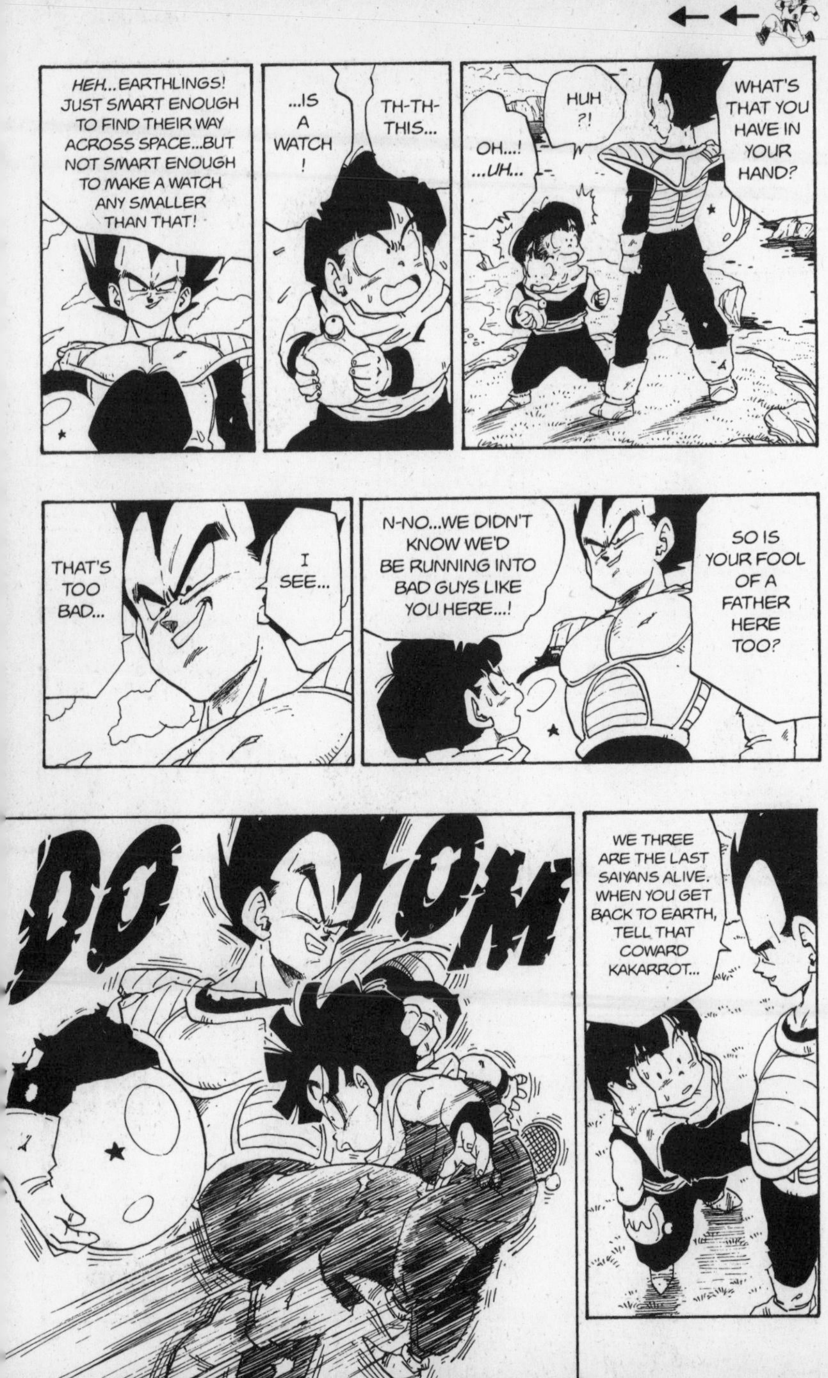
WHAT'S THAT YOU HAVE IN YOUR HAND?
HUH ?!
OH...! ...UH...
TH-TH-THIS...
...IS A WATCH !
HEH... EARTHLINGS! JUST SMART ENOUGH TO FIND THEIR WAY ACROSS SPACE...BUT NOT SMART ENOUGH TO MAKE A WATCH ANY SMALLER THAN THAT!
SO IS YOUR FOOL OF A FATHER HERE TOO?
N-NO...WE DIDN'T KNOW WE'D BE RUNNING INTO BAD GUYS LIKE YOU HERE...!
I SEE...
THAT'S TOO BAD...
WE THREE ARE THE LAST SAIYANS ALIVE. WHEN YOU GET BACK TO EARTH, TELL THAT COWARD KAKARROT...
DOOM

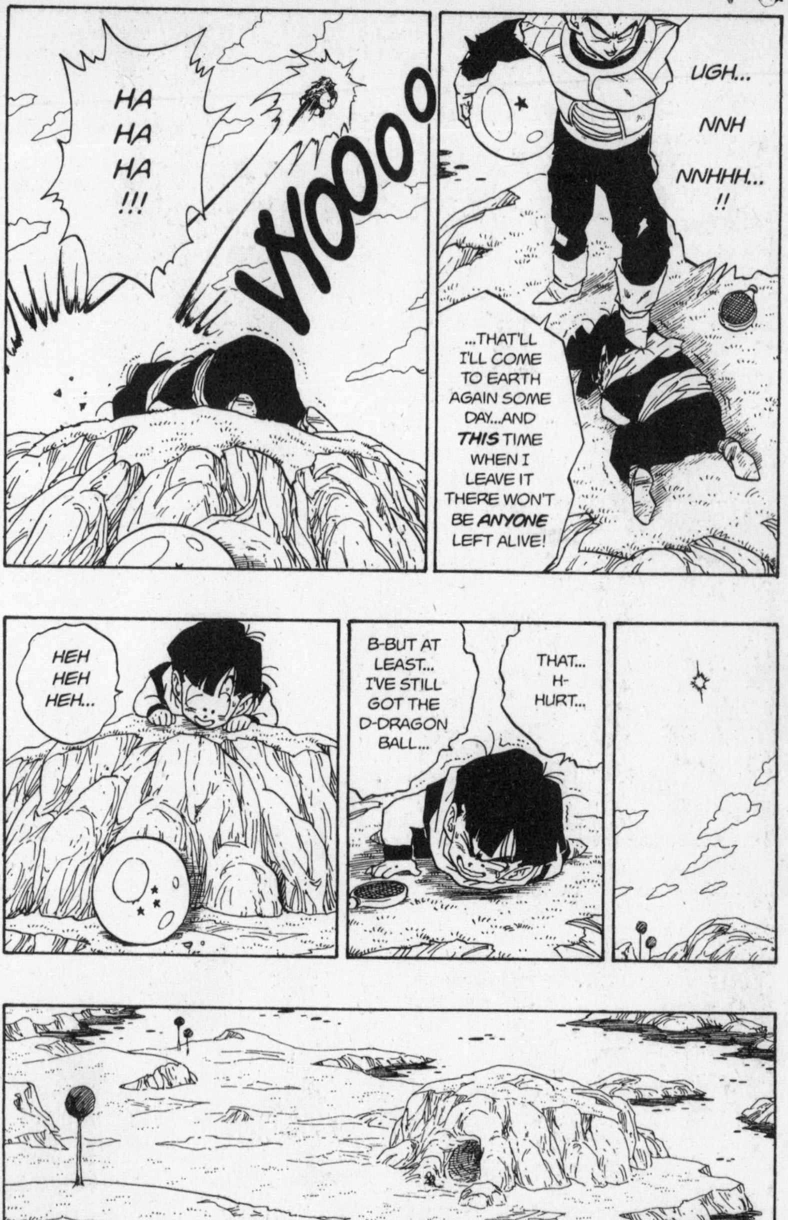
UGH...
NNH
NNHHH... !!
...THAT'LL I'LL COME TO EARTH AGAIN SOME DAY...AND **THIS** TIME WHEN I LEAVE IT THERE WON'T BE **ANYONE** LEFT ALIVE!
VOOOO
HA HA HA !!!
THAT... H- HURT...
B-BUT AT LEAST... I'VE STILL GOT THE D-DRAGON BALL...
HEH HEH HEH...

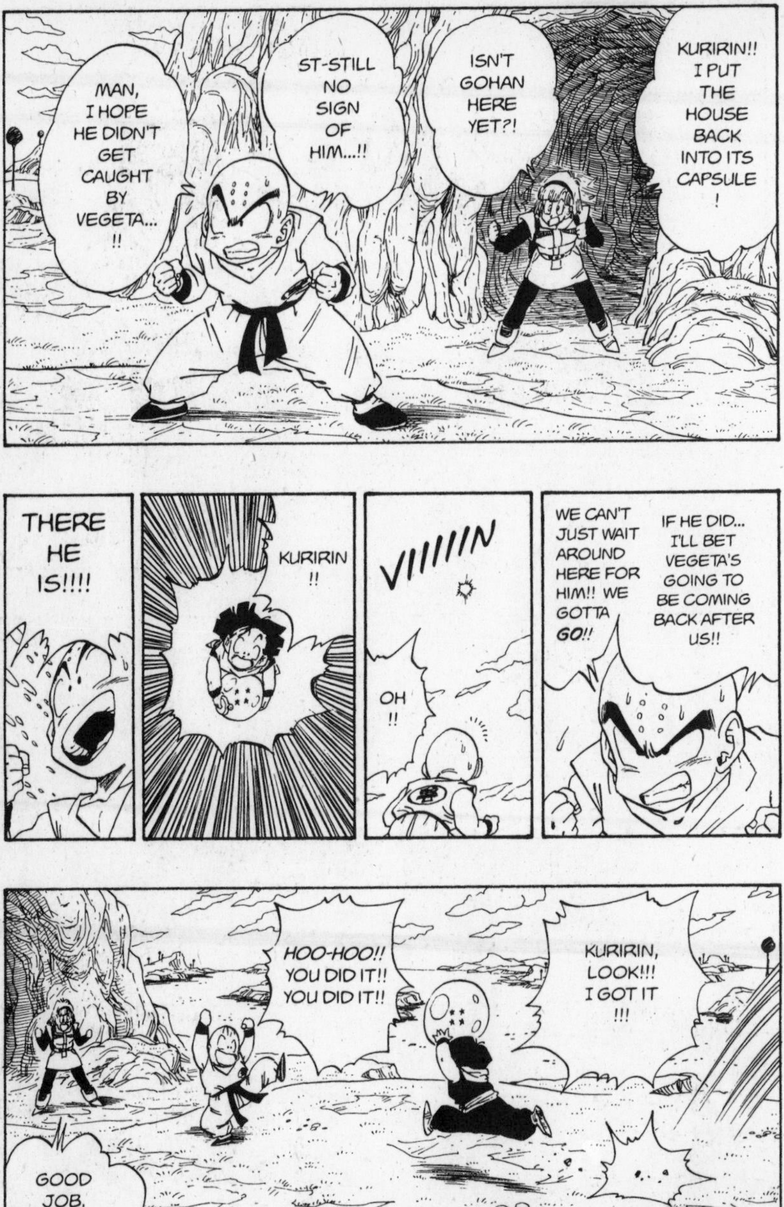

KURIRIN!! I PUT THE HOUSE BACK INTO ITS CAPSULE!
ISN'T GOHAN HERE YET?!
ST-STILL NO SIGN OF HIM...!!
MAN, I HOPE HE DIDN'T GET CAUGHT BY VEGETA...!!
IF HE DID... I'LL BET VEGETA'S GOING TO BE COMING BACK AFTER US!!
WE CAN'T JUST WAIT AROUND HERE FOR HIM!! WE GOTTA *GO*!!
VIIIIIN
OH !!
KURIRIN !!
THERE HE IS!!!!
KURIRIN, LOOK!!! I GOT IT !!!
HOO-HOO!! YOU DID IT!! YOU DID IT!!
GOOD JOB, GOHAN !!!

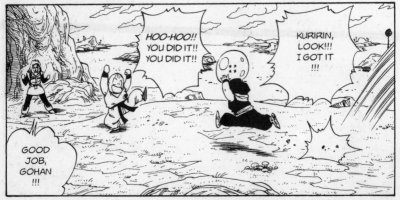

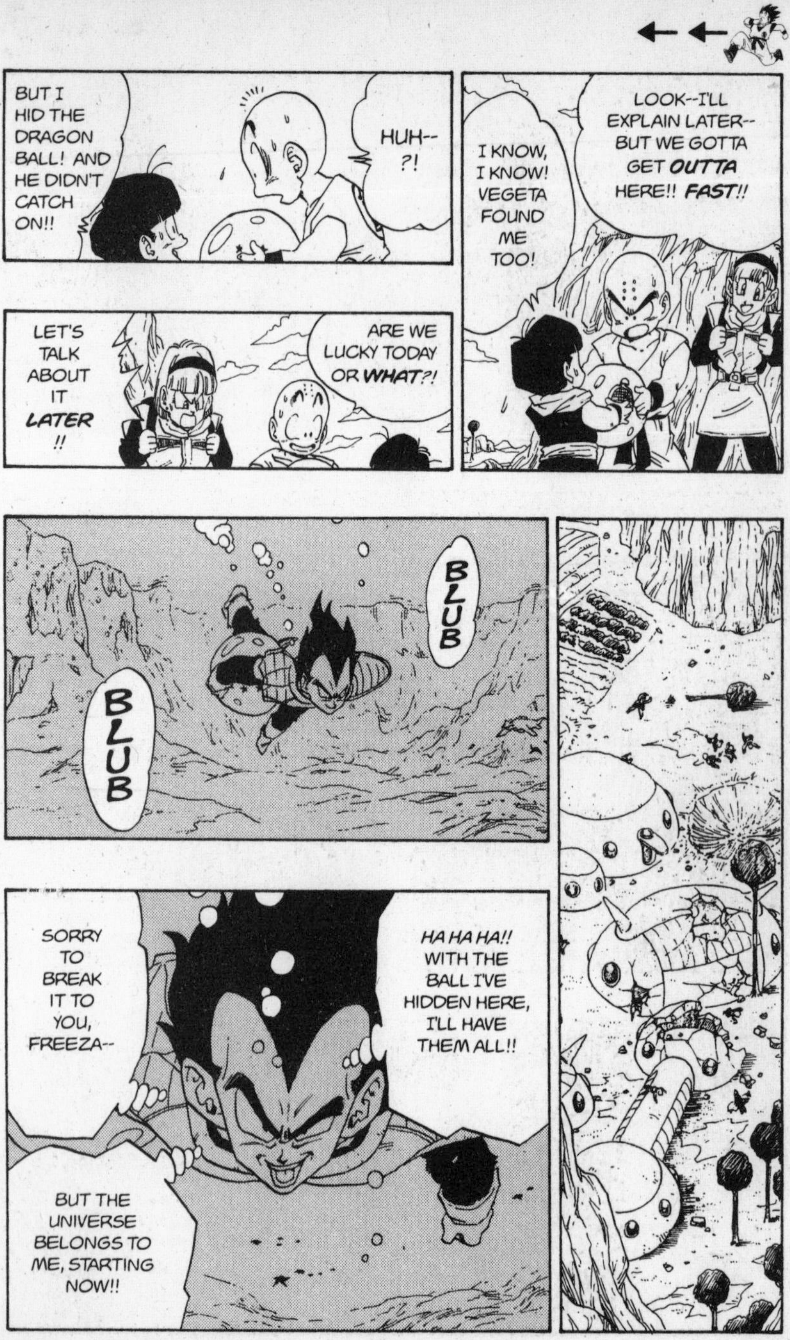
LOOK--I'LL EXPLAIN LATER-- BUT WE GOTTA GET **OUTTA** HERE!! ***FAST!!***
I KNOW, I KNOW! VEGETA FOUND ME TOO!
HUH-- ?!
BUT I HID THE DRAGON BALL! AND HE DIDN'T CATCH ON!!
ARE WE LUCKY TODAY OR ***WHAT?!***
LET'S TALK ABOUT IT ***LATER*** !!
BLUB
BLUB
HA HA HA!! WITH THE BALL I'VE HIDDEN HERE, I'LL HAVE THEM ALL!!
SORRY TO BREAK IT TO YOU, FREEZA--
BUT THE UNIVERSE BELONGS TO ME, STARTING NOW!!

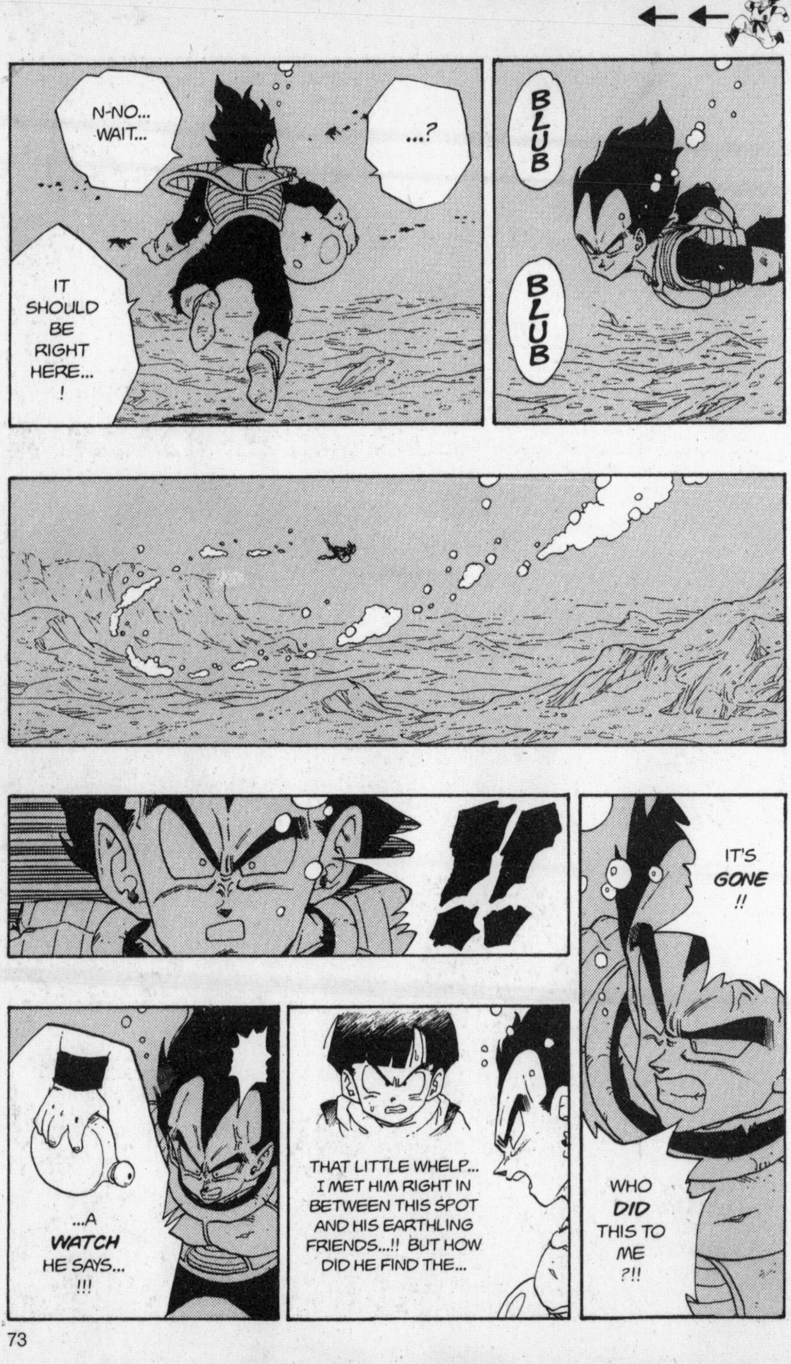
BLUB
BLUB
...?
N-NO... WAIT...
IT SHOULD BE RIGHT HERE... !
IT'S GONE !!
WHO DID THIS TO ME ?!!
THAT LITTLE WHELP... I MET HIM RIGHT IN BETWEEN THIS SPOT AND HIS EARTHLING FRIENDS...!! BUT HOW DID HE FIND THE...
...A WATCH HE SAYS... !!!

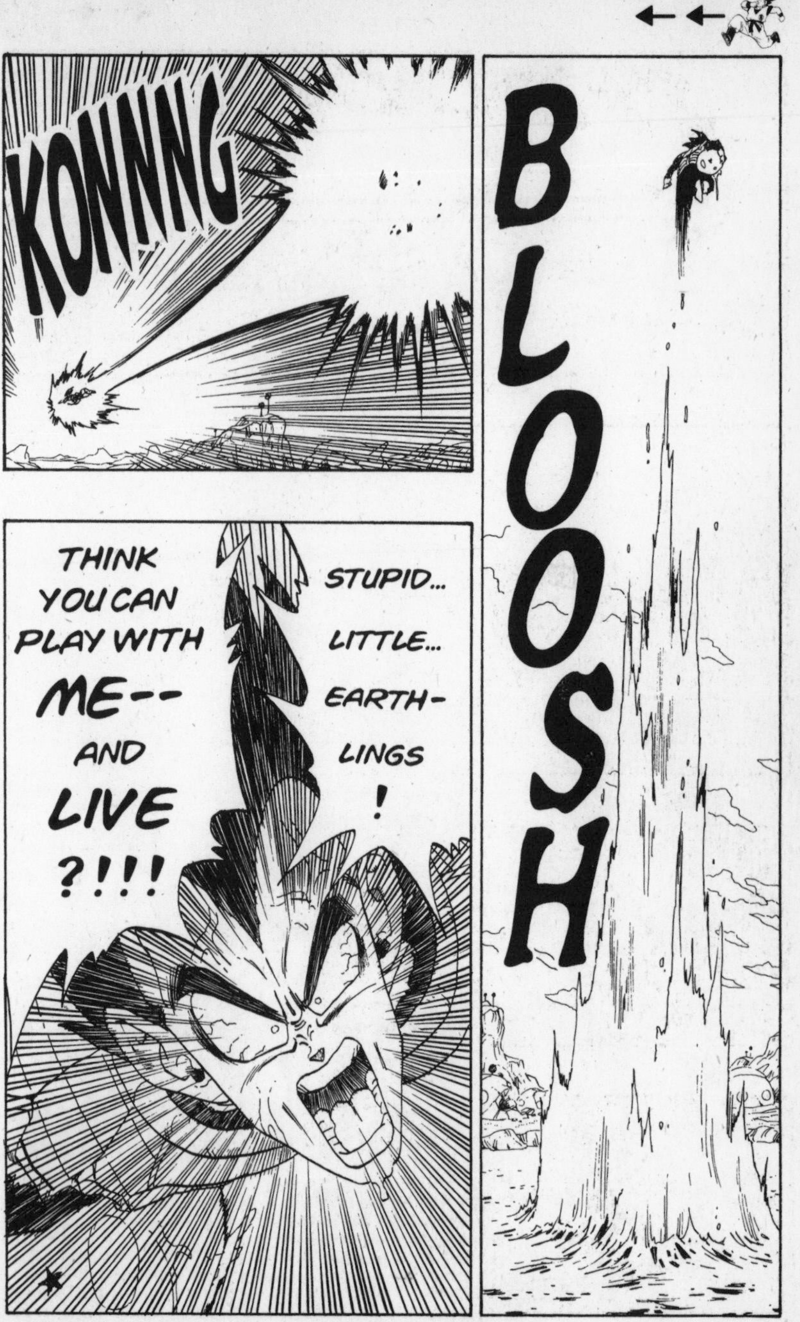
BLOOSH
KONNNG
STUPID... LITTLE... EARTH-LINGS!
THINK YOU CAN PLAY WITH ME-- AND LIVE ?!!!

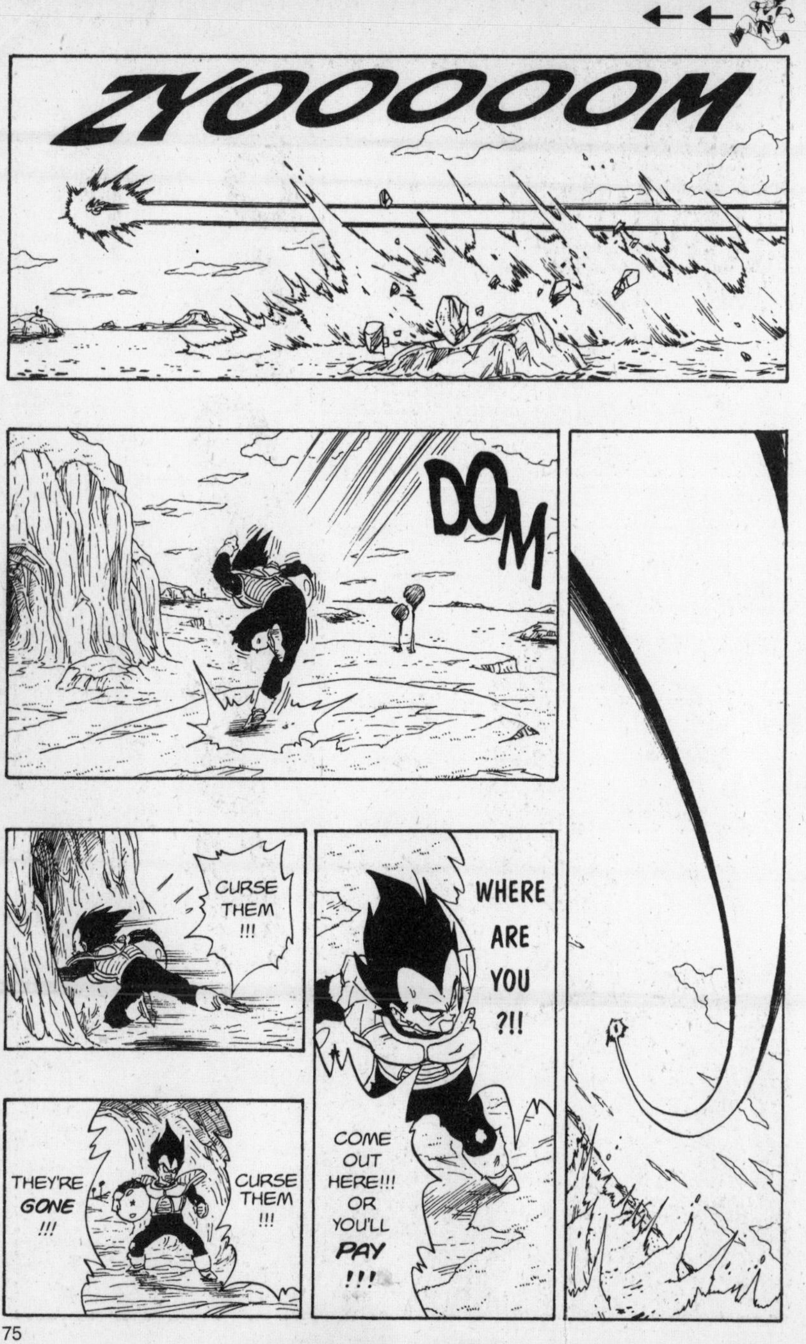

ZYOOOOOM
DOM
WHERE ARE YOU ?!!
COME OUT HERE!!! OR YOU'LL PAY !!!
CURSE THEM !!!
CURSE THEM !!!
THEY'RE GONE !!!

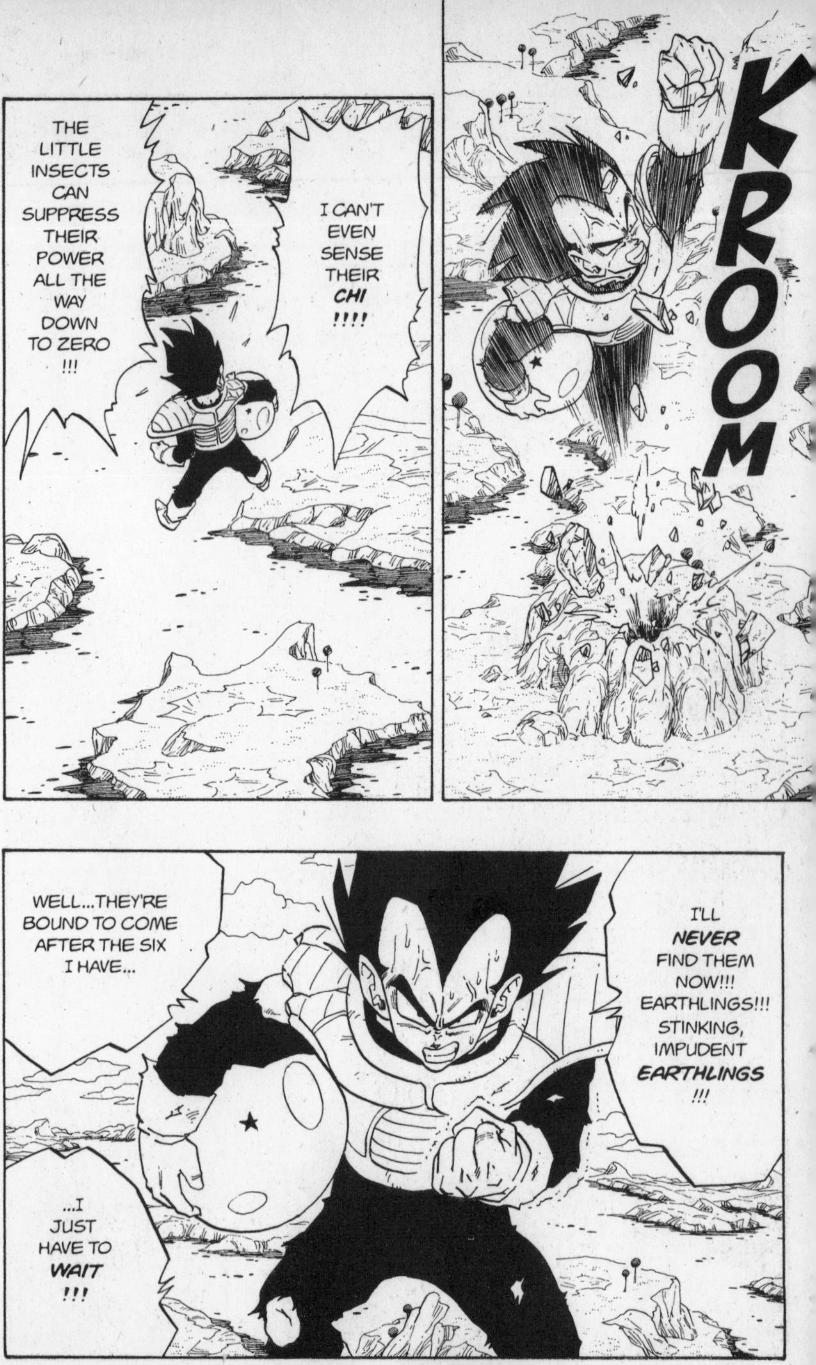
KROOM
I CAN'T EVEN SENSE THEIR CHI!!!!
THE LITTLE INSECTS CAN SUPPRESS THEIR POWER ALL THE WAY DOWN TO ZERO!!!
I'LL NEVER FIND THEM NOW!!! EARTHLINGS!!! STINKING, IMPUDENT EARTHLINGS!!!
WELL...THEY'RE BOUND TO COME AFTER THE SIX I HAVE...
...I JUST HAVE TO WAIT!!!

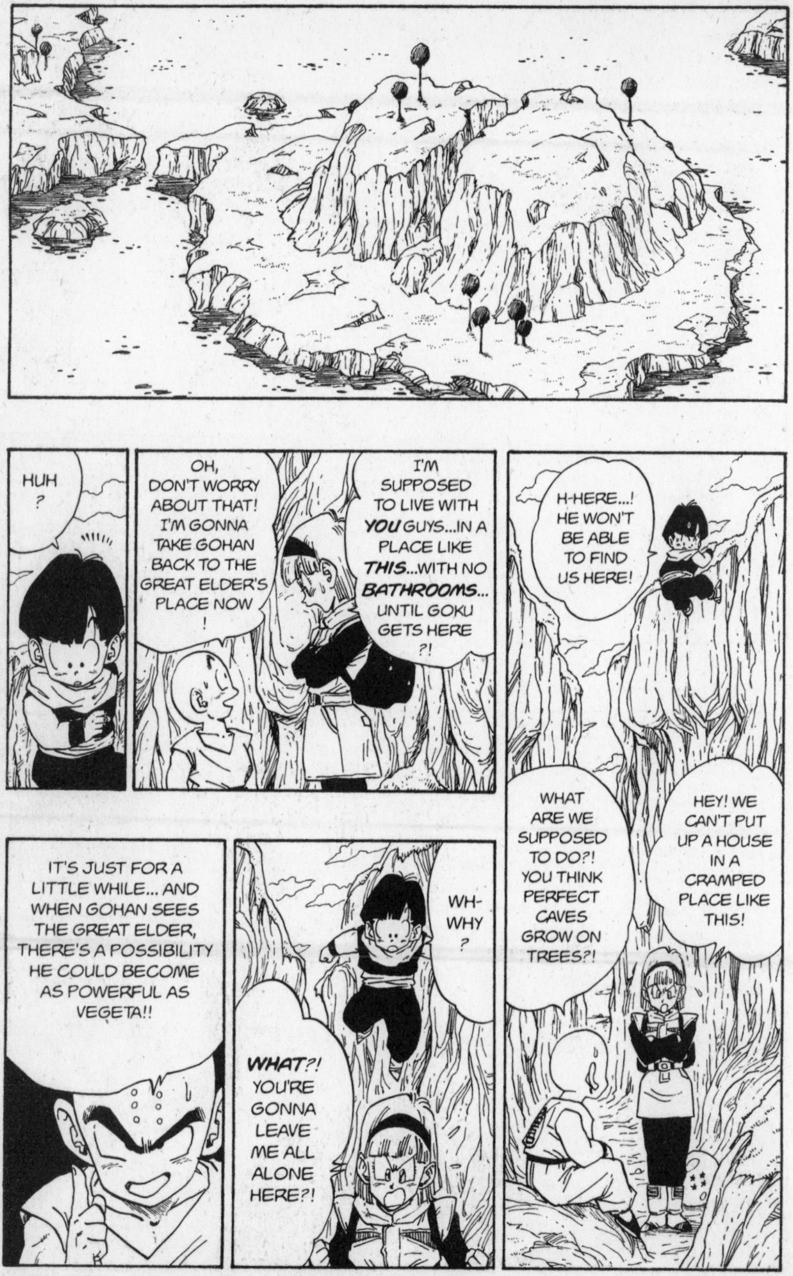
H-HERE...! HE WON'T BE ABLE TO FIND US HERE!
I'M SUPPOSED TO LIVE WITH **YOU** GUYS...IN A PLACE LIKE **THIS**...WITH NO **BATHROOMS**... UNTIL GOKU GETS HERE ?!
OH, DON'T WORRY ABOUT THAT! I'M GONNA TAKE GOHAN BACK TO THE GREAT ELDER'S PLACE NOW !
HUH ?
HEY! WE CAN'T PUT UP A HOUSE IN A CRAMPED PLACE LIKE THIS!
WHAT ARE WE SUPPOSED TO DO?! YOU THINK PERFECT CAVES GROW ON TREES?!
WH- WHY ?
WHAT?! YOU'RE GONNA LEAVE ME ALL ALONE HERE?!
IT'S JUST FOR A LITTLE WHILE... AND WHEN GOHAN SEES THE GREAT ELDER, THERE'S A POSSIBILITY HE COULD BECOME AS POWERFUL AS VEGETA!!

NEXT: High Gravity Goku!!!

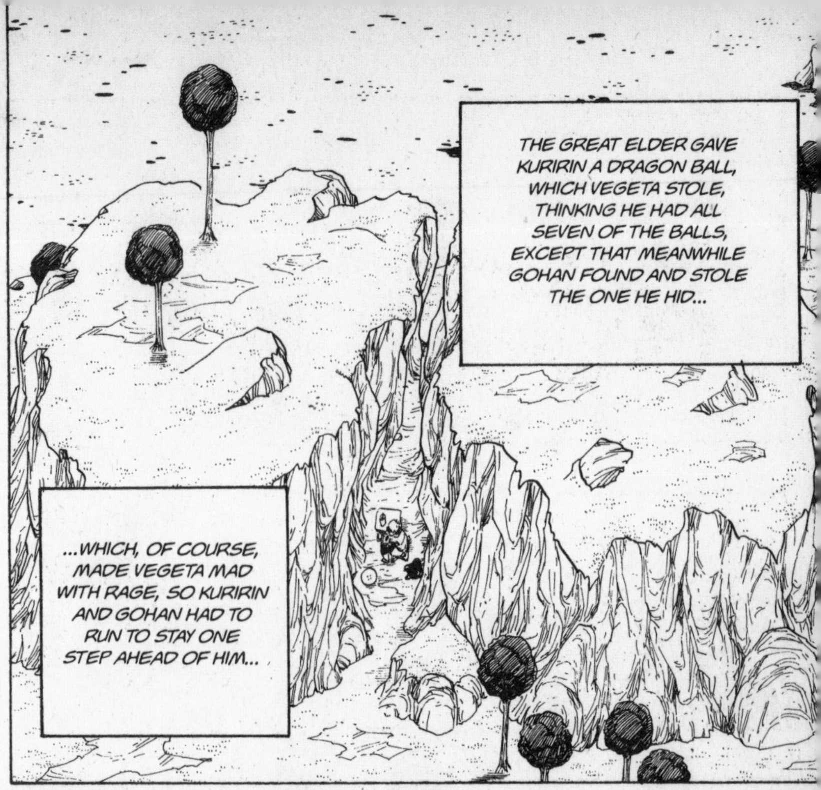
THE GREAT ELDER GAVE KURIRIN A DRAGON BALL, WHICH VEGETA STOLE, THINKING HE HAD ALL SEVEN OF THE BALLS, EXCEPT THAT MEANWHILE GOHAN FOUND AND STOLE THE ONE HE HID...
...WHICH, OF COURSE, MADE VEGETA MAD WITH RAGE, SO KURIRIN AND GOHAN HAD TO RUN TO STAY ONE STEP AHEAD OF HIM...

DBZ:76 • Premonitions of War

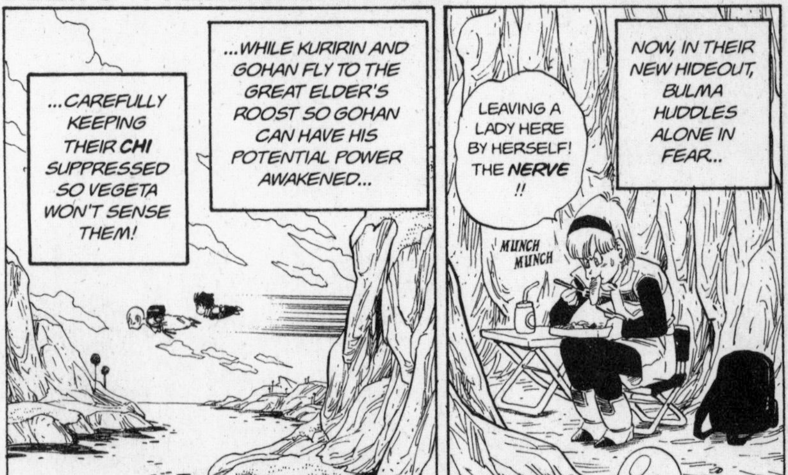
NOW, IN THEIR NEW HIDEOUT, BULMA HUDDLES ALONE IN FEAR...
LEAVING A LADY HERE BY HERSELF! THE **NERVE** !!
MUNCH MUNCH
...WHILE KURIRIN AND GOHAN FLY TO THE GREAT ELDER'S ROOST SO GOHAN CAN HAVE HIS POTENTIAL POWER AWAKENED...
...CAREFULLY KEEPING THEIR **CHI** SUPPRESSED SO VEGETA WON'T SENSE THEM!

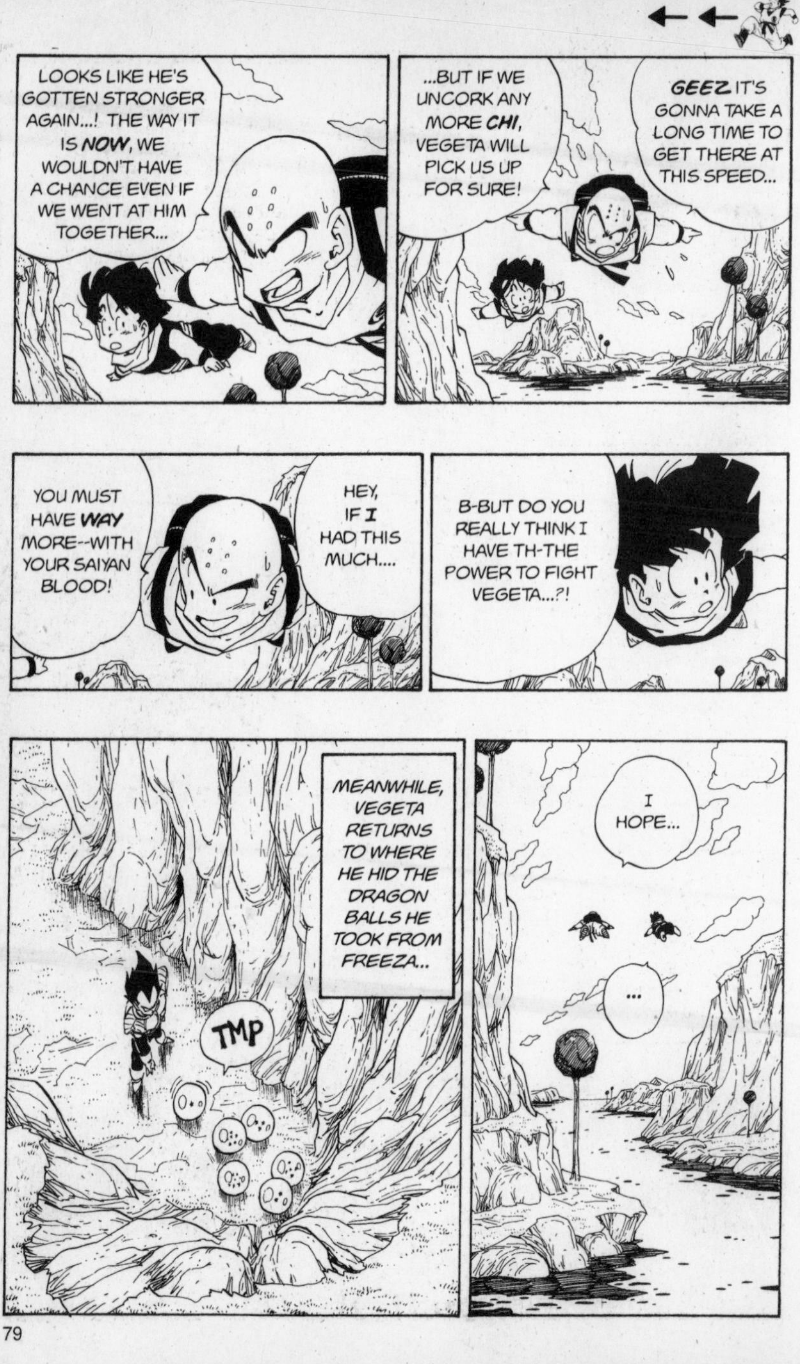

GEEZ IT'S GONNA TAKE A LONG TIME TO GET THERE AT THIS SPEED...
...BUT IF WE UNCORK ANY MORE CHI, VEGETA WILL PICK US UP FOR SURE!
LOOKS LIKE HE'S GOTTEN STRONGER AGAIN...! THE WAY IT IS NOW, WE WOULDN'T HAVE A CHANCE EVEN IF WE WENT AT HIM TOGETHER...
B-BUT DO YOU REALLY THINK I HAVE TH-THE POWER TO FIGHT VEGETA...?!
HEY, IF I HAD THIS MUCH....
YOU MUST HAVE WAY MORE--WITH YOUR SAIYAN BLOOD!
I HOPE...
...
MEANWHILE, VEGETA RETURNS TO WHERE HE HID THE DRAGON BALLS HE TOOK FROM FREEZA...
TMP

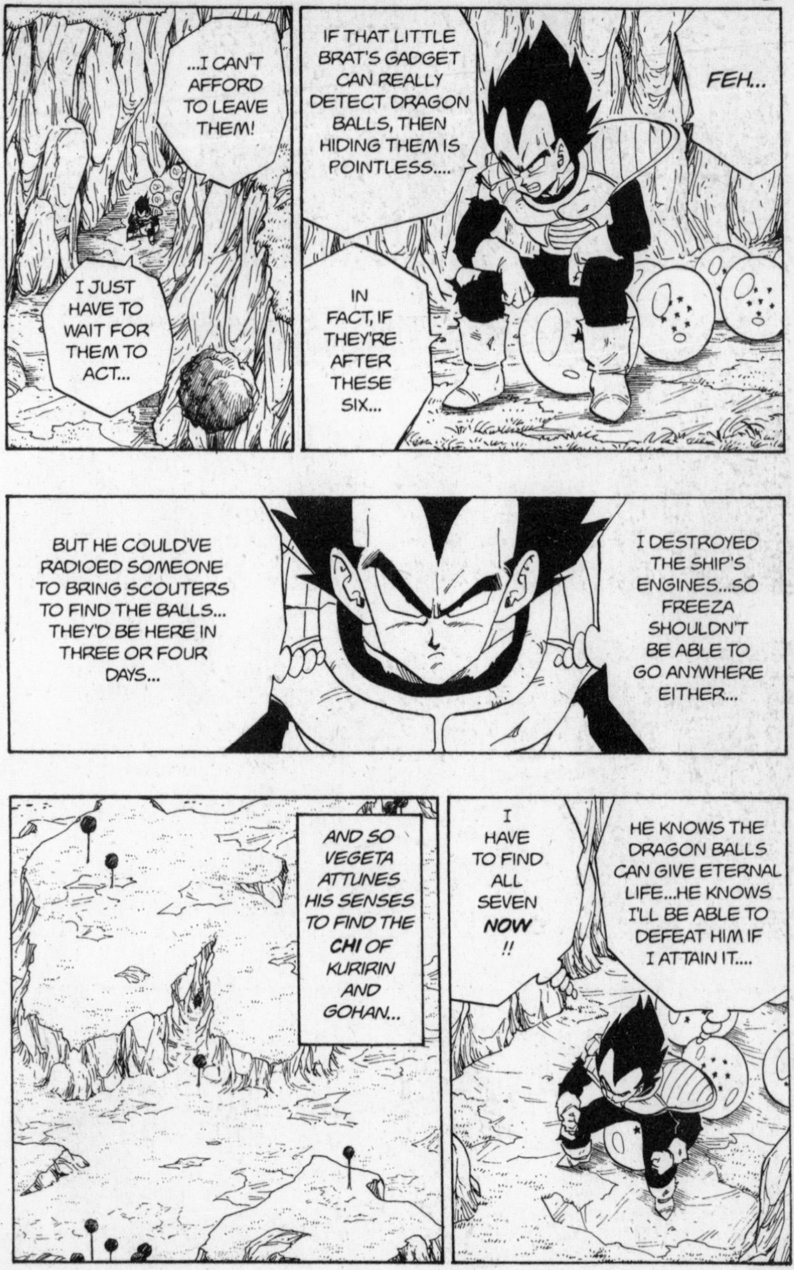
FEH...
IF THAT LITTLE BRAT'S GADGET CAN REALLY DETECT DRAGON BALLS, THEN HIDING THEM IS POINTLESS....
IN FACT, IF THEY'RE AFTER THESE SIX...
...I CAN'T AFFORD TO LEAVE THEM!
I JUST HAVE TO WAIT FOR THEM TO ACT...
I DESTROYED THE SHIP'S ENGINES...SO FREEZA SHOULDN'T BE ABLE TO GO ANYWHERE EITHER...
BUT HE COULD'VE RADIOED SOMEONE TO BRING SCOUTERS TO FIND THE BALLS... THEY'D BE HERE IN THREE OR FOUR DAYS...
HE KNOWS THE DRAGON BALLS CAN GIVE ETERNAL LIFE...HE KNOWS I'LL BE ABLE TO DEFEAT HIM IF I ATTAIN IT....
I HAVE TO FIND ALL SEVEN *NOW* !!
*AND SO VEGETA ATTUNES HIS SENSES TO FIND THE **CHI** OF KURIRIN AND GOHAN...*

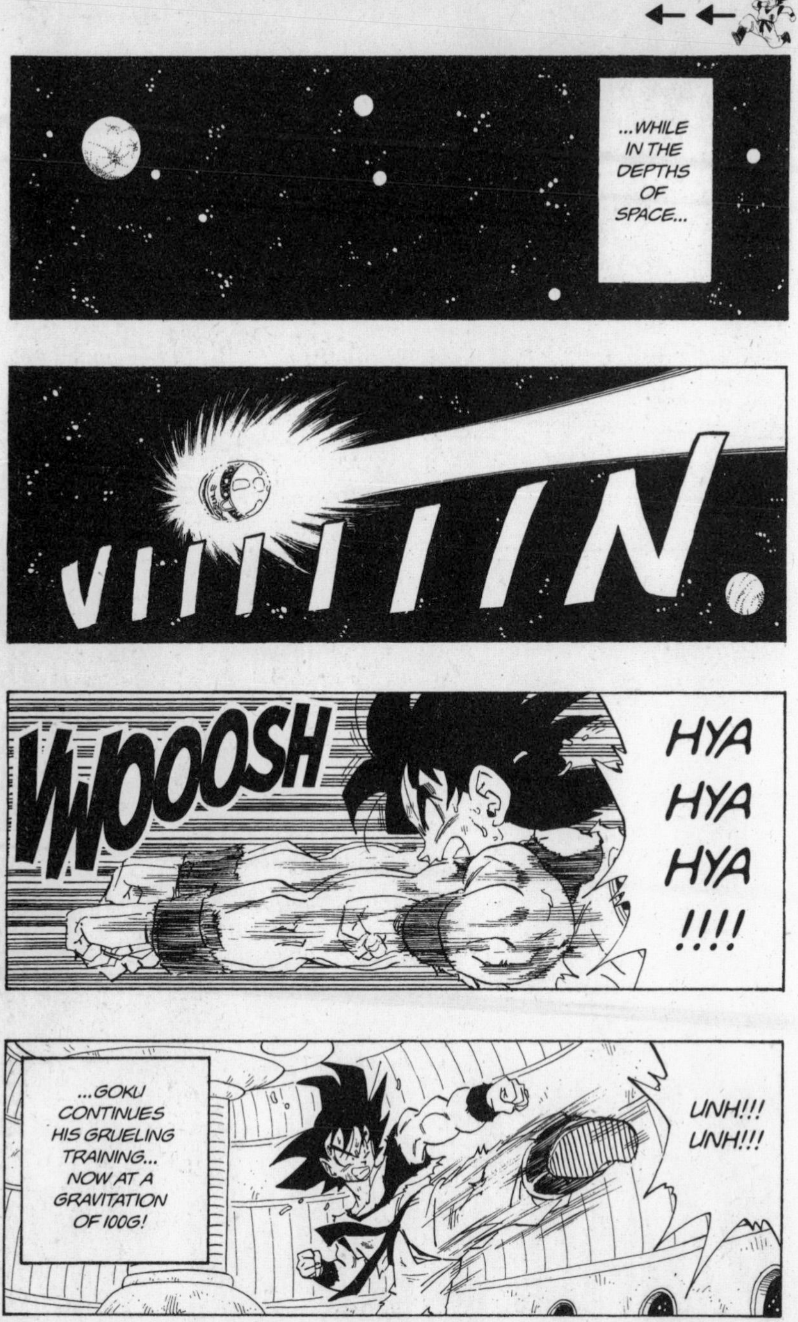
...WHILE IN THE DEPTHS OF SPACE...
VIIIIIIN
HYA HYA HYA !!!!
WOOOSH
...GOKU CONTINUES HIS GRUELING TRAINING... NOW AT A GRAVITATION OF 100G!
UNH!!! UNH!!!

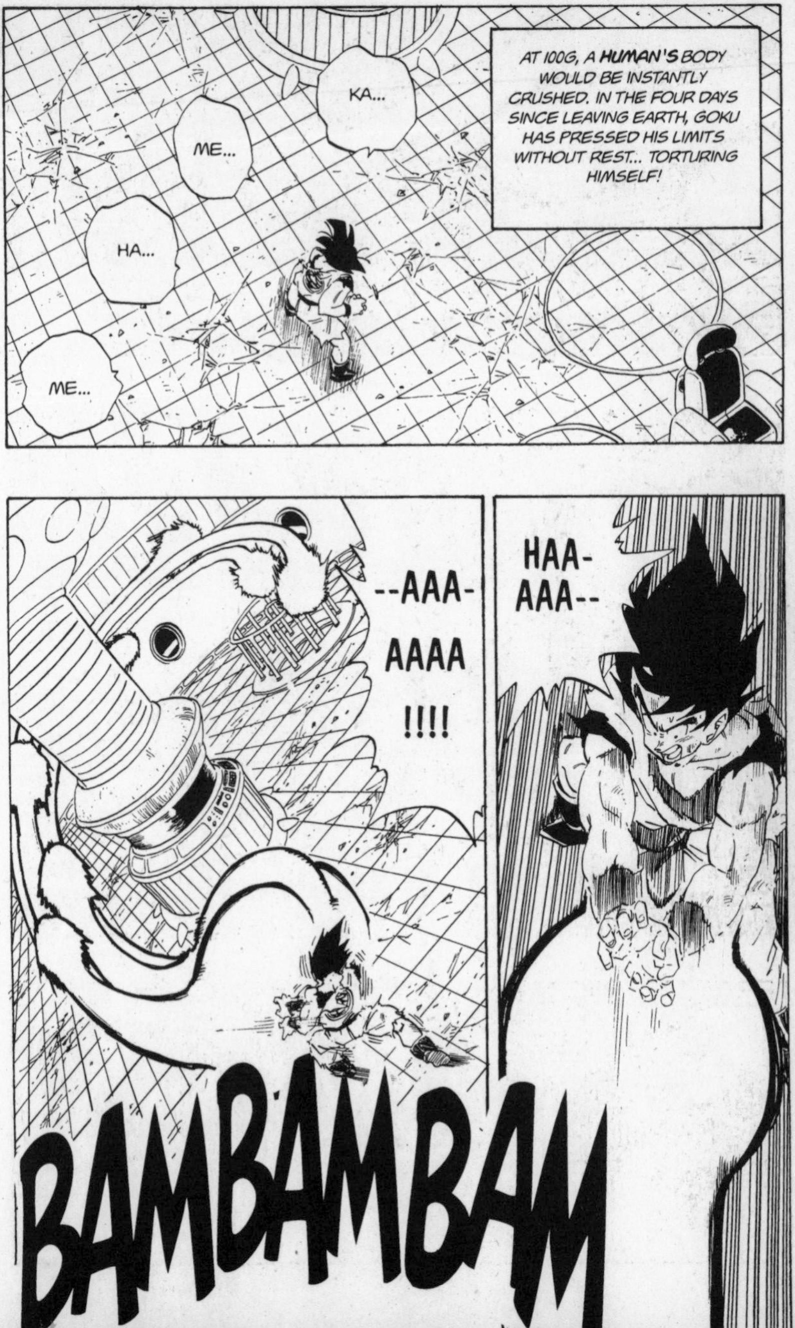
AT 100G, A **HUMAN'S** BODY WOULD BE INSTANTLY CRUSHED. IN THE FOUR DAYS SINCE LEAVING EARTH, GOKU HAS PRESSED HIS LIMITS WITHOUT REST... TORTURING HIMSELF!
KA...
ME...
HA...
ME...
HAA- AAA--
--AAA- AAAA !!!!
BAMBAMBAM

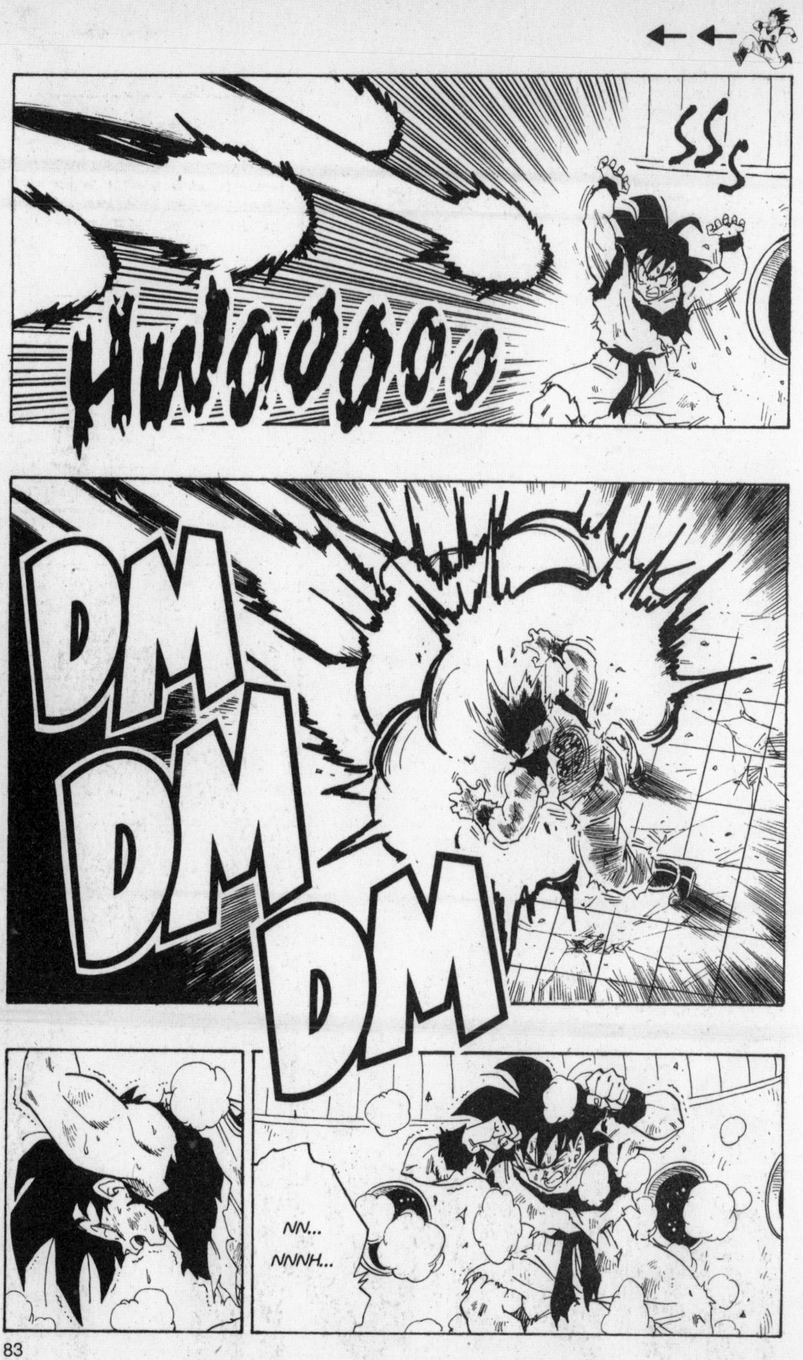
SSS
HWOOOOO
DM DM DM
NN...
NNNH...

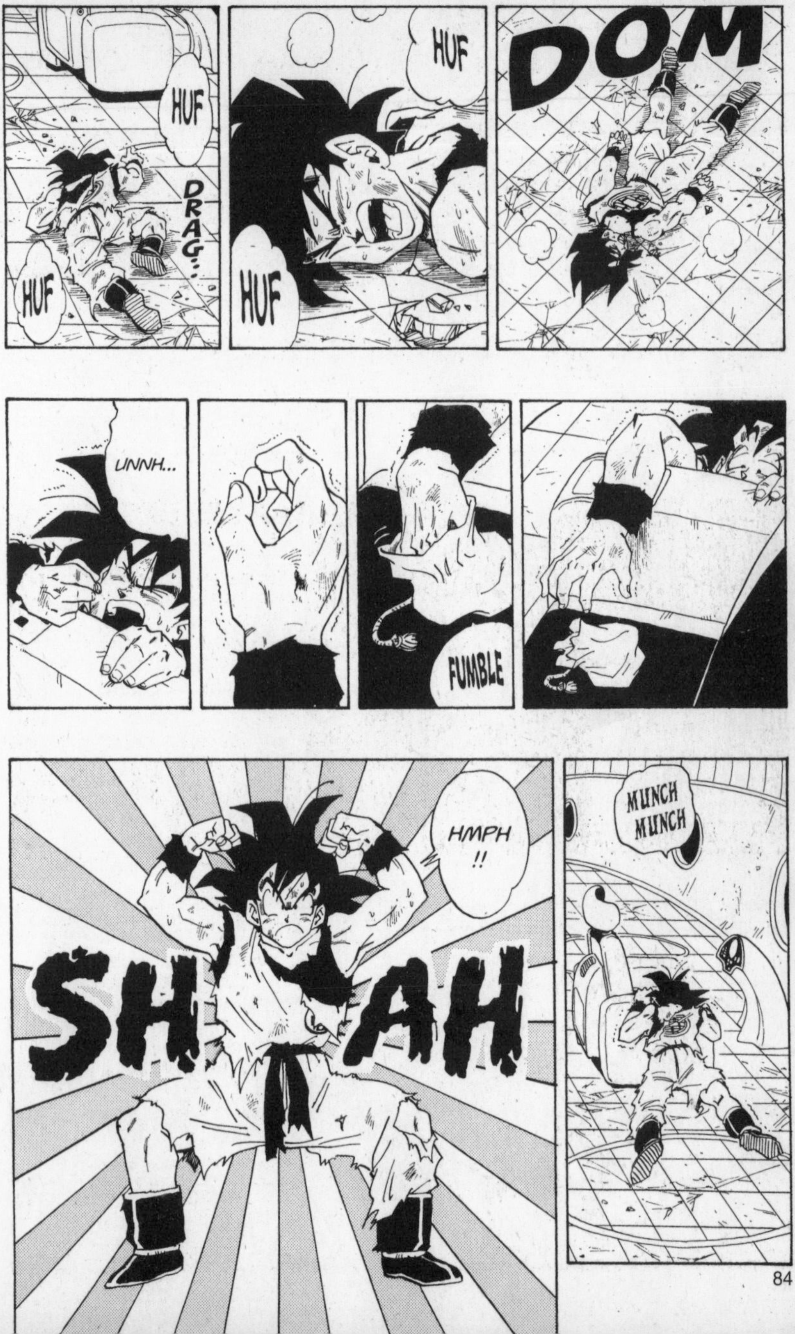

DOM
HUF
HUF
HUF
DRAG...
HUF
FUMBLE
UNNH...
MUNCH MUNCH
HMPH!!
SHAH

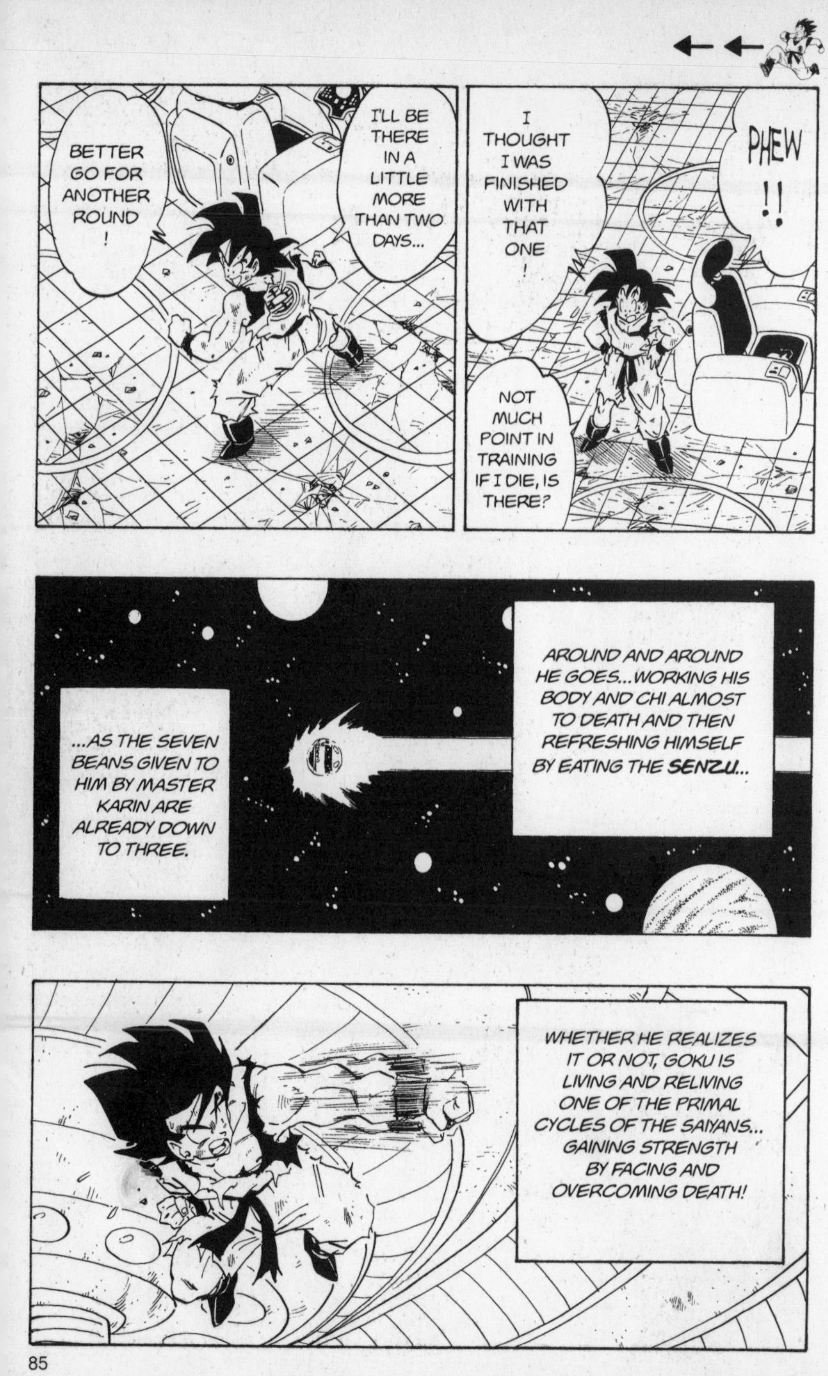
PHEW !!
I THOUGHT I WAS FINISHED WITH THAT ONE !
NOT MUCH POINT IN TRAINING IF I DIE, IS THERE?
I'LL BE THERE IN A LITTLE MORE THAN TWO DAYS...
BETTER GO FOR ANOTHER ROUND !
AROUND AND AROUND HE GOES...WORKING HIS BODY AND CHI ALMOST TO DEATH AND THEN REFRESHING HIMSELF BY EATING THE **SENZU**...
...AS THE SEVEN BEANS GIVEN TO HIM BY MASTER KARIN ARE ALREADY DOWN TO THREE.
WHETHER HE REALIZES IT OR NOT, GOKU IS LIVING AND RELIVING ONE OF THE PRIMAL CYCLES OF THE SAIYANS... GAINING STRENGTH BY FACING AND OVERCOMING DEATH!

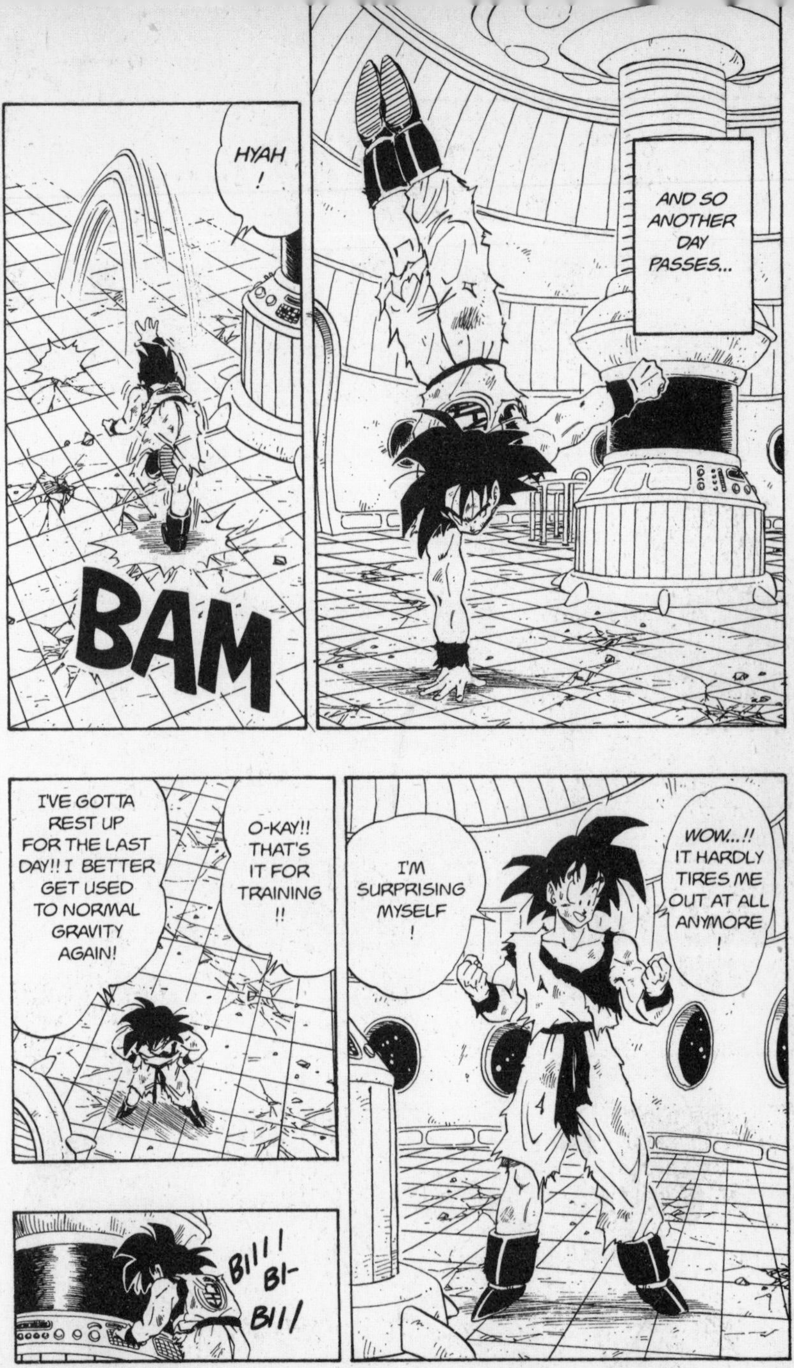
AND SO ANOTHER DAY PASSES...
HYAH!
BAM
WOW...!! IT HARDLY TIRES ME OUT AT ALL ANYMORE!
I'M SURPRISING MYSELF!
O-KAY!! THAT'S IT FOR TRAINING!!
I'VE GOTTA REST UP FOR THE LAST DAY!! I BETTER GET USED TO NORMAL GRAVITY AGAIN!
BI!! BI-BI!!

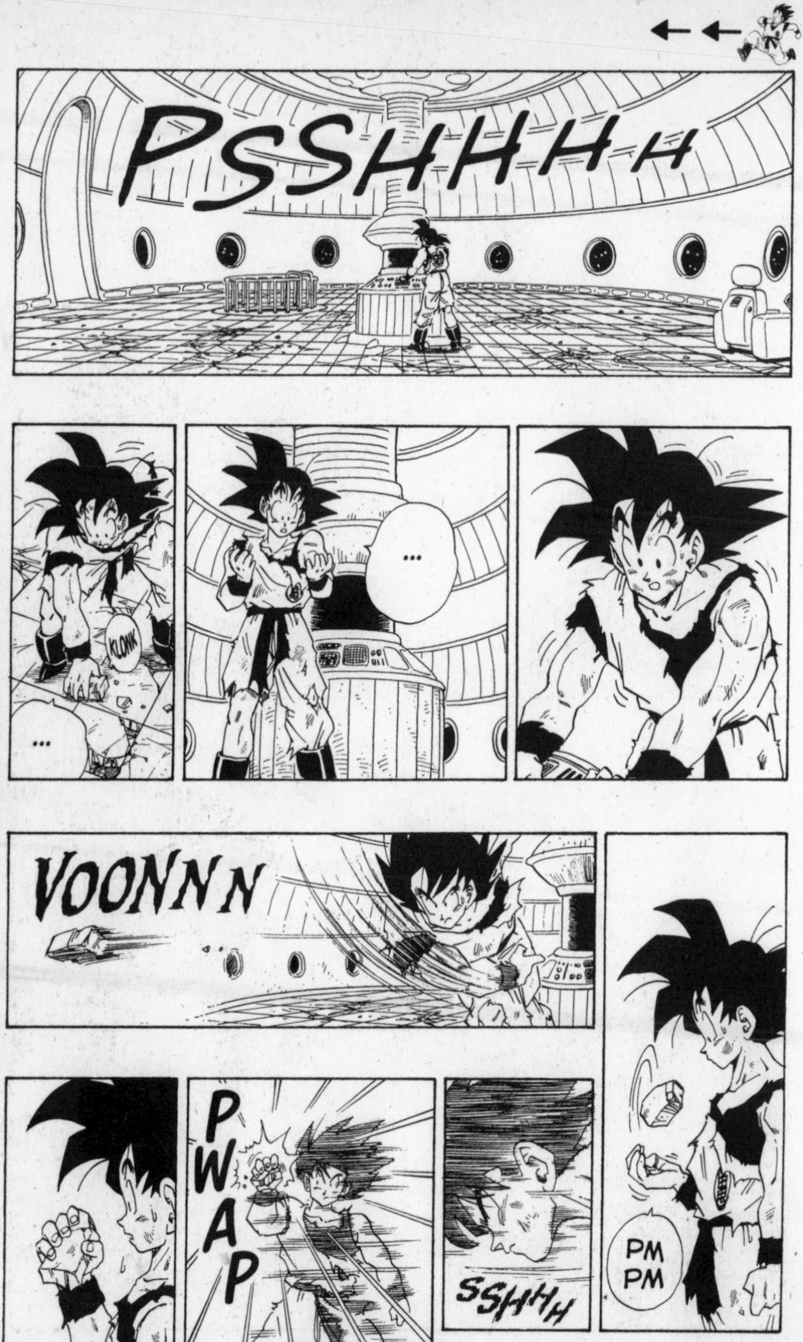

PSSHHHH
...
KLONK
...
PM PM
VOONNN
SSHHHH
PWAP

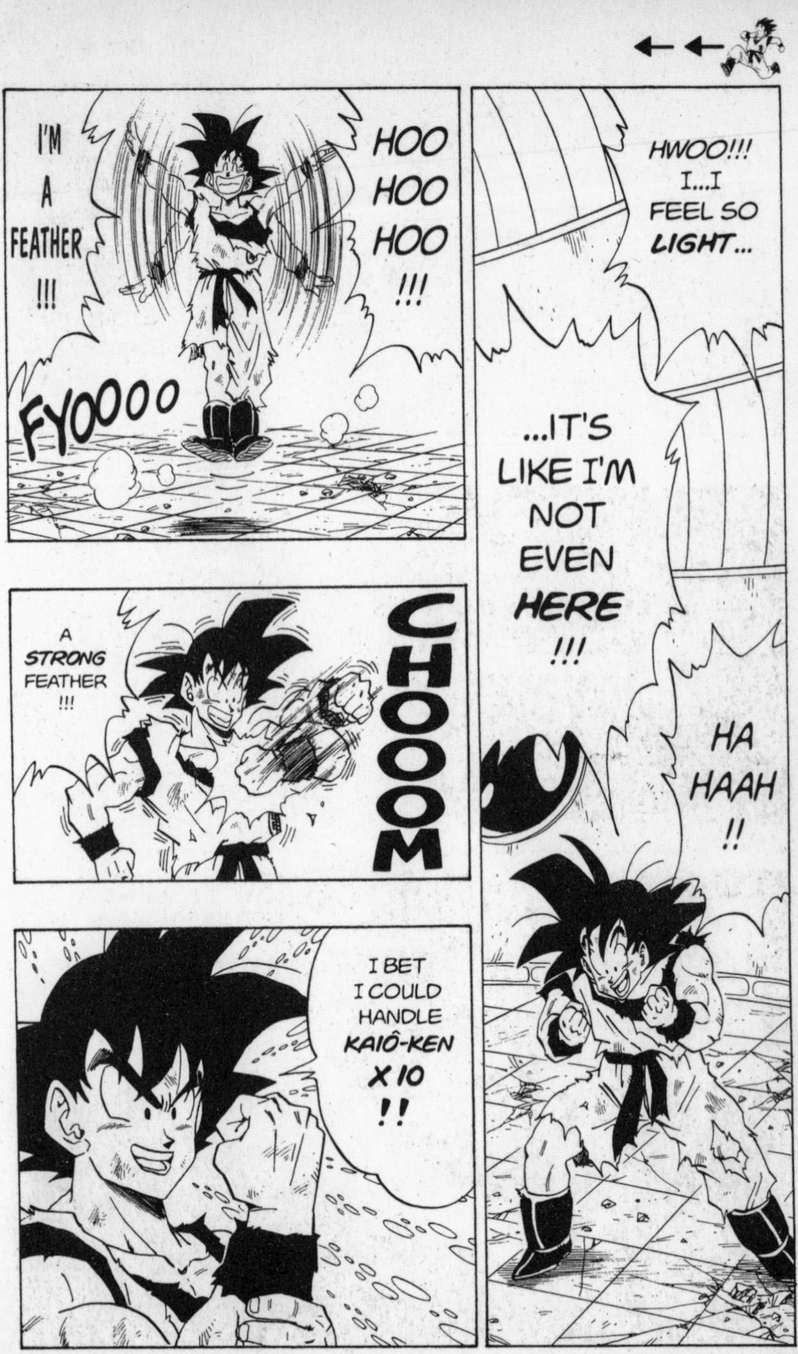
HWOO!!! I...I FEEL SO LIGHT...
...IT'S LIKE I'M NOT EVEN HERE!!!
HA HAAH!!
HOO HOO HOO!!!
I'M A FEATHER!!!
FYOOOO
CHOOOOM
A STRONG FEATHER!!!
I BET I COULD HANDLE KAIÔ-KEN X10!!

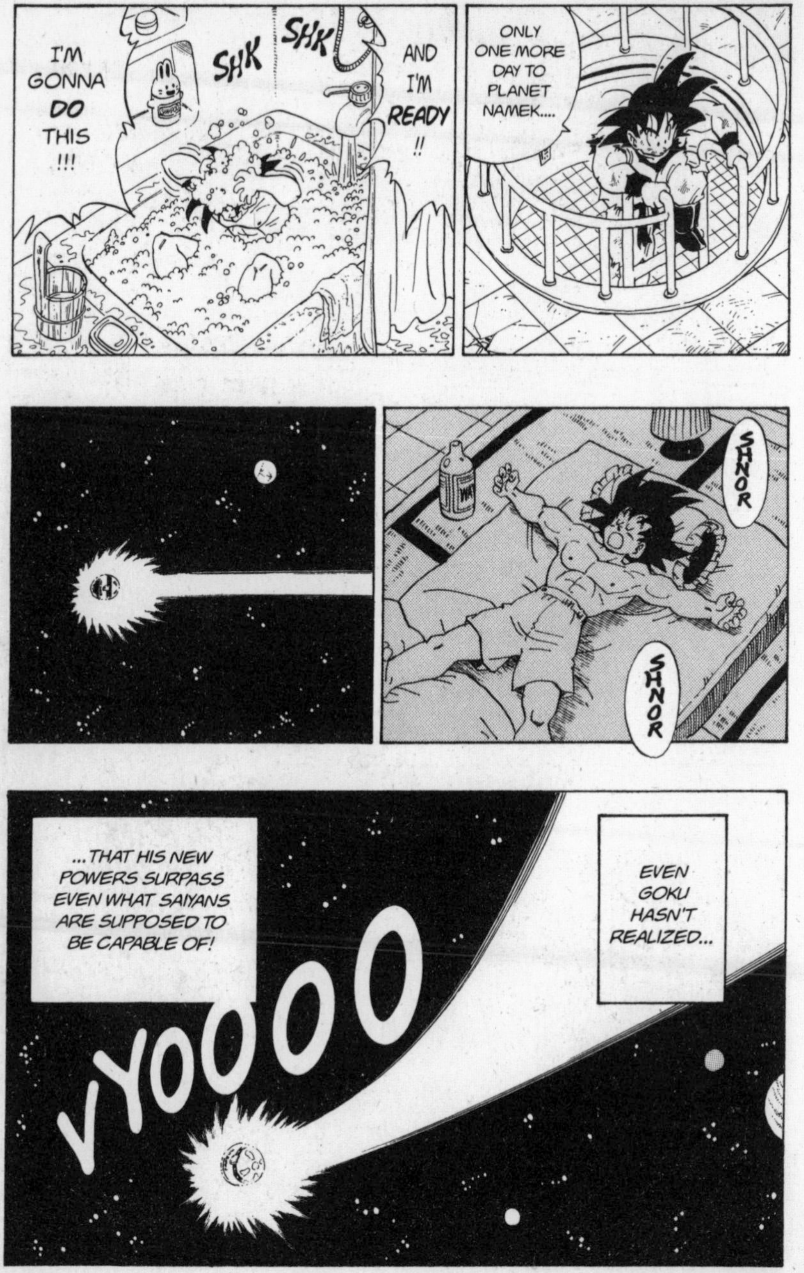
ONLY ONE MORE DAY TO PLANET NAMEK....
SHK SHK
I'M GONNA DO THIS !!!
AND I'M READY !!
SHNOR
SHNOR
EVEN GOKU HASN'T REALIZED...
...THAT HIS NEW POWERS SURPASS EVEN WHAT SAIYANS ARE SUPPOSED TO BE CAPABLE OF!
VYOOOO

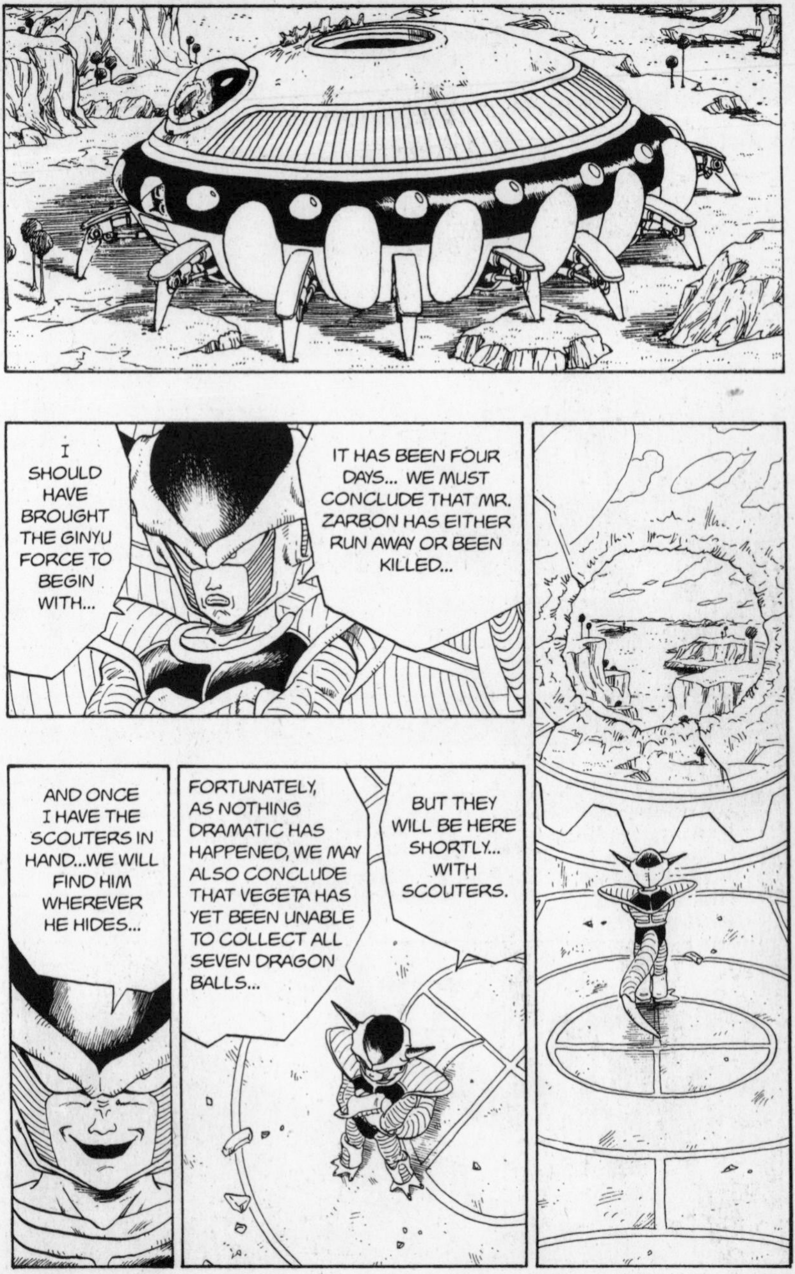
IT HAS BEEN FOUR DAYS... WE MUST CONCLUDE THAT MR. ZARBON HAS EITHER RUN AWAY OR BEEN KILLED...
I SHOULD HAVE BROUGHT THE GINYU FORCE TO BEGIN WITH...
BUT THEY WILL BE HERE SHORTLY... WITH SCOUTERS.
FORTUNATELY, AS NOTHING DRAMATIC HAS HAPPENED, WE MAY ALSO CONCLUDE THAT VEGETA HAS YET BEEN UNABLE TO COLLECT ALL SEVEN DRAGON BALLS...
AND ONCE I HAVE THE SCOUTERS IN HAND...WE WILL FIND HIM WHEREVER HE HIDES...

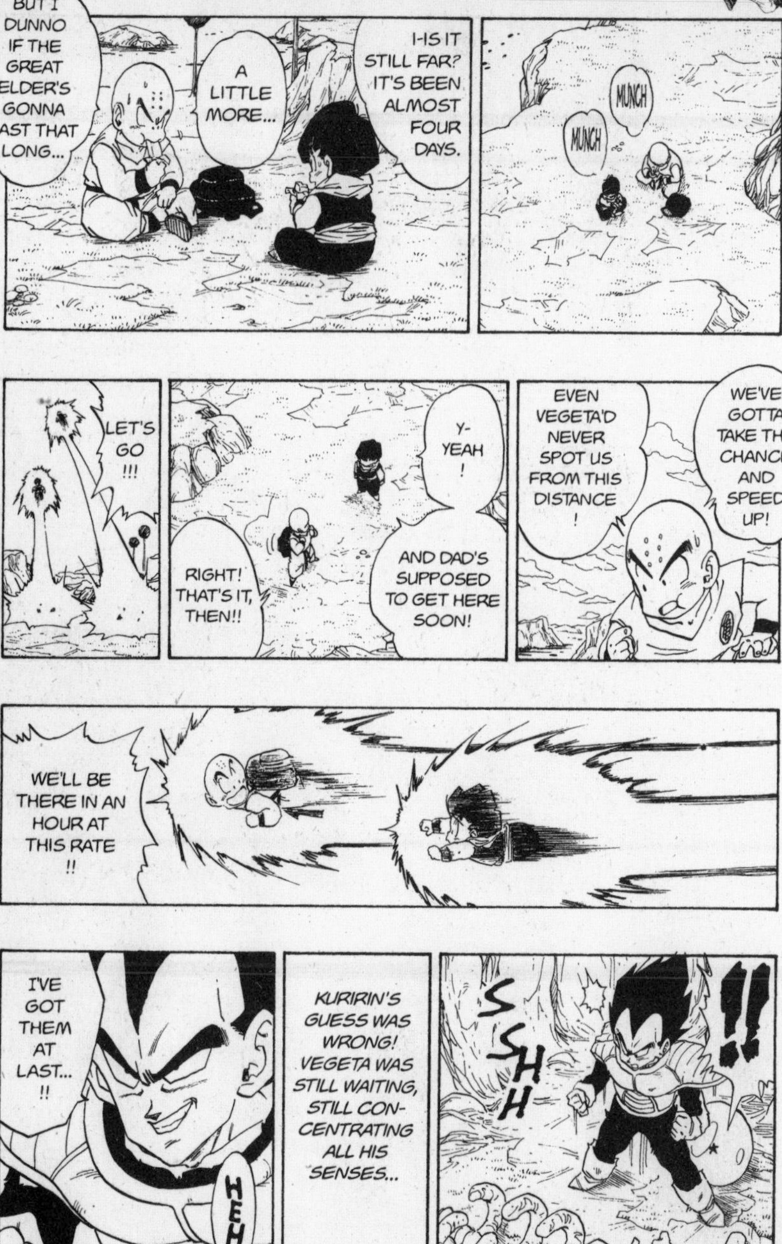
MUNCH
MUNCH
I-IS IT STILL FAR? IT'S BEEN ALMOST FOUR DAYS.
A LITTLE MORE...
BUT I DUNNO IF THE GREAT ELDER'S GONNA LAST THAT LONG...
WE'VE GOTTA TAKE THE CHANCE AND SPEED UP!
EVEN VEGETA'D NEVER SPOT US FROM THIS DISTANCE!
Y-YEAH!
AND DAD'S SUPPOSED TO GET HERE SOON!
RIGHT! THAT'S IT, THEN!!
LET'S GO!!!
WE'LL BE THERE IN AN HOUR AT THIS RATE!!
SSHH
!!
KURIRIN'S GUESS WAS WRONG! VEGETA WAS STILL WAITING, STILL CON-CENTRATING ALL HIS SENSES...
I'VE GOT THEM AT LAST...!!
HEH

NEXT: The Ginyu Force!

DBZ:77 • The Enemy of My Enemy…

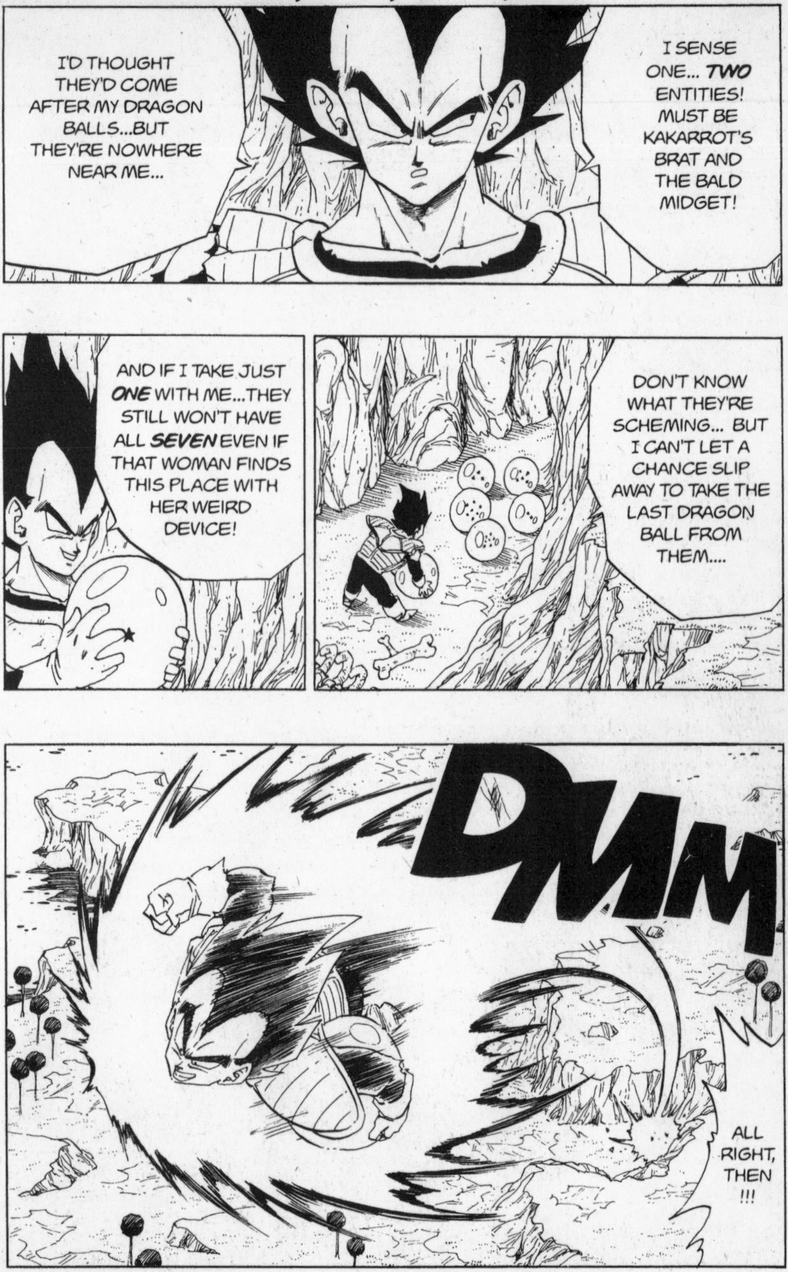

I SENSE ONE... TWO ENTITIES! MUST BE KAKARROT'S BRAT AND THE BALD MIDGET!
I'D THOUGHT THEY'D COME AFTER MY DRAGON BALLS...BUT THEY'RE NOWHERE NEAR ME...
DON'T KNOW WHAT THEY'RE SCHEMING... BUT I CAN'T LET A CHANCE SLIP AWAY TO TAKE THE LAST DRAGON BALL FROM THEM....
AND IF I TAKE JUST ONE WITH ME...THEY STILL WON'T HAVE ALL SEVEN EVEN IF THAT WOMAN FINDS THIS PLACE WITH HER WEIRD DEVICE!
DMM!
ALL RIGHT, THEN !!!

THIS TIME...I LET *NOTHING* STAND IN MY WAY!!!

HYAAAH ～!!!!

VOOOSH

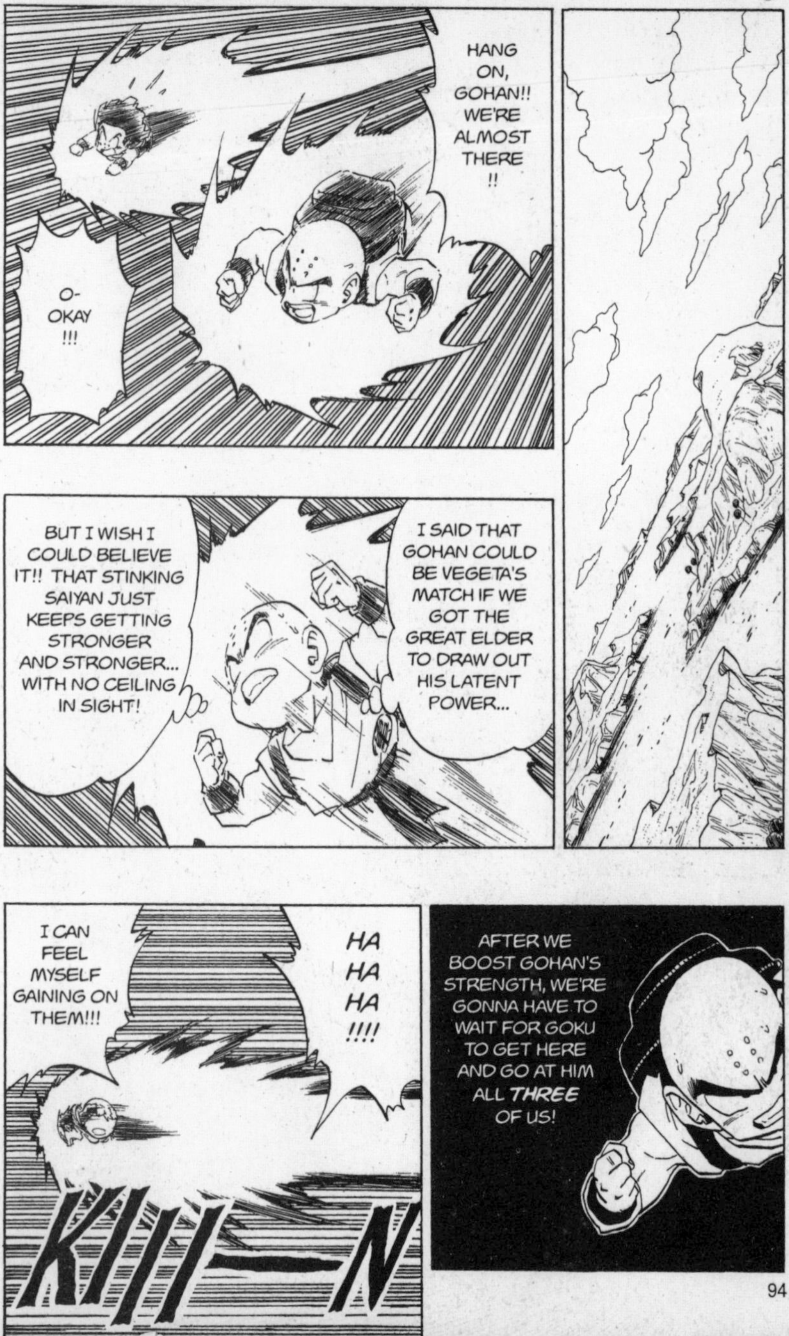
HANG ON, GOHAN!! WE'RE ALMOST THERE !!
O-OKAY !!!
I SAID THAT GOHAN COULD BE VEGETA'S MATCH IF WE GOT THE GREAT ELDER TO DRAW OUT HIS LATENT POWER...
BUT I WISH I COULD BELIEVE IT!! THAT STINKING SAIYAN JUST KEEPS GETTING STRONGER AND STRONGER... WITH NO CEILING IN SIGHT!
AFTER WE BOOST GOHAN'S STRENGTH, WE'RE GONNA HAVE TO WAIT FOR GOKU TO GET HERE AND GO AT HIM ALL *THREE* OF US!
HA HA HA !!!!
I CAN FEEL MYSELF GAINING ON THEM!!!
KIII—N

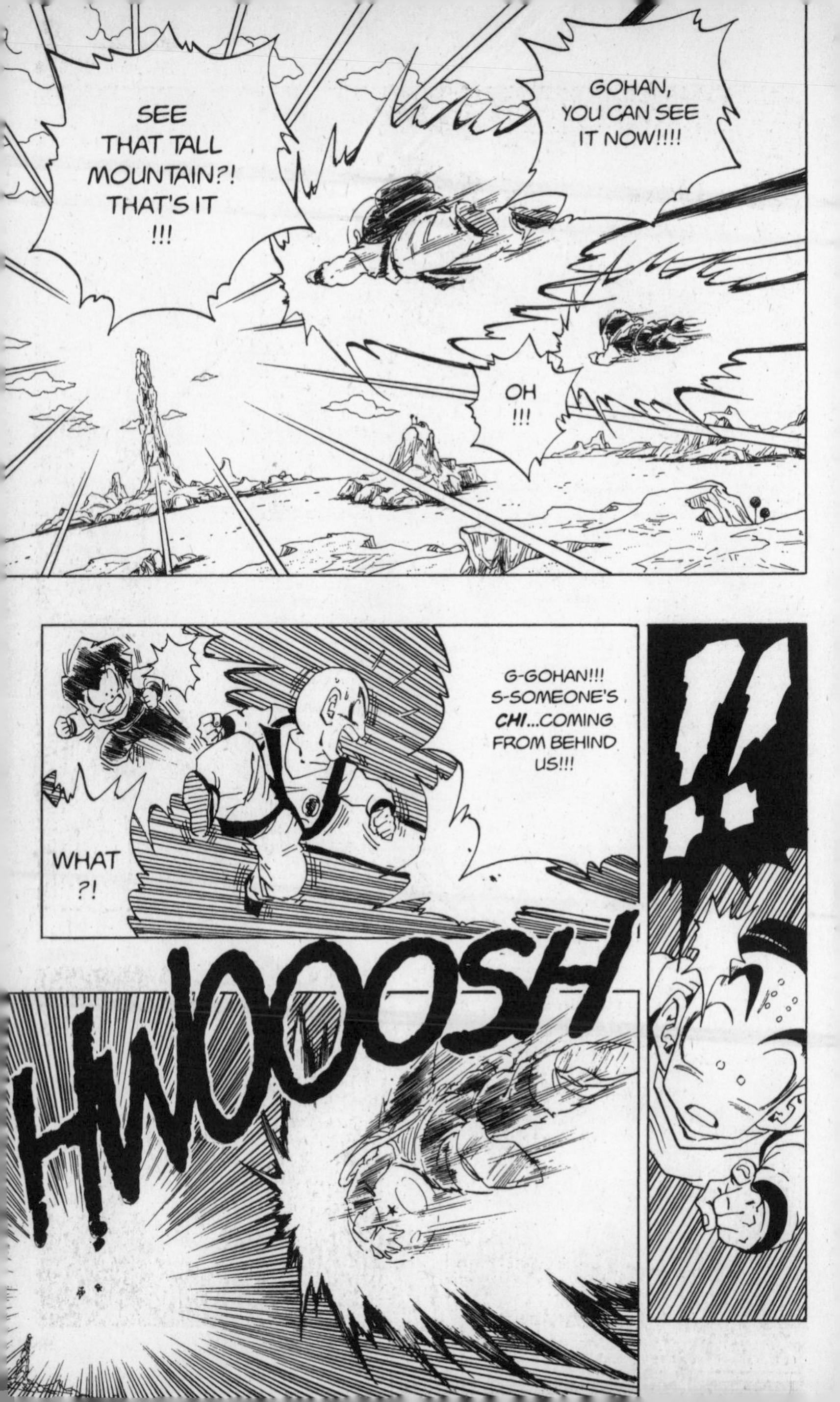
GOHAN, YOU CAN SEE IT NOW!!!!
SEE THAT TALL MOUNTAIN?! THAT'S IT !!!
OH !!!
!!
G-GOHAN!!! S-SOMEONE'S ***CHI***...COMING FROM BEHIND US!!!
WHAT ?!
HWOOOSH

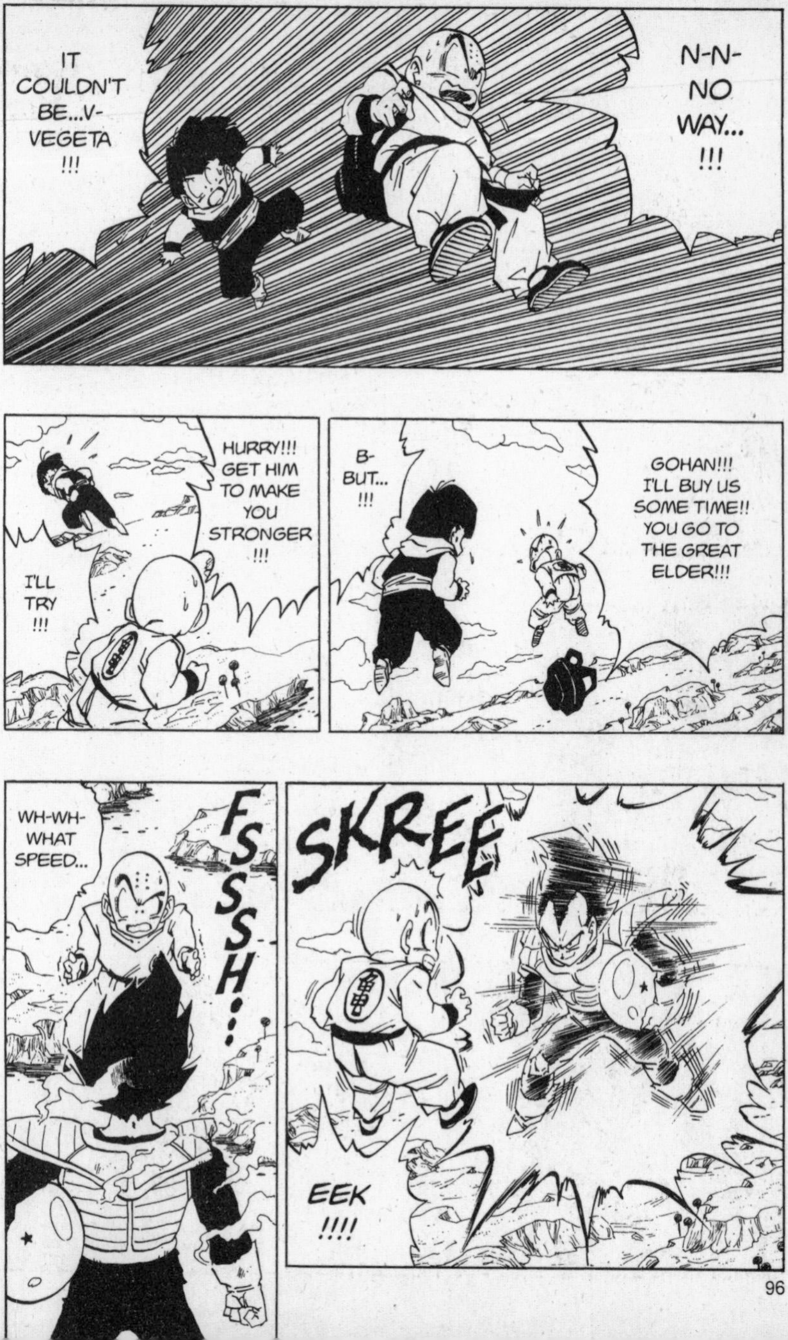
N-N- NO WAY... !!!
IT COULDN'T BE...V- VEGETA !!!
GOHAN!!! I'LL BUY US SOME TIME!! YOU GO TO THE GREAT ELDER!!!
B- BUT... !!!
HURRY!!! GET HIM TO MAKE YOU STRONGER !!!
I'LL TRY !!!
SKREE
EEK !!!!
FSSSH...
WH-WH- WHAT SPEED...

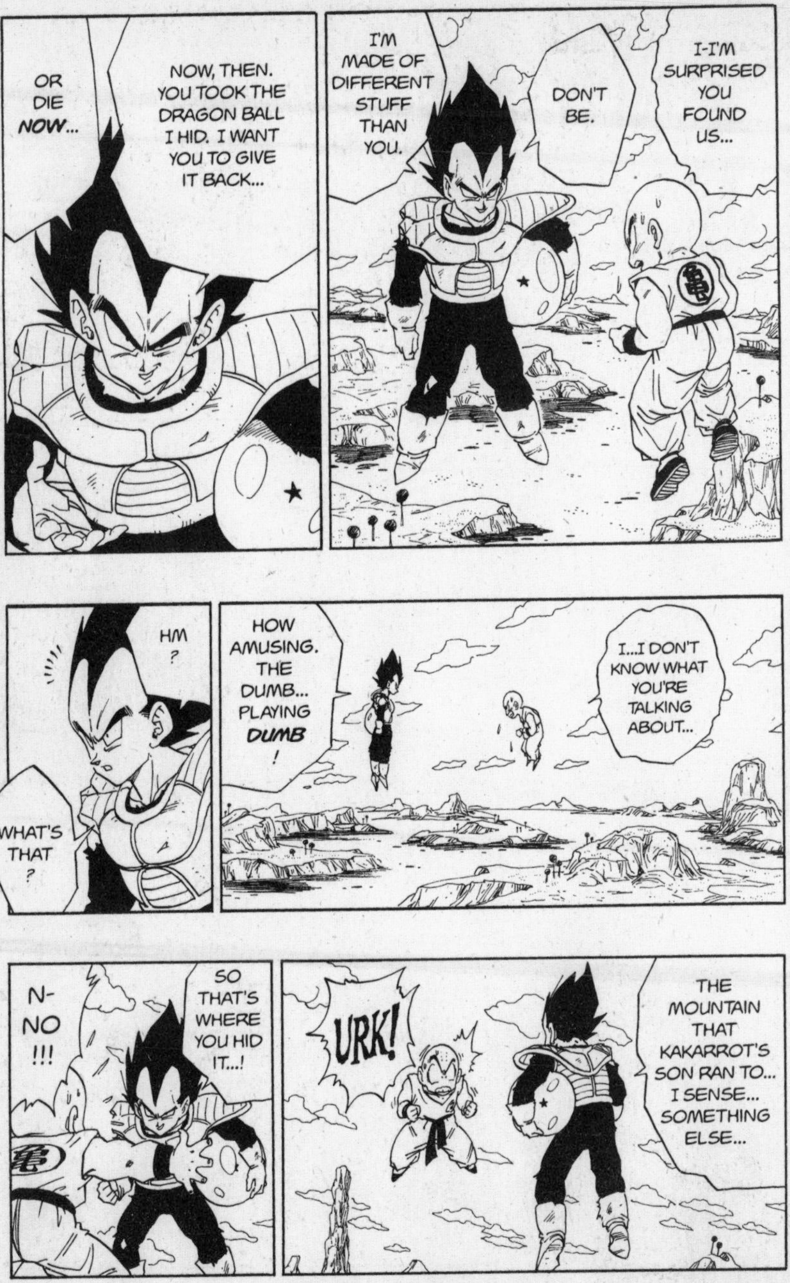

I-I'M SURPRISED YOU FOUND US...
DON'T BE.
I'M MADE OF DIFFERENT STUFF THAN YOU.
NOW, THEN. YOU TOOK THE DRAGON BALL I HID. I WANT YOU TO GIVE IT BACK...
OR DIE NOW...
I...I DON'T KNOW WHAT YOU'RE TALKING ABOUT...
HOW AMUSING. THE DUMB... PLAYING DUMB!
HM?
WHAT'S THAT?
THE MOUNTAIN THAT KAKARROT'S SON RAN TO... I SENSE... SOMETHING ELSE...
URK!
SO THAT'S WHERE YOU HID IT...!
N-NO!!!

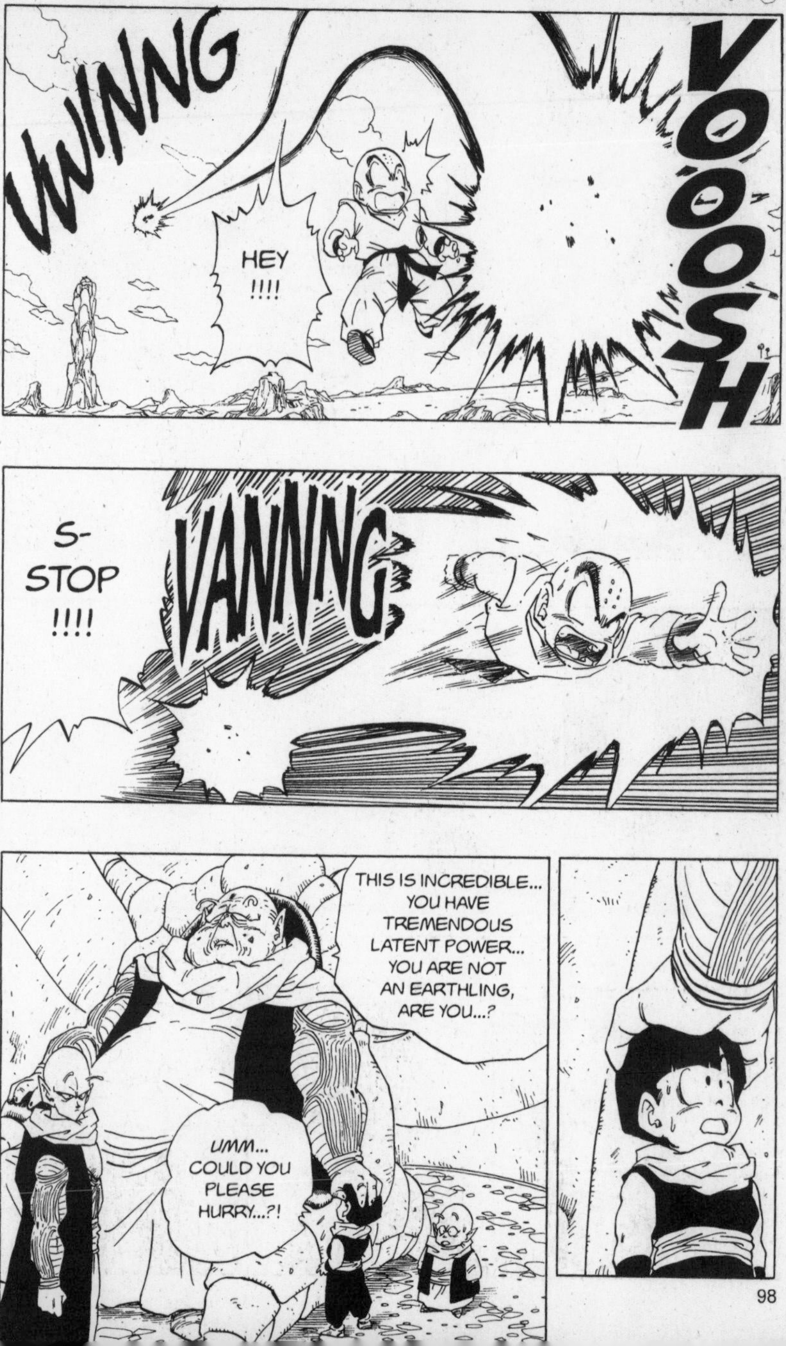
VOOOSH
HEY !!!!
WINNG
VANNNG
S- STOP !!!!
THIS IS INCREDIBLE... YOU HAVE TREMENDOUS LATENT POWER... YOU ARE NOT AN EARTHLING, ARE YOU...?
UMM... COULD YOU PLEASE HURRY...?!

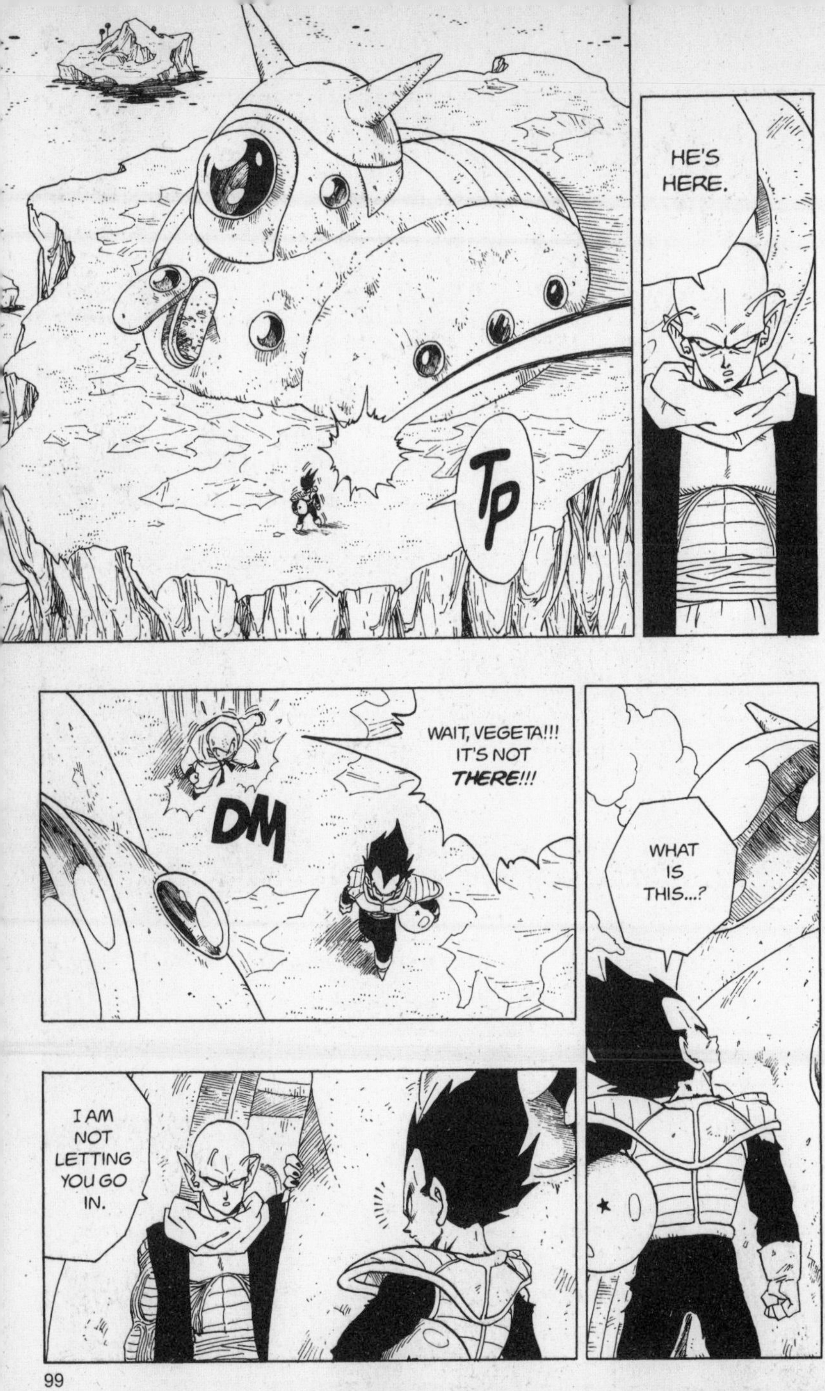
HE'S HERE.
TP
WHAT IS THIS...?
WAIT, VEGETA!!! IT'S NOT *THERE*!!!
DM
I AM NOT LETTING YOU GO IN.

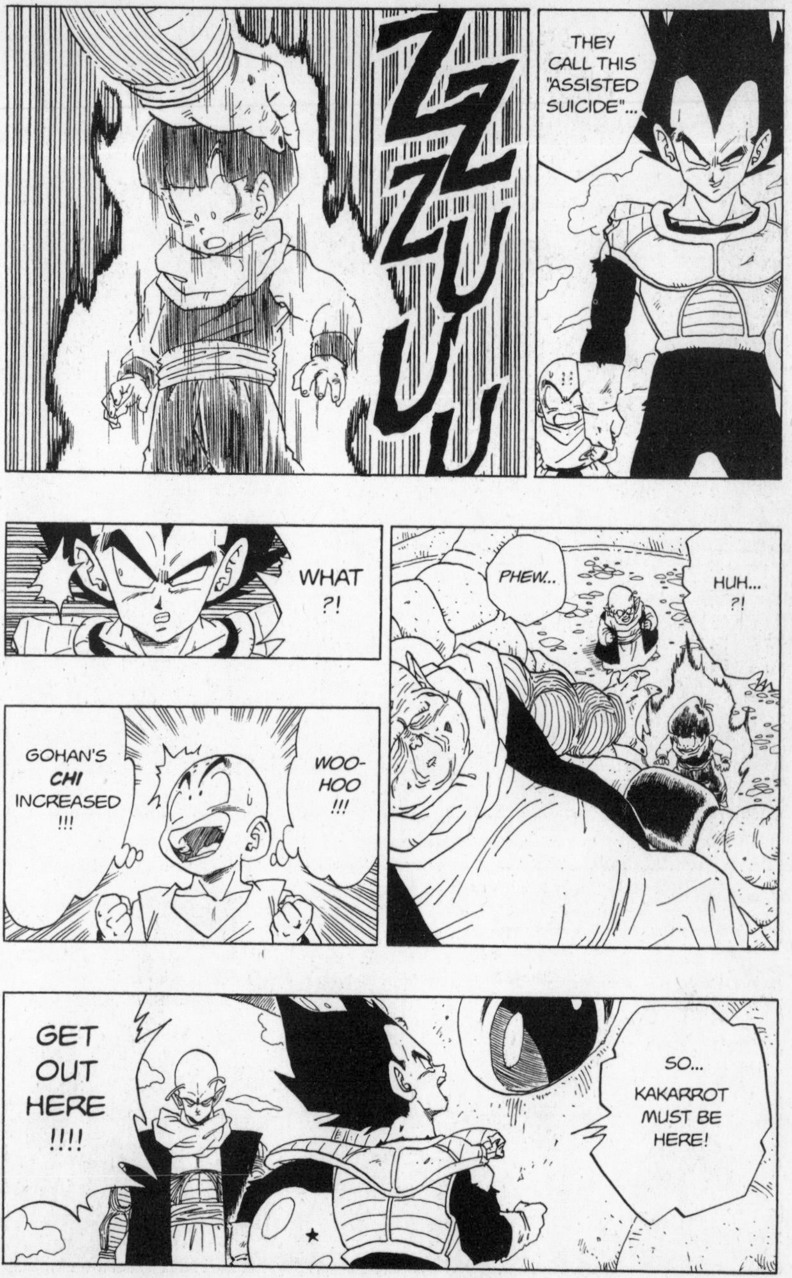

THEY CALL THIS "ASSISTED SUICIDE"...
ZZZUUU
HUH... ?!
PHEW...
WHAT ?!
WOO-HOO !!!
GOHAN'S **CHI** INCREASED !!!
SO... KAKARROT MUST BE HERE!
GET OUT HERE !!!!

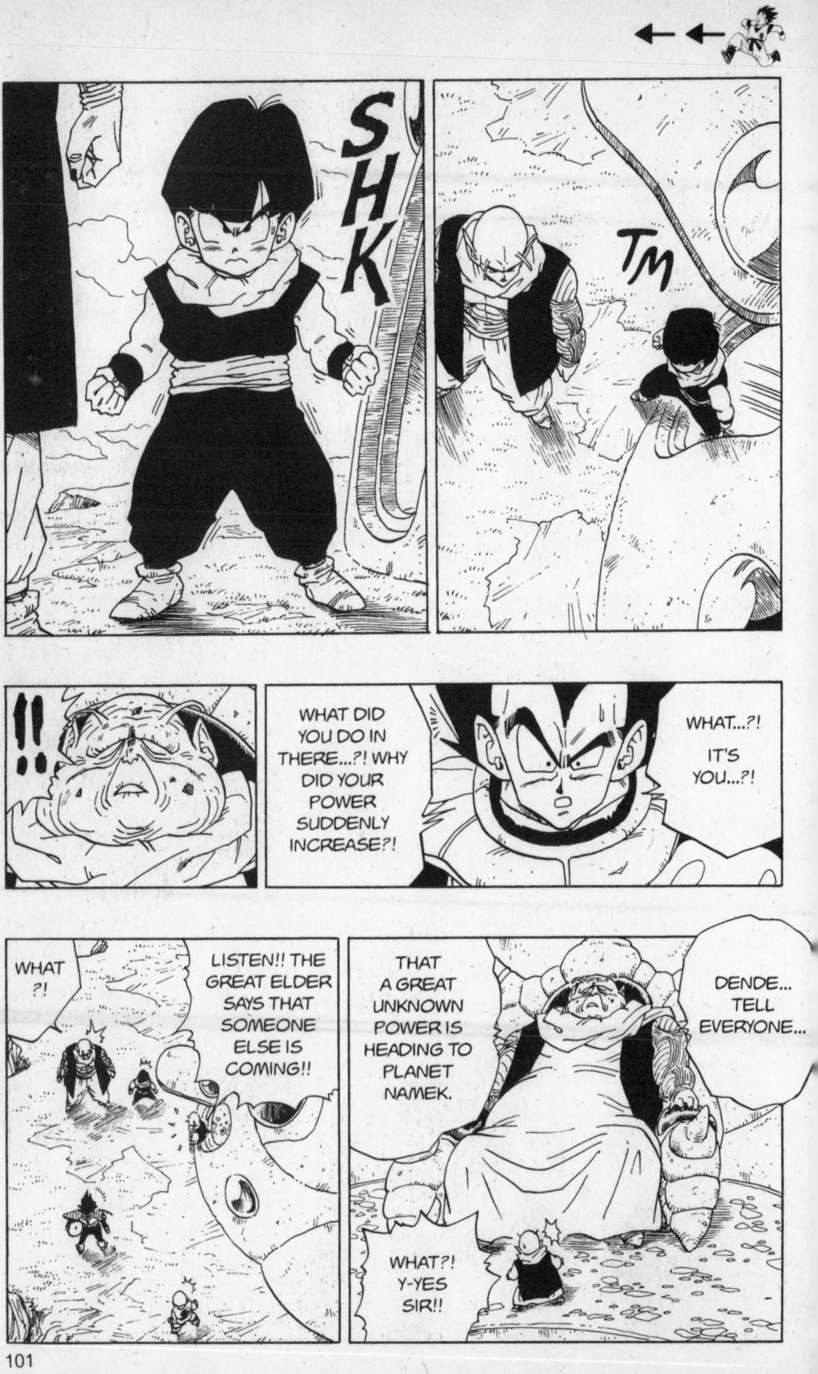
TM
SHK
WHAT...?!
IT'S YOU...?!
WHAT DID YOU DO IN THERE...?! WHY DID YOUR POWER SUDDENLY INCREASE?!
!!
DENDE... TELL EVERYONE...
THAT A GREAT UNKNOWN POWER IS HEADING TO PLANET NAMEK.
WHAT?! Y-YES SIR!!
LISTEN!! THE GREAT ELDER SAYS THAT SOMEONE ELSE IS COMING!!
WHAT ?!

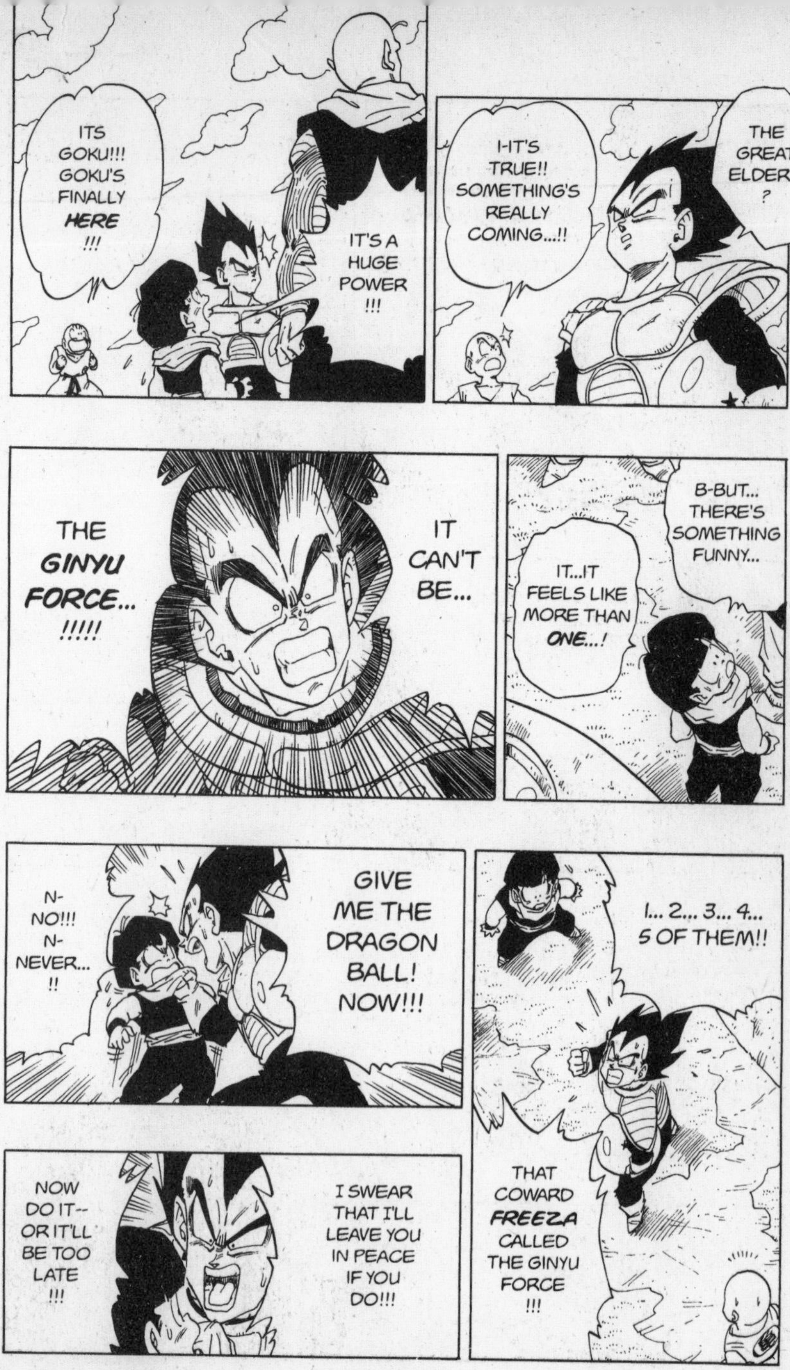

THE GREAT ELDER... ?
I-IT'S TRUE!! SOMETHING'S REALLY COMING...!!
IT'S A HUGE POWER !!!
ITS GOKU!!! GOKU'S FINALLY HERE !!!
B-BUT... THERE'S SOMETHING FUNNY...
IT...IT FEELS LIKE MORE THAN ONE...!
IT CAN'T BE...
THE GINYU FORCE... !!!!!
1... 2... 3... 4... 5 OF THEM!!
THAT COWARD FREEZA CALLED THE GINYU FORCE !!!
GIVE ME THE DRAGON BALL! NOW!!!
N-NO!!! N-NEVER... !!
I SWEAR THAT I'LL LEAVE YOU IN PEACE IF YOU DO!!!
NOW DO IT-- OR IT'LL BE TOO LATE !!!

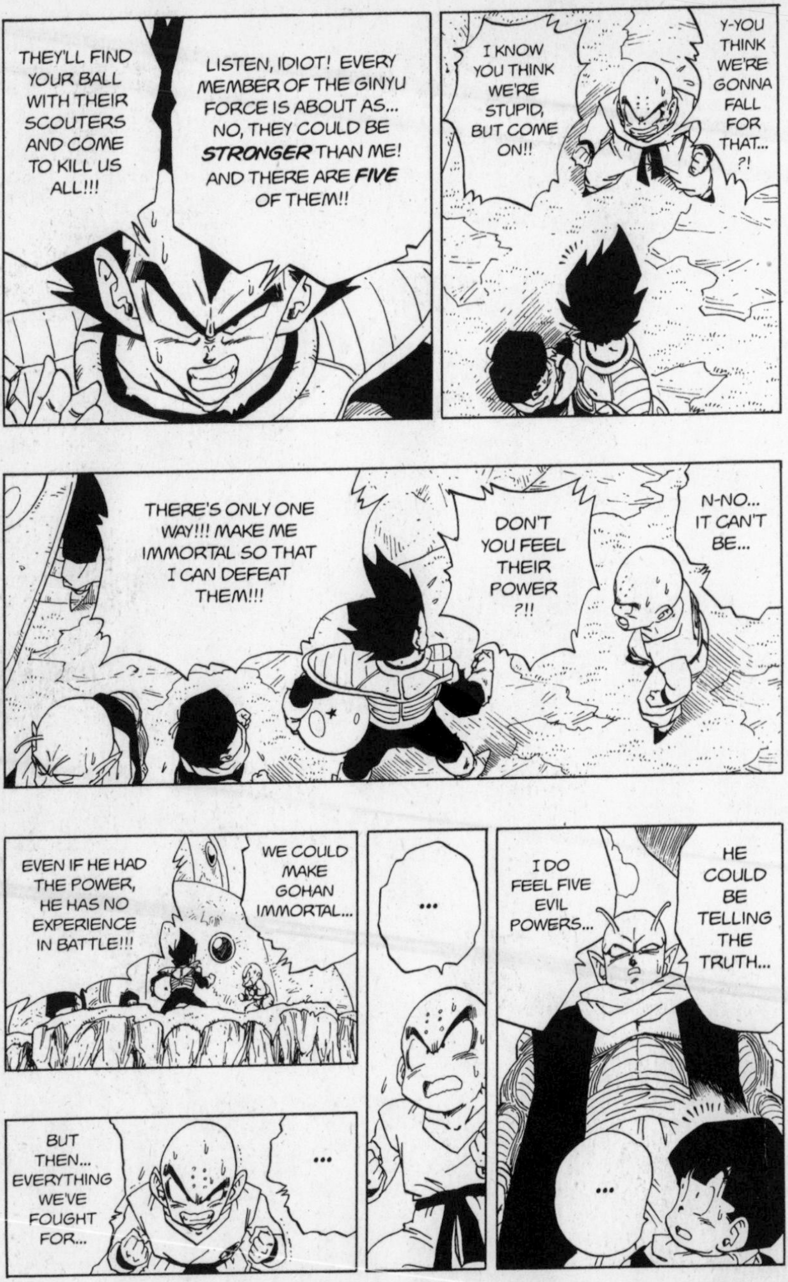
Y-YOU THINK WE'RE GONNA FALL FOR THAT...?!
I KNOW YOU THINK WE'RE STUPID, BUT COME ON!!
LISTEN, IDIOT! EVERY MEMBER OF THE GINYU FORCE IS ABOUT AS... NO, THEY COULD BE STRONGER THAN ME! AND THERE ARE FIVE OF THEM!!
THEY'LL FIND YOUR BALL WITH THEIR SCOUTERS AND COME TO KILL US ALL!!!
N-NO... IT CAN'T BE...
DON'T YOU FEEL THEIR POWER?!!
THERE'S ONLY ONE WAY!!! MAKE ME IMMORTAL SO THAT I CAN DEFEAT THEM!!!
HE COULD BE TELLING THE TRUTH...
I DO FEEL FIVE EVIL POWERS...
...
...
WE COULD MAKE GOHAN IMMORTAL...
EVEN IF HE HAD THE POWER, HE HAS NO EXPERIENCE IN BATTLE!!!
...
BUT THEN... EVERYTHING WE'VE FOUGHT FOR...

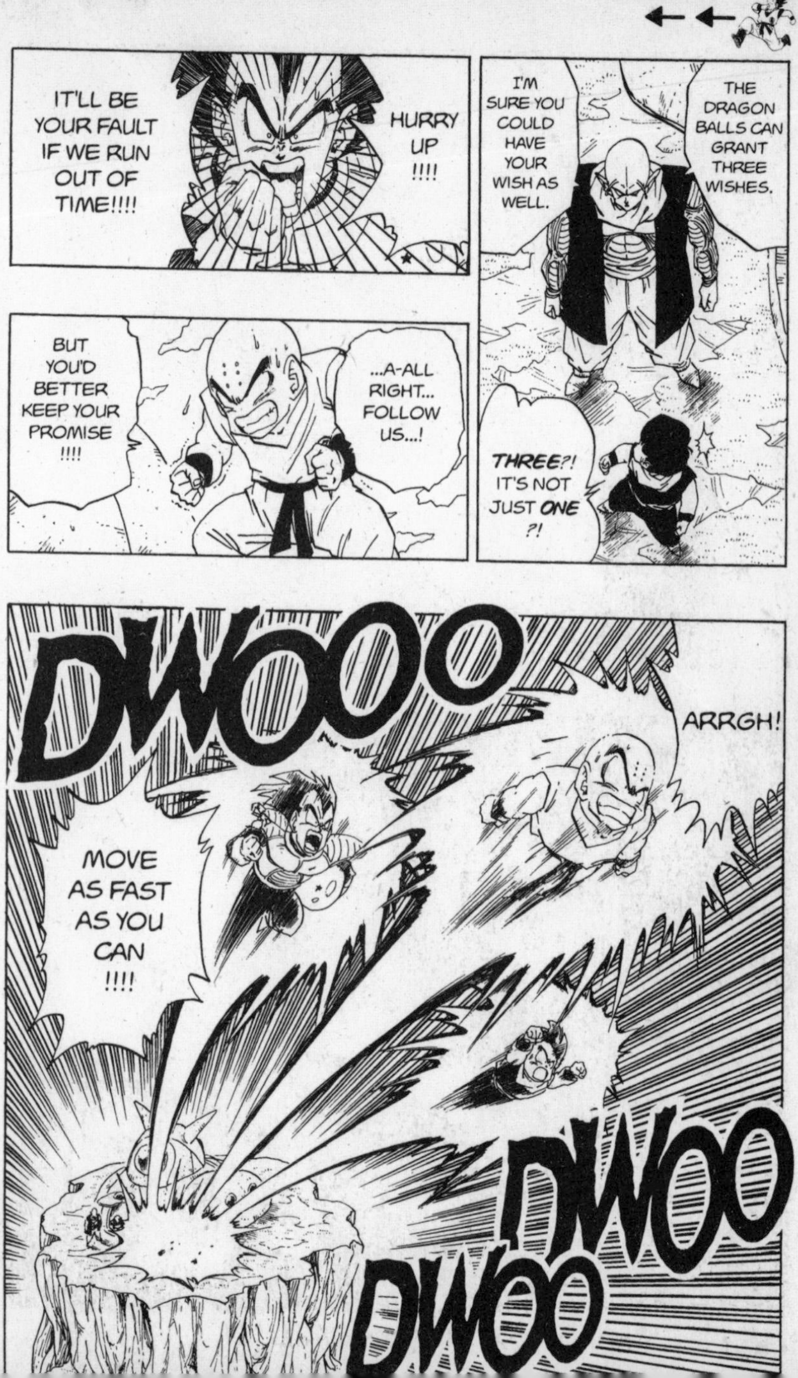
THE DRAGON BALLS CAN GRANT THREE WISHES.
I'M SURE YOU COULD HAVE YOUR WISH AS WELL.
THREE?! IT'S NOT JUST ONE ?!
HURRY UP !!!!
IT'LL BE YOUR FAULT IF WE RUN OUT OF TIME!!!!
...A-ALL RIGHT... FOLLOW US...!
BUT YOU'D BETTER KEEP YOUR PROMISE !!!!
DWOOO
ARRGH!
MOVE AS FAST AS YOU CAN !!!!
DWOO
DWOO

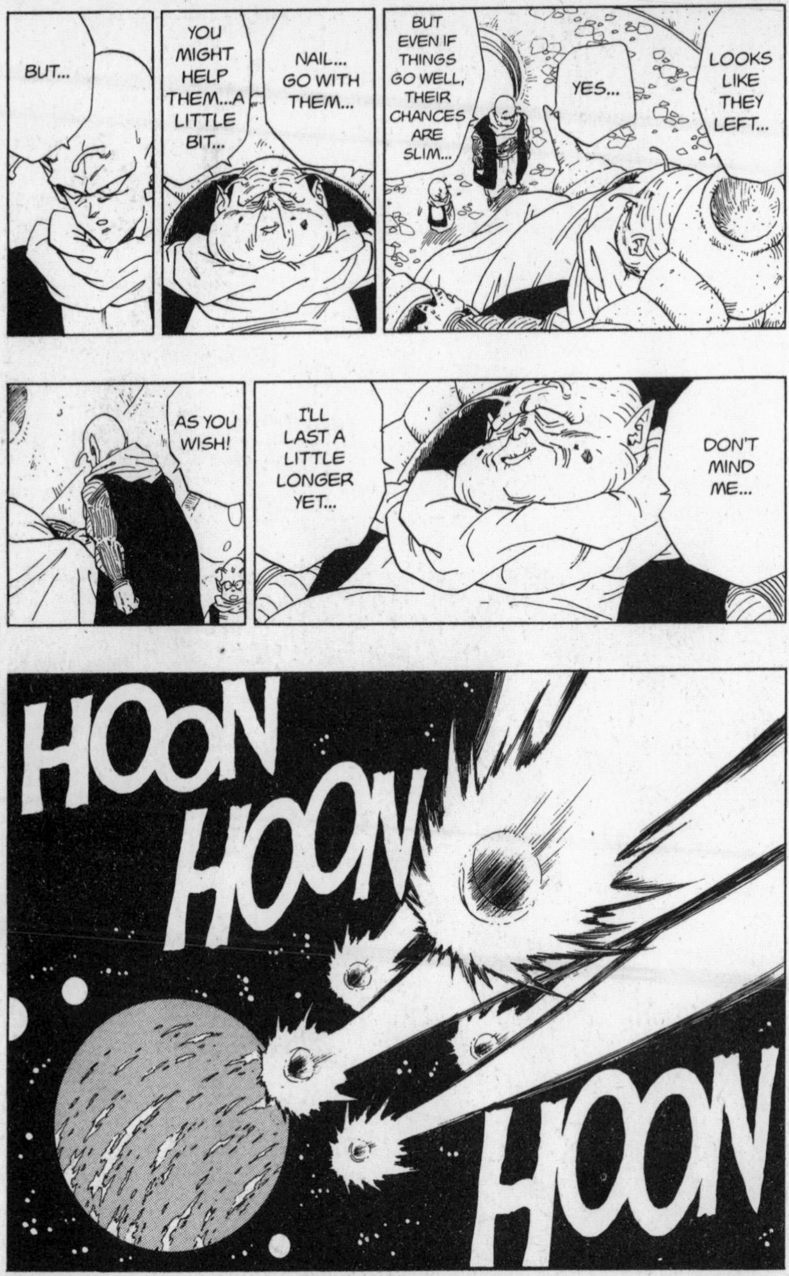
LOOKS LIKE THEY LEFT...
YES...
BUT EVEN IF THINGS GO WELL, THEIR CHANCES ARE SLIM...
NAIL... GO WITH THEM...
YOU MIGHT HELP THEM...A LITTLE BIT...
BUT...
DON'T MIND ME...
I'LL LAST A LITTLE LONGER YET...
AS YOU WISH!
HOON
HOON
HOON

NEXT: *Race for the Dragon Balls!!!*

DBZ:78 • The Ginyu Force

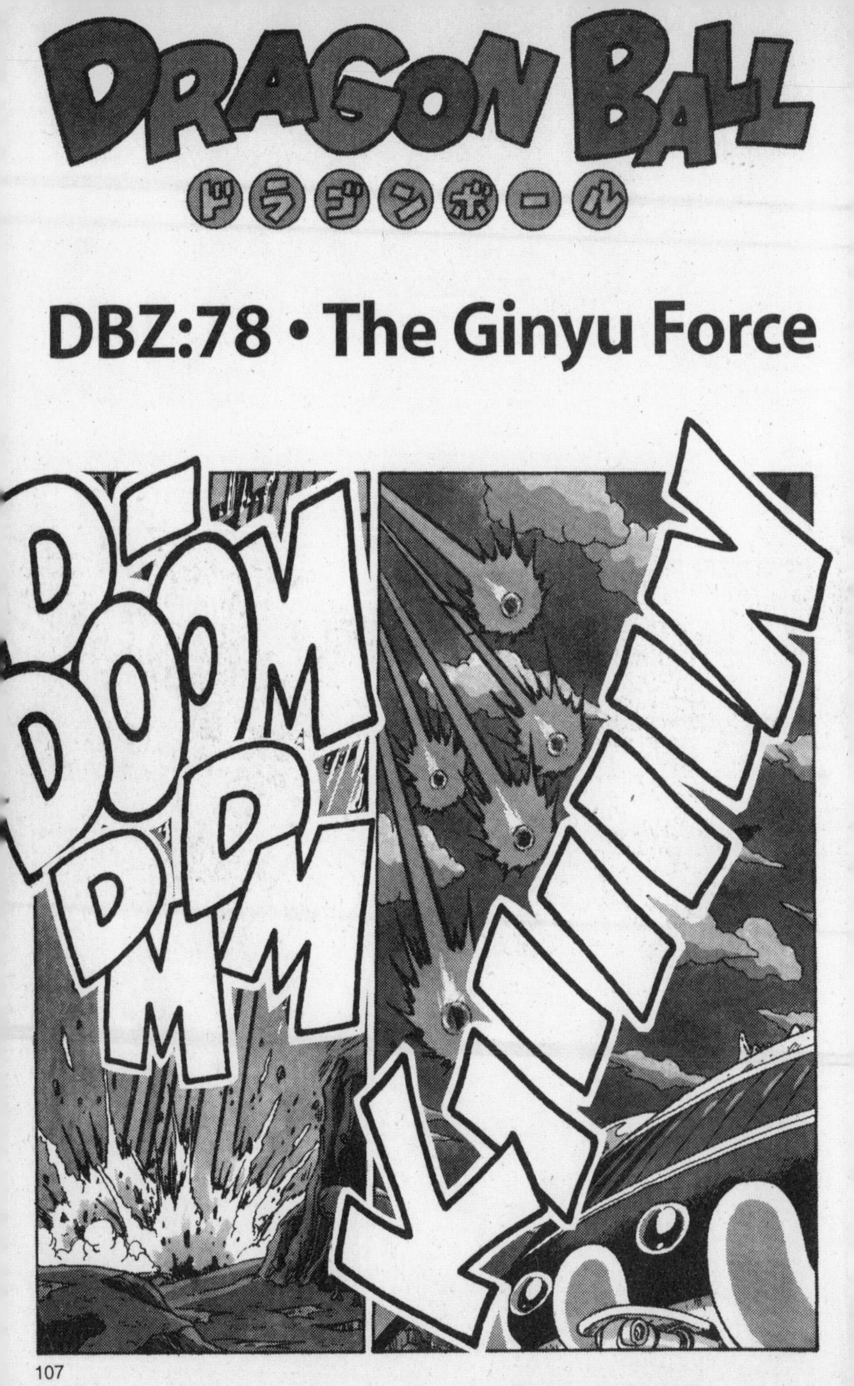

DOOM
DOOM

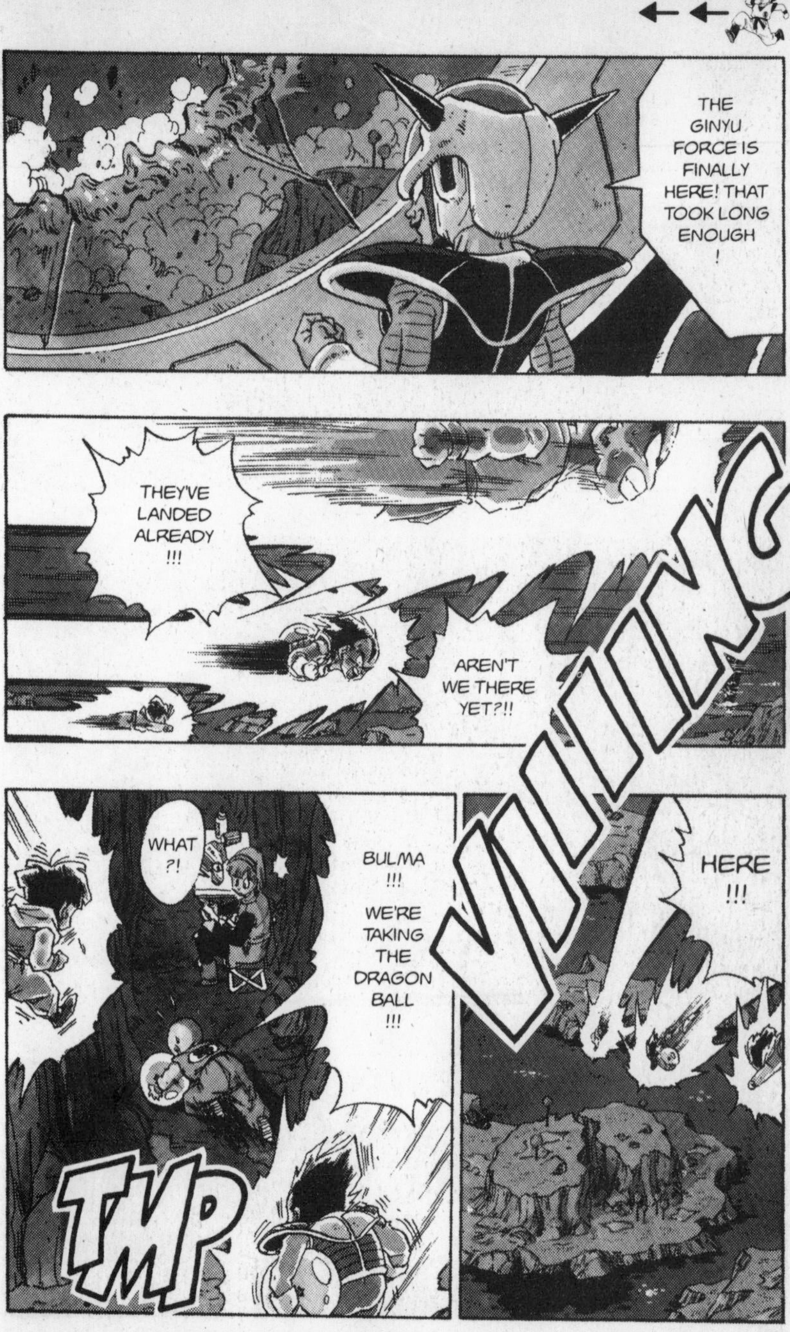

THE GINYU FORCE IS FINALLY HERE! THAT TOOK LONG ENOUGH!
AREN'T WE THERE YET?!!
THEY'VE LANDED ALREADY!!!
VIIIING
HERE!!!
BULMA!!! WE'RE TAKING THE DRAGON BALL!!!
WHAT?!
TMP

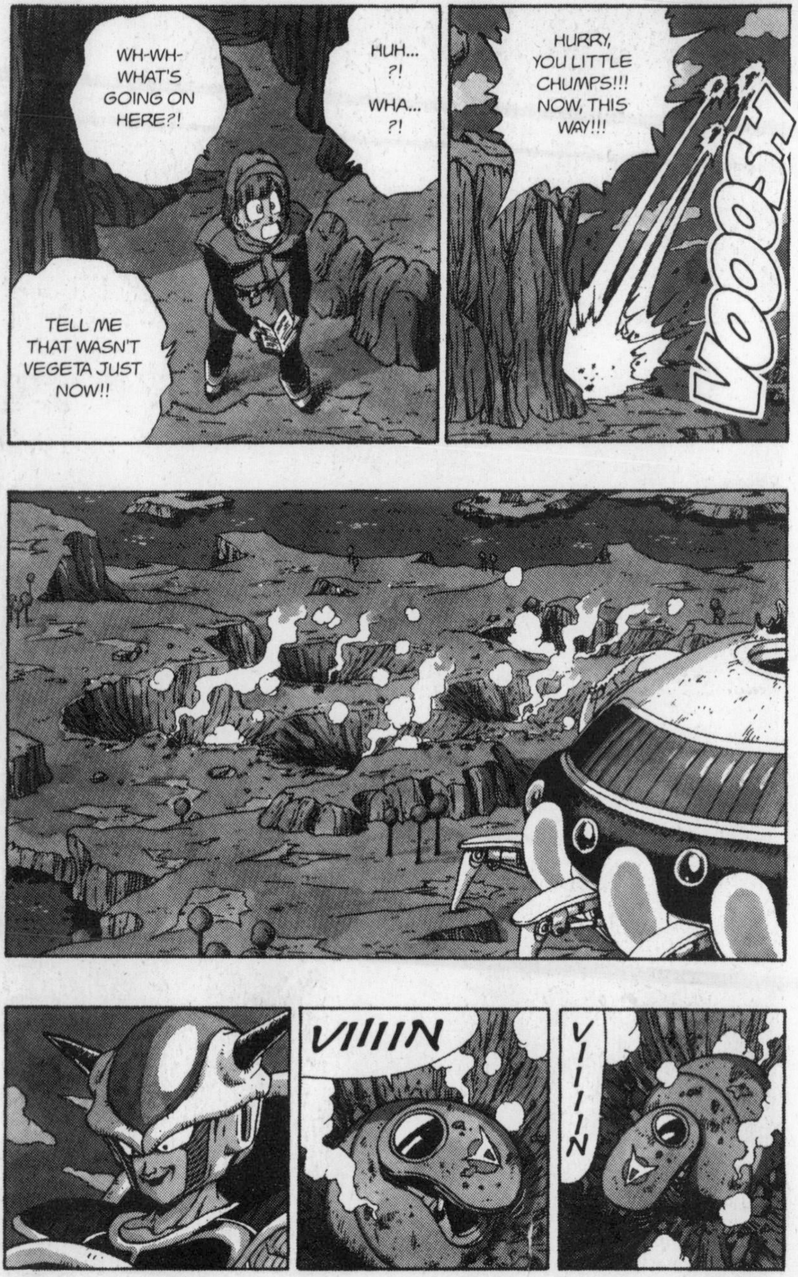
HURRY, YOU LITTLE CHUMPS!!! NOW, THIS WAY!!!
VOOOSH
HUH... ?!
WHA... ?!
WH-WH-WHAT'S GOING ON HERE?!
TELL ME THAT WASN'T VEGETA JUST NOW!!
VIIIIN
VIIIN

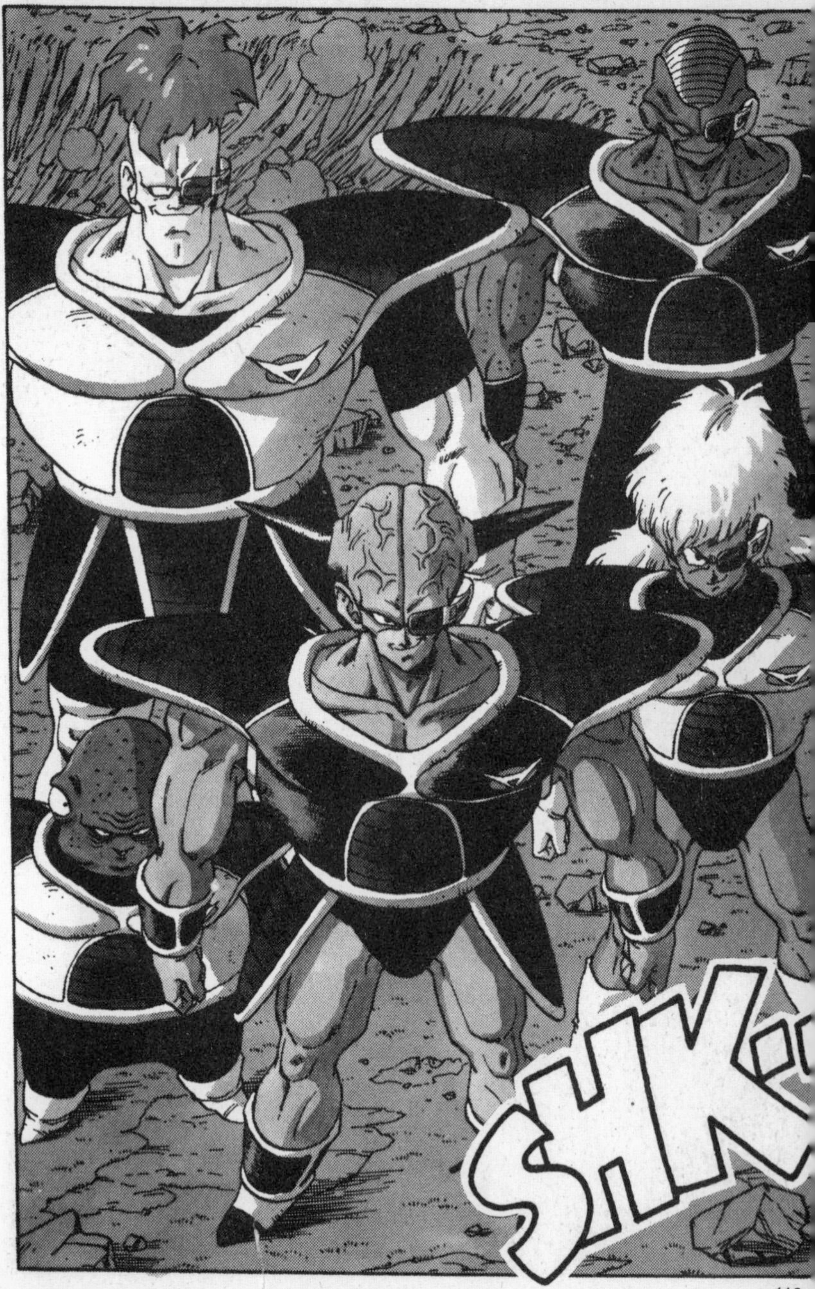
SHK

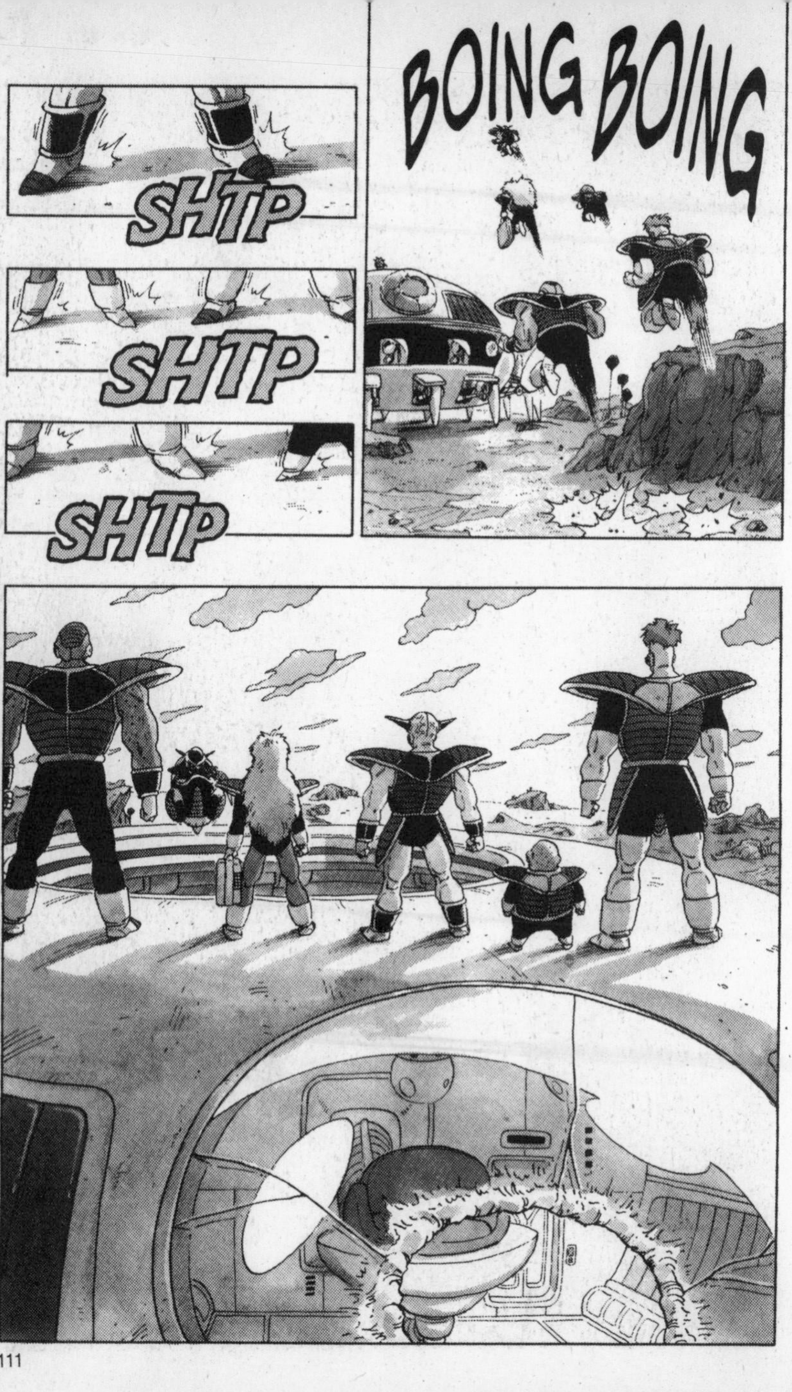

BOING BOING
SHTP
SHTP
SHTP

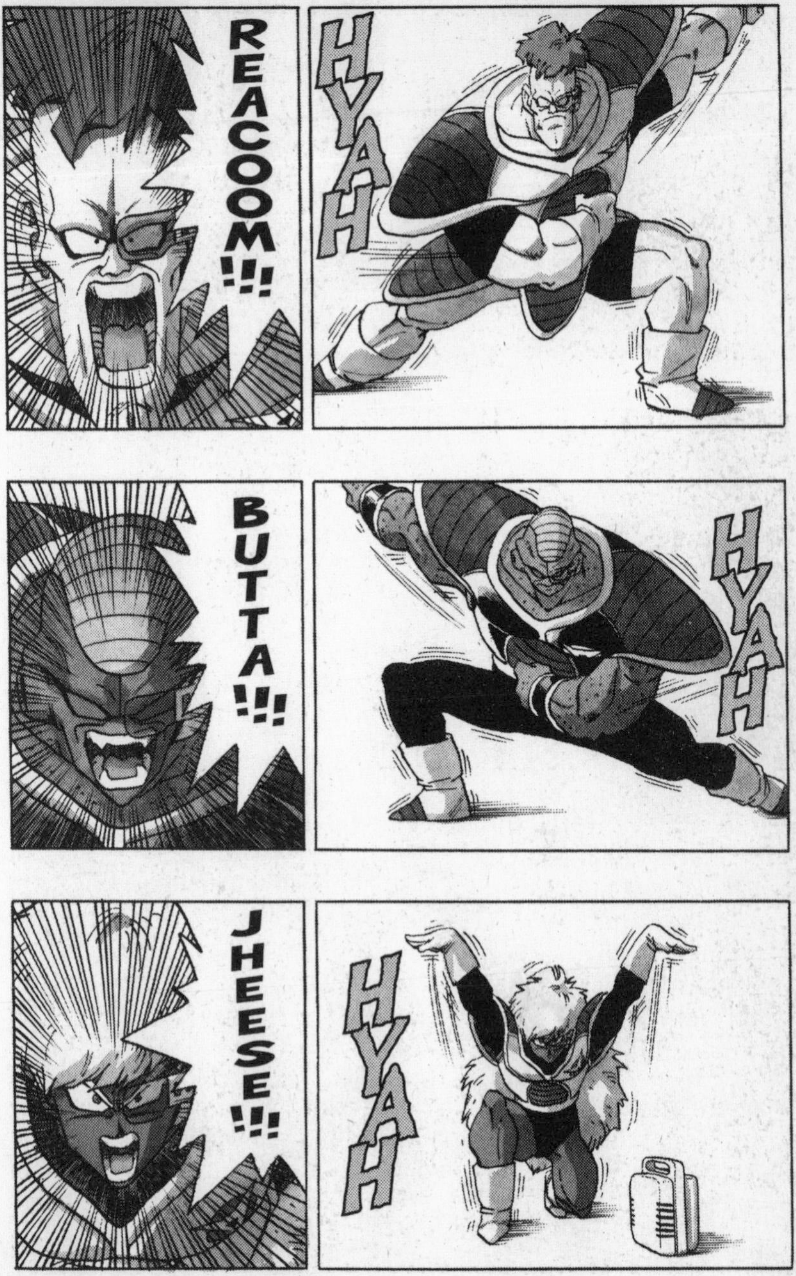
HYAH
REACOOM!!!
HYAH
BUTTA!!!
HYAH
JHEESE!!!

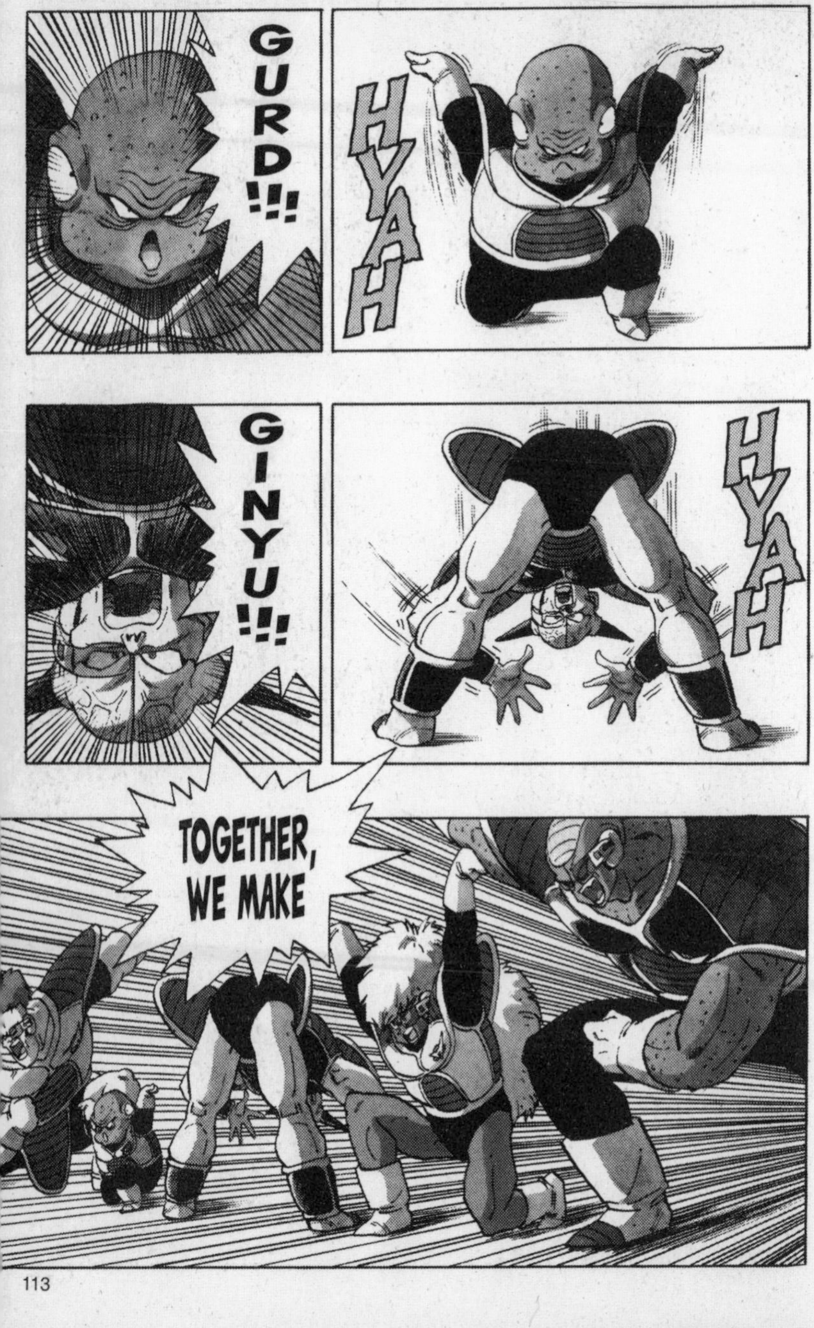
HYAH
GURD!!!
HYAH
GINYU!!!
TOGETHER, WE MAKE

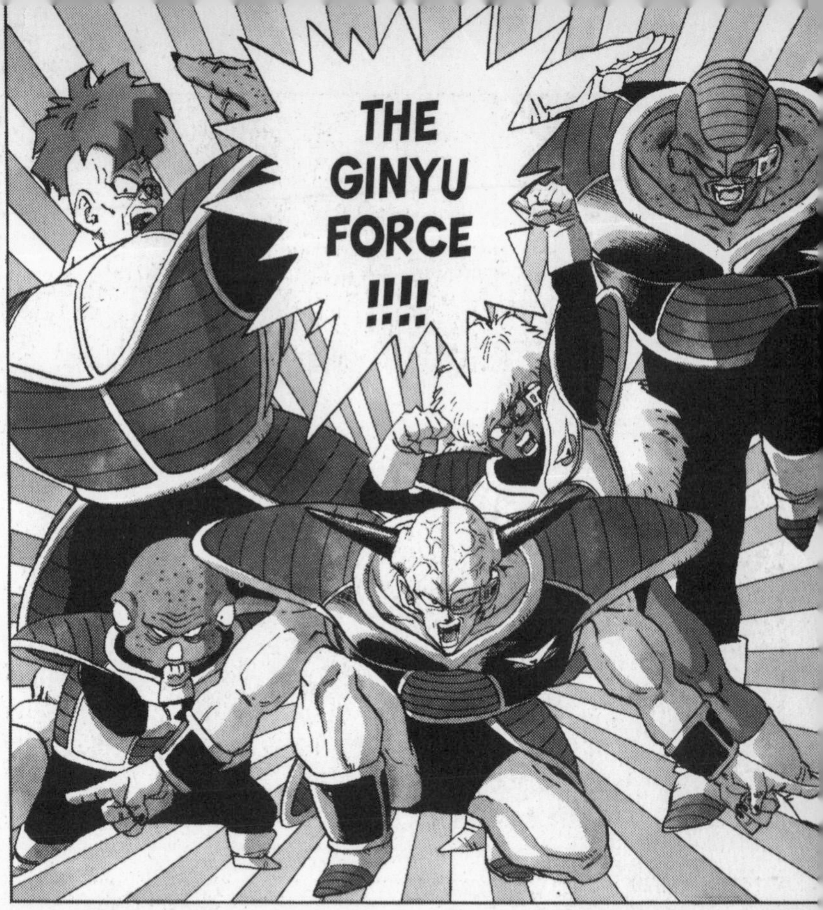
THE GINYU FORCE !!!!
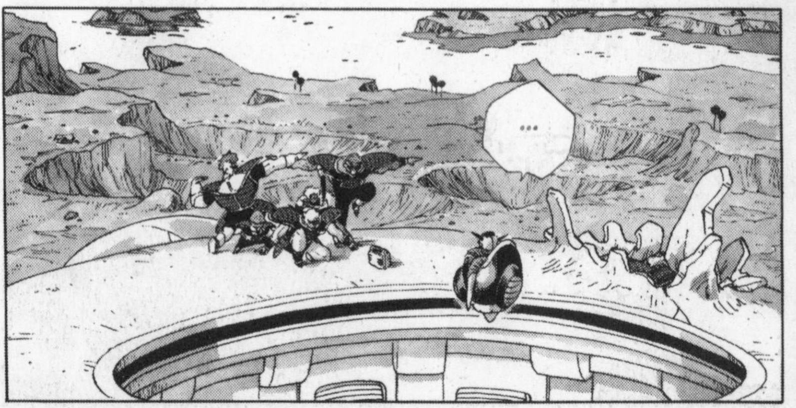
...

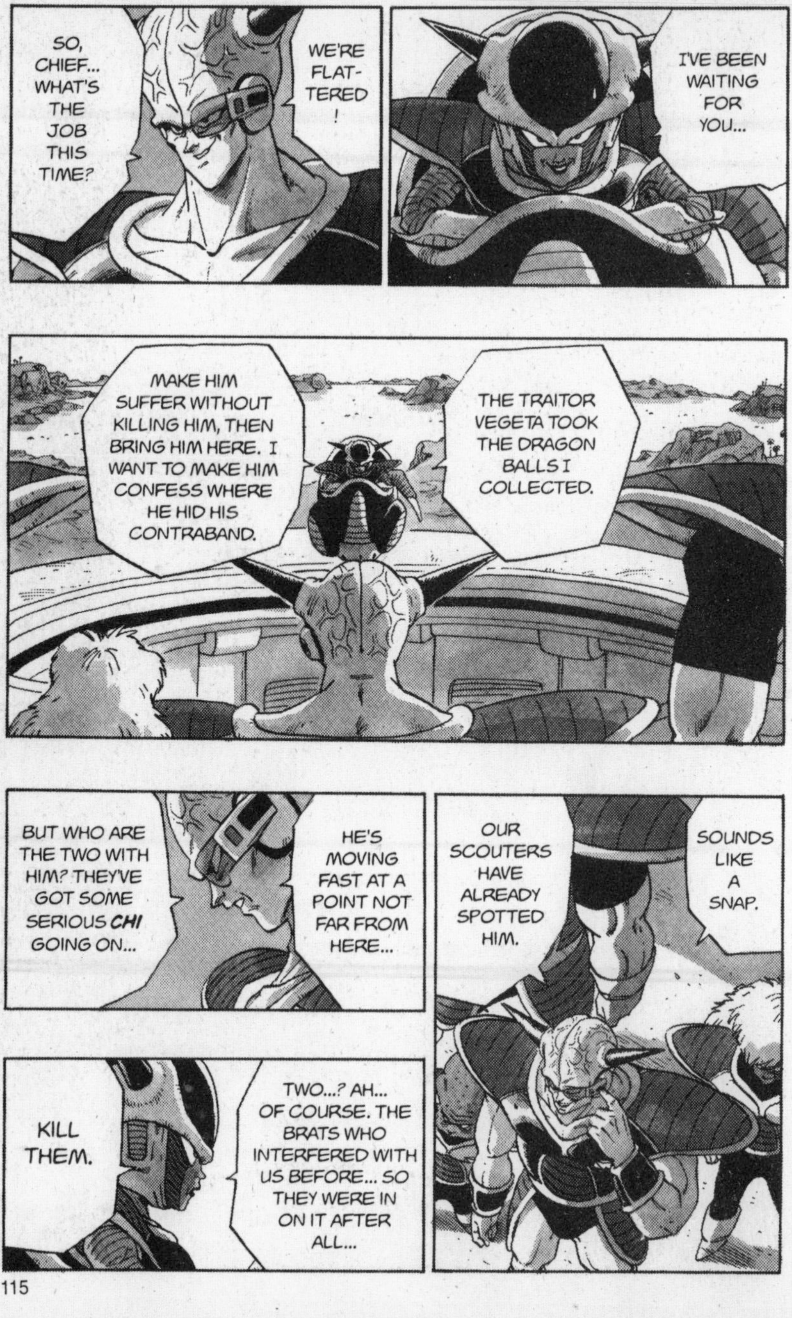
I'VE BEEN WAITING FOR YOU...
WE'RE FLATTERED!
SO, CHIEF... WHAT'S THE JOB THIS TIME?
THE TRAITOR VEGETA TOOK THE DRAGON BALLS I COLLECTED.
MAKE HIM SUFFER WITHOUT KILLING HIM, THEN BRING HIM HERE. I WANT TO MAKE HIM CONFESS WHERE HE HID HIS CONTRABAND.
SOUNDS LIKE A SNAP.
OUR SCOUTERS HAVE ALREADY SPOTTED HIM.
HE'S MOVING FAST AT A POINT NOT FAR FROM HERE...
BUT WHO ARE THE TWO WITH HIM? THEY'VE GOT SOME SERIOUS ***CHI*** GOING ON...
TWO...? AH... OF COURSE. THE BRATS WHO INTERFERED WITH US BEFORE... SO THEY WERE IN ON IT AFTER ALL...
KILL THEM.

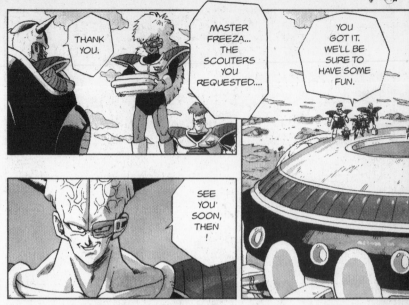

YOU GOT IT. WE'LL BE SURE TO HAVE SOME FUN.
MASTER FREEZA... THE SCOUTERS YOU REQUESTED....
THANK YOU.
SEE YOU' SOON, THEN !
FIGHT !!!
TOGETHER--
SHHOOOM

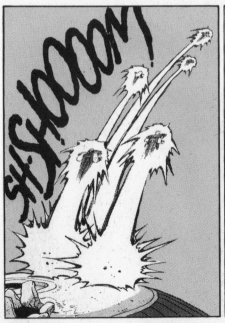

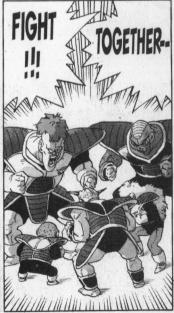

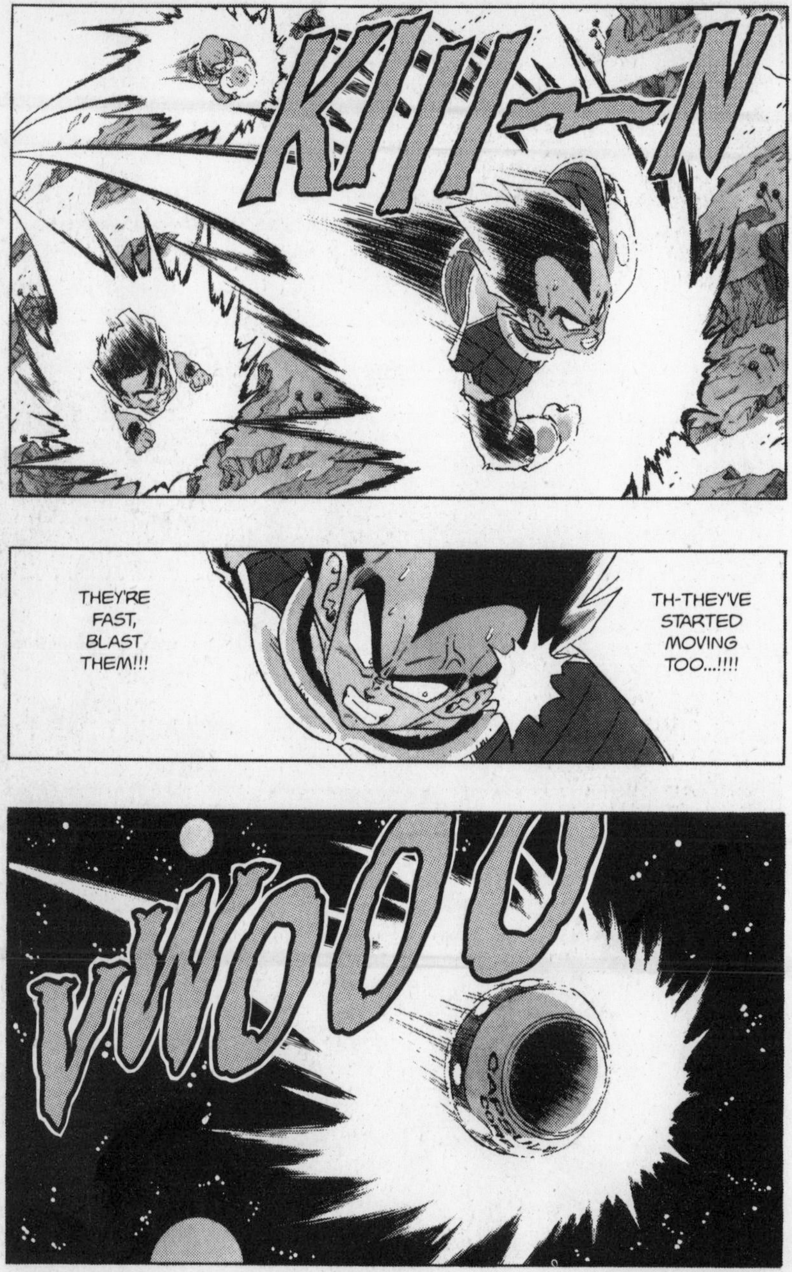
KIII~N
TH-THEY'VE STARTED MOVING TOO...!!!!
THEY'RE FAST, BLAST THEM!!!
VWOOOO

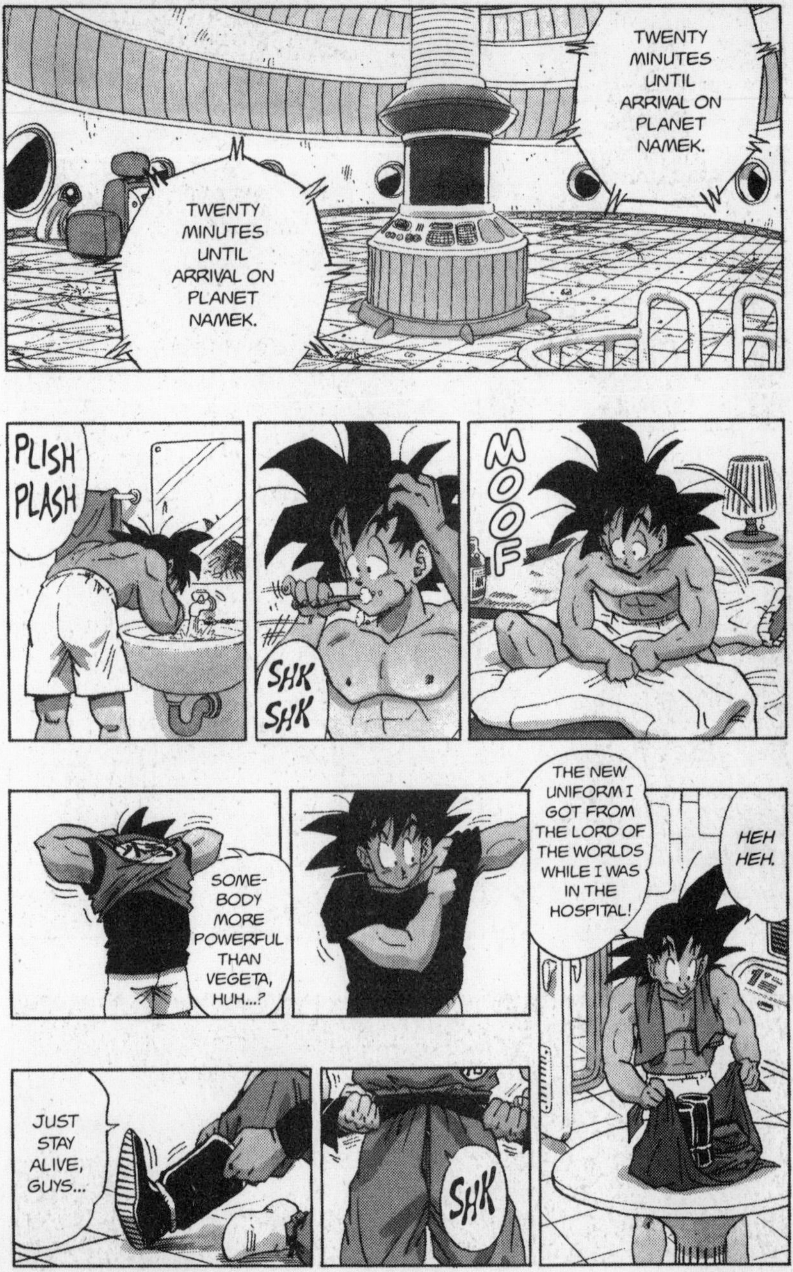
TWENTY MINUTES UNTIL ARRIVAL ON PLANET NAMEK.
TWENTY MINUTES UNTIL ARRIVAL ON PLANET NAMEK.
MOOF
SHK SHK
PLISH PLASH
THE NEW UNIFORM I GOT FROM THE LORD OF THE WORLDS WHILE I WAS IN THE HOSPITAL!
HEH HEH.
SOME-BODY MORE POWERFUL THAN VEGETA, HUH...?
SHK
JUST STAY ALIVE, GUYS...

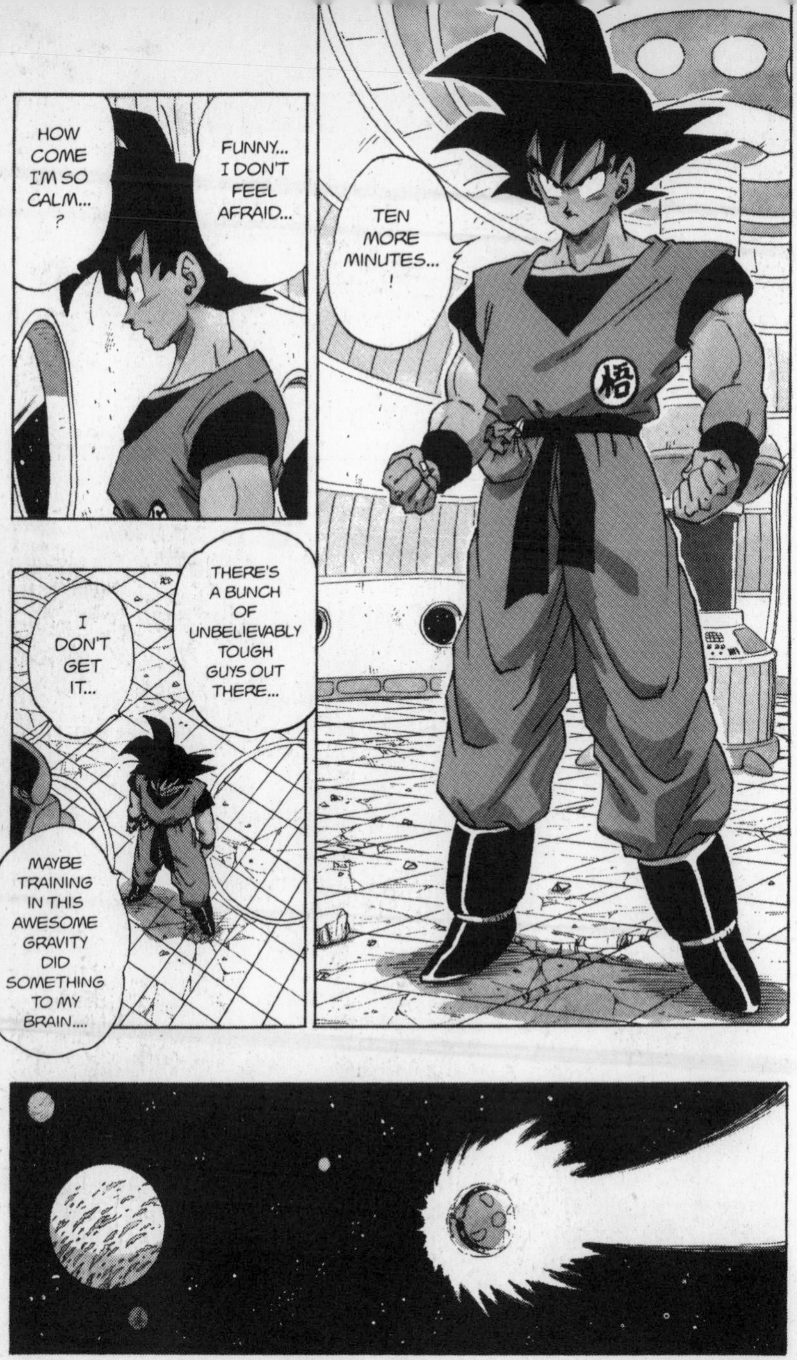
TEN MORE MINUTES...!
FUNNY... I DON'T FEEL AFRAID...
HOW COME I'M SO CALM...?
THERE'S A BUNCH OF UNBELIEVABLY TOUGH GUYS OUT THERE...
I DON'T GET IT...
MAYBE TRAINING IN THIS AWESOME GRAVITY DID SOMETHING TO MY BRAIN....

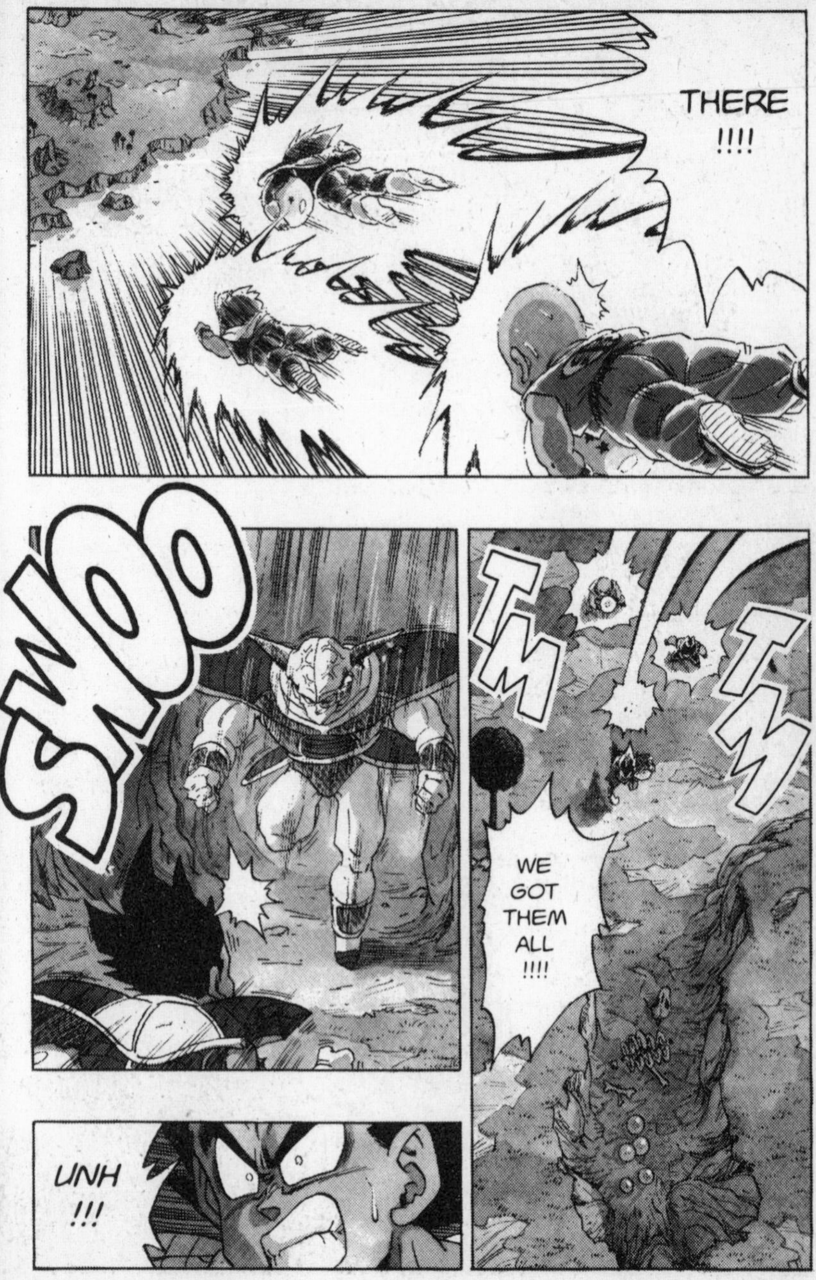
THERE !!!!
TM
TM
WE GOT THEM ALL !!!!
SWOO
UNH !!!

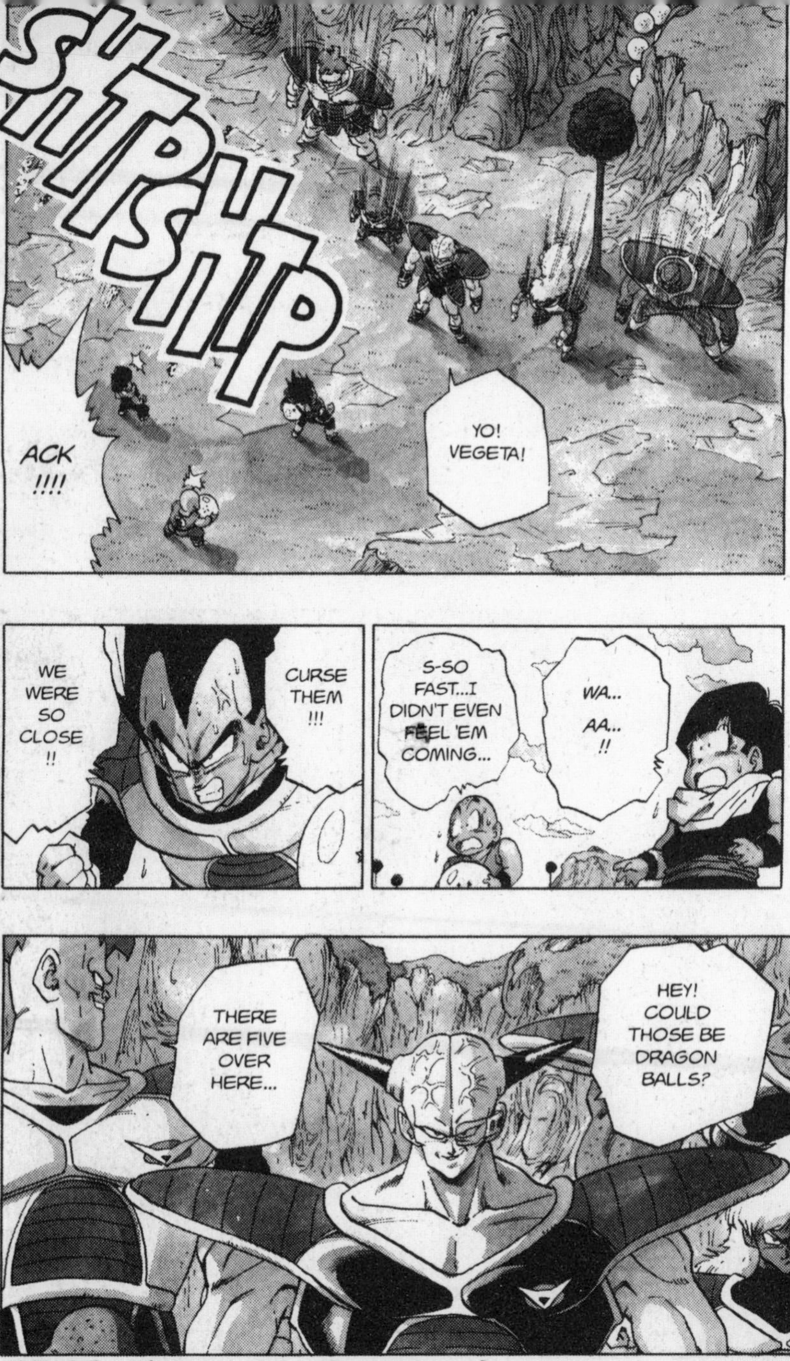
SHTPSHTP
YO! VEGETA!
ACK !!!!
S-SO FAST...I DIDN'T EVEN FEEL 'EM COMING...
WA... AA... !!
CURSE THEM !!!
WE WERE SO CLOSE !!
HEY! COULD THOSE BE DRAGON BALLS?
THERE ARE FIVE OVER HERE...

NEXT: Milking the Suspense!

DBZ:79 • Five Deadly Fighters

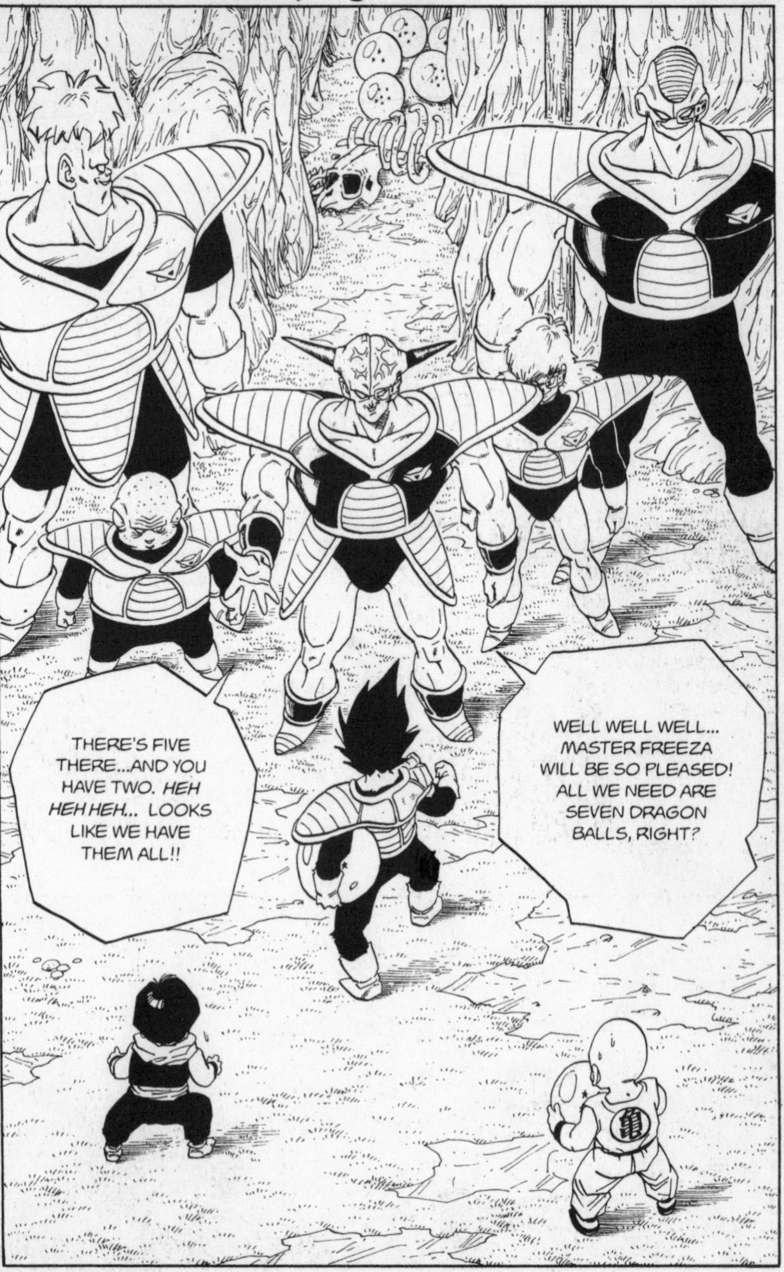
WELL WELL WELL... MASTER FREEZA WILL BE SO PLEASED! ALL WE NEED ARE SEVEN DRAGON BALLS, RIGHT?
THERE'S FIVE THERE...AND YOU HAVE TWO. *HEH HEH HEH...* LOOKS LIKE WE HAVE THEM ALL!!

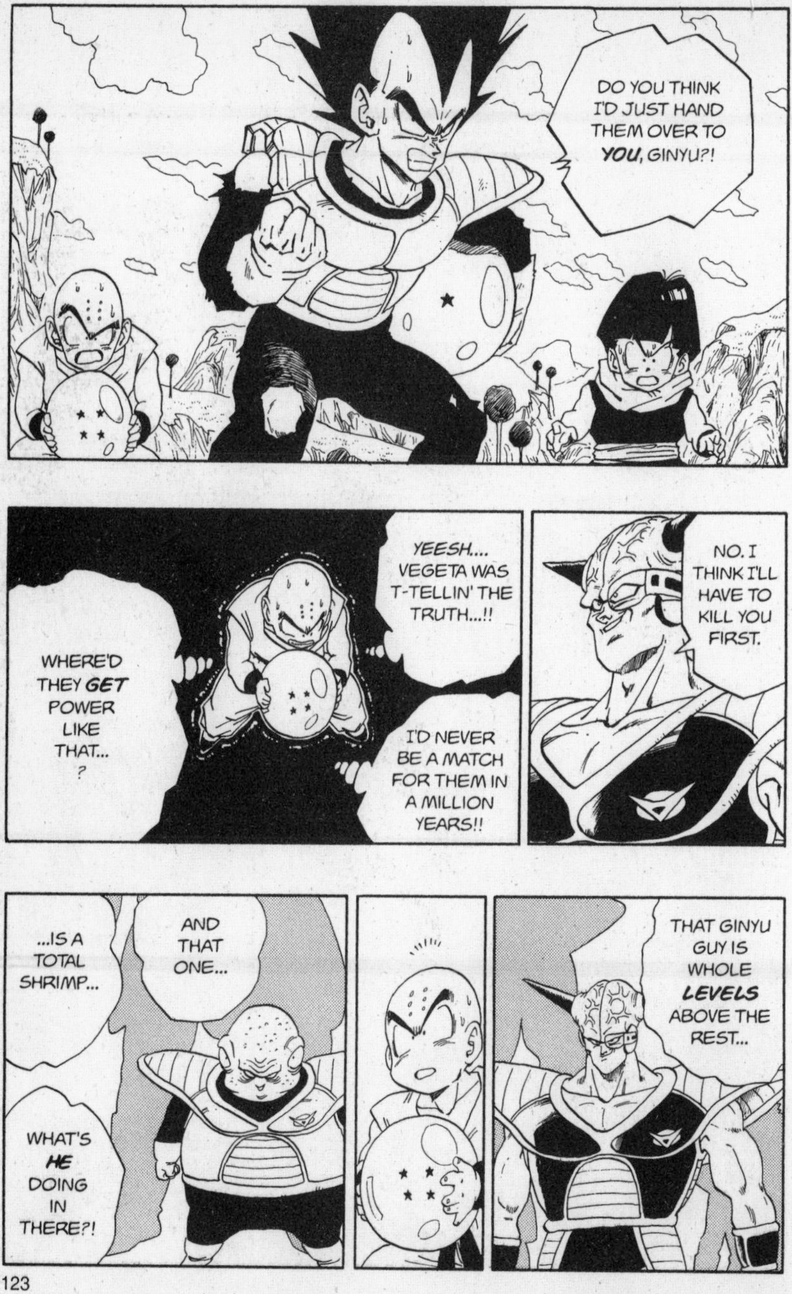
DO YOU THINK I'D JUST HAND THEM OVER TO ***YOU***, GINYU?!
NO. I THINK I'LL HAVE TO KILL YOU FIRST.
YEESH.... VEGETA WAS T-TELLIN' THE TRUTH...!!
I'D NEVER BE A MATCH FOR THEM IN A MILLION YEARS!!
WHERE'D THEY ***GET*** POWER LIKE THAT...?
THAT GINYU GUY IS WHOLE ***LEVELS*** ABOVE THE REST...
AND THAT ONE...
...IS A TOTAL SHRIMP...
WHAT'S ***HE*** DOING IN THERE?!

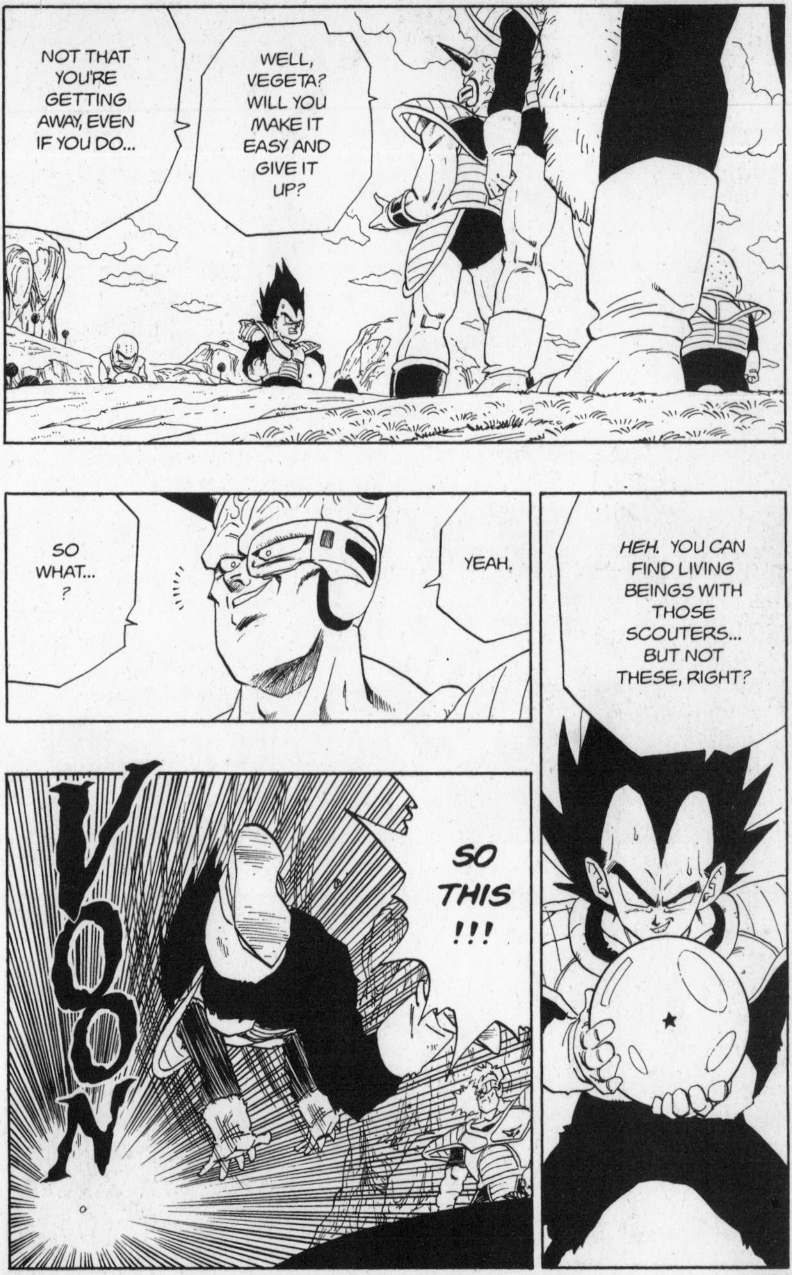
WELL, VEGETA? WILL YOU MAKE IT EASY AND GIVE IT UP?
NOT THAT YOU'RE GETTING AWAY, EVEN IF YOU DO...
HEH. YOU CAN FIND LIVING BEINGS WITH THOSE SCOUTERS... BUT NOT THESE, RIGHT?
YEAH.
SO WHAT... ?
SO THIS !!!
VOOM

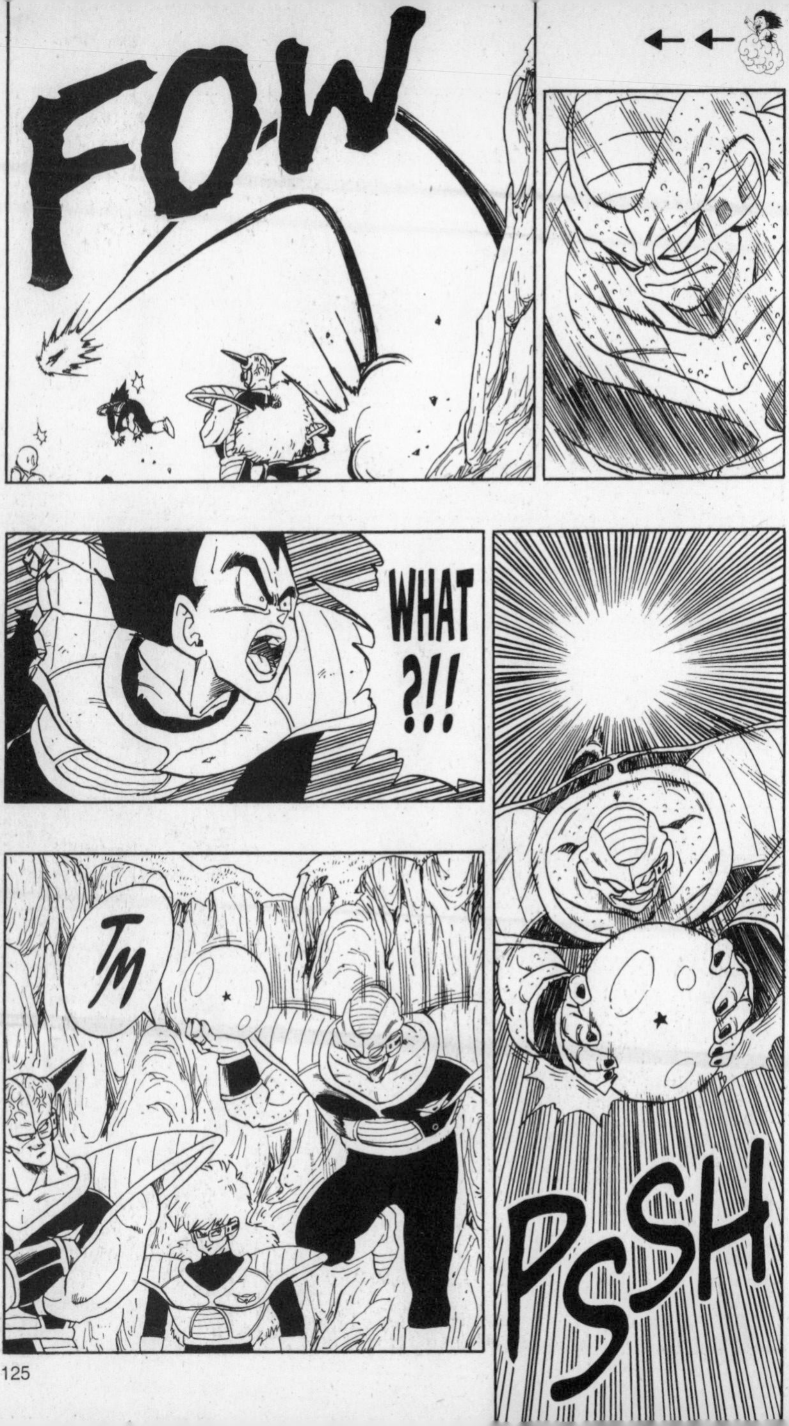
FO-W
PSH
WHAT ?!!
TM

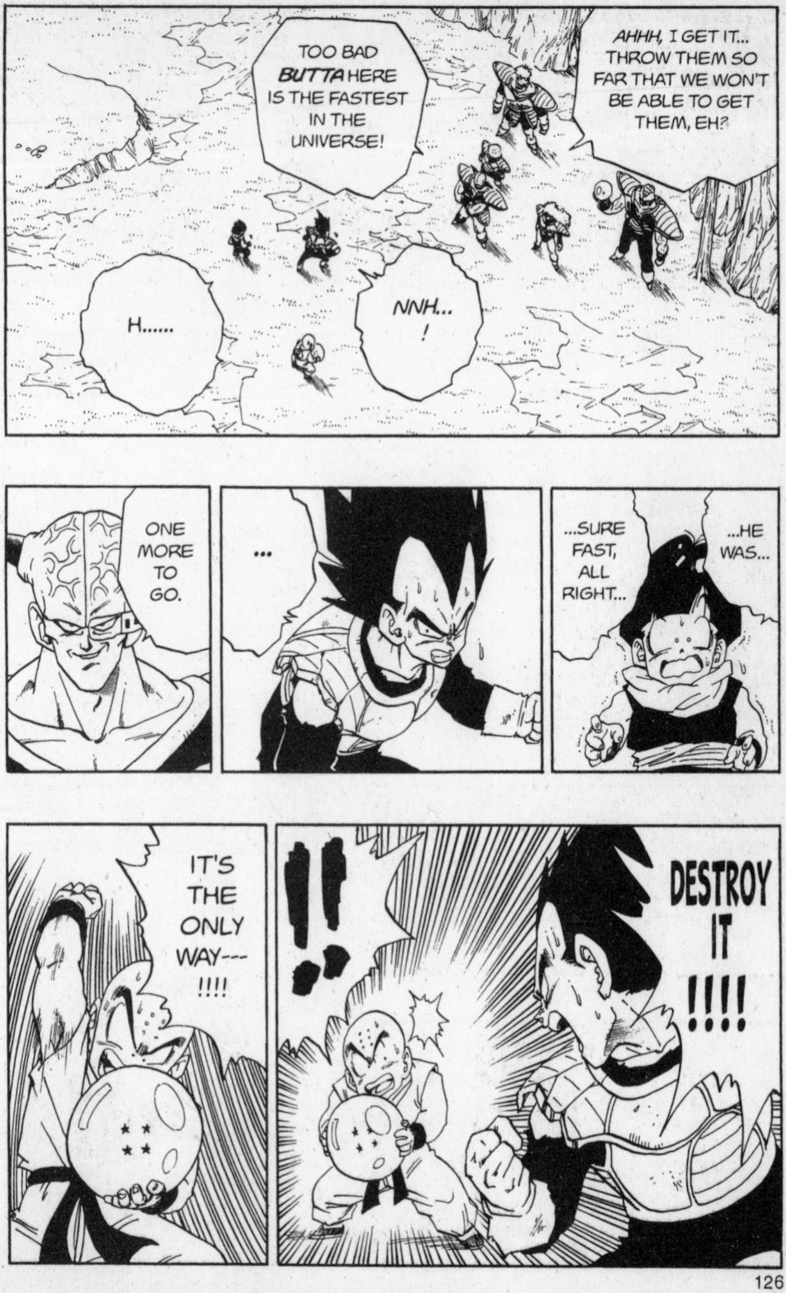
AHHH, I GET IT... THROW THEM SO FAR THAT WE WON'T BE ABLE TO GET THEM, EH?
TOO BAD BUTTA HERE IS THE FASTEST IN THE UNIVERSE!
NNH... !
H......
...HE WAS...
...SURE FAST, ALL RIGHT...
...
ONE MORE TO GO.
DESTROY IT !!!!
!!
IT'S THE ONLY WAY--- !!!!

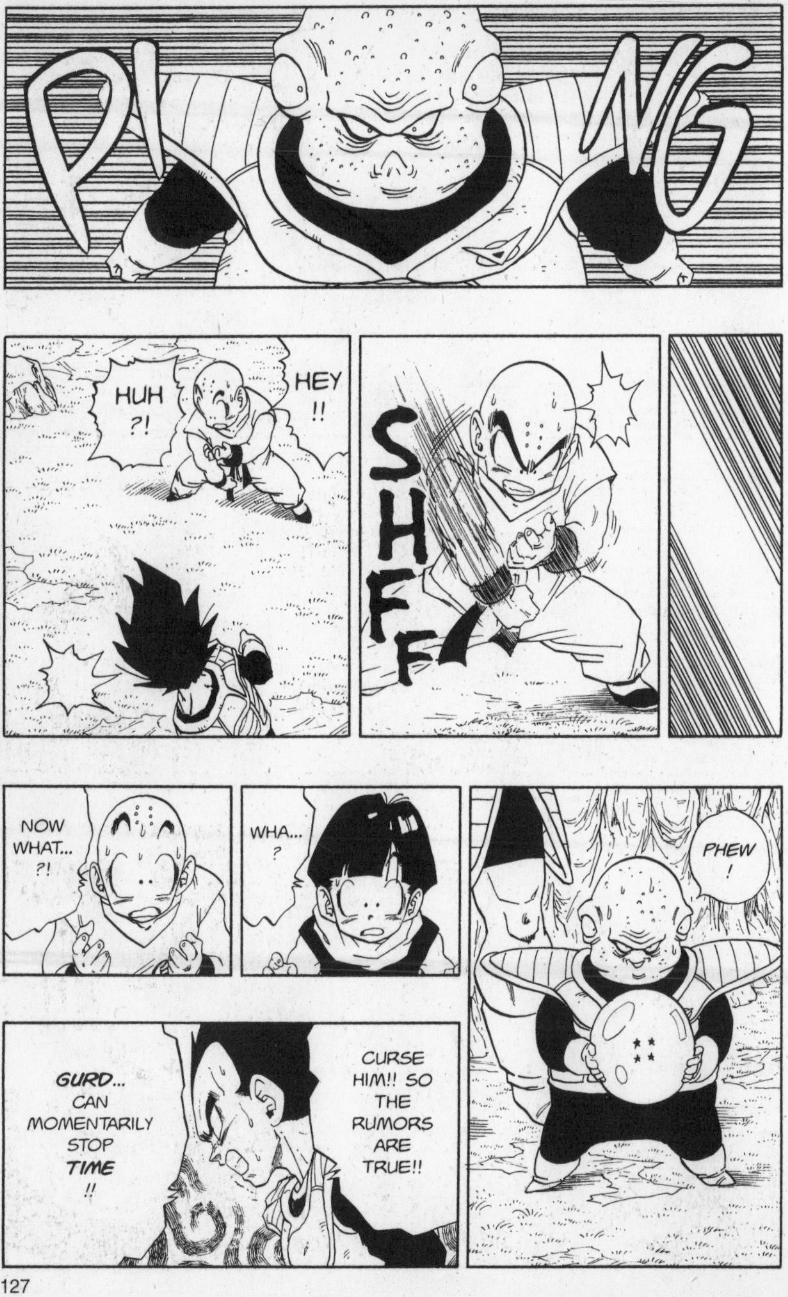
PING
SHFF
HEY !!
HUH ?!
PHEW !
WHA... ?
NOW WHAT... ?!
CURSE HIM!! SO THE RUMORS ARE TRUE!!
GURD... CAN MOMENTARILY STOP TIME !!

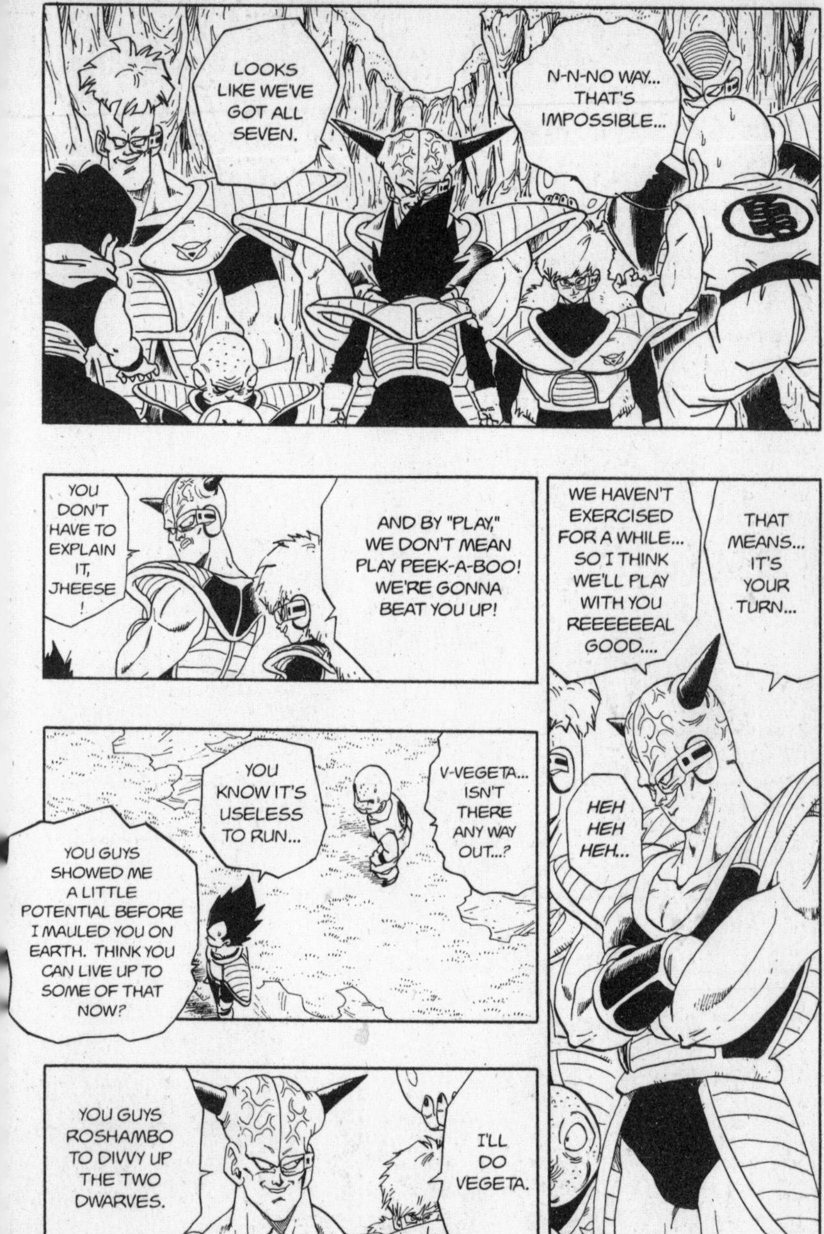
N-N-NO WAY... THAT'S IMPOSSIBLE...
LOOKS LIKE WE'VE GOT ALL SEVEN.
THAT MEANS... IT'S YOUR TURN...
WE HAVEN'T EXERCISED FOR A WHILE... SO I THINK WE'LL PLAY WITH YOU REEEEEEAL GOOD....
HEH HEH HEH...
AND BY "PLAY," WE DON'T MEAN PLAY PEEK-A-BOO! WE'RE GONNA BEAT YOU UP!
YOU DON'T HAVE TO EXPLAIN IT, JHEESE!
V-VEGETA... ISN'T THERE ANY WAY OUT...?
YOU KNOW IT'S USELESS TO RUN...
YOU GUYS SHOWED ME A LITTLE POTENTIAL BEFORE I MAULED YOU ON EARTH. THINK YOU CAN LIVE UP TO SOME OF THAT NOW?
I'LL DO VEGETA.
YOU GUYS ROSHAMBO TO DIVVY UP THE TWO DWARVES.

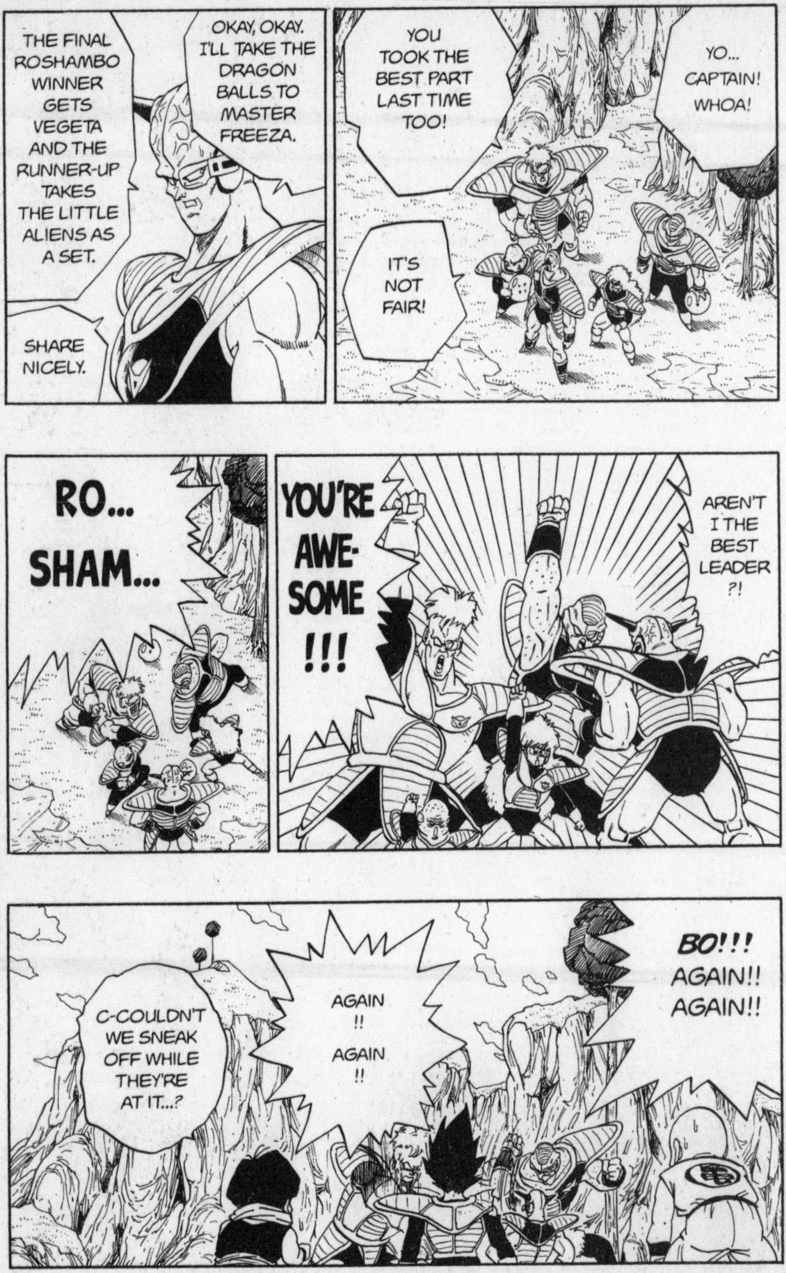

YO... CAPTAIN! WHOA!
YOU TOOK THE BEST PART LAST TIME TOO!
IT'S NOT FAIR!
OKAY, OKAY. I'LL TAKE THE DRAGON BALLS TO MASTER FREEZA.
THE FINAL ROSHAMBO WINNER GETS VEGETA AND THE RUNNER-UP TAKES THE LITTLE ALIENS AS A SET.
SHARE NICELY.
AREN'T I THE BEST LEADER?!
YOU'RE AWESOME!!!
RO... SHAM...
BO!!! AGAIN!! AGAIN!!
AGAIN!! AGAIN!!
C-COULDN'T WE SNEAK OFF WHILE THEY'RE AT IT...?

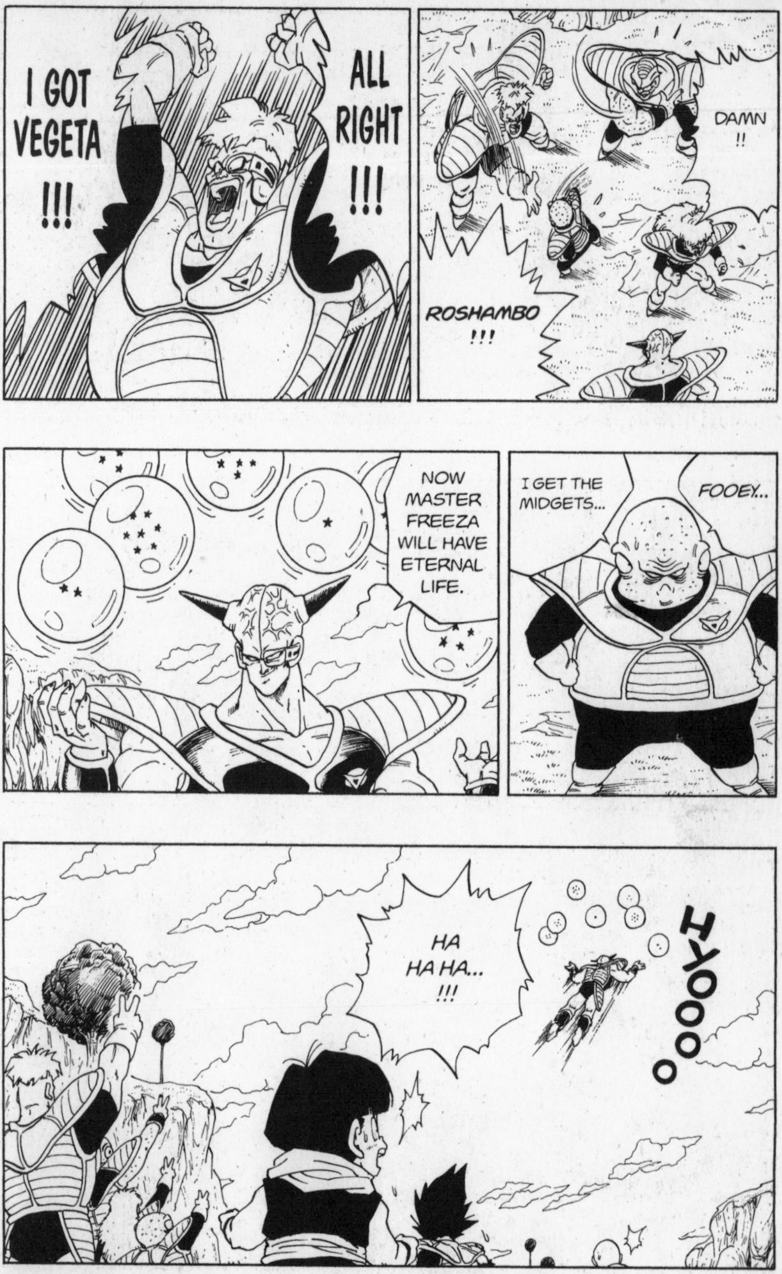
DAMN !!
ROSHAMBO !!!
ALL RIGHT !!!
I GOT VEGETA !!!
FOOEY...
I GET THE MIDGETS...
NOW MASTER FREEZA WILL HAVE ETERNAL LIFE.
HYOOOOO
HA HA HA... !!!

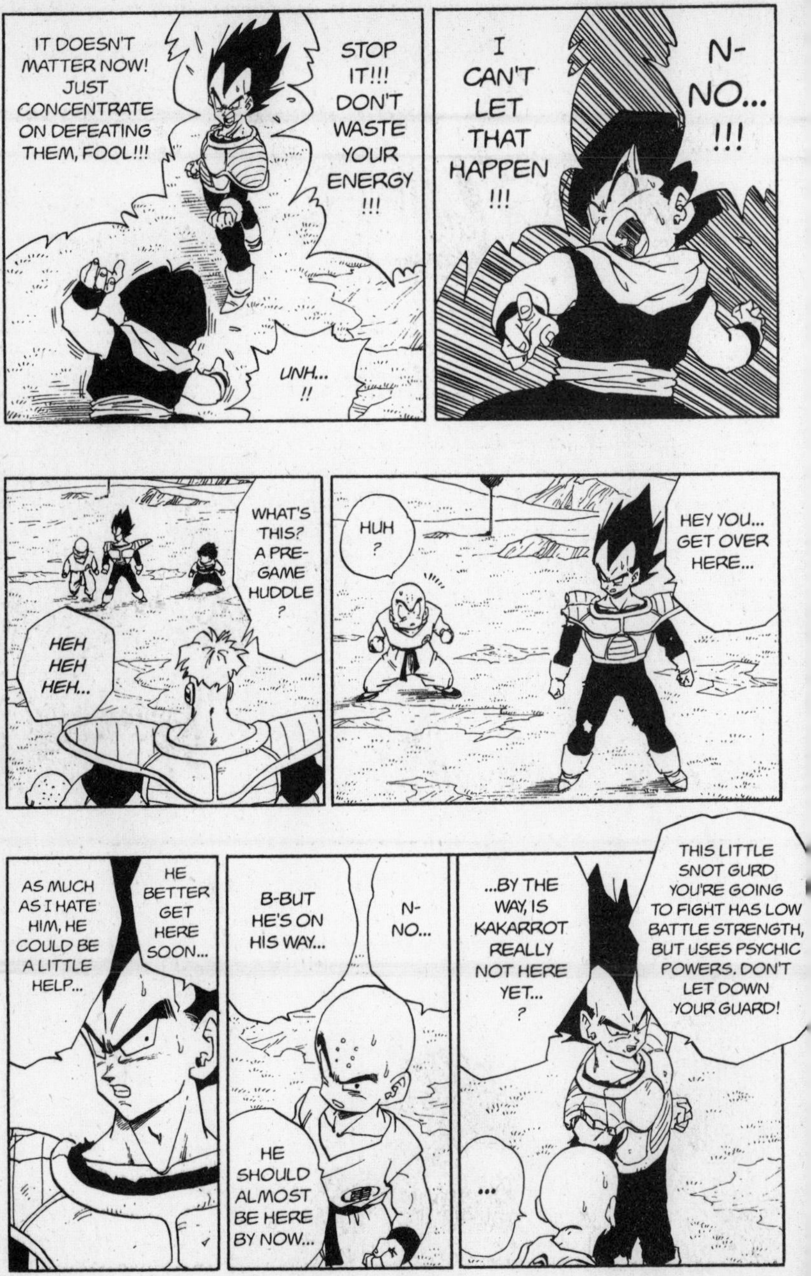
N-NO... !!!
I CAN'T LET THAT HAPPEN !!!
STOP IT!!! DON'T WASTE YOUR ENERGY !!!
IT DOESN'T MATTER NOW! JUST CONCENTRATE ON DEFEATING THEM, FOOL!!!
UNH... !!
HEY YOU... GET OVER HERE...
HUH ?
WHAT'S THIS? A PRE-GAME HUDDLE ?
HEH HEH HEH...
THIS LITTLE SNOT GURD YOU'RE GOING TO FIGHT HAS LOW BATTLE STRENGTH, BUT USES PSYCHIC POWERS. DON'T LET DOWN YOUR GUARD!
...BY THE WAY, IS KAKARROT REALLY NOT HERE YET... ?
...
N-NO...
B-BUT HE'S ON HIS WAY...
HE SHOULD ALMOST BE HERE BY NOW...
HE BETTER GET HERE SOON...
AS MUCH AS I HATE HIM, HE COULD BE A LITTLE HELP...

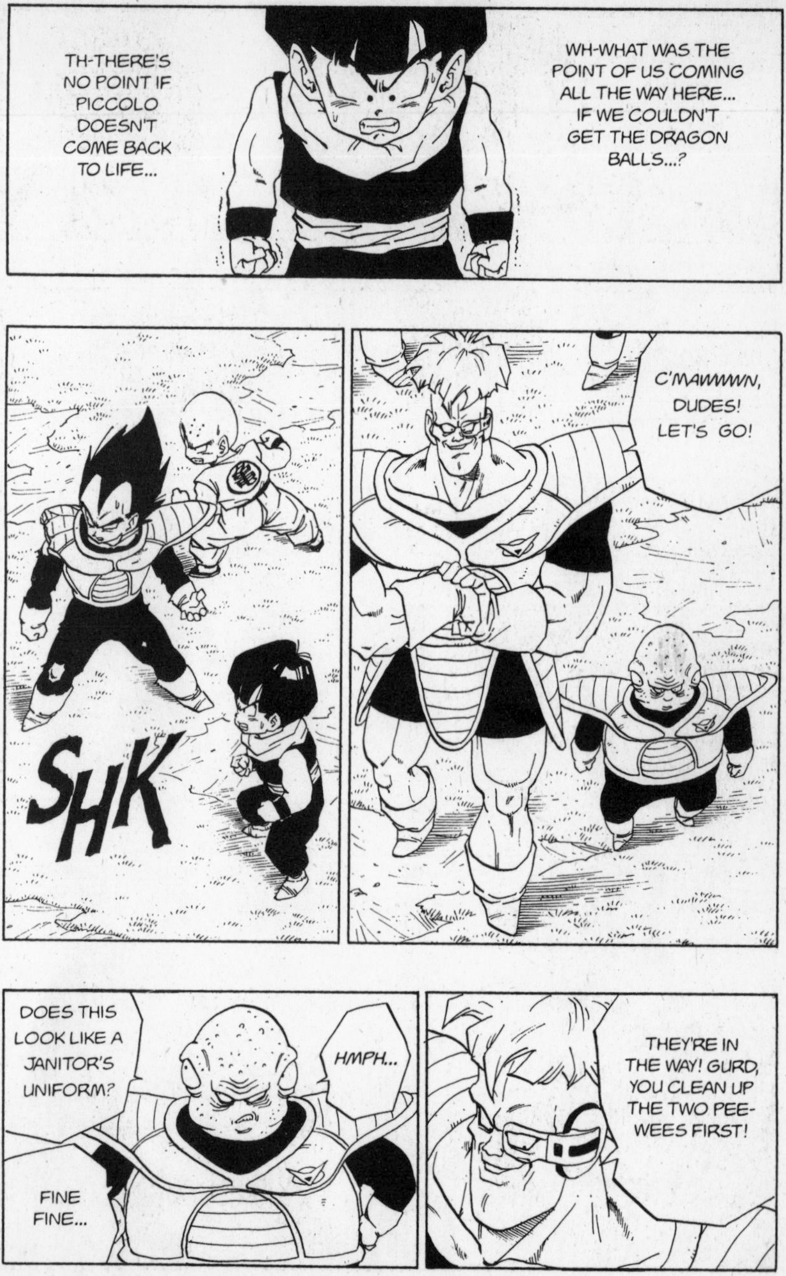
WH-WHAT WAS THE POINT OF US COMING ALL THE WAY HERE... IF WE COULDN'T GET THE DRAGON BALLS...?
TH-THERE'S NO POINT IF PICCOLO DOESN'T COME BACK TO LIFE...
C'MAWWWN, DUDES! LET'S GO!
SHK
THEY'RE IN THE WAY! GURD, YOU CLEAN UP THE TWO PEE-WEES FIRST!
HMPH...
DOES THIS LOOK LIKE A JANITOR'S UNIFORM?
FINE FINE...

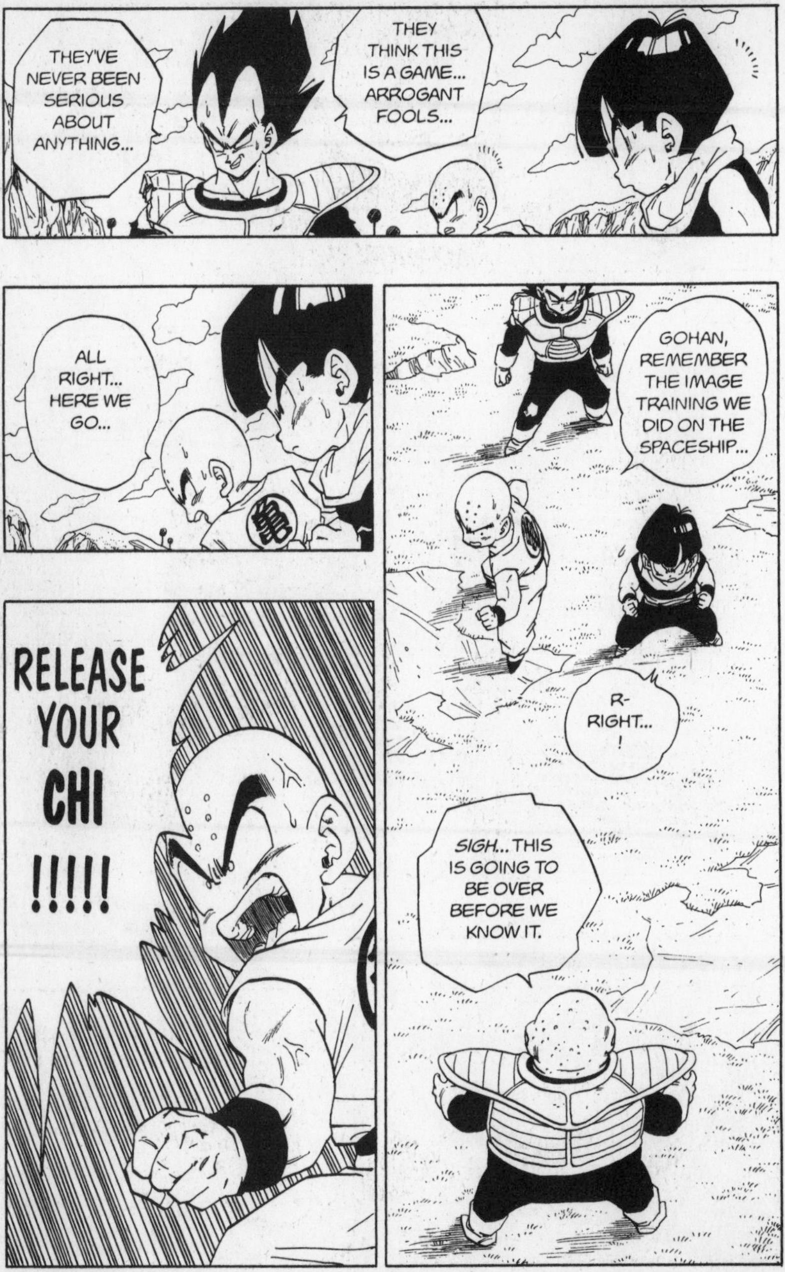

THEY THINK THIS IS A GAME... ARROGANT FOOLS...
THEY'VE NEVER BEEN SERIOUS ABOUT ANYTHING...
GOHAN, REMEMBER THE IMAGE TRAINING WE DID ON THE SPACESHIP...
R- RIGHT... !
SIGH... THIS IS GOING TO BE OVER BEFORE WE KNOW IT.
ALL RIGHT... HERE WE GO...
RELEASE YOUR CHI !!!!!

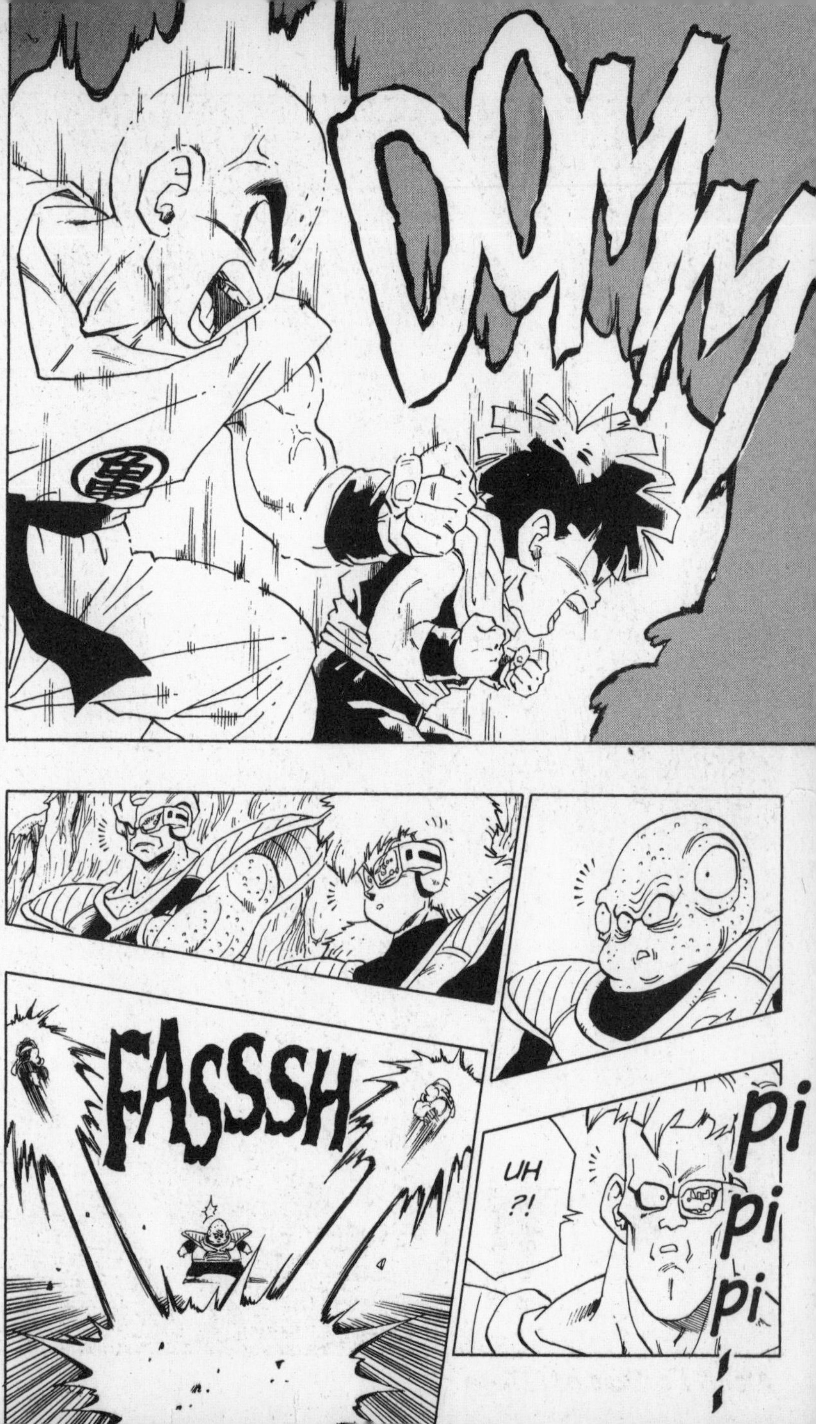
DOMM
UH ?!
pi pi pi!
FASSSH

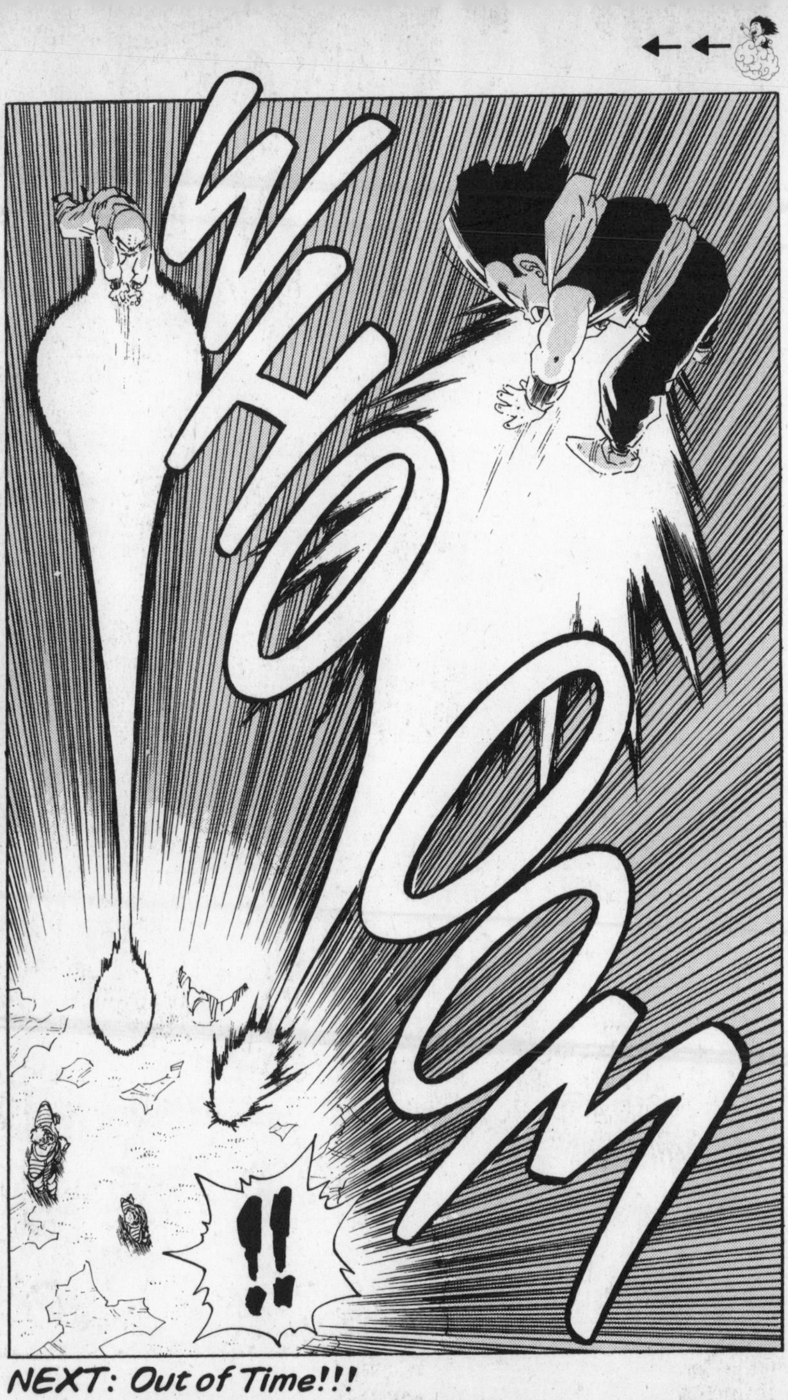
WHOOOM
!!

NEXT: Out of Time!!!

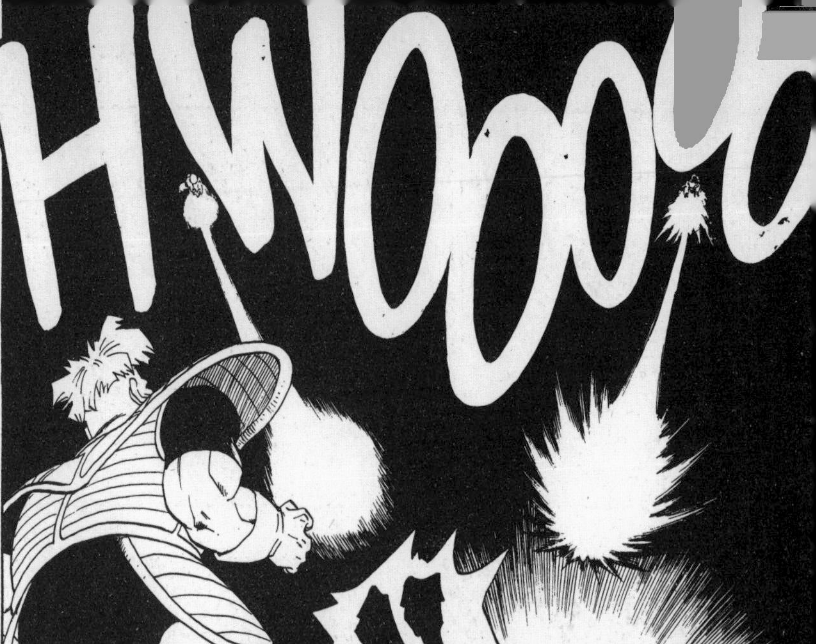
HWOOOO
!!

DBZ:80 • Gurd's Psychic Powers

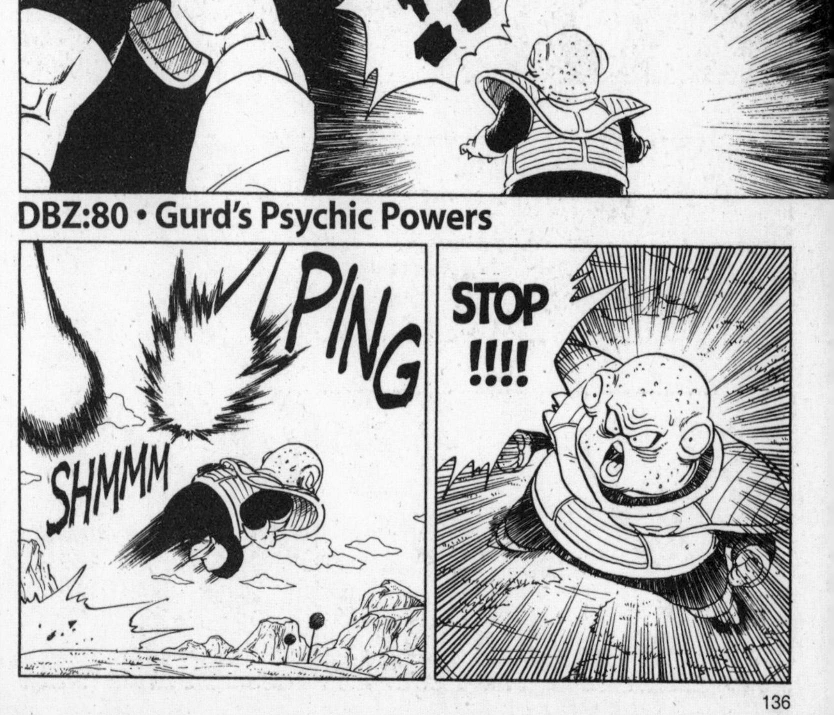
STOP
!!!!
PING
SHMMM

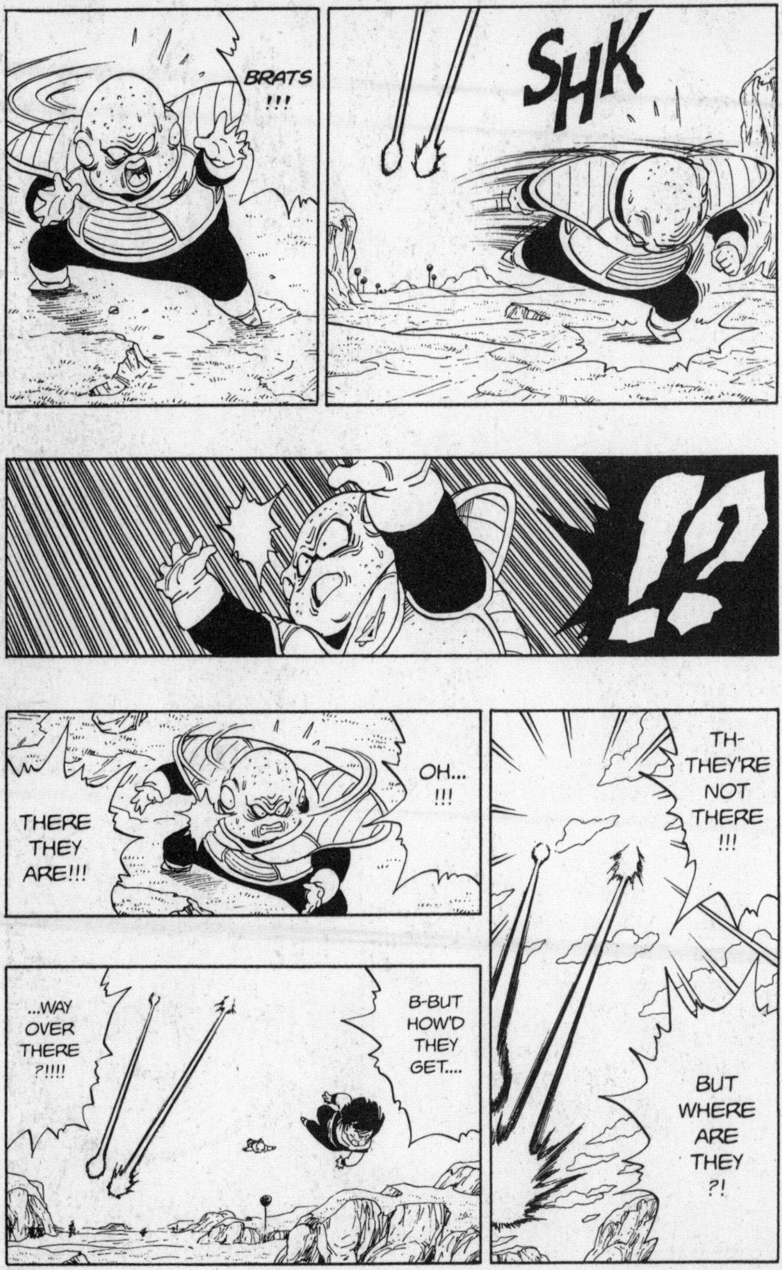
SHK
BRATS !!!
!?
TH-THEY'RE NOT THERE !!!
BUT WHERE ARE THEY ?!
OH... !!!
THERE THEY ARE!!!
B-BUT HOW'D THEY GET....
...WAY OVER THERE ?!!!!

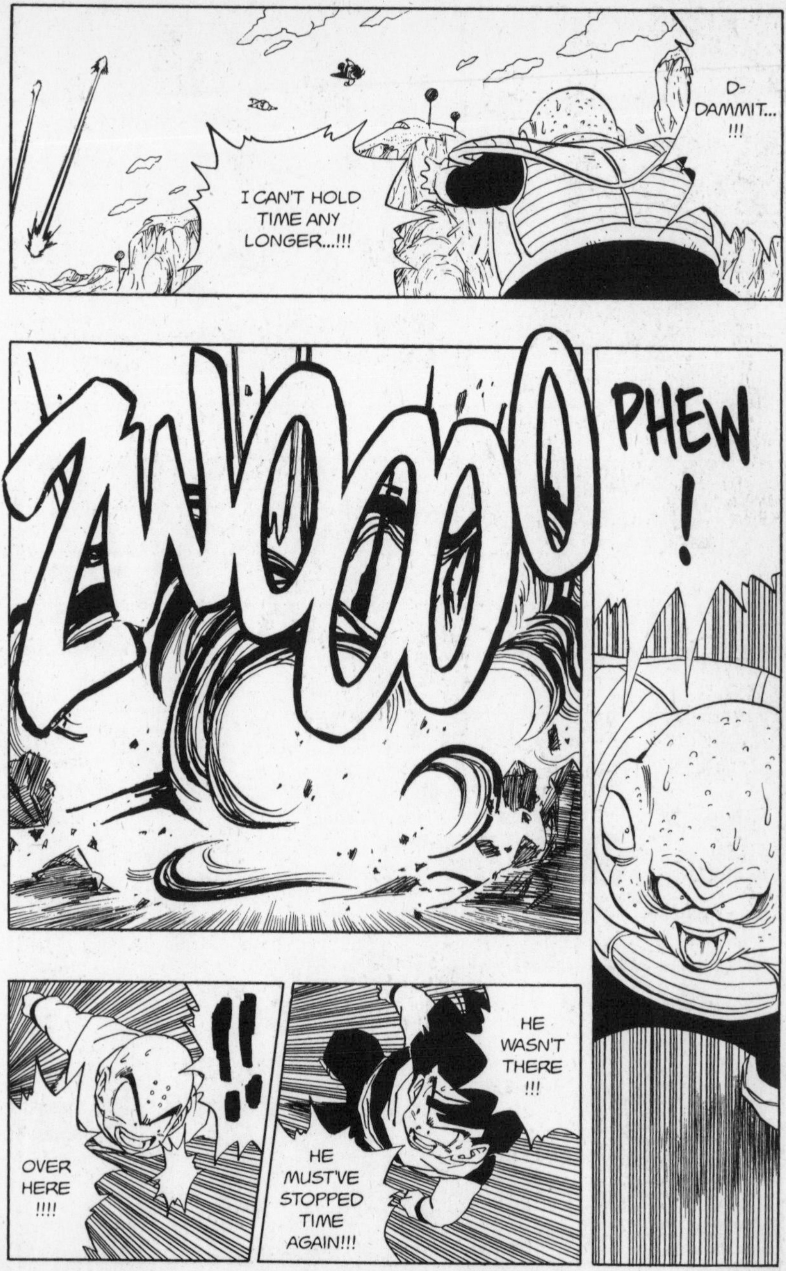
D-DAMMIT...!!!
I CAN'T HOLD TIME ANY LONGER...!!!
PHEW!
ZWOOOOO
HE WASN'T THERE!!!
HE MUST'VE STOPPED TIME AGAIN!!!
!!
OVER HERE!!!!

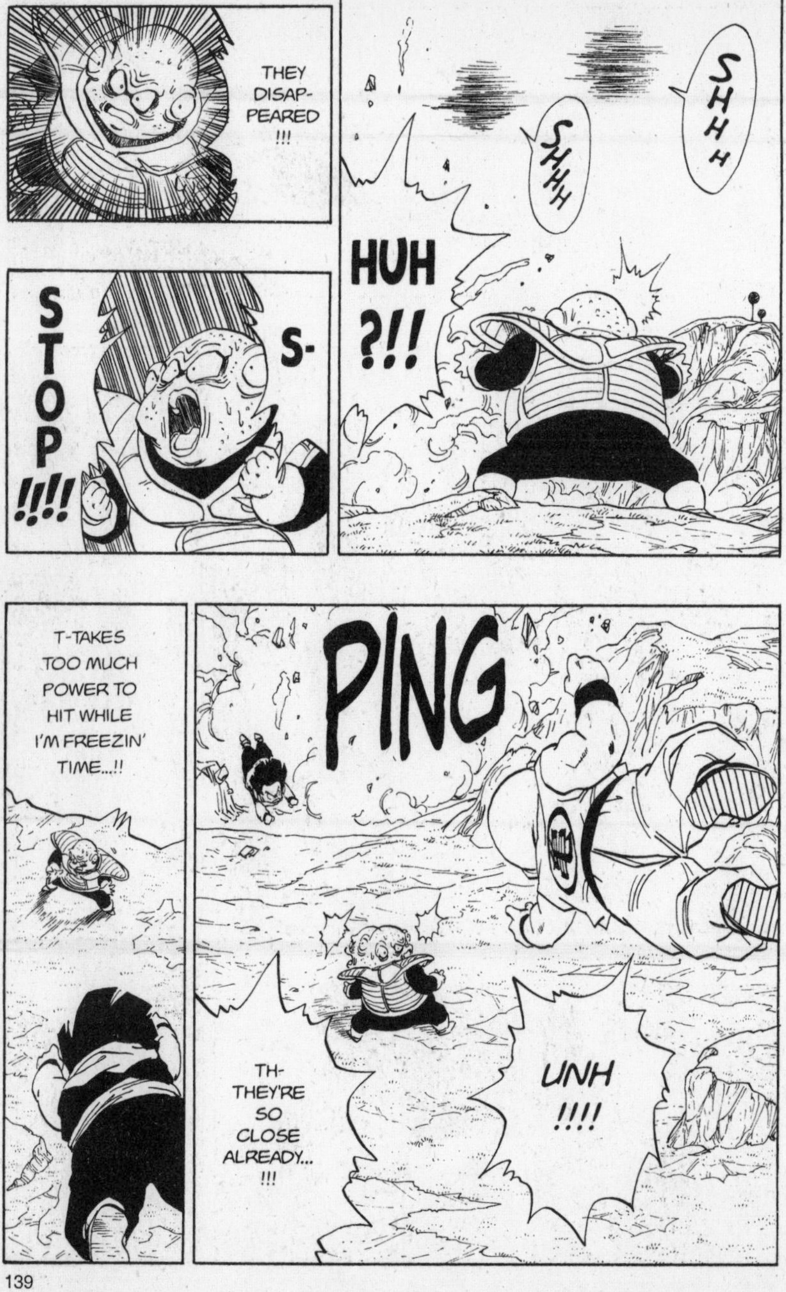
SHHH
SHHH
HUH?!!
THEY DISAP-PEARED!!!
S-
STOP!!!!
PING
UNH!!!!
TH-THEY'RE SO CLOSE ALREADY...!!!
T-TAKES TOO MUCH POWER TO HIT WHILE I'M FREEZIN' TIME...!!

GOTTA.... HIDE BEHIND THE ROCKS... ATTACK WHILE THEY'RE CONFUSED!!

* HUF *
* HUF *

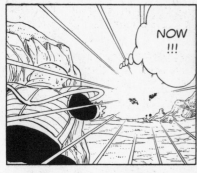

NOW !!!

NNNH !!!!

THERE !!!

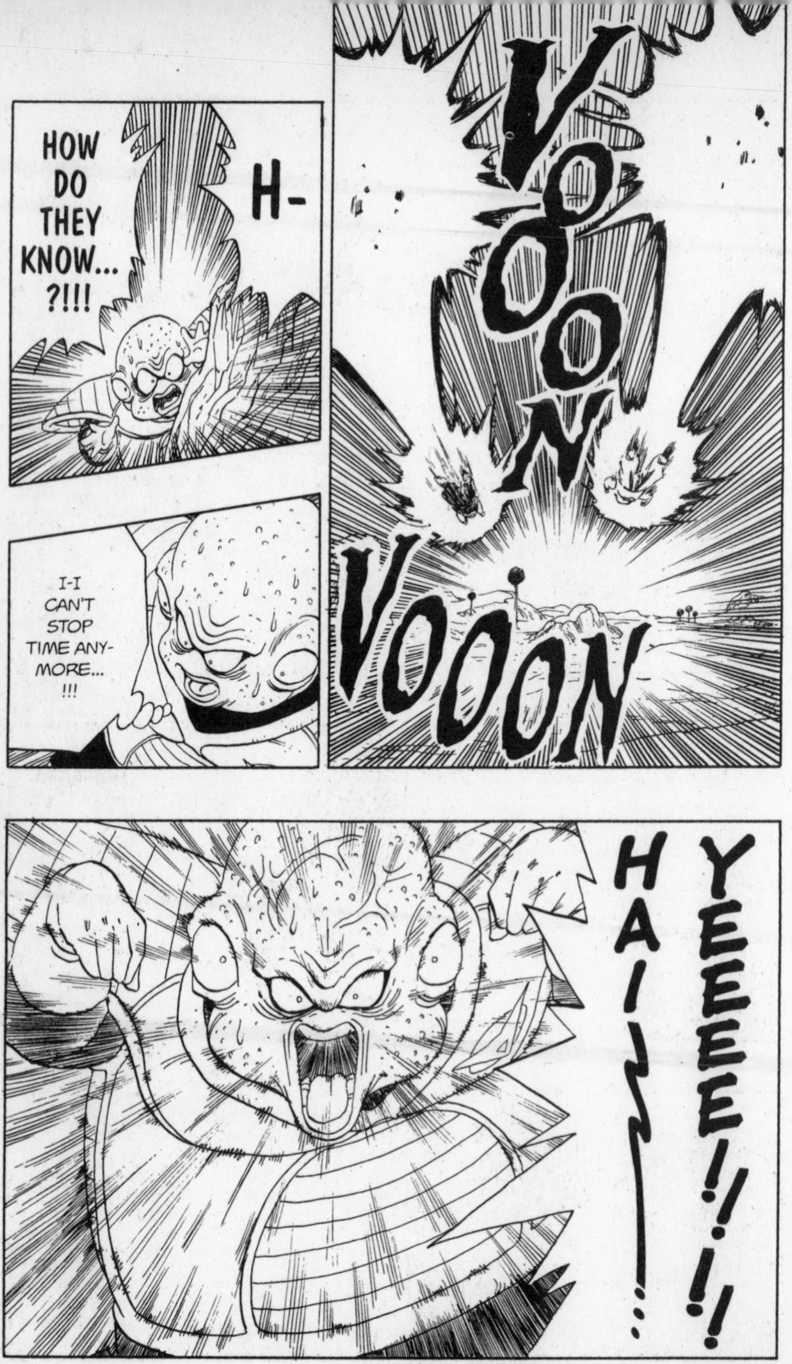
VOOON
VOOON
H-
HOW DO THEY KNOW...?!!!
I-I CAN'T STOP TIME ANY-MORE...!!!
YEEEE!!!!
HAI~~...

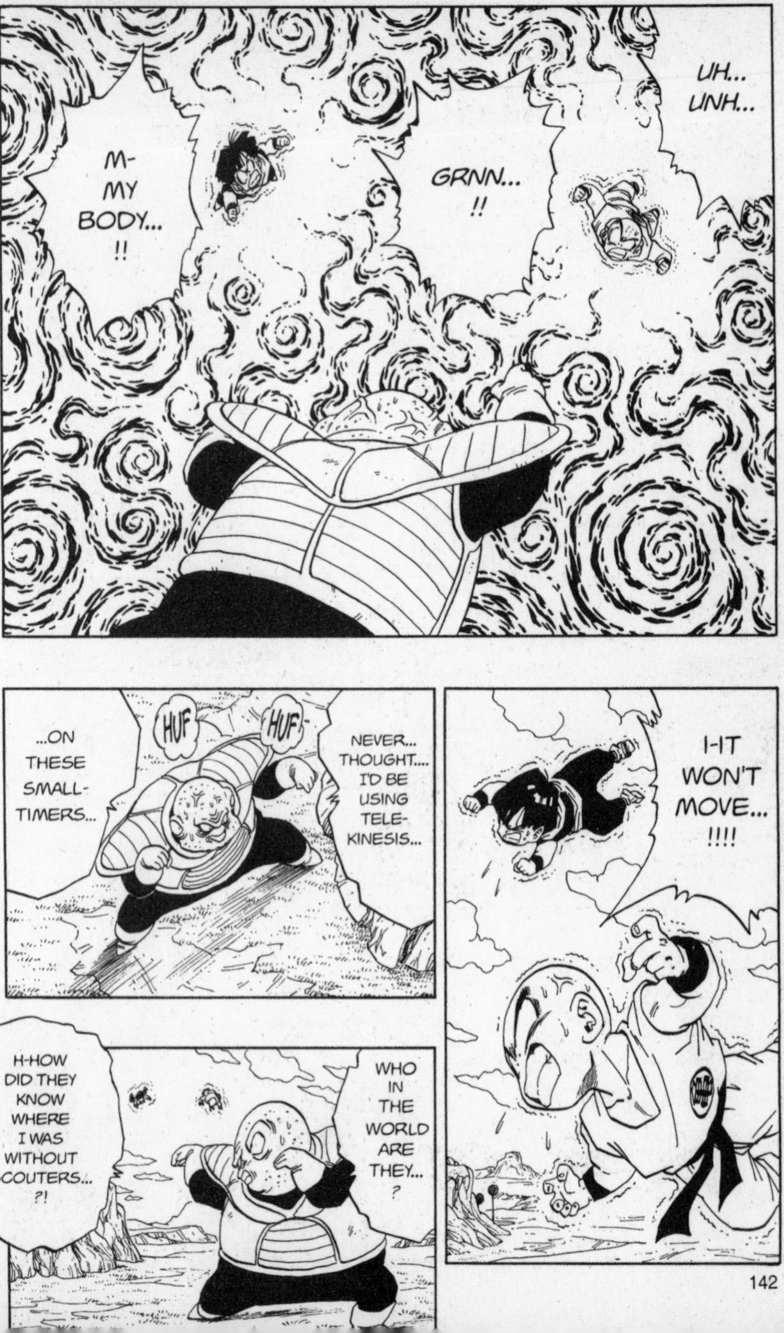
UH... UNH...
GRNN... !!
M- MY BODY... !!
I-IT WON'T MOVE... !!!!
NEVER... THOUGHT.... I'D BE USING TELE-KINESIS...
HUF
HUF
...ON THESE SMALL-TIMERS...
WHO IN THE WORLD ARE THEY... ?
H-HOW DID THEY KNOW WHERE I WAS WITHOUT SCOUTERS... ?!

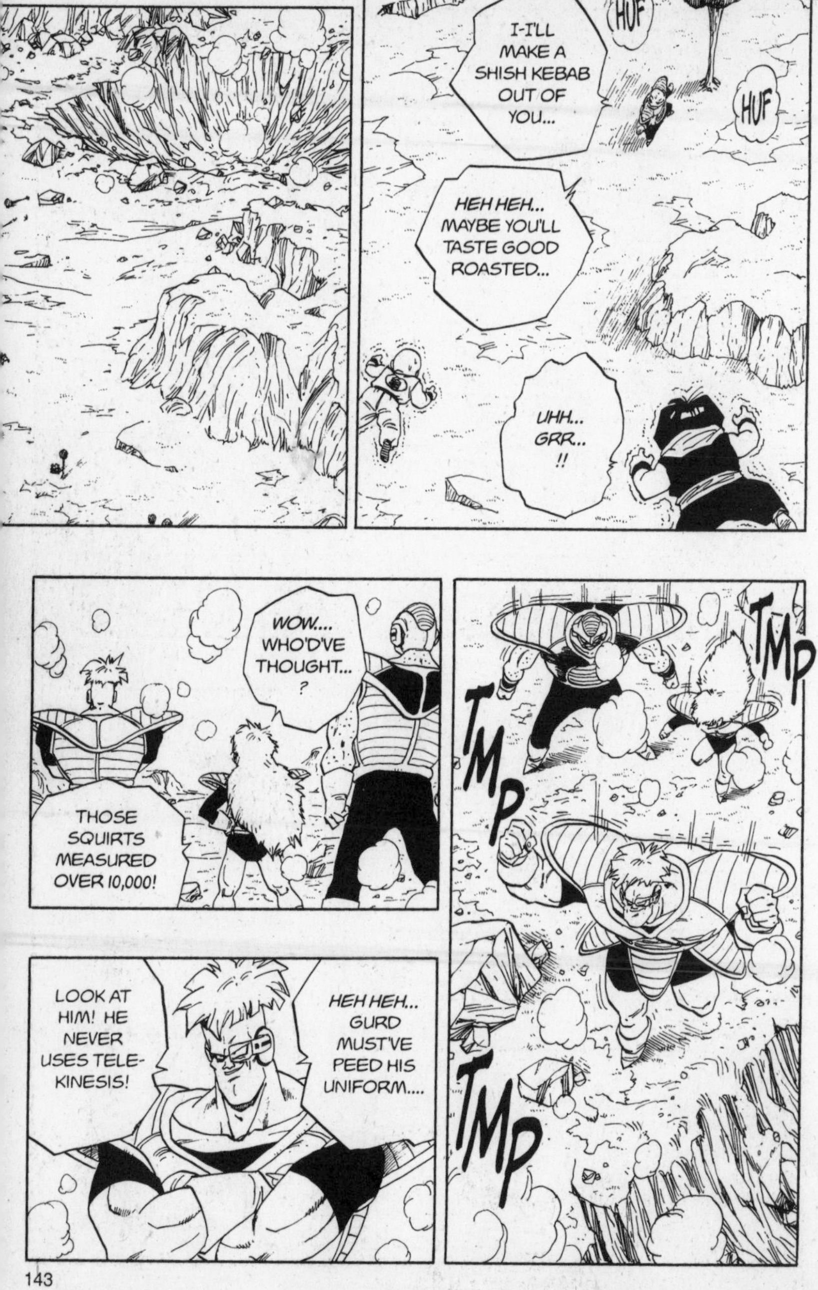
HUF
I-I'LL MAKE A SHISH KEBAB OUT OF YOU...
HUF
HEH HEH... MAYBE YOU'LL TASTE GOOD ROASTED...
UHH... GRR... !!
TMP
TMP
TMP
TMP
WOW.... WHO'D'VE THOUGHT...?
THOSE SQUIRTS MEASURED OVER 10,000!
HEH HEH... GURD MUST'VE PEED HIS UNIFORM....
LOOK AT HIM! HE NEVER USES TELE-KINESIS!

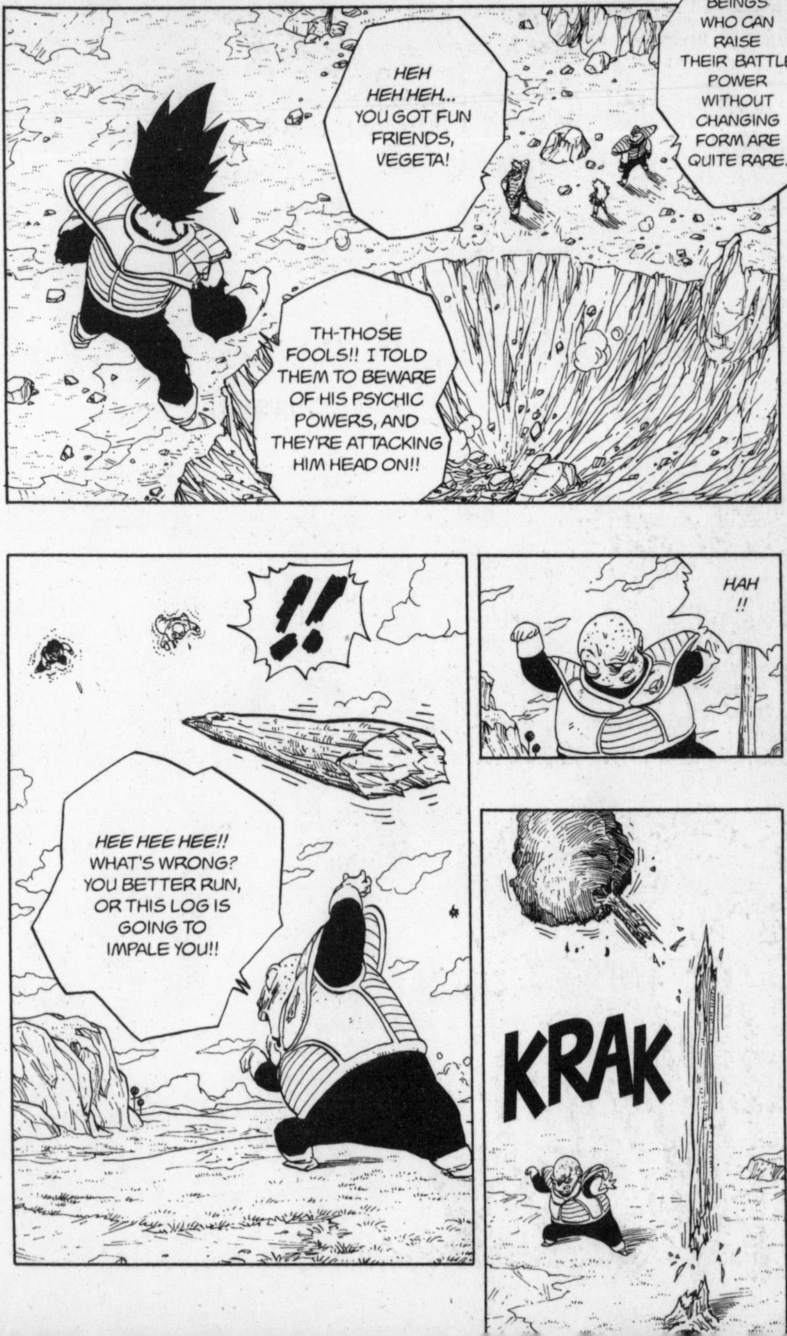
BEINGS WHO CAN RAISE THEIR BATTLE POWER WITHOUT CHANGING FORM ARE QUITE RARE.
HEH HEH HEH... YOU GOT FUN FRIENDS, VEGETA!
TH-THOSE FOOLS!! I TOLD THEM TO BEWARE OF HIS PSYCHIC POWERS, AND THEY'RE ATTACKING HIM HEAD ON!!
HAH !!
KRAK
!!
HEE HEE HEE!! WHAT'S WRONG? YOU BETTER RUN, OR THIS LOG IS GOING TO IMPALE YOU!!

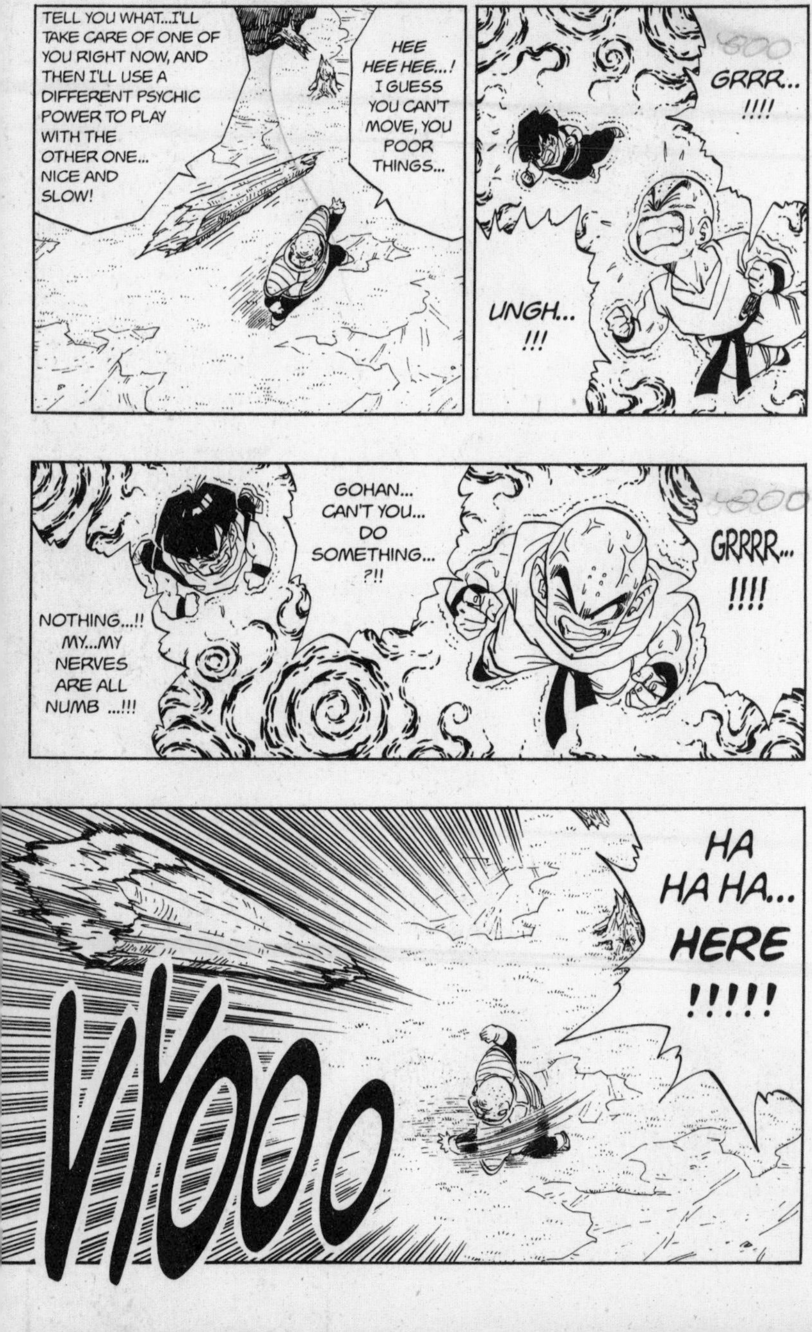
GRRR... !!!!
UNGH... !!!
HEE HEE HEE...! I GUESS YOU CAN'T MOVE, YOU POOR THINGS...
TELL YOU WHAT...I'LL TAKE CARE OF ONE OF YOU RIGHT NOW, AND THEN I'LL USE A DIFFERENT PSYCHIC POWER TO PLAY WITH THE OTHER ONE... NICE AND SLOW!
GRRRR... !!!!
GOHAN... CAN'T YOU... DO SOMETHING... ?!!
NOTHING...!! MY...MY NERVES ARE ALL NUMB ...!!!
HA HA HA... HERE !!!!!
WOOO

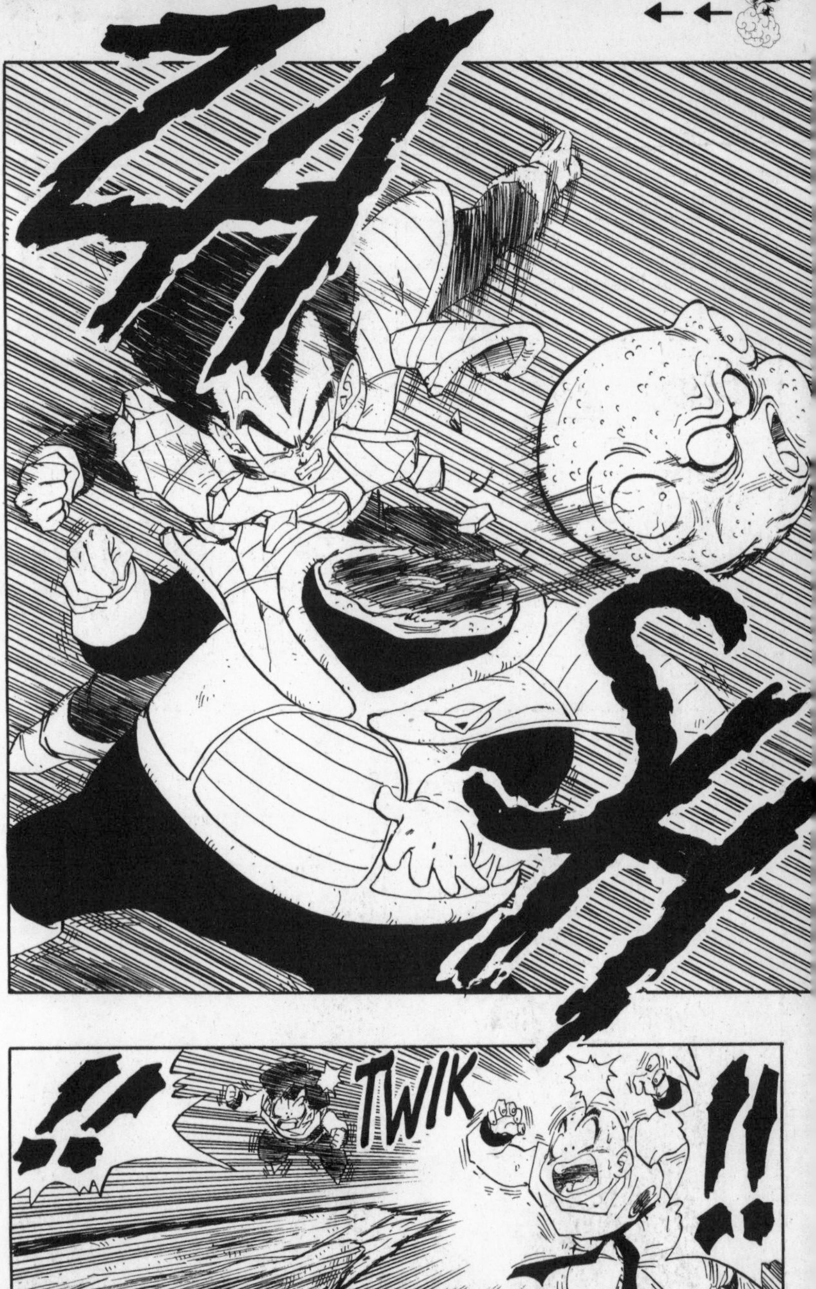
TWIK

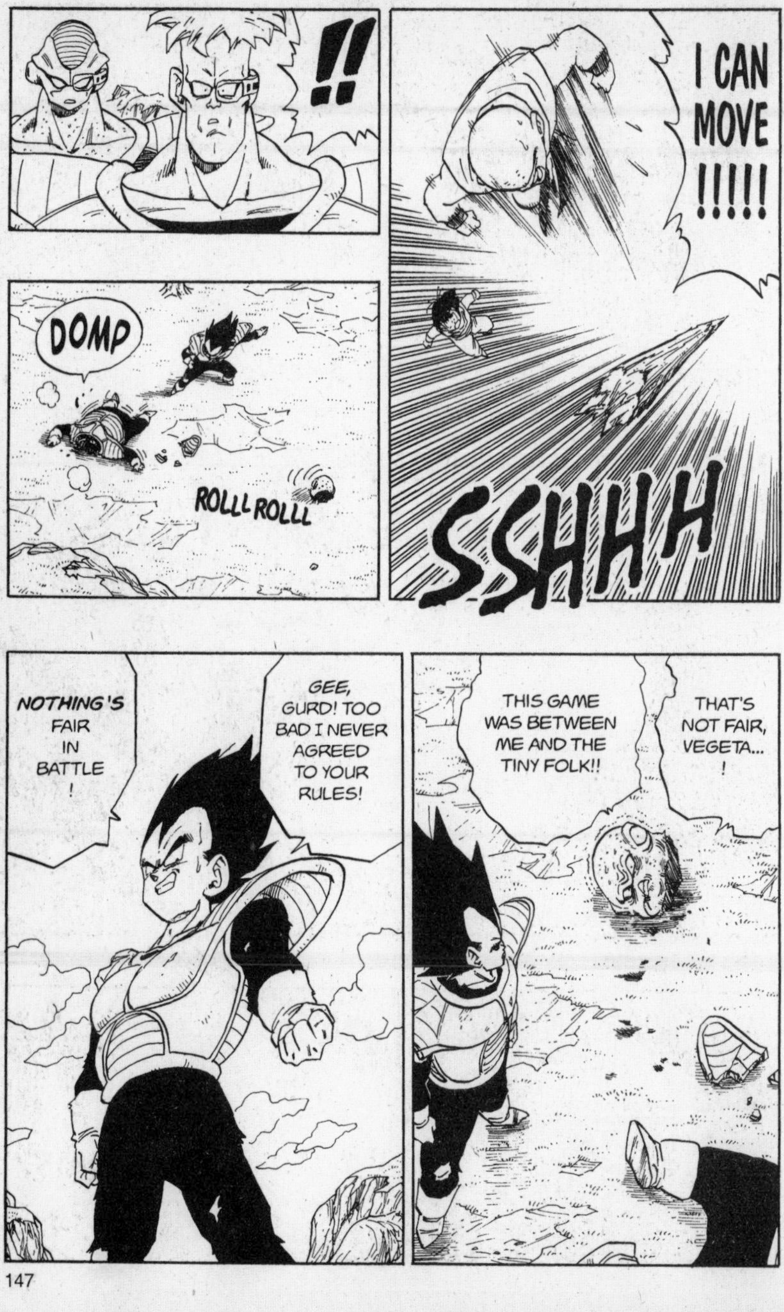
I CAN MOVE !!!!!
SSHHH
!!
DOMP
ROLLL ROLLL
THAT'S NOT FAIR, VEGETA... !
THIS GAME WAS BETWEEN ME AND THE TINY FOLK!!
GEE, GURD! TOO BAD I NEVER AGREED TO YOUR RULES!
NOTHING'S FAIR IN BATTLE !

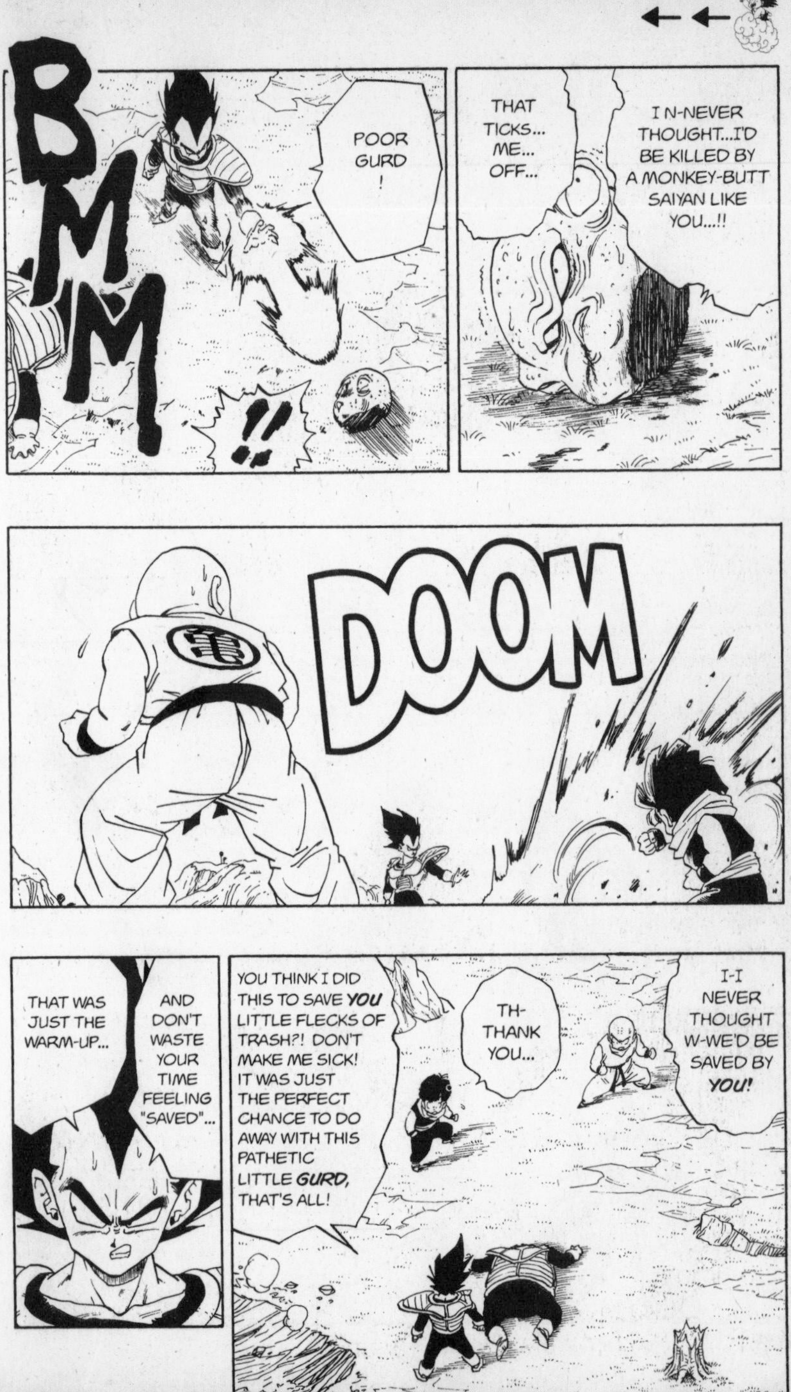
I N-NEVER THOUGHT...I'D BE KILLED BY A MONKEY-BUTT SAIYAN LIKE YOU...!!
THAT TICKS... ME... OFF...
POOR GURD !
BMM
!!
DOOM
I-I NEVER THOUGHT W-WE'D BE SAVED BY YOU!
TH-THANK YOU...
YOU THINK I DID THIS TO SAVE YOU LITTLE FLECKS OF TRASH?! DON'T MAKE ME SICK! IT WAS JUST THE PERFECT CHANCE TO DO AWAY WITH THIS PATHETIC LITTLE GURD, THAT'S ALL!
THAT WAS JUST THE WARM-UP...
AND DON'T WASTE YOUR TIME FEELING "SAVED"...

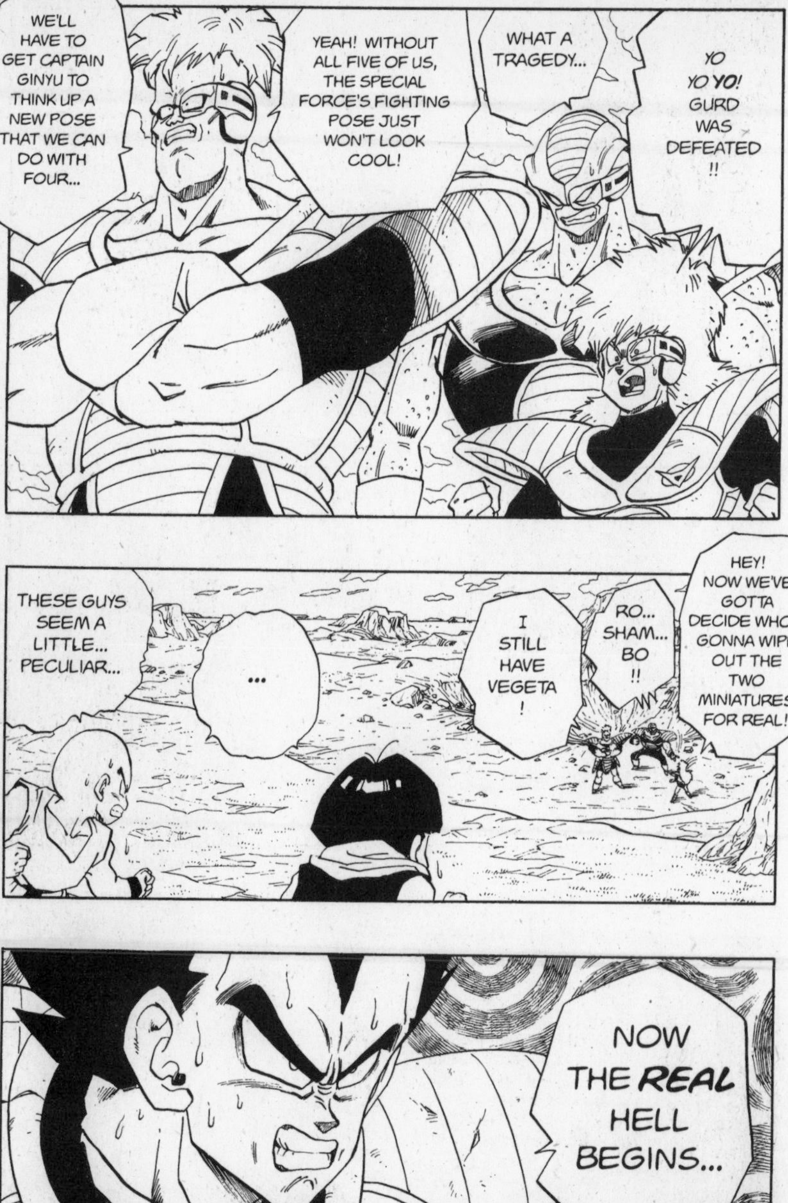
YO YO YO! GURD WAS DEFEATED!!
WHAT A TRAGEDY...
YEAH! WITHOUT ALL FIVE OF US, THE SPECIAL FORCE'S FIGHTING POSE JUST WON'T LOOK COOL!
WE'LL HAVE TO GET CAPTAIN GINYU TO THINK UP A NEW POSE THAT WE CAN DO WITH FOUR...
HEY! NOW WE'VE GOTTA DECIDE WHO'S GONNA WIPE OUT THE TWO MINIATURES FOR REAL!
RO... SHAM... BO!!
I STILL HAVE VEGETA!
...
THESE GUYS SEEM A LITTLE... PECULIAR...
NOW THE *REAL* HELL BEGINS...

NEXT: Vegeta Strikes First!!!

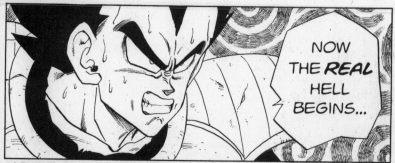

DBZ:81 • Vegeta vs. Reacoom

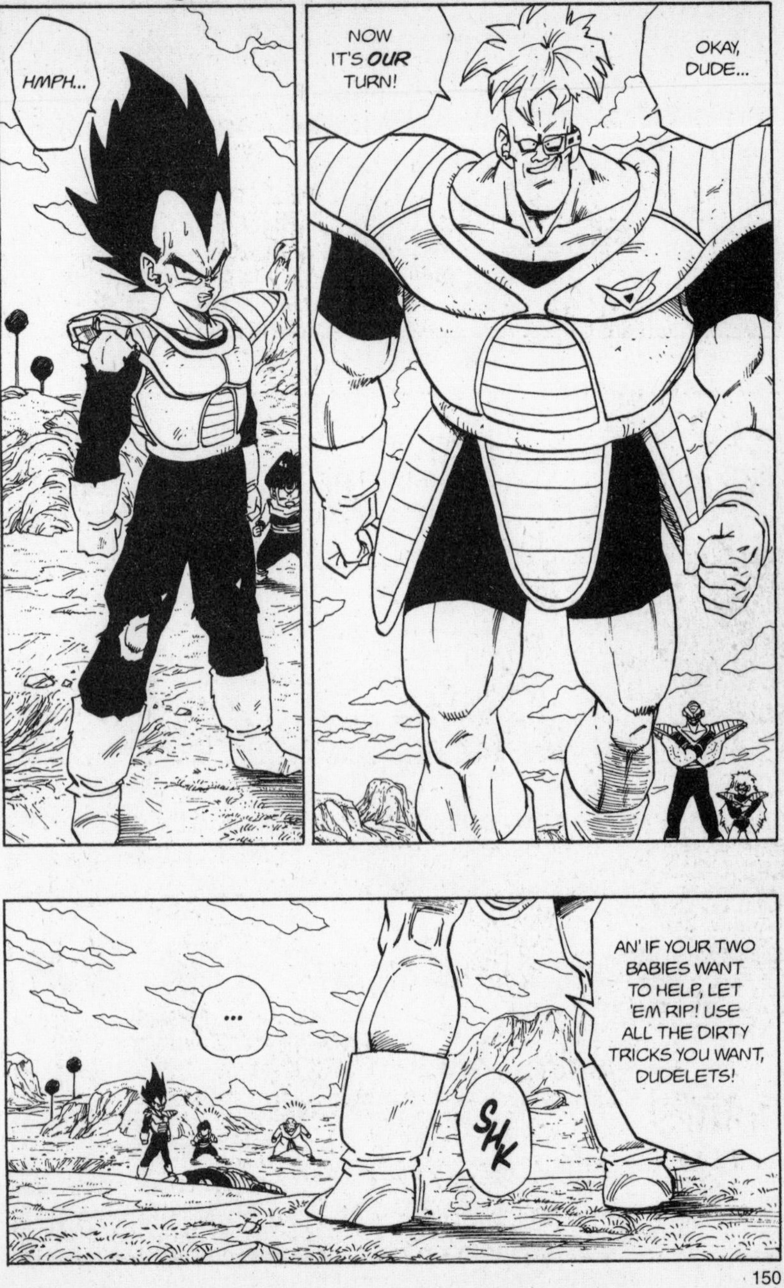
OKAY, DUDE...
NOW IT'S OUR TURN!
HMPH...
AN' IF YOUR TWO BABIES WANT TO HELP, LET 'EM RIP! USE ALL THE DIRTY TRICKS YOU WANT, DUDELETS!
SHK
...

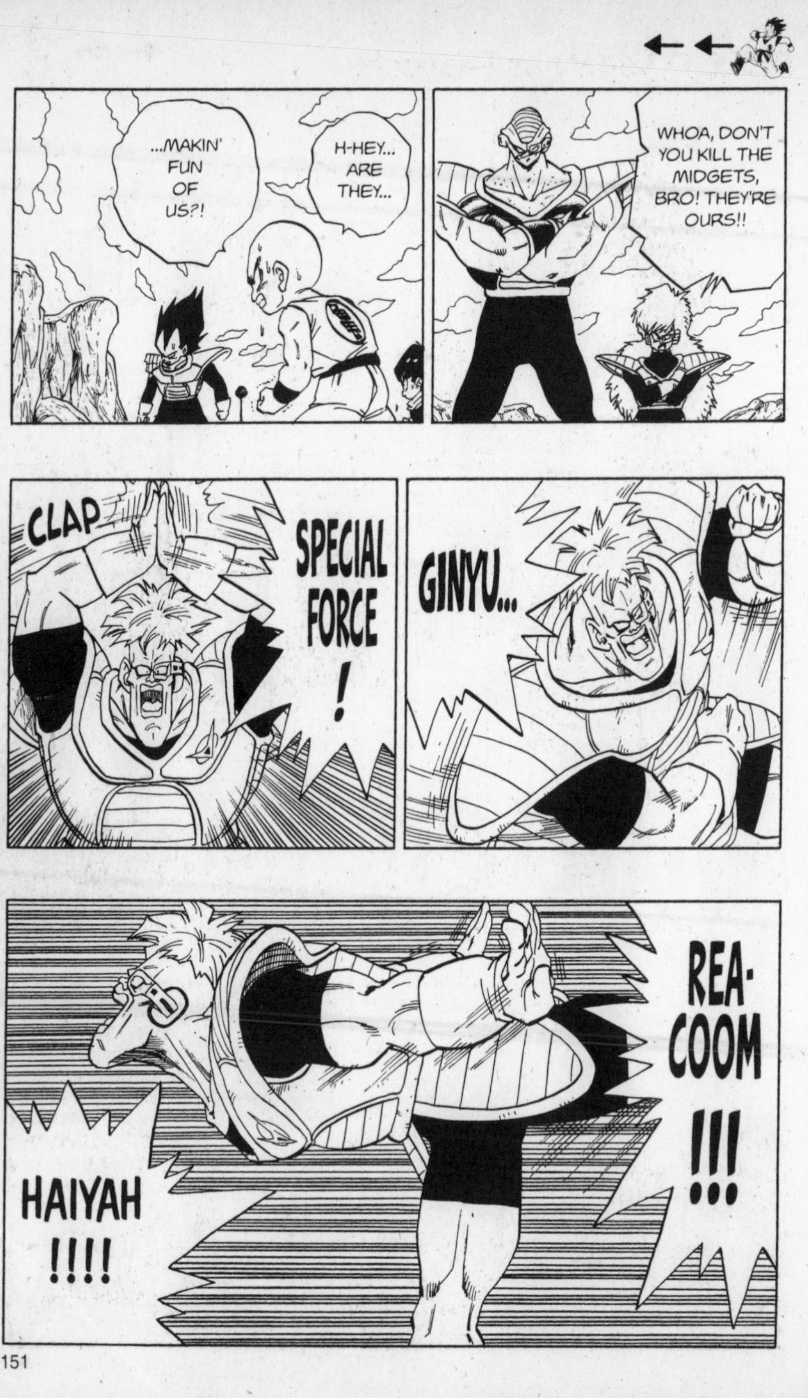

WHOA, DON'T YOU KILL THE MIDGETS, BRO! THEY'RE OURS!!
H-HEY... ARE THEY...
...MAKIN' FUN OF US?!
GINYU...
SPECIAL FORCE !
CLAP
REA-COOM !!!
HAIYAH !!!!

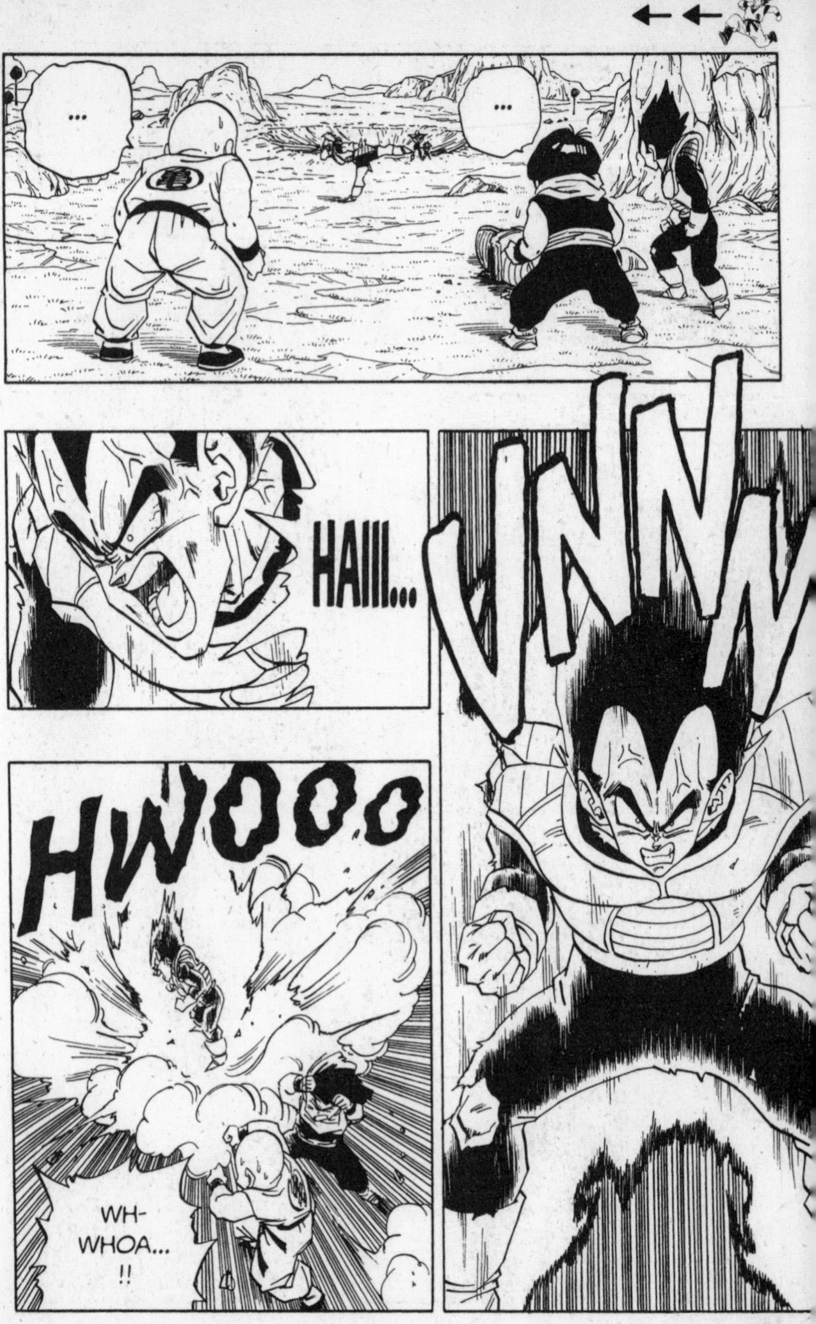
...
...
UNNN
HAIII...
HWOOO
WH-
WHOA...
!!

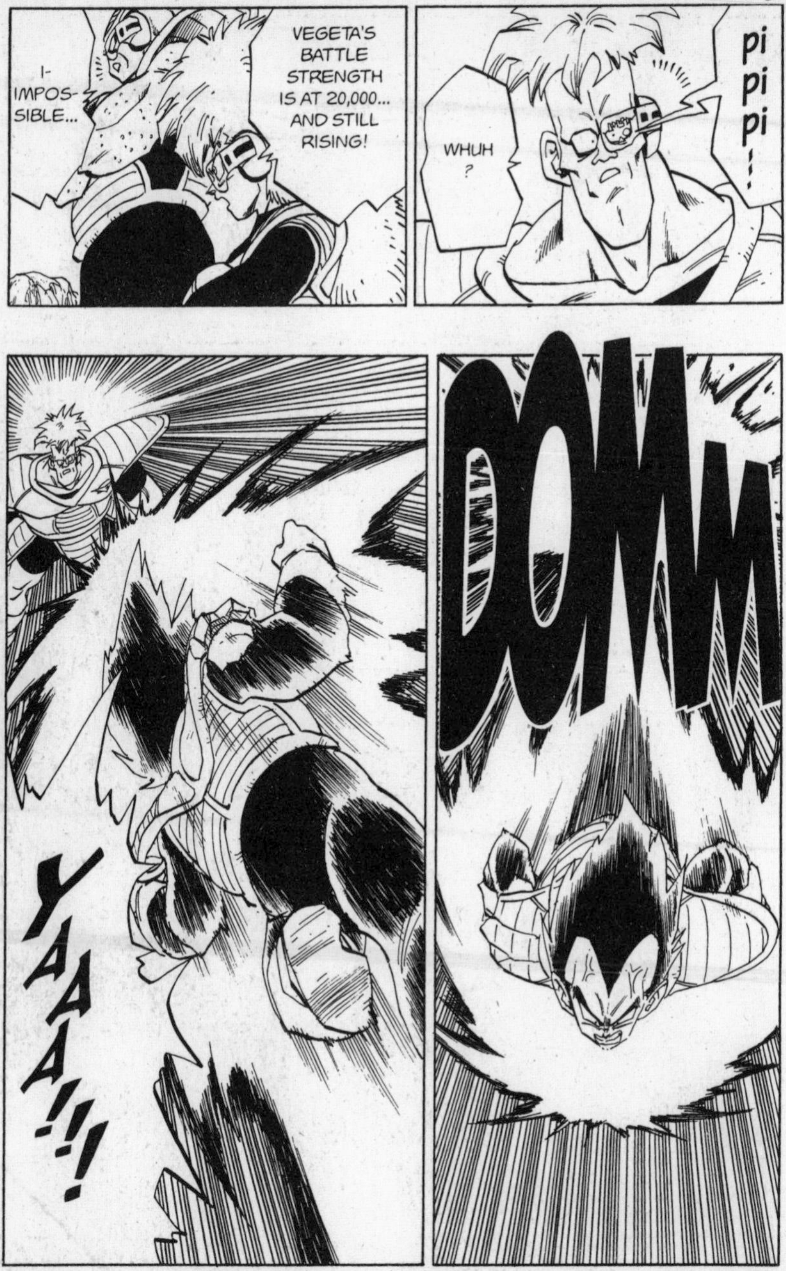
pi pi pi!!
WHUH?
VEGETA'S BATTLE STRENGTH IS AT 20,000... AND STILL RISING!
I- IMPOSSIBLE...
DOMM
YAAA!!!

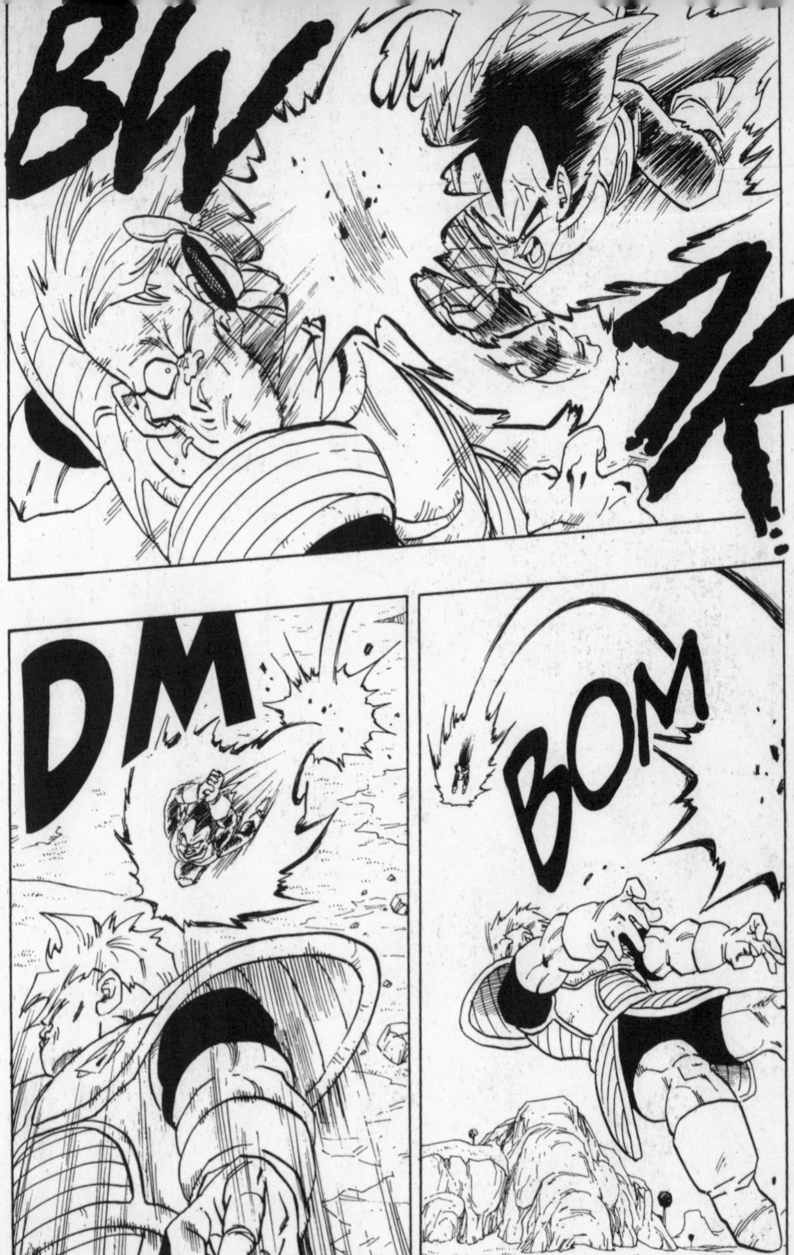
BWAK!!
BOM
DM

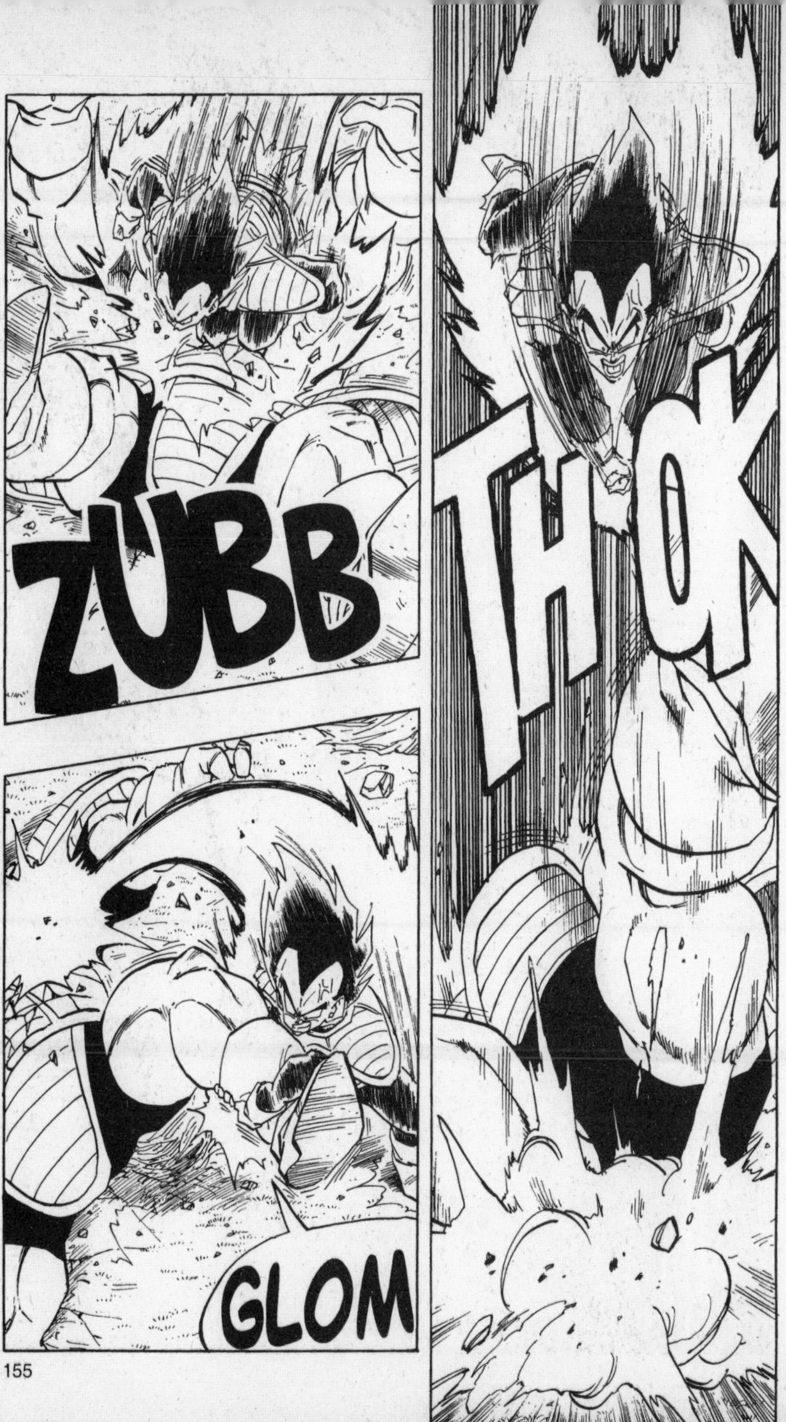
THOK
ZUBB
GLOM

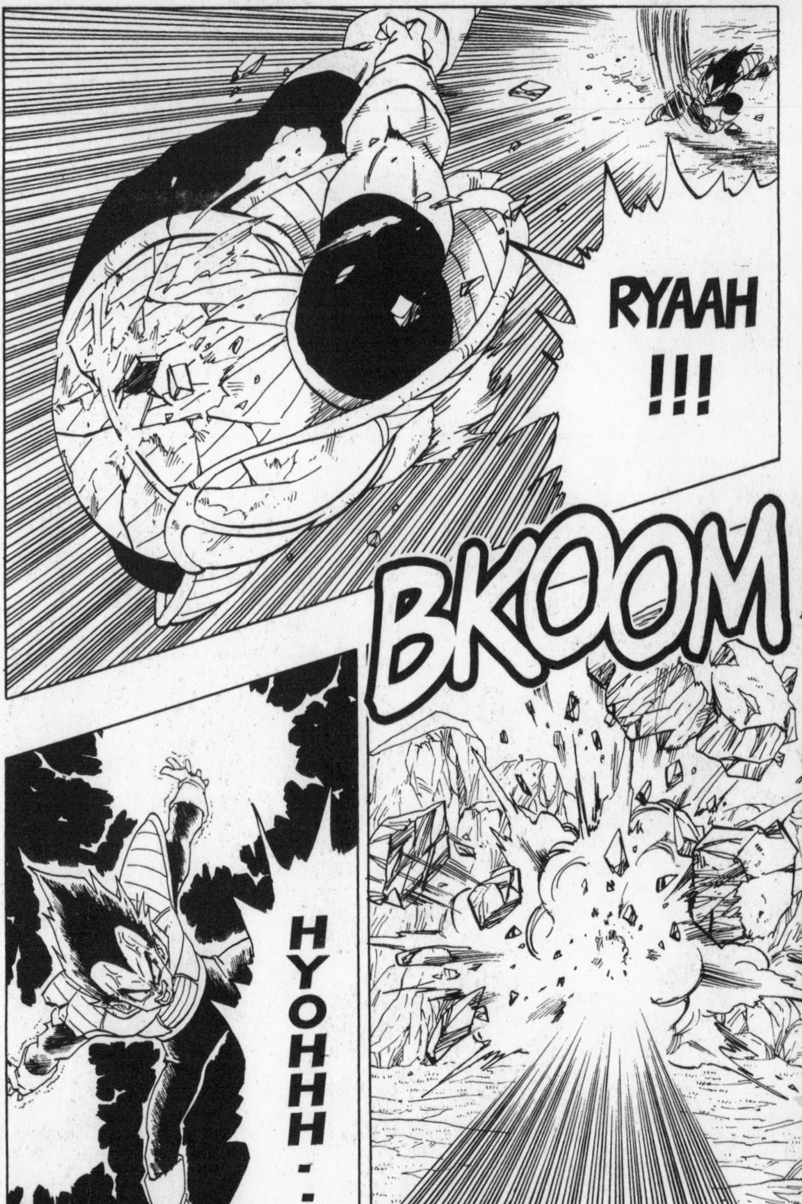
RYAAH !!!
BKOOM
HYOHHH...

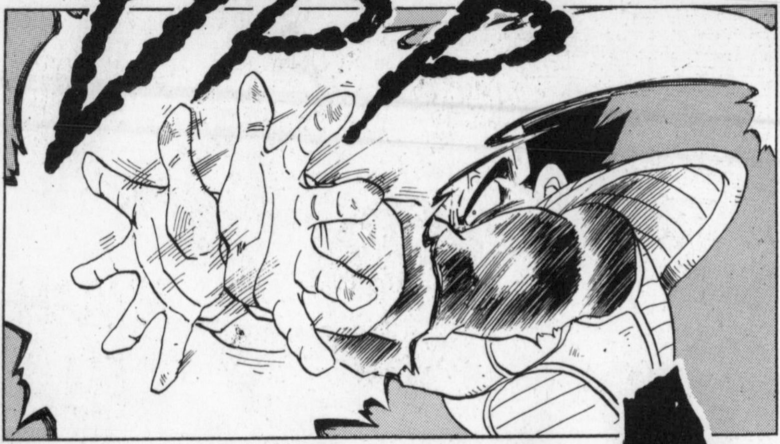
VIPP

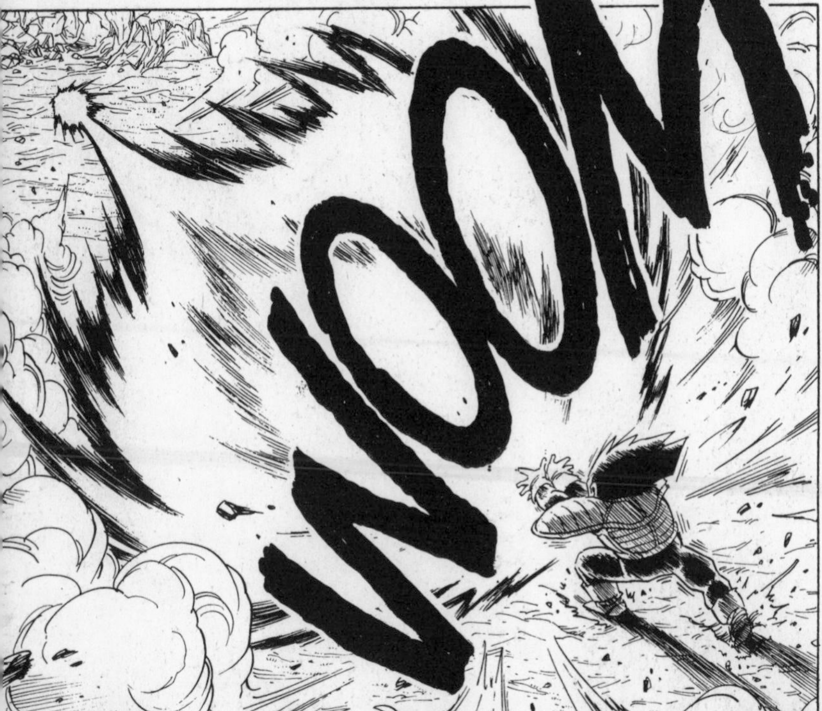
VOOM

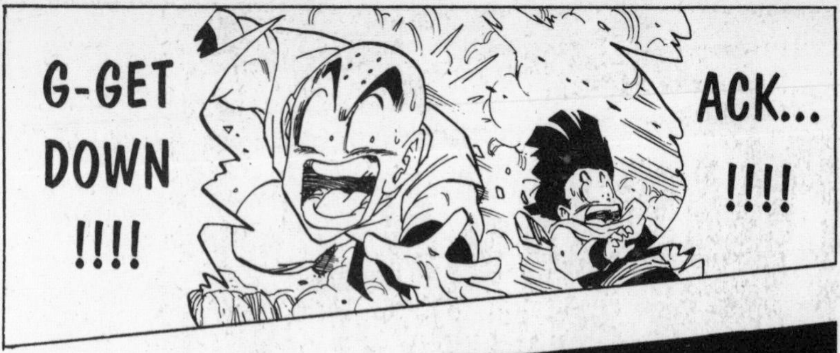
ACK... !!!!
G-GET DOWN !!!!
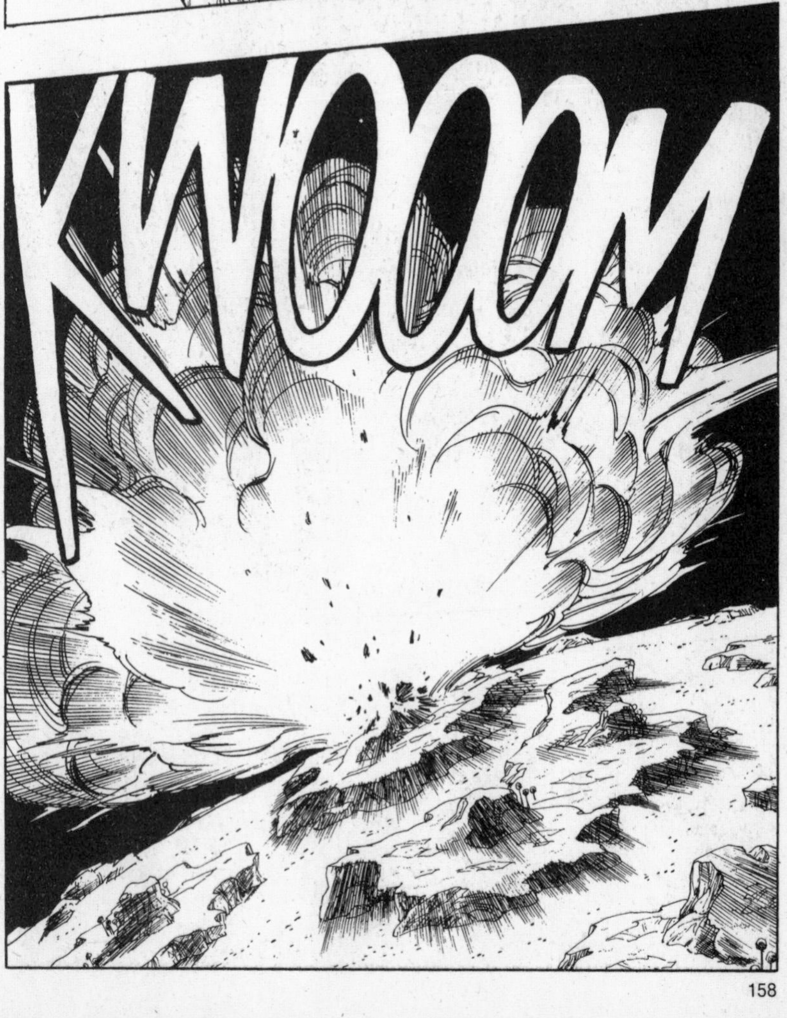
KWOOOM

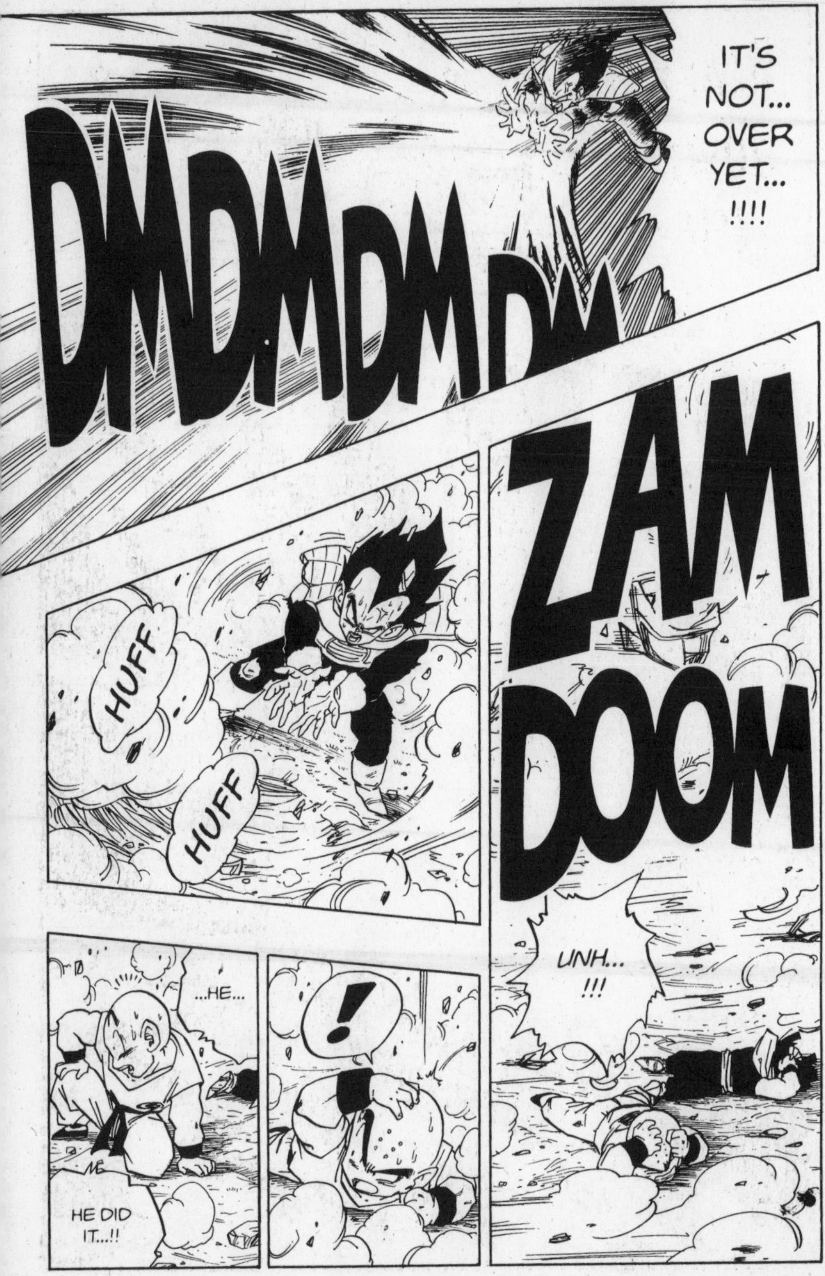
IT'S NOT... OVER YET... !!!!
DMDMDMDM
ZAM
DOOM
UNH... !!!
HUFF
HUFF
!
...HE...
HE DID IT...!!

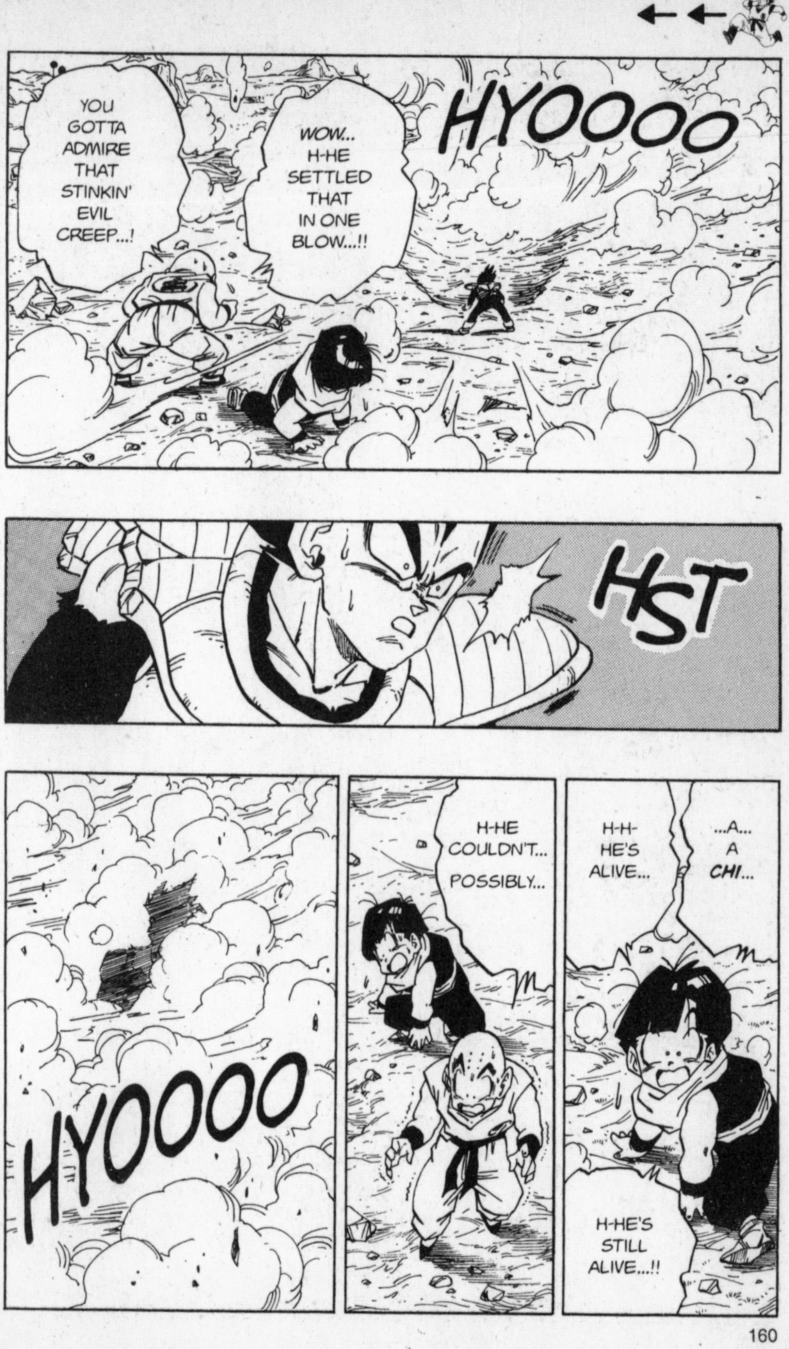
HYOOOO
WOW... H-HE SETTLED THAT IN ONE BLOW...!!
YOU GOTTA ADMIRE THAT STINKIN' EVIL CREEP...!
HST
...A... A *CHI*...
H-H-HE'S ALIVE...
H-HE'S STILL ALIVE...!!
H-HE COULDN'T... POSSIBLY...
HYOOOO

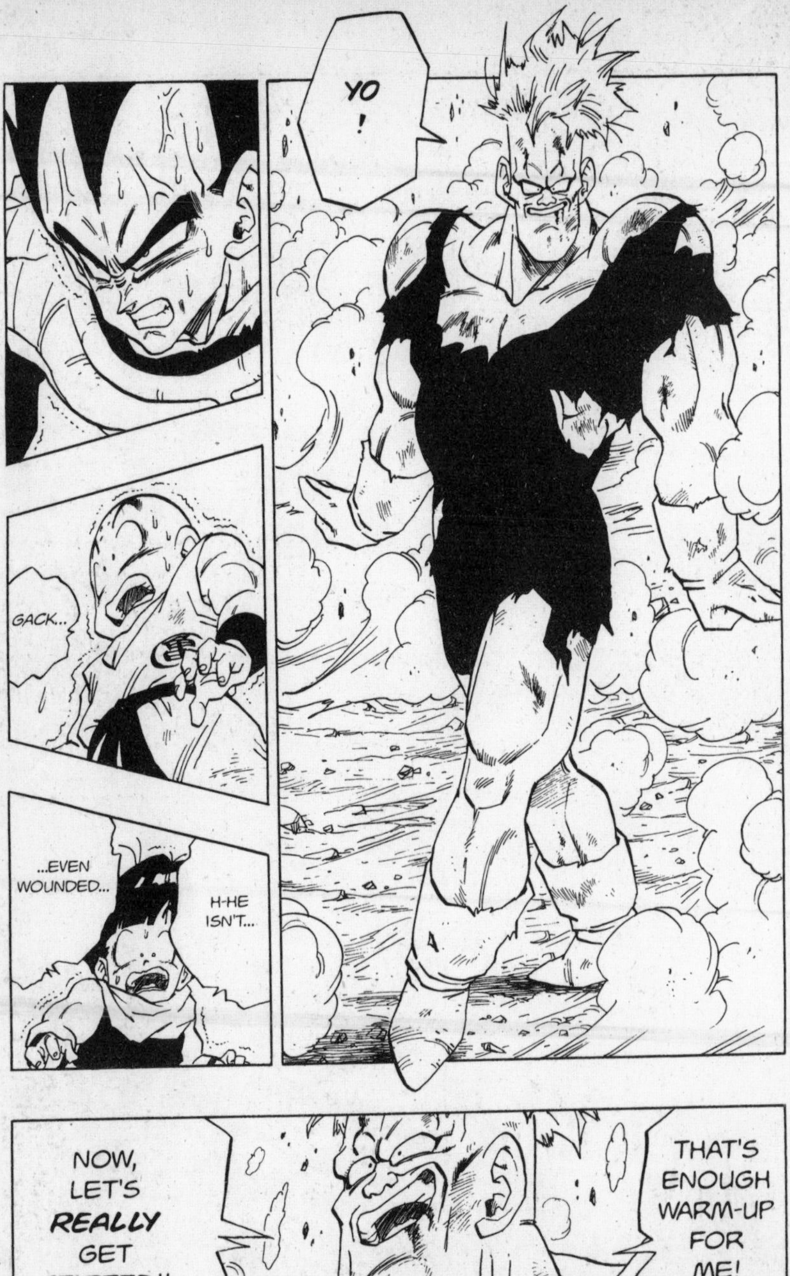
YO!
GACK...
H-HE ISN'T...
...EVEN WOUNDED...
THAT'S ENOUGH WARM-UP FOR ME!
NOW, LET'S REALLY GET STARTED!!

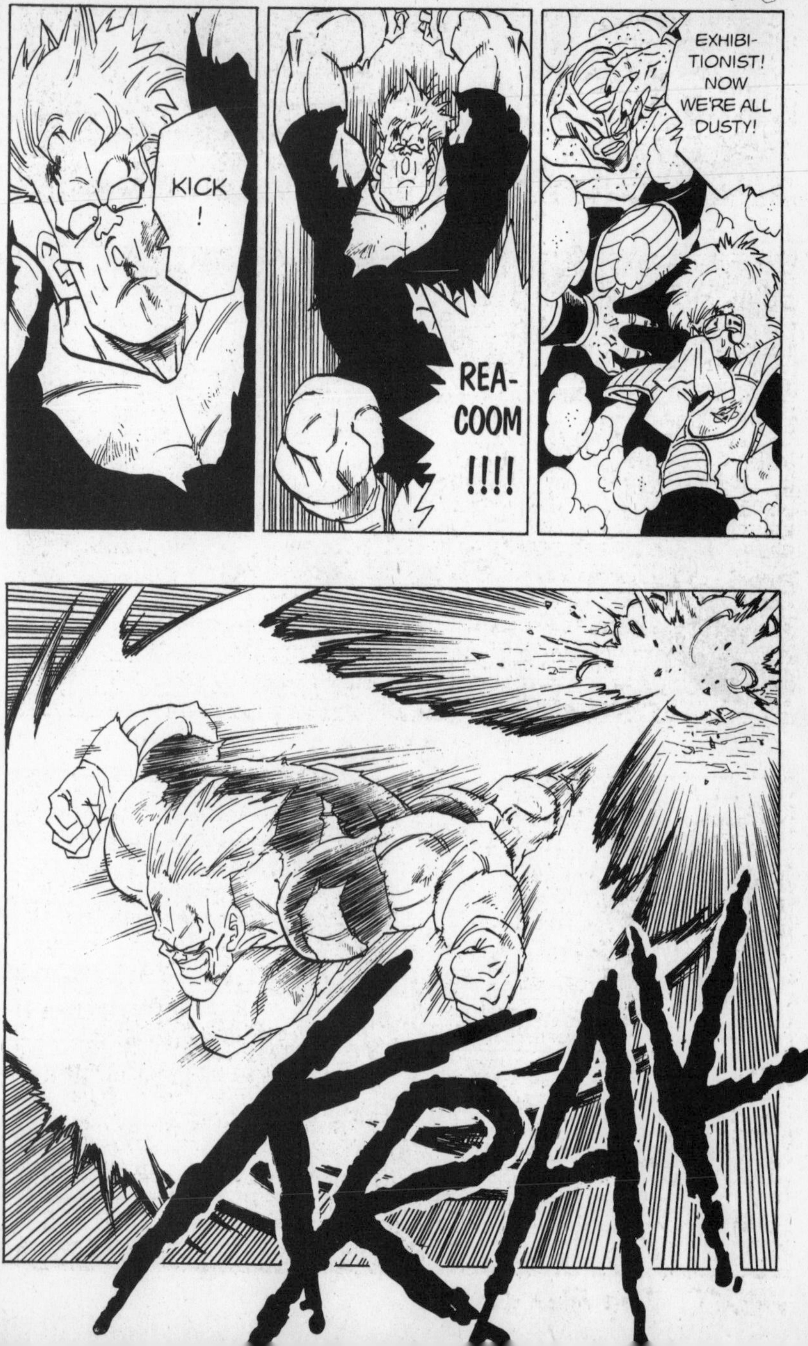
EXHIBITIONIST! NOW WE'RE ALL DUSTY!
REA-COOM!!!!
KICK!
KRAK!

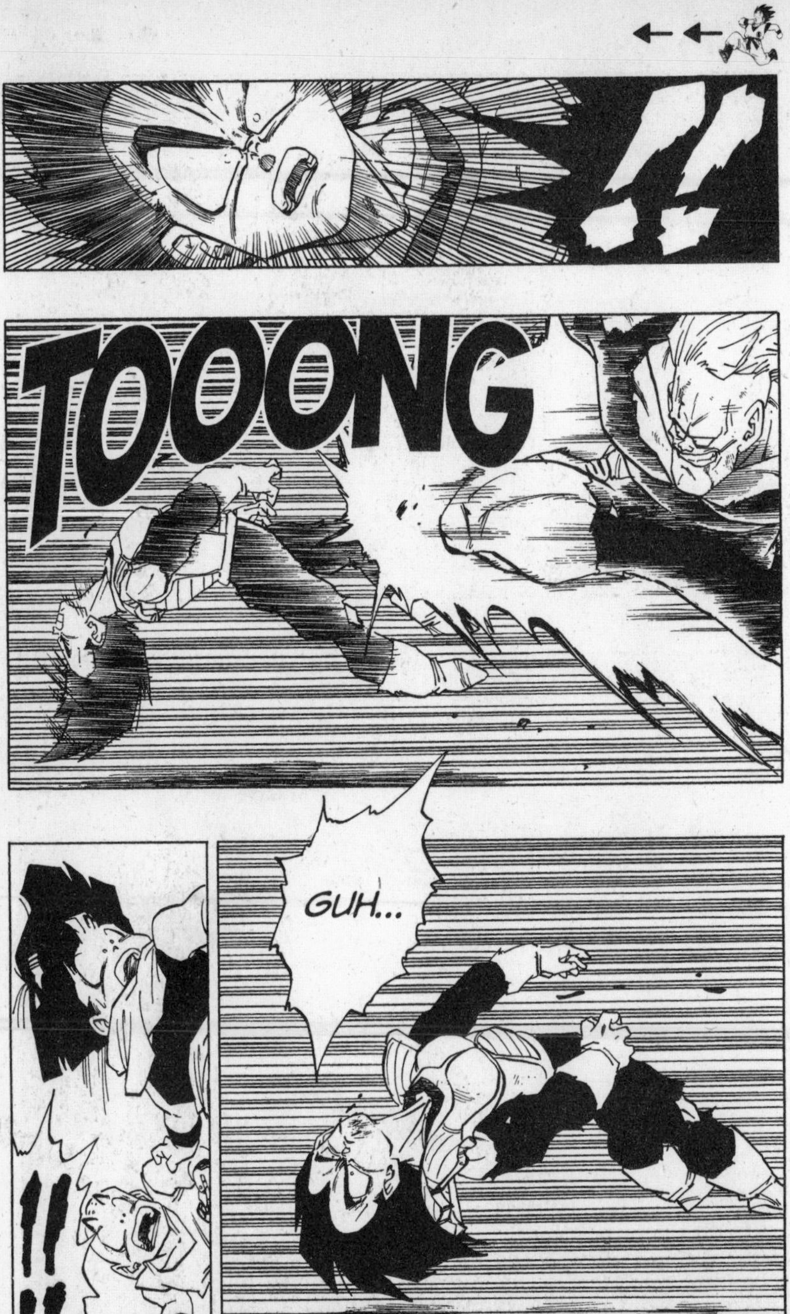
!!
TOOONG
GUH...
!!

NEXT: The Real Battle!

DBZ:82 • Vegeta vs. Reacoom, Part 2

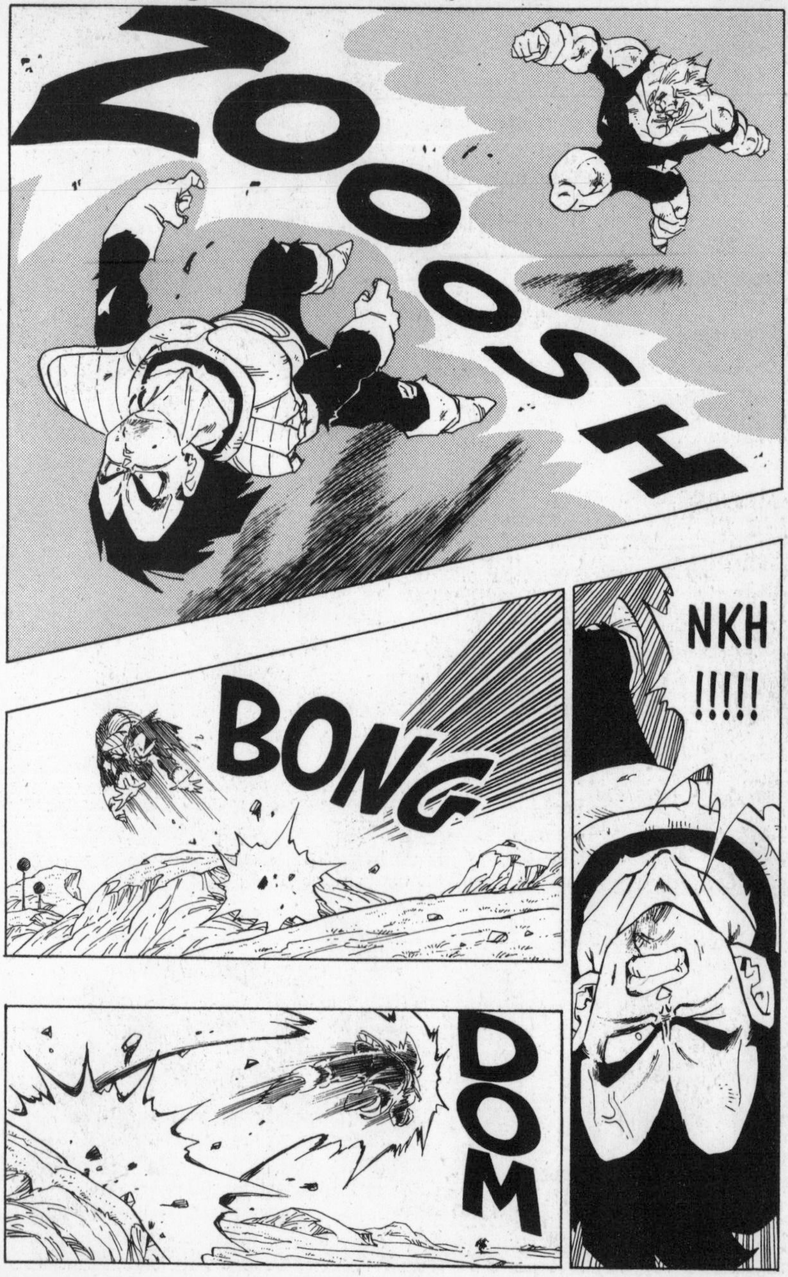
ZOOOSH
NKH !!!!!
BONG
DOM

GYAAAH

!!!!

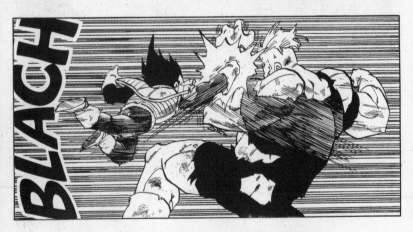

BLACH

GNG

165

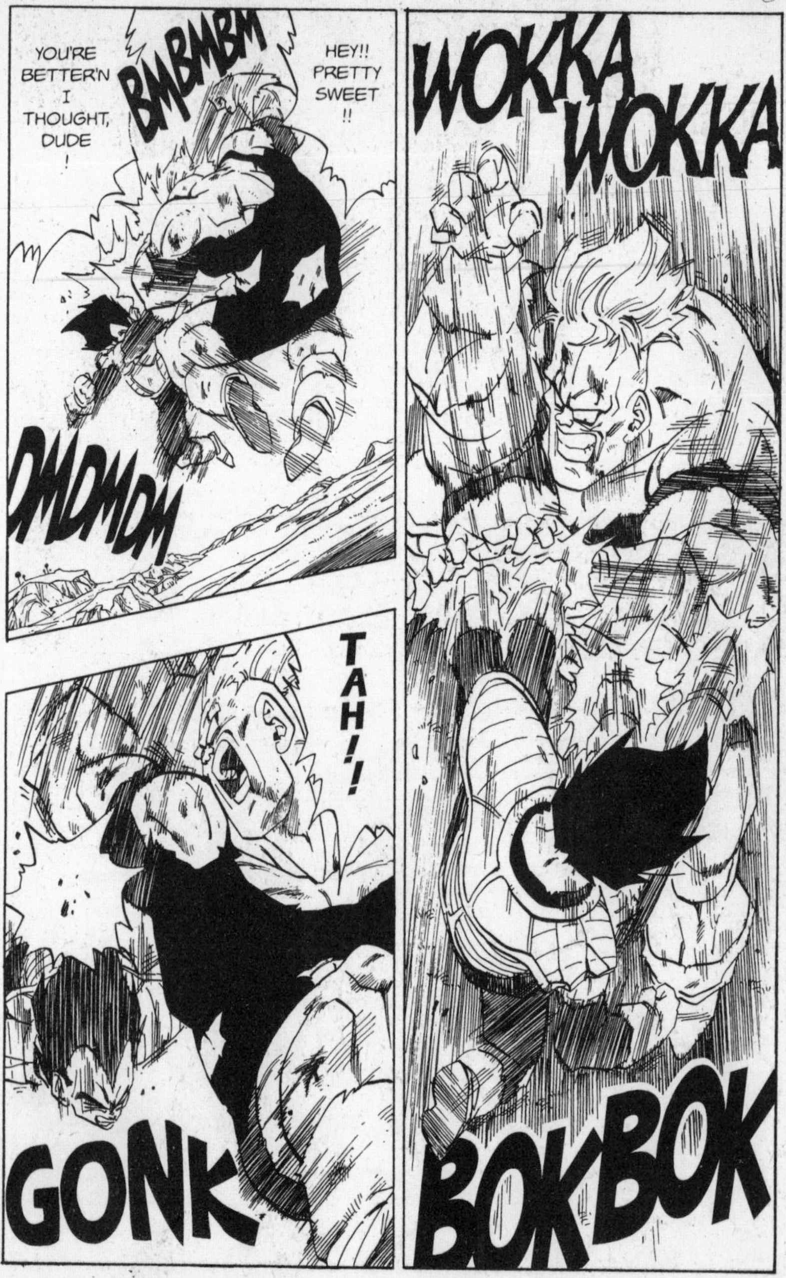
WOKKA WOKKA
BOKBOK
HEY!! PRETTY SWEET!!
BMBMBM
YOU'RE BETTER'N I THOUGHT, DUDE!
DMDMDM
TAH!!
GONK

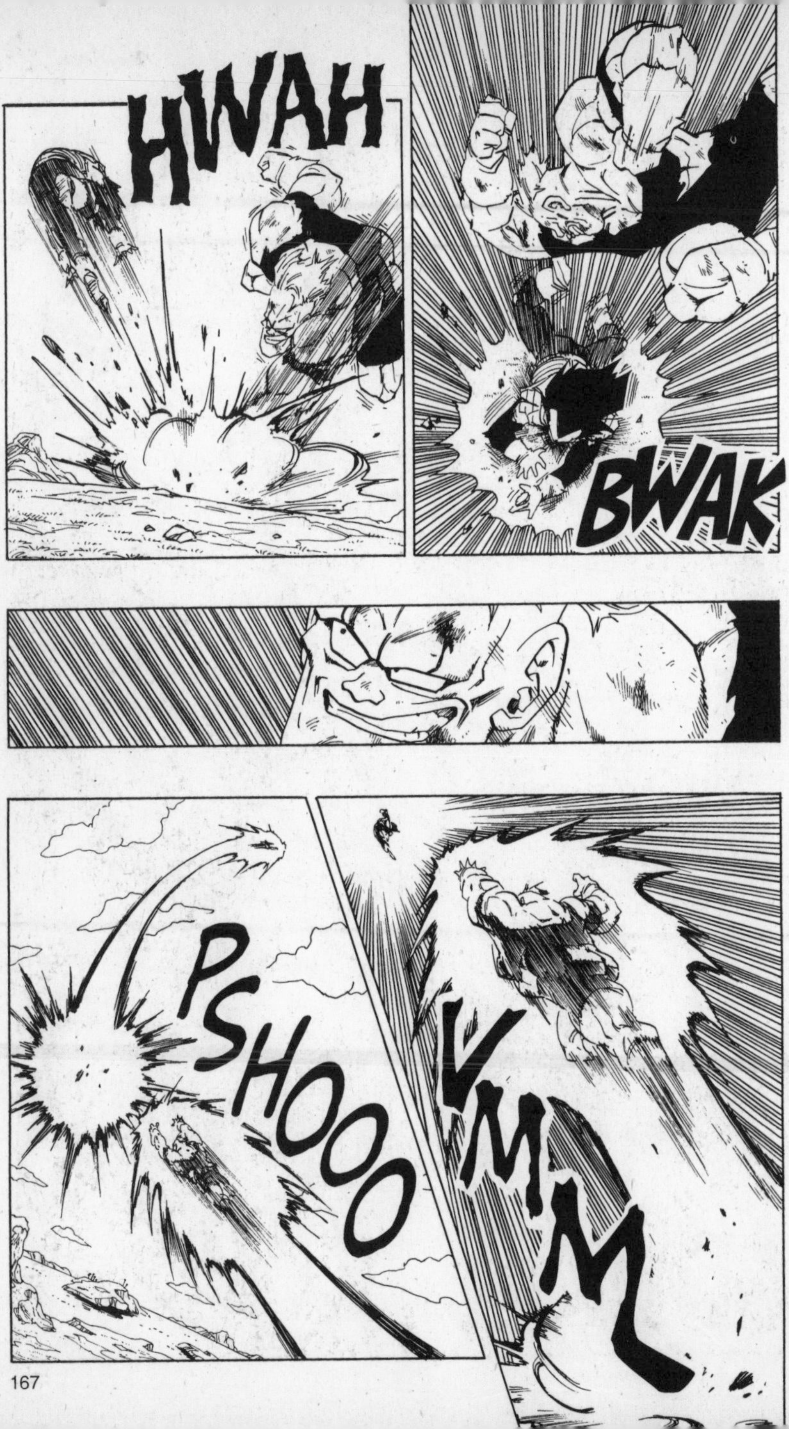
BWAK
HWAH
VMMM
PSHOOO

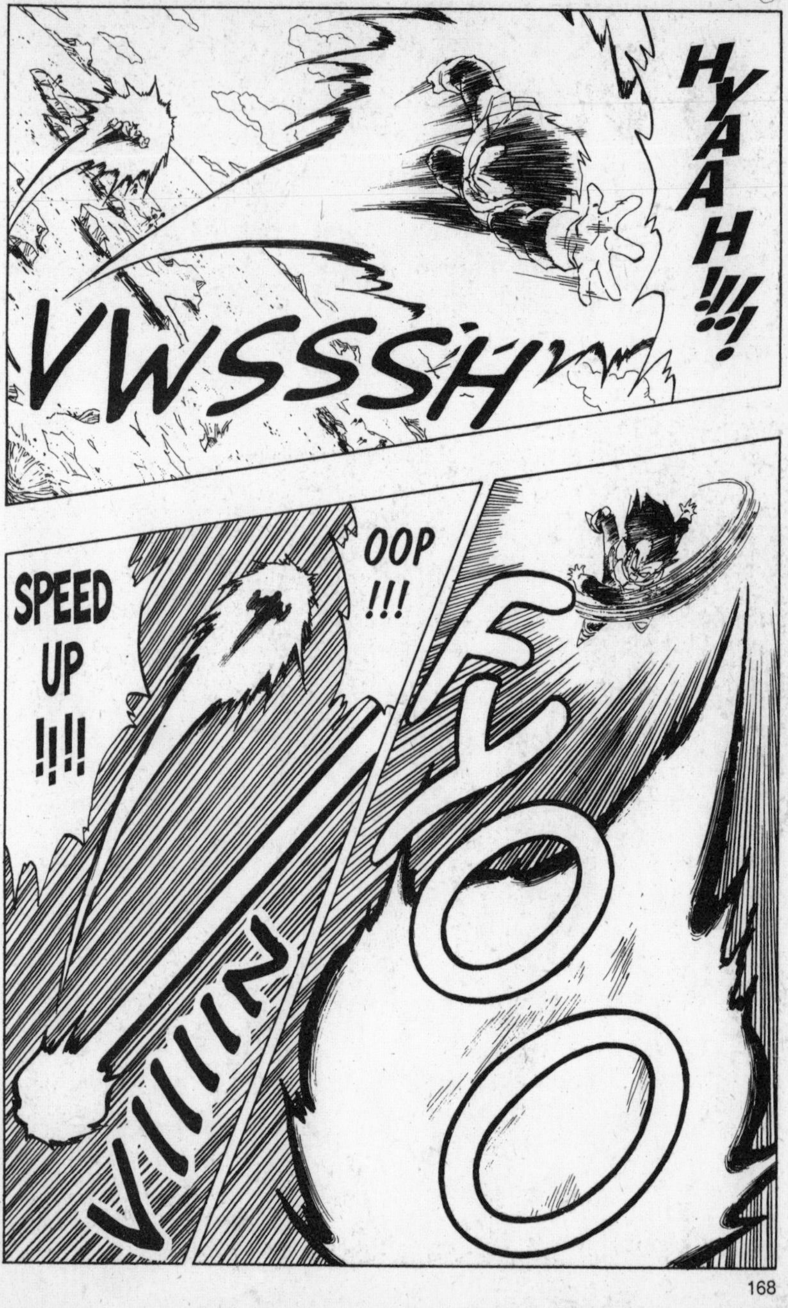
HYAAH!!!!
VWSSSH
FWOO
SPEED UP !!!!
OOP !!!
VIIIIN

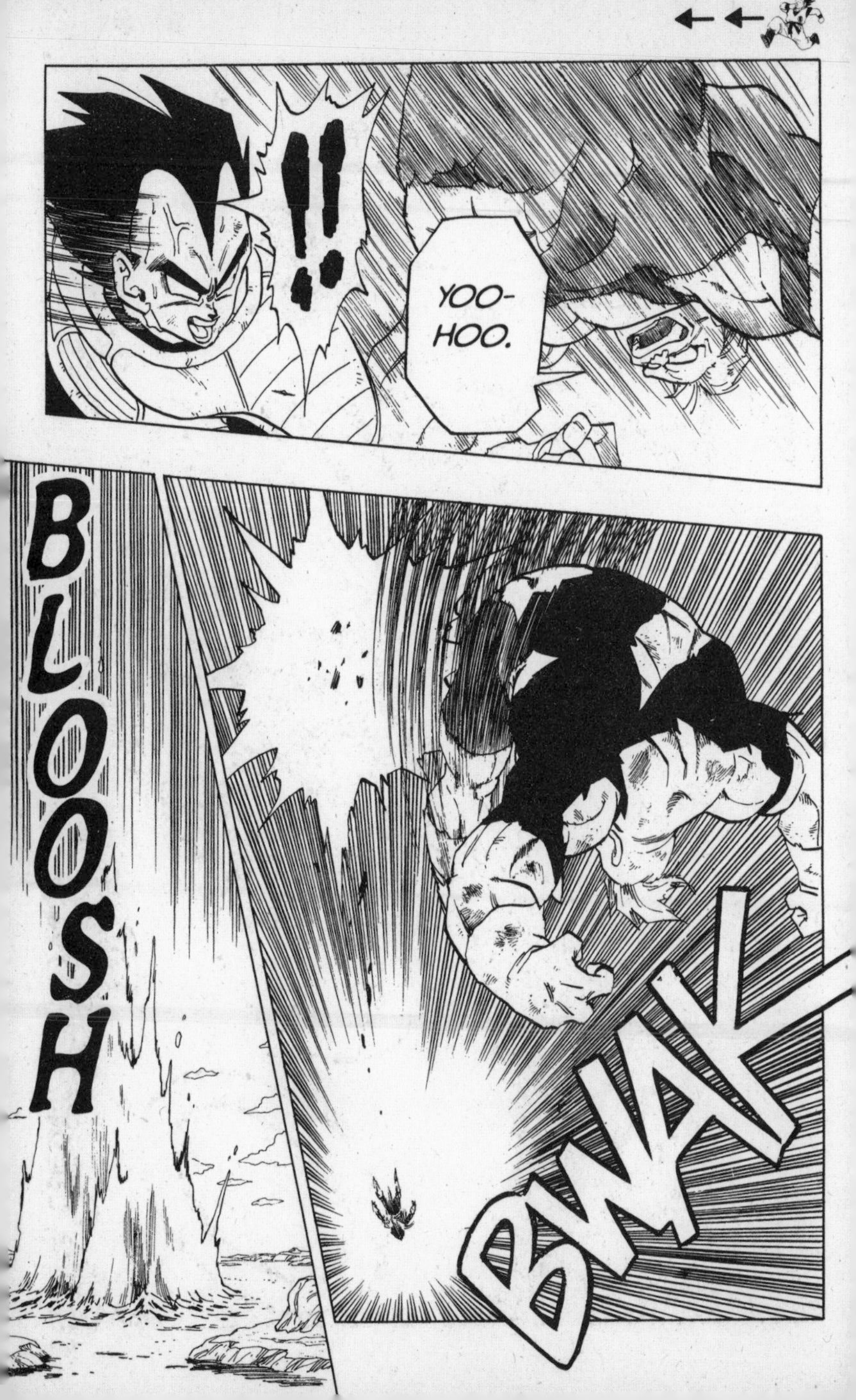
!!
YOO-HOO.
BWAK
BLOOSH

SLUSSSHHH

HEE HEE HEE...!

UH... UH...!

BO MF

PSHOOOOO

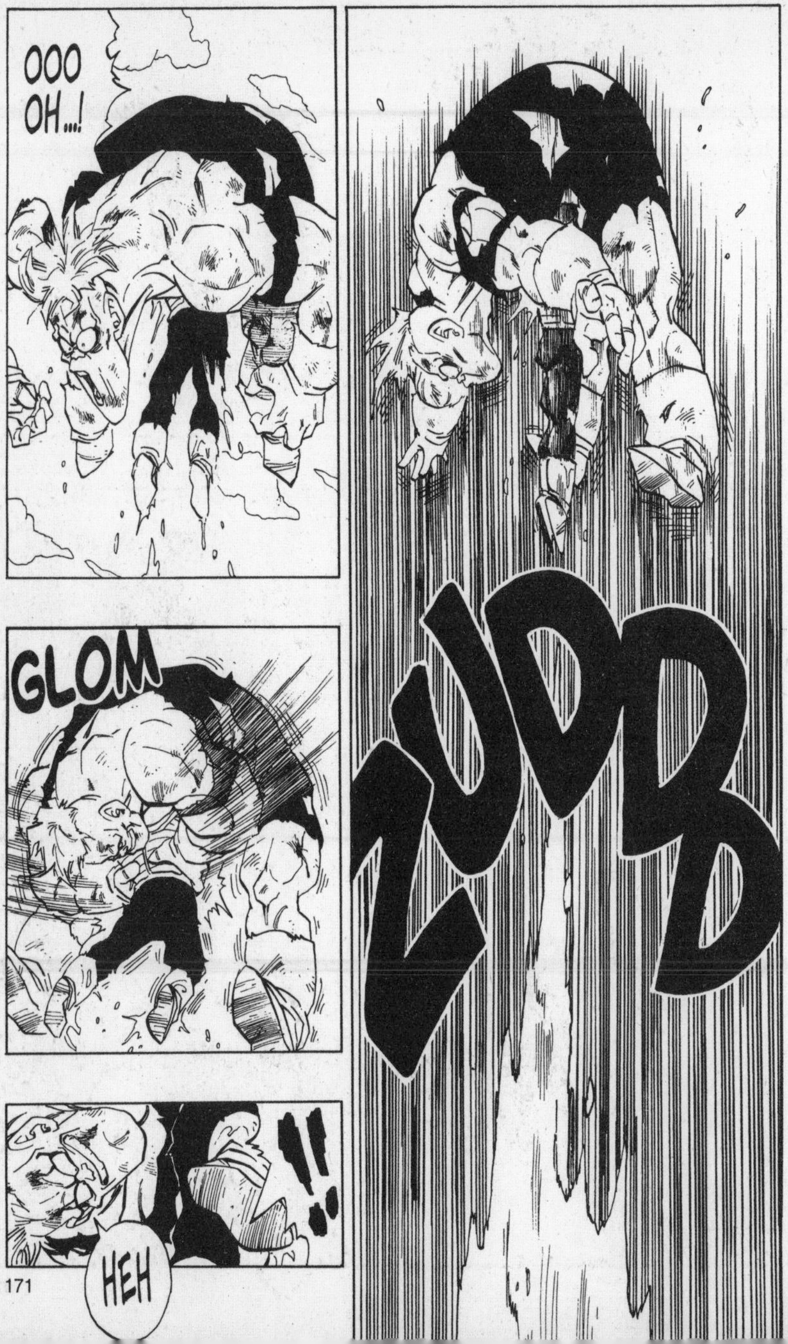
ZUDB
OOO OH...!
GLOM
!!
HEH

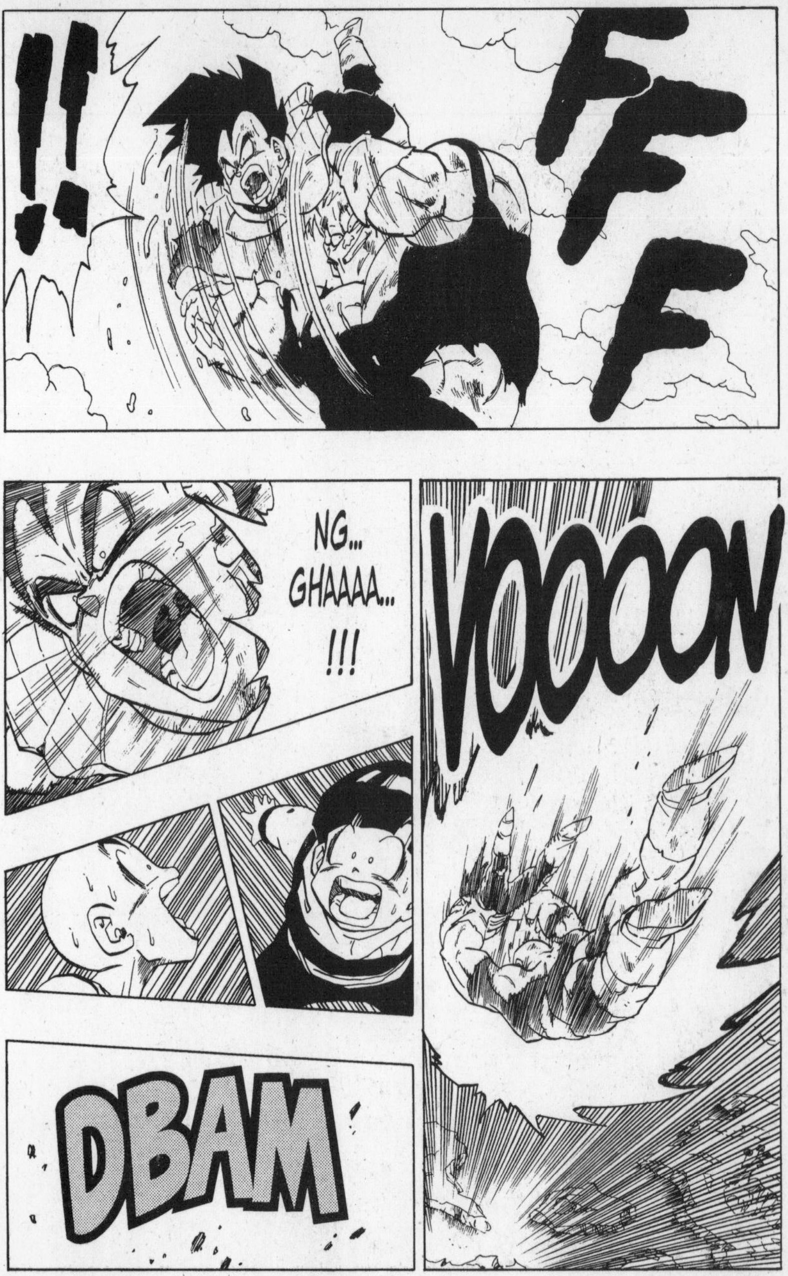
FFF
!!
VOOOON
NG... GHAAAA... !!!
DBAM

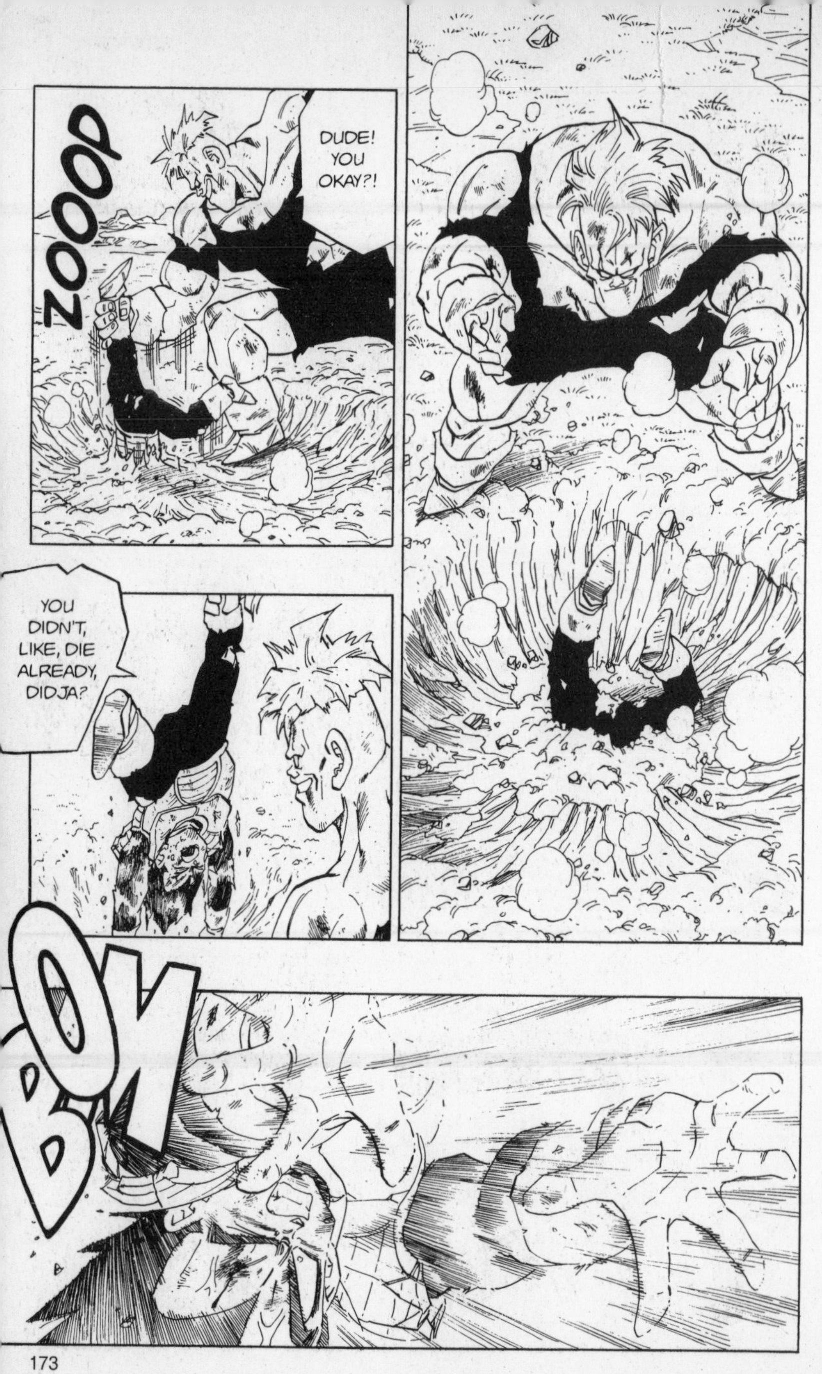
ZOOOP
DUDE! YOU OKAY?!
YOU DIDN'T, LIKE, DIE ALREADY, DIDJA?
BOM

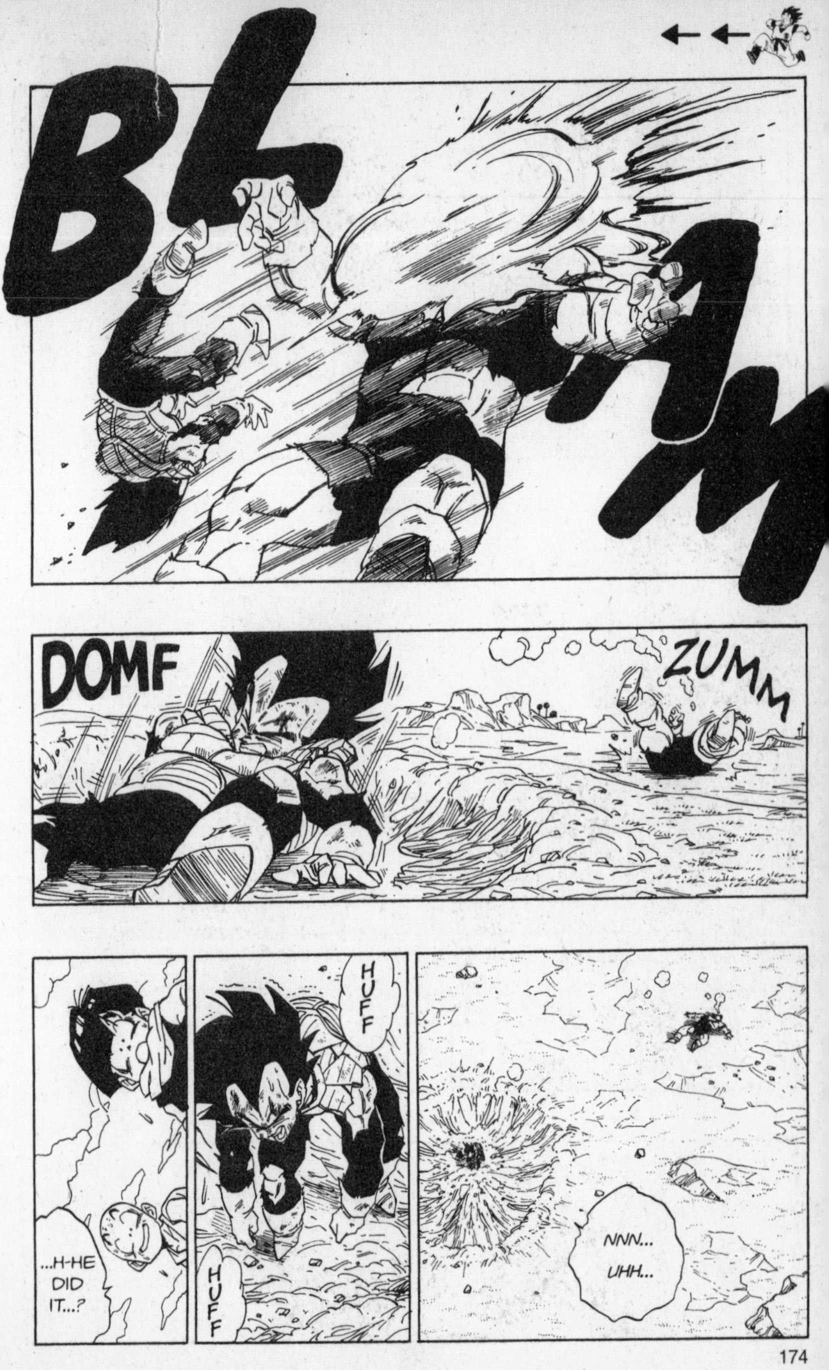
BLAMM
ZUMM
DOMF
NNN... UHH...
HUFF
HUFF
...H-HE DID IT...?

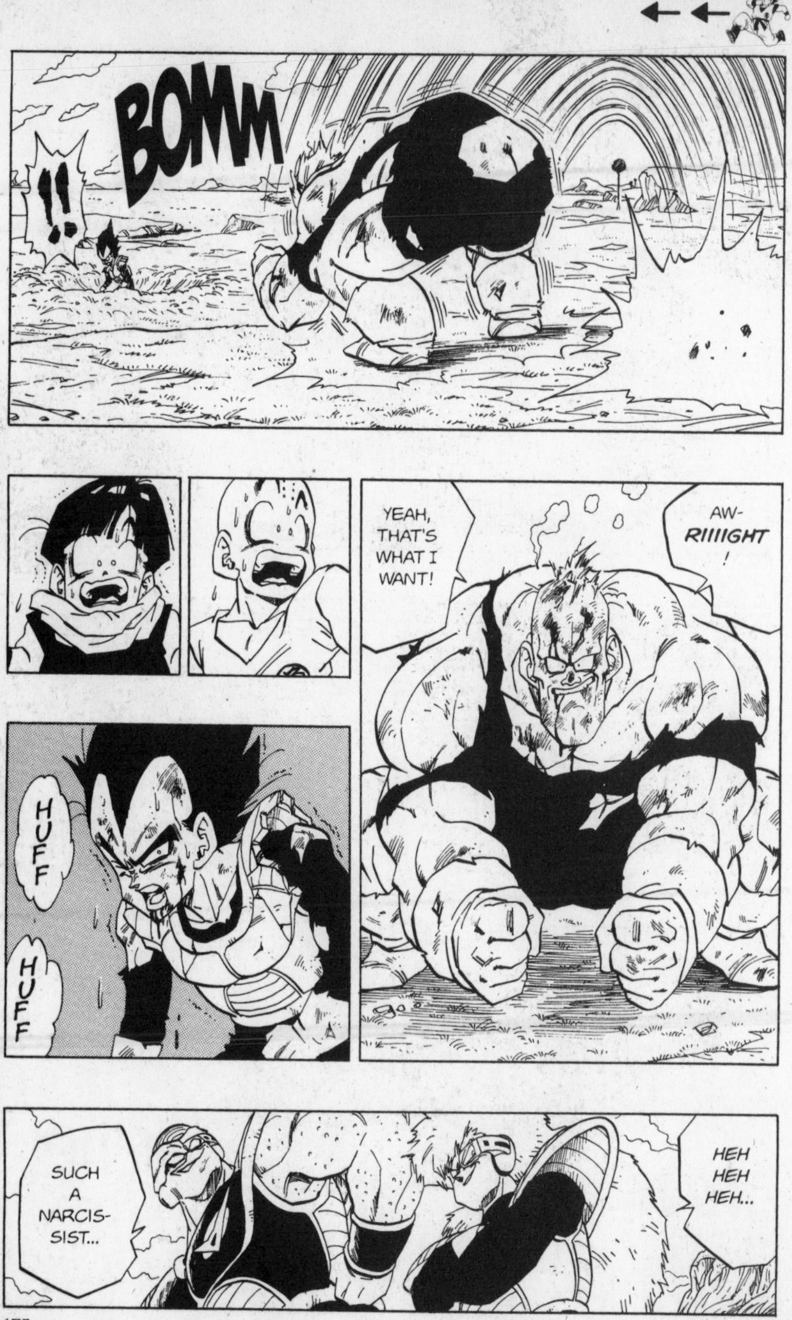
BOMM
!!
AW-RIIIIGHT!
YEAH, THAT'S WHAT I WANT!
HUFF
HUFF
HEH HEH HEH...
SUCH A NARCIS-SIST...

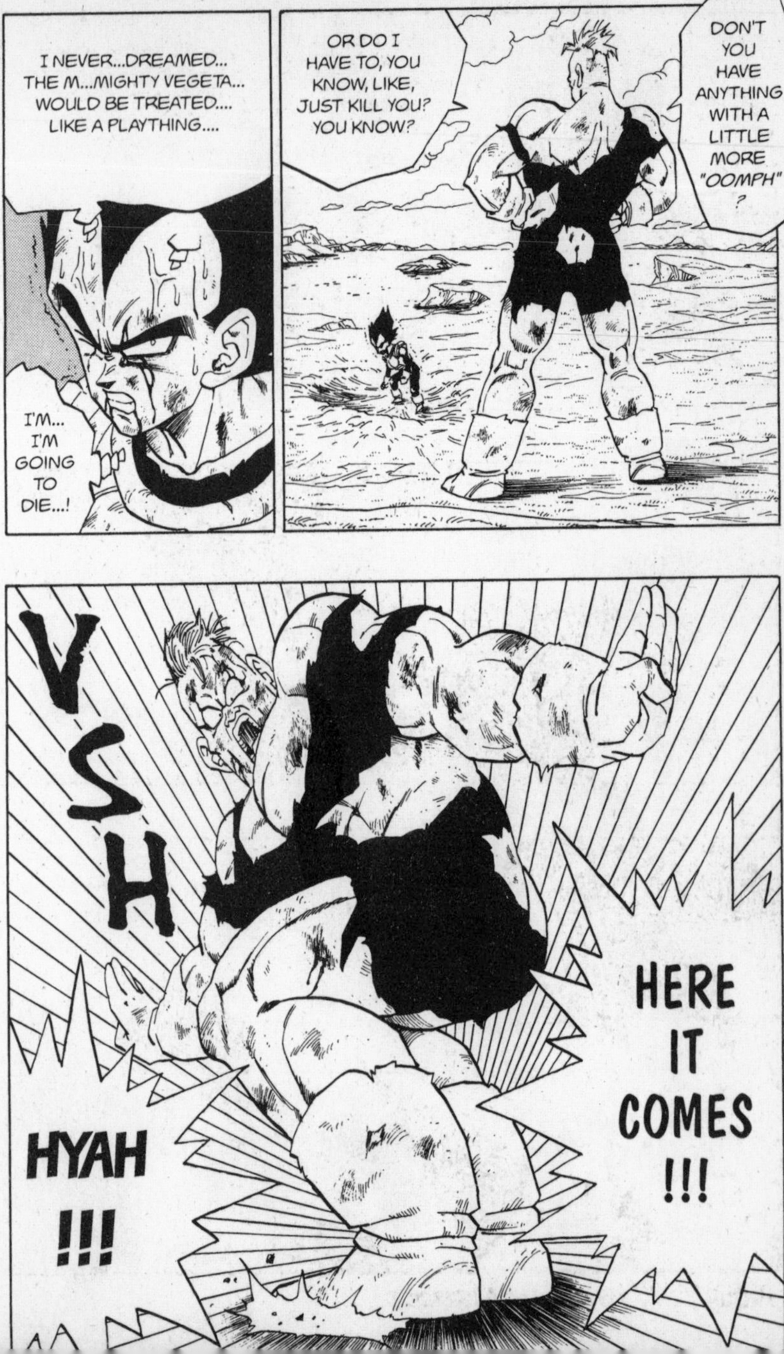
DON'T YOU HAVE ANYTHING WITH A LITTLE MORE "OOMPH" ?
OR DO I HAVE TO, YOU KNOW, LIKE, JUST KILL YOU? YOU KNOW?
I NEVER...DREAMED... THE M...MIGHTY VEGETA... WOULD BE TREATED.... LIKE A PLAYTHING....
I'M... I'M GOING TO DIE...!
HERE IT COMES !!!
VSH
HYAH !!!

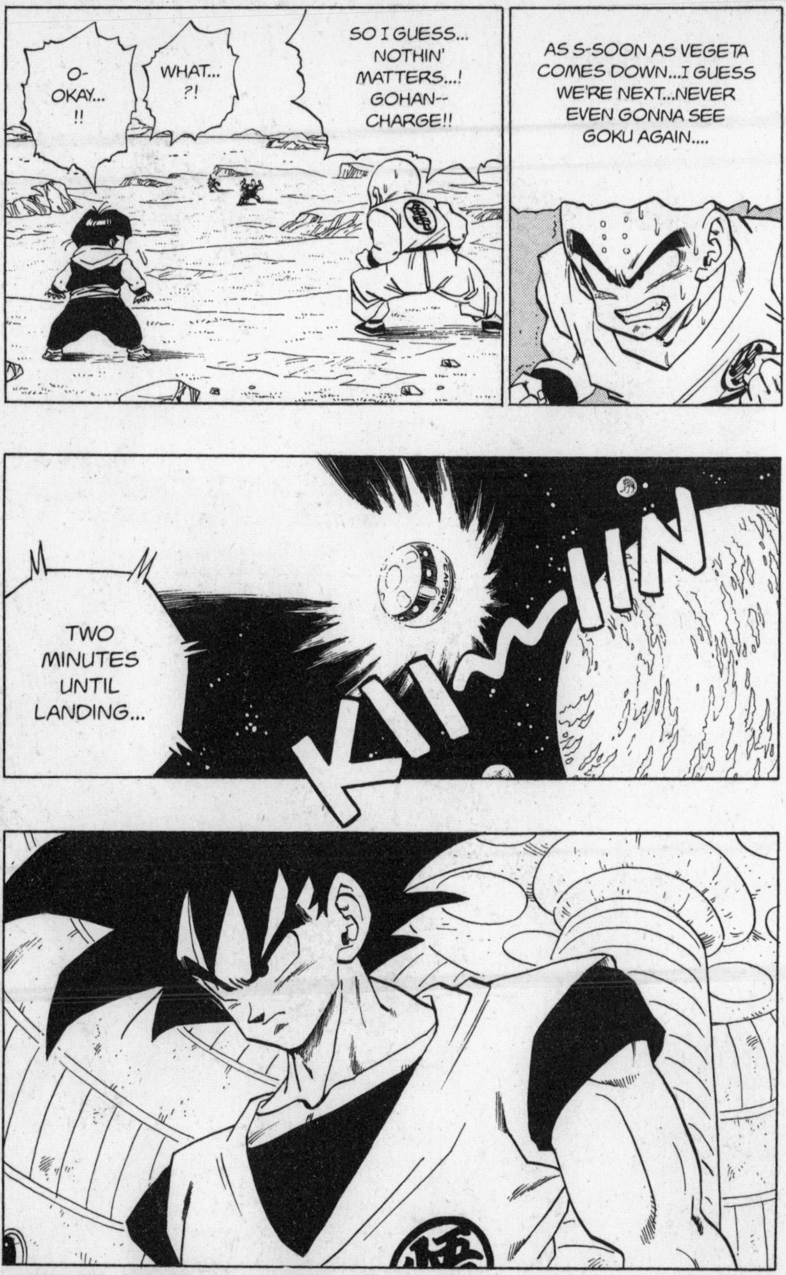
AS S-SOON AS VEGETA COMES DOWN...I GUESS WE'RE NEXT...NEVER EVEN GONNA SEE GOKU AGAIN....
SO I GUESS... NOTHIN' MATTERS...! GOHAN--CHARGE!!
WHAT...?!
O-OKAY...!!
CAPSULE
KII~IIN
TWO MINUTES UNTIL LANDING...

NEXT: The Last Stand!!!

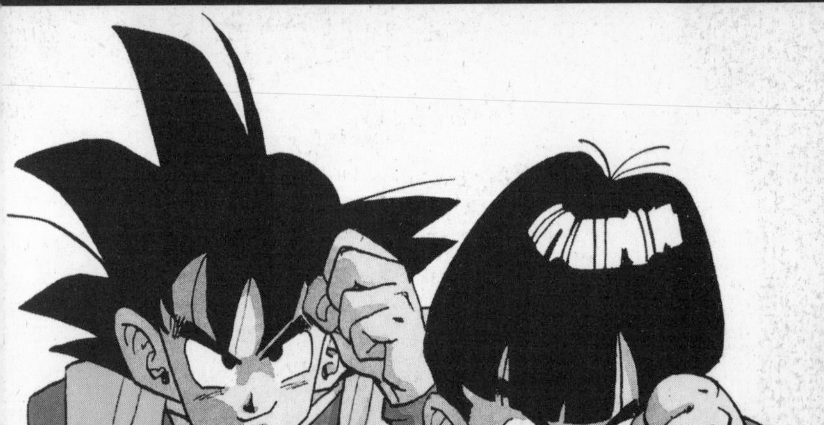
亀

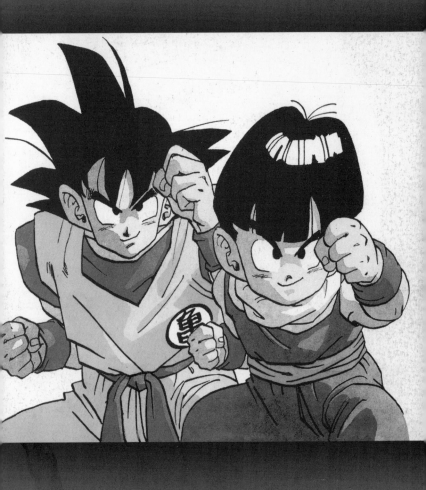

TITLE PAGE GALLERY

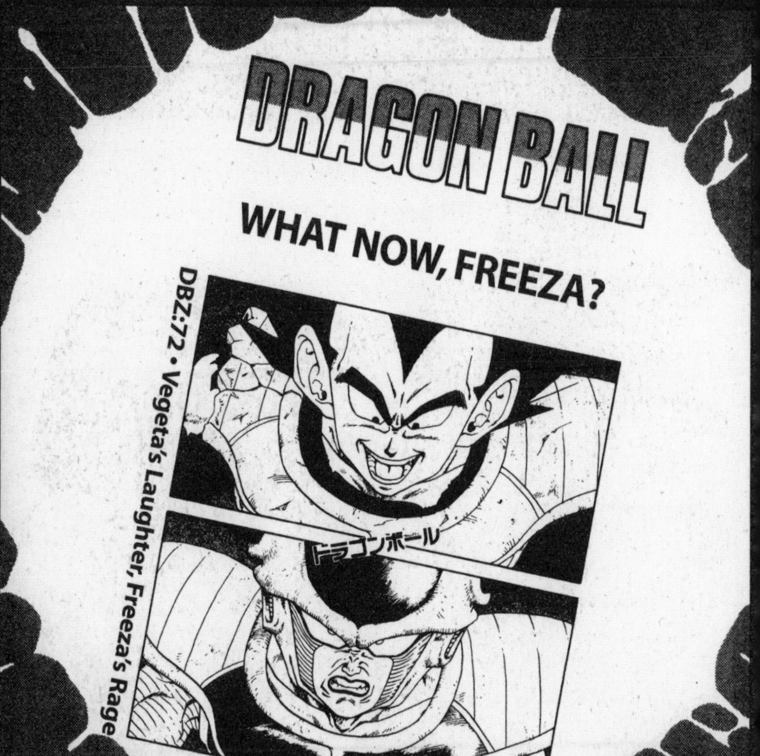
DRAGON BALL
WHAT NOW, FREEZA?
DBZ:72 • Vegeta's Laughter, Freeza's Rage
ドラゴンボール
Akira Toriyama
BIRD 鳥山明 STUDIO

Here are the title pages which were used when these chapters of **Dragon Ball Z** were originally published in Japan in 1990 in **Weekly Shonen Jump** magazine.

DRAGON BALL

DBZ:73 • Reunion of Terror!

BETWEEN A ROCK AND A HARD PLACE!! BULMA & KURIRIN'S CHOICE OF TWO DEATHS!!!

Akira Toriyama
鳥山明
BIRD STUDIO

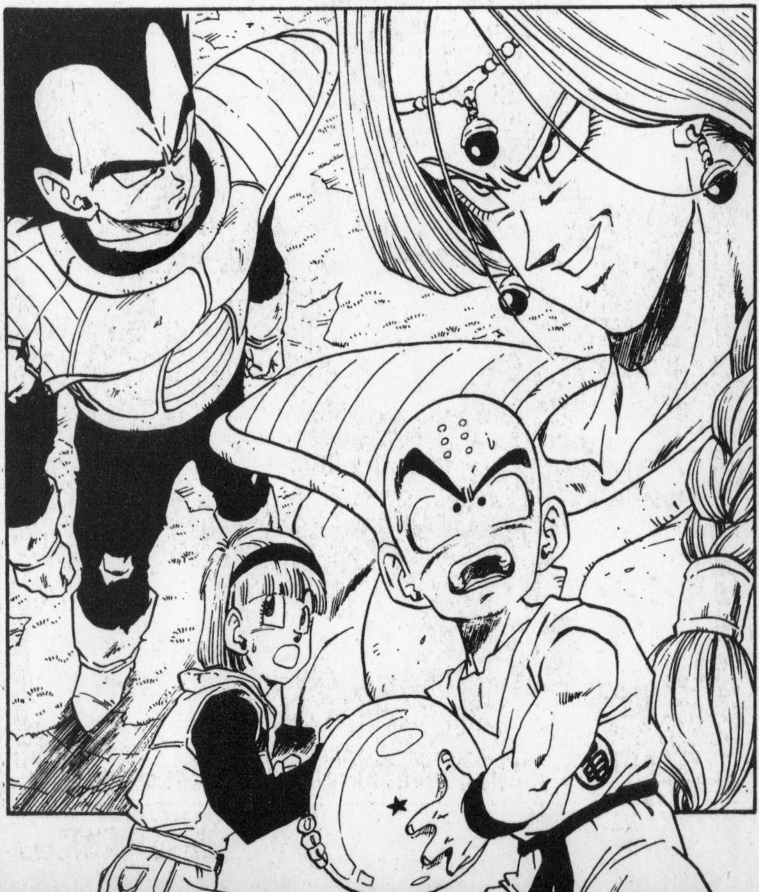

DRAGON BALL

SOON, ALL THE DRAGON BALLS WILL BE MINE!

DBZ:74 • Vegeta in Overdrive!

Akira Toriyama
鳥山明 BIRD STUDIO

DRAGON BALL

DBZ:75 • Brains and Brawn

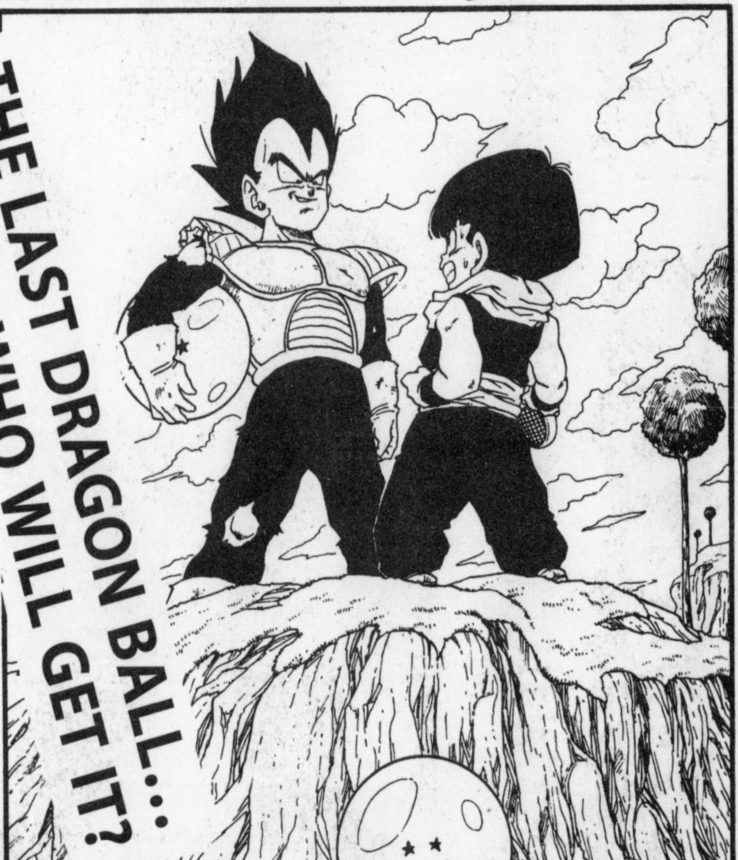
THE LAST DRAGON BALL...
WHO WILL GET IT?

Akira Toriyama
鳥山明 BIRD STUDIO

DRAGON BALL

JUST WAIT...I'LL SHOW YOU MY NEW POWER!

DBZ:76 • Premonitions of War

Akira Toriyama
鳥山明
BIRD STUDIO

DRAGON BALL

EVEN VEGETA'S AFRAID OF... THE GINYU FORCE!!!

DBZ:77 • The Enemy of My Enemy

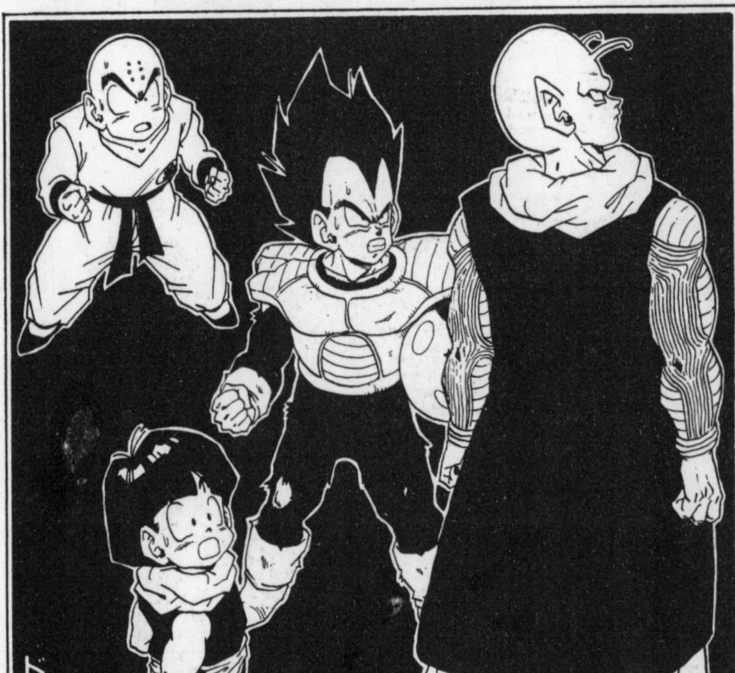
ドラゴンボール

Akira Toriyama

BIRD 鳥山明 STUDIO

DRAGON BALL

DEATH BY ROSHAMBO!!!

DBZ:79 • Five Deadly Fighters

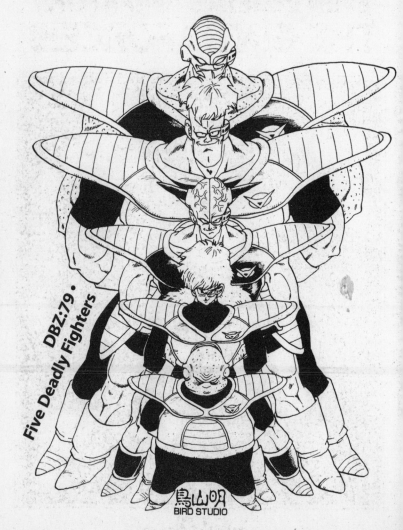

BIRD STUDIO

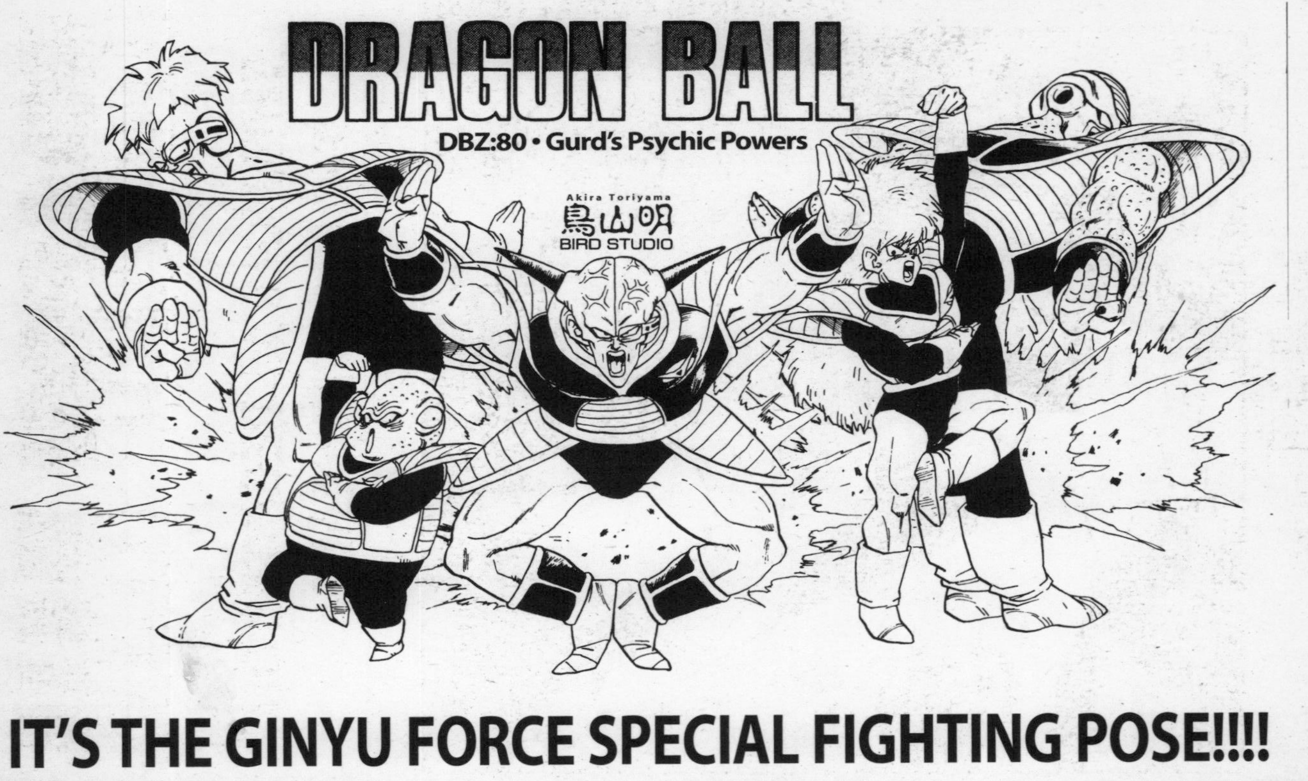
DRAGON BALL
DBZ:80 • Gurd's Psychic Powers
Akira Toriyama
鳥山明
BIRD STUDIO
IT'S THE GINYU FORCE SPECIAL FIGHTING POSE!!!!

DRAGON BALL

THIS FIGHT'LL REGISTER ON THE RICHTER SCALE...

DBZ:81 • Vegeta vs. Reacoom

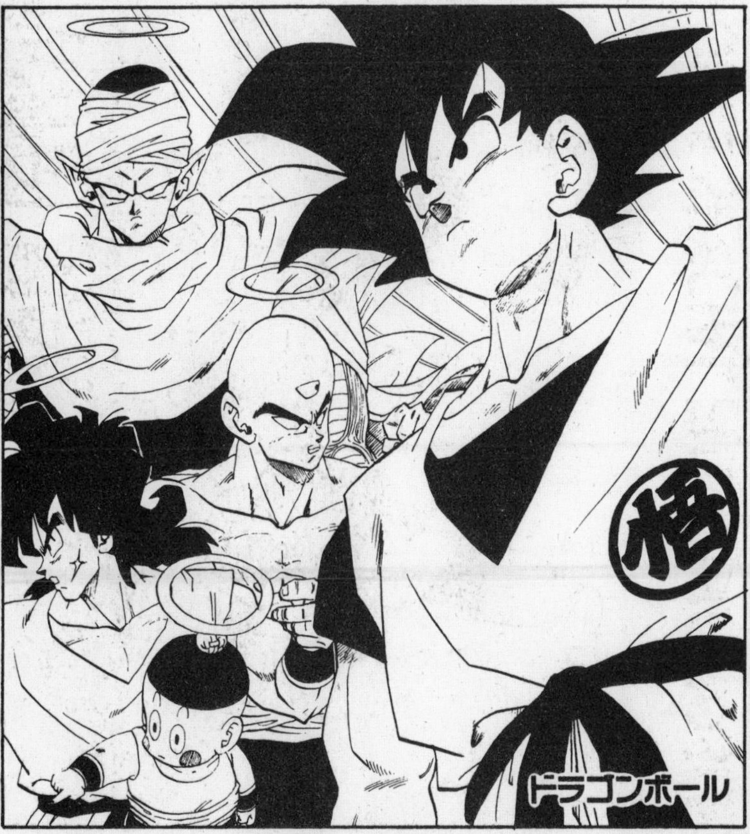
悟
ドラゴンボール

Akira Toriyama

BIRD 鳥山明 STUDIO

DRAGON BALL

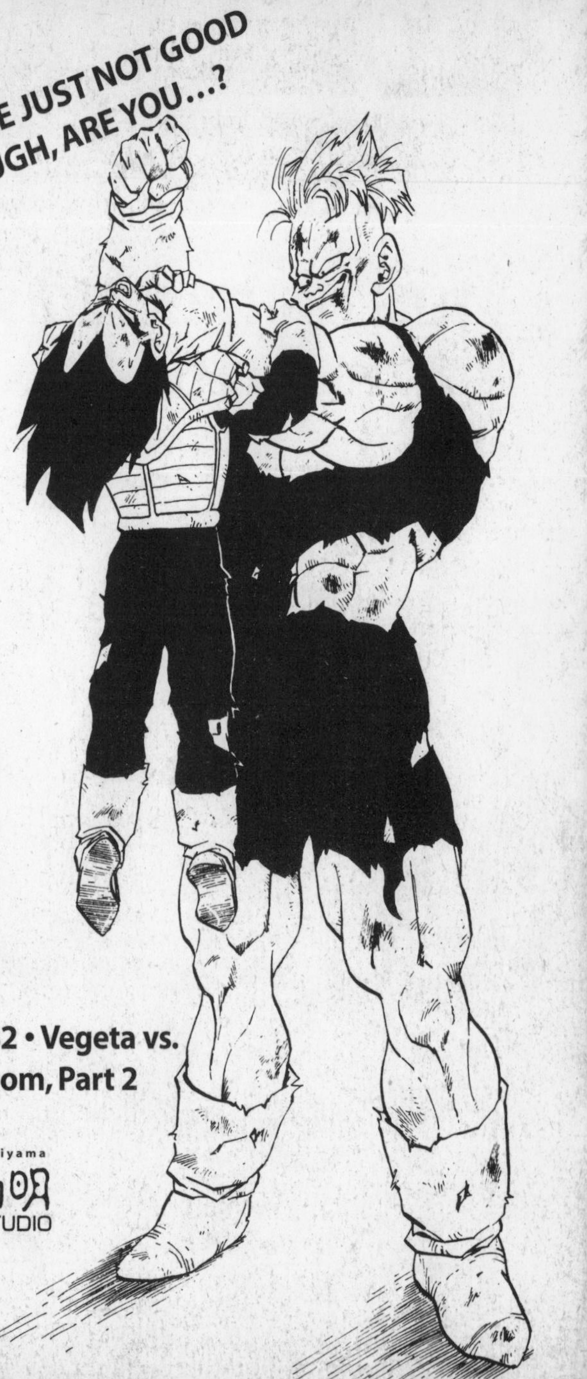
YOU'RE JUST NOT GOOD ENOUGH, ARE YOU...?

DBZ:82 • Vegeta vs. Reacoom, Part 2

Akira Toriyama
鳥山明
BIRD STUDIO

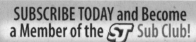

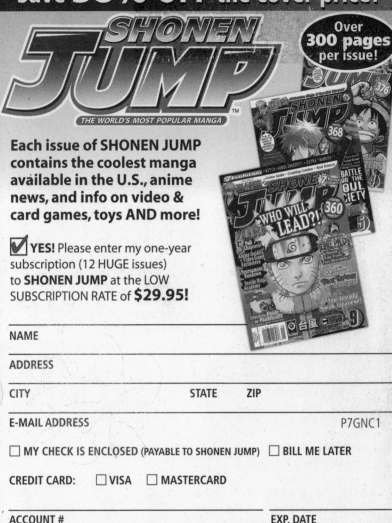